CORPORATE COLLAPSE

Regulatory, Accounting and Ethical Failure

F.L. CLARKE

Faculty of Commerce
University of Newcastle
Central Coast Campus

G.W. DEAN

Department of Accounting
University of Sydney

K.G. OLIVER

CAMBRIDGE
UNIVERSITY PRESS

PUBLISHED BY THE PRESS SYNDICATE OF THE UNIVERSITY OF CAMBRIDGE
The Pitt Building, Trumpington Street, Cambridge CB2 1RP, United Kingdom

CAMBRIDGE UNIVERSITY PRESS
The Edinburgh Building, Cambridge CB2 2RU, UK   http://www.cup.cam.ac.uk
40 West 20th Street, New York, NY 10011–4211, USA   http://ww.cup.org
10 Stamford Road, Oakleigh, Melbourne 3166, Australia

© F.L. Clarke, G.W. Dean and K.G. Oliver 1997

First published 1997
Reprinted 1998

Printed in Australia by Brown Prior Anderson

Typeset in New Baskerville 10/12 pt

National Library of Australia Cataloguing in Publication data

Clark, Frank L.
Corporate collapse: regulatory, accounting and ethical
failure.
Includes bibliographical references and index.
1. Accounting. 2. Business failures. 3. Business losses.
I. Dean, G. W. II. Oliver, Kyle. III. Title.
657.95

Library of Congress Cataloguing in Publication data

Clarke, Frank L.
Corporate collapse: regulatory, accounting and ethical failure/
F.L. Clarke, G.W. Dean, K.G. Oliver.
      p.   cm.
Includes bibliographical references and index.
1. Business failures – United States. 2. Corporations – United
States – Accounting. 3. Business ethics – United States. I. Dean.
G.W. II. Oliver, Kyle Gaius, 1965– . III. Title.
HG3766.C53 1997
174'.9657–dc21   96–39880

A catalogue record for this book is available from the British Library

ISBN 0 521 58520 1 hardback

Contents

Illustrations

Figures

Tables

Acknowledgements

This book would not be, if not for the assistance received from numerous sources. In particular, we owe a debt to many colleagues for their critiques of our interpretations of observations and ideas for reform; known and unknown reviewers of the manuscript; Ron Ringer for his technical help and advice; Amanda Threlfo and Kim Johnstone who were successive research assistants on the project; those too numerous to name who alerted us to various aspects of the events we address; and to those whose valuable works we cite – some we agree with and many that we do not, but which always provided a test for our interpretations and conclusions. In particular, we are deeply grateful for the guidance of the editorial and production team at Cambridge University Press. Finally, we publicly acknowledge our gratitude to Angelika and Nicole Dean, and to Jeanette Clarke, for their encouragement and forbearance over the several years it took to bring our examination of the relationship between corporate collapse and accounting to this point, and to Emeritus Professor Raymond Chambers without whose mentorship and inspiration it would never have commenced.

FRANK CLARKE
GRAEME DEAN
KYLE OLIVER

Tables 5.1 and 5.2, and Figures 5.1 and 5.2 appear courtesy of the Victorian government. The material reproduced there is not an official copy of Crown copyright material and the Victorian government accepts no responsibility for its accuracy.

Tables 12.1, 12.2, 13.3 and 14.2 appear courtesy of the Australian Stock Exchange. ASX or ASXO accept no responsibility for their accuracy.

Preface

Over more than three decades of corporate collapse, continued criticism of accounting is the result of ineffective action by regulators in general and the accounting profession in particular. Complaints regarding the unserviceability of accounting and published financial data pervade commercial discourse, notwithstanding changes from accounting self-regulation in the 1950s to the present regime of mixed government and professional intervention. A miscellany of Accounting Standards has been issued and legislatively endorsed. Diversity in the outcomes of accounting for similar commercial events remains, misleading data prevail – creative accounting reigns supreme. Our *leitmotif* is that corporate consumers – that is, the users of corporate accounts – have not been served well.

Standardisation of the inputs to the accounting process has been based on an incorrect premise that controlling the input necessarily enhances the quality of the output. Uniformity of process has been substituted for the serviceability of output. Unless there is a shift away from the present thinking and the practice it nurtures, the current criticisms of the products of accounting and auditing filling the financial press are destined to continue. The increased litigation in the 1990s is bound to be repeated during the next round in the cycle of economic boom and subsequent corporate failures.

Corporate collapses uniquely provide the raw material for a post-mortem of the *system* of accounting and auditing currently endorsed. Liquidators' accounts, and the official reports of inspectors into failures, give an unusually candid insight into the administration of companies and provide a contrast between the financial truth of their positions at various times and what they reported them to be. Whilst perhaps not the primary cause of corporate collapse and financial shenanigans, accounting has systematically failed to inform adequately, and in a timely fashion, of the drift of the financial affairs of businesses towards impending failure, leading to wealth mal-distributions along the way and, in some cases, exacerbating the extent of the financial losses.

The buck-passing feature of the accountancy profession's response to company failures is a repeated theme. Nine major Australian corporate collapses from the 1960s, 1970s and 1980s are examined in detail in Chapters 3 to 14, while others are referred to briefly. These were purposely selected for the specific instances they illustrate, the universality of the organisational and accounting practices they entailed, and the defects in the financial data which resulted. They flesh out the role played by accounting in the financing, investing and other managerial moves prior to a corporate collapse. Accounting is shown to have been a willing traveller, revealing in many instances surprisingly very little along the corporate path to failure. Many of the companies examined collapsed unexpectedly, just after reporting healthy audited profit figures. Ineffective regulatory action also is shown to have played a role.

Whilst not highlighted in the collapses covered here, we do not wish to down-play the possibility of managers' intent to deceive using, amongst other things in the 1980s, new financial instruments such as derivatives, and put and call options, sometimes off-balance sheet.

Chapter 2 precedes those analyses by inquiring into the notion and significance of *creative accounting*. This contrasts with what we have coined *feral accounting*, the use of a specific accounting practice with the intention to mislead. But the effects of creative accounting are equally insidious. Whilst there is equivocation within accounting and regulatory circles regarding the precise meaning of creative accounting, there are sound reasons why it has arisen repeatedly as a matter of importance in corporate post-mortems. Those only interested in the 1980s collapses may wish to go directly to Chapter 11.

Specialists in accounting matters may wish to begin at Chapter 3. There it is shown that the utterances of the accountancy profession over the last 30-odd years to complaint and criticism of the product of conventional accounting are an old refrain. Effectively the profession has remained reactive in responding to the need to have accounting produce financial data serviceable for assessing the wealth and progress of corporations. Professional attention has been directed to important, but mainly peripheral, issues. Overall, the generic defects which have beset conventional accounting practice for decades have survived virtually intact into the 1990s. Particular practices have been outlawed, but the generic organisational and accounting defects to which they contributed remain.

Official Standards-setting bodies have been established and modified over time. Due process for forging Accounting Standards has been devised and revised, but the quality of the end products has not

improved. Arguably it has deteriorated. A miscellany of often in-
consistent procedural and valuation rules continues to form the basis of
the compulsory conventional accounting procedures and policies.
Diversity in accounting practice persists. There is retention by the
profession of its long-stated position that the balance sheet is not a
statement of net worth and that all that is required is that the public be
educated as to the limitation of accounts. When there is an inquiry,
invariably the public is fed the notion that the financial data are misleading and creative, by virtue of practitioners deviating from, or
deliberately misinterpreting, the prescribed Accounting Standards.
Those analyses have lacked the Jesuitical verve so necessary to get to the
truth. The reality from our perspective is that compliance with Accounting Standards is as likely a major cause of accounting creativity. Unquestionably, there is chaos in the counting-house.

A siege mentality has prevailed when analysing various accounting
anomalies, including those associated with corporate failures. Repeatedly, blame has been sheeted home in the financial press and the
professional literature to the nebulous 'bad management', inadequate
compliance with Accounting Standards and ineffective regulatory
monitoring of that compliance, contiguous with criticisms of declining
business ethics and even poor accounting education. Everything, it
would seem, has been at fault, except the patchwork bases of accounting
and its unserviceable products. Chapters 15–18 examine those matters in
some detail. Buck-passing is endemic to an immature profession – the
current system of accounting deserves to be put on trial; hence our
subtitle, *Regulatory, Accounting and Ethical Failure.*

Anecdote supports the view that a virulent form of social injustice has
emerged within the commercial and business community by virtue of the
compulsory production of financial data unfit for the purposes for which
they are commonly used. Radical restructuring of conventional accounting practice is needed, a matter pursued in Chapters 15–18.

Effective reconstruction of accounting is impossible without reform
of the legal and social structure in which it operates. Some of the current
legal structures demonstrably need to be abandoned. Others need
remodelling if they are to fulfil their traditional objectives. In this context,
Chapters 15 and 16 contest the role of, and continued need for, subsidiaries and labyrinthine corporate group structures. Some of the pervading practices of accounting require a closer look by a critical eye than
the regulators appear to have given them. In Chapter 17 it is demonstrated
that some approved practices are without commercial foundation, others
without a coherent structure, many without either foundation or
structure, in the social setting of property rights and a financial system in
which money, prices, price levels, price structures and markets have a
dominant place.

This case for reform emphasises various aspects of corporate failure, especially the commingling of accounting, financing and investing in the managerial process. In that process the market worth of physical assets is an essential element in assessing a firm's solvency, its capacity to borrow, whether to liquidate specific assets and redirect resources and otherwise adapt to changing circumstances, as well as to any calculation of its wealth and financial progress. Neither internal nor external *informed* financial decisions can be taken without that information mix. This commingling provides the context for analysing the role of accounting. The reform proposal proceeds with the firm conviction that the public at large are consumers of financial information regarding the companies they deal with, are employed by, invest in, and otherwise are related to in the wider economy. That information product is currently of poor quality.

What follows may cause offence to those who hold dear the conventional practices and conventions of accounting. There are mental blinkers or a shutter on an open debate when it comes to being critical of accounting practice *from within*. Questioning the *status quo* is often denigrated, false motives are often attributed, the character of those who question is often impugned. Yet, the reality is that practitioners, the professional accountancy bodies, and the legislative and quasi-legislative agencies regulating corporate activity have not scored too highly in developing and monitoring a system which meets consumers' needs. Accountants *per se* are not under attack here. It is our profession too and we are less than happy with the way it is regressing. Accountants have to practise with a system which places them at great risk – damned by the consumers of accounting in many cases if they comply with approved Standards and damned by their governing bodies if they do not. Mostly, none of that is their fault – it is the *system* we put on trial here.

It is reasonable for the wider community to wonder why this situation has arisen. Why, given accountants' specialised knowledge of their craft – its *differentia specifica*, an inside view of the difficulties they face and the litigation danger they confront – practitioners have not forced corrective action before now.

Likely as not, many believe the current Standards-setting exercise is corrective action. Our thesis is that the proliferation of official Standards and mandatory compliance has not addressed the problem. Perhaps accountants have not mastered the intricacies of their own inventions – the accounting artifacts. Perhaps they are too close to the action, not sufficiently detached or independently placed, to see it for what it is – warts and all. Oscar Wilde captured that quirk of human behaviour in his *An Ideal Husband* – perhaps they have had all the experience but not had the privilege of 'making' the observations.

Our hope is that the observations which follow will jolt accountants and company regulators into long overdue action.

Dramatis Personae

Adsteam	Adsteam conglomerate with the flagship company, The Adelaide Steamship Co. Limited. John Spalvins was at its helm from 1977 to 1990. It was perceived as a 1980s corporate 'high-flier'.
Ansett	Ansett Transport Industries Ltd, a major transport company and 49 per cent shareholder in ASL, was headed by Sir Reginald Ansett. In 1978, Ansett declined to finance further ASL's operations, thereby precipitating its ultimate collapse.
ASL	Associated Securities Limited (ASL group).
BCH	Bond Corp (or Bond Corporation Holdings Limited), renamed in 1993 Southern Equities Corporation Limited, was one of Australia's largest and most internationally known entrepreneurial companies of the 1980s. Alan Bond was its founder and chairman from 1967 to 1991.
Bosch, Henry	Chairman of the NCSC (1985–1990) and major spokesperson on corporate governance in the 1990s. He was extremely critical of the accounting practices of Westmex and Bond Corporation.
Brierley, Sir Ron	Founder of Industrial Equity Limited and a major antipodean investor from the 1970s to the 1990s. A takeover 'whiz kid', Brierley proved to be a major factor in the downfall of Adsteam, especially his fatal 'consolidated' account of the conglomerate's state of affairs.

Cambridge	Cambridge Credit Corporation Limited (Cambridge group), run by R.E.M. (Mort) Hutcheson.
Dallhold	Dallhold Investments Proprietary Limited (Alan Bond's family company).
H.G. Palmer	H.G. Palmer (Consolidated) Limited, named after its founder Herbie Palmer. Palmer refers to H.G. Palmer (Consolidated) Limited (Palmer group).
Insull	Insull Utility Investments Inc., a major 1920s US utility conglomerate which took its name from its founder, Samuel Insull.
Kreuger	Kreuger and Toll Inc., a major 1920s multinational match company headed by Ivar Kreuger.
Manet, Edouard	Impressionist painter of *La Promenade*, the acquisition and sale of which by Bond Corporation was central to the gaoling of Alan Bond in 1996 on conspiracy to defraud charges.
Maxwell, Robert	British newspaper and communications baron throughout the 1970s and 1980s, who was found drowned in 1991 thereby sparking a series of investigations, a mountain of corporate debt and many unanswered questions about *his* financial empire.
Minsec	Mineral Securities of Australia Limited, or MSAL, refers to a loose collection of companies known as the Minsec group managed by Ken McMahon and Tom Nestel in the late 1960s and early 1970s.
Murphy, Peter (QC)	Investigator appointed by the Victorian government to inquire into the affairs of Stanhill Development Finance Limited and related companies.
Murray, B.L. & B.J. Shaw (QCs)	Investigators appointed by the Victorian government to inquire into the affairs of the Reid Murray Holdings group.
Reid Murray	RMH, or Reid Murray Holdings Limited (Reid Murray group), headed by Ossie O'Grady.
RMA	Reid Murray Acceptance Limited, formed to act as a corporate 'banker' for RMH.

Rothwells — Western Australian-based merchant bank headed by the colourful financier Laurie Connell. Rothwells was pejoratively described as a 'lender of last resort' for high-risk ventures. Rothwells' activities and Connell's were scrutinised during the WA Royal Commission into WA Inc.

Rowland, Tiny — Founder of the multinational Lonrho and a crucial player in the final downfall of Bond Corporation, especially the world-wide distribution in late 1988 of the notorious 'Financial Analysis' document detailing Bond Corporation's 'insolvent' state of affairs.

Royal Mail — Royal Mail group, headed by the Royal Mail Steam Packet Company Ltd – the world's largest 1920s UK ocean liner group run by the former Governor of the City of London, Lord Kylsant.

Stanhill — Stanhill Proprietary Ltd, family company of Stanley Korman, founder of the SDF group including SCL (Stanhill Consolidated Limited), SDF (Stanhill Development Finance Limited), Chevron (Chevron Limited) and SD Pty Ltd (Stanhill Development Proprietary Ltd).

Van Gogh, Vincent — Impressionist painter of *Irises*, which was acquired in the mid-1980s by the Bond Corporation group.

Westmex — Westmex Limited was a 1980s conglomerate 'high-flier' headed by Russell Goward during its brief rise and fall from 1986 to 1990.

Whiz kids — Phrase coined to describe those takeover wizards of the securities market who engaged in conglomerate takeovers in the mid-1960s and more conventional acquisitions in the early 1970s. They included Sir Ronald Brierley and Alexander Barton in Australia, Harold Geneen of ITT fame and Sir James Goldsmith (Britain). Subsequently applied to some Australian 1980s 'high-fliers', including Russell Goward.

Abbreviations

AARF	Australian Accounting Research Foundation, formed in 1966 as part of the profession's response to the spate of 1960s corporate collapses
AAS	Australian Accounting Standards, which have had the force of law under Australia's Corporations Law since 1992
AASB	Australian Accounting Standards Board, the major Standards-setting body since 1992
AFC	Australian Finance Conference
AICPA	American Institute of Certified Public Accountants
APB	Accounting Principles Board (United States Accounting Principles-setting body, 1959–1971)
ASA	Australian Society of Accountants (predecessor body of the ASCPA)
ASA General Council	General Council of the Australian Society of Accountants
ASC	Australian Securities Commission, the successor to the NCSC as Australia's national corporate regulator (1991–)
ASCPA	Australian Society of Certified Practicising Accountants
ASX	Australian Stock Exchange Ltd, formed in 1990 from an amalgamation of Australia's state Stock Exchanges
CEO	Chief Executive Officer
FASB	Financial Accounting Standards Board (United States Accounting Standards-setting body, 1972–)
Financial Review	*Australian Financial Review*
FITB	Future income tax benefit

FRC	Financial Reporting Council of the London Stock Exchange (1990–)
IASC	International Accounting Standards Committee (International Accounting Standards-setting body, 1973–)
ICAA	The Institute of Chartered Accountants in Australia (1928–)
ICAEW	The Institute of Chartered Accountants in England and Wales (1880–)
ISOYD	Inverse sum of the years' digits depreciation method
NCSC	National Companies and Securities Commission – national corporate regulatory body (1981–1990)
NPV	Net present value
POB	Public Oversight Board (part of the SEC Practice Section of the AICPA)
Rule of 78	A recognised arbitrary method of apportioning interest on term contracts, such as hire purchase finance
SEC	Securities Exchange Commission, formed in the United States in 1933 following the Depression as part of America's 'New Deal'. It took many functions previously held by the Federal Trade Commission.
UIG	Urgent Issues Group, formed at the end of 1994 with the aim of 'providing timely guidance on urgent financial reporting issues'

PART I

Chaos in the Counting-house

ONE

Swindlers' List?

It was the best of days, yet the worst of days! On 12 October 1989 the
7.40 a.m. train pulled out of Wahroonga station, on its way to the city. It was
like every other workday. Those who had stood on the station in Sydney's
executive belt, sheltering under its neatly clipped trees to avoid the
morning sun, attaché-case in hand, squash racquet under arm, now
slipped into seats in a mock orderly fashion. Getting a seat at that time of
the day is always a lottery. But they knew it would be unbecoming to appear
anxious about such a small matter. It would not be the sort of stuff that the
upwardly mobile – the *yuppies, dinks, snags* and the like – are made of, not
the sort of thing you would expect to see a *Bond,* a *Skase,* a *Holmes à Court,*
a *Goward,* a *Brierley* or a *Spalvins* do in similar circumstances.

It had been the normal ritual. Car left parked beside the station; or the
wife, husband or companion, whipping up to the kerb in the leased
BMW or the like, a quick peck on the cheek and then the intending com-
muter breaking into a commanding stride down the steps to the platform, mobile phone at the ready. Once in a seat the attaché-case was
opened. Usually there was not much in it; a brown-bag lunch comprising
all the latest Heart Foundation suggestions, a piece of fruit perched in
one of the slots as if it were made for it, the mandatory copy of *Yachting
World,* or *Mode,* the *Financial Review,* a calculator and, of course, the
reading glasses neatly filed.

But that morning there was a difference.

Gasps of amazement echoed throughout the rattling carriages as
Sydney's up-and-coming business glitterati read the headlines in the
Review – Bond Corporation, the group led by the man who several years
earlier had been Australia's 'Businessman of the Year', more recently
'Father of the Year', and of course always a hero for bankrolling the 1983
unscrewing of the America's Cup from its Rhode Island mantelpiece, was

3

reported to have incurred almost a billion-dollar loss! Bond himself was under a cloud in respect of certain transactions. Bond Corporation's assets (it seemed) were not gold-plated at all. Indeed, it was being said that they were mostly *water*. One top-value asset, the accounting-created future income tax benefits, had a massive $453.4 million written off it. Unbelievable! Well, at least so to those having an inadequate understanding of the annals of corporate history. And that, it seemed, included almost everyone.

Yes, it had all happened before; many times, over many decades, all around the world. Different characters, different settings, different companies in different industries – but with similar circumstances and under a common pervading regulatory philosophy: procedural input processing rules and sanctions for non-compliance, even when non-compliance made more sense in reporting an entity's financial state of affairs.

What was soon to happen after that day was common, too. Media commentators would zoom in on the personalities, intrude on their private lives, pick up and highlight the gossip regarding their peccadilloes. A *regulatory theatre* would provide an old refrain of indignation, outrage, promises of retribution to offenders, justice to the aggrieved. The *cult of the individual* would be revived. Connell, Yuill, Goldberg, Bond, Skase, Goward and other major players in the failures that followed would be labelled 'corporate cowboys'. Their life in the saddle would become more newsworthy and receive more media exposure than anything else relating to the collapses. Huge sums would be spent attempting to bring the high-fliers to ground or to extract them from their hideaways. Of course, the search for scapegoats would be time-consuming. But again, attention would be on individuals: individual auditors, individual accountants – or the firms of which they were partners; individual directors – or the boards of which they were members; individual bankers and financial intermediaries – or the financial institutions of which they were head. Their business morality, their ethics, would be raked over and called into question. It is an exemplar of what critic of mass media's influence on social attitudes, Neil Postman, described in his *Amusing Ourselves to Death* as entertainment. But entertainment that reduces to the point where the seriousness of the affairs is lost from sight in the short term and completely forgotten in the longer term.

For most observers, drawing up a list of 'bad guys' was, as it always has been, an imperative; apprehending and punishing them for not following the regulatory codes was again the approach. Everyone in the early 1990s, it seemed, wanted to draw up the definitive *Swindlers' List*.

Whilst resources were increased to assist regulatory bodies, virtually nowhere would there be concerted attention to rectifying the system that permitted it all to occur, even facilitated it – the generic imperfections in the mechanisms supposedly regulating corporate activities, their financial reporting, permissive corporate structures under our law, or the pervading ideas on corporate governance.

A window on corporate failure

Calls for regulatory and quasi-regulatory reform of accounting and auditing practices have been the norm for several decades in Australia and overseas. Whereas there have been flurries of action, there has been little progress.

Recurrent instances of bankruptcies and liquidations in the early years of the 1990s evoked the familiar rhetoric, but little in the way of effective, preventive action. Financial and social fallout from larger Australian company failures in the latter part of the 1980s – the failures of Ariadne, Hooker, Qintex, Westmex, Parry Corporation, Judge Corporation, Adsteam, Budget Corporation, Tricontinental, Pyramid Building Society, Rothwells, National Safety Council of Australia, the State Banks of Victoria and South Australia, Spedley Securities, the Battery, Duke, Girvan and Linter groups, Estate Mortgage and Aust-Wide Trusts, and in the early years of the 1990s the partial, then complete liquidation of Southern Equities Corporation (formerly Bond Corporation), and the commercial dilemmas at Harlin/Fosters Brewing, Westpac and Coles Myer, for example – have been well documented in the financial press. Generally these journalistic accounts have been rigorous in respect to technical issues. They run contrary to the frequent commentaries on how to achieve business elegance and invite the question: 'Why undertake inquiry into failure, rather than success?'

'Success' is pursued in countless how-to-get-rich books. Indeed, virtually all of the prominent companies which failed over the past decade or so (and their leaders) could earlier have been written up as paragons of how to be successful, like Bob Ansett in Australia and Donald Trump in the United States. Alan Bond was 'Businessman of the Year' in 1978. Asil Nadir rode high when Polly Peck was in its prime in the United Kingdom. Everyone wanted to be Michael Milken's mate when junk bonds were the flavour-of-the month in the 1980s. Many courted Robert Maxwell's friendship. Few shied away from involvement with Qintex, Adsteam, Equiticorp or Hooker Corporation during their good times. More than often, those who failed had been heralded and lauded earlier as a major success. Adsteam was a model for many, before it ran aground. So, in a sense, examining the process of failure is merely the other end of examining success – though for a number of reasons, primarily related to access to more objective data, failure is likely to be more capable of an objective, autoptic evaluation.

Table 1.1   Corporate insolvencies, selected years, 1976 to 1995

Year end	Number	Year end	Number
1976	1,178	1991	8,366
1981	1,565	1992	10,361
1987	5,816	1993	8,859
1988	4,836	1994	7,772
1989	6,189	1995	7,240
1990	7,394		

Source: Corporate Affairs Commission, *Annual Reports*, 1976 and 1981;
1987–1995 data compiled from NCSC and ASC releases.

The increase in the number of corporate failures in Australia during
the late 1980s and early 1990s is evident in Table 1.1. In 1991 the AMP
Society estimated that 'the collapse of our corporate high-fliers has cost
shareholders more than $8 billion'.[1] Others have claimed the figure to
have been nearer $20 billion.[2]

What's a billion or two between corporate friends? The 1980s' high-
priests of corporate finance, now the disgraced entrepreneurs, certainly
had no qualms about lending millions to each other.

Some specific results of Australia's largest companies revealed in
Table 1.2 further highlight the extent of the battering Australia's
corporate profile took during the early 1990s. Little wonder that the
corporate cowboys tag is commonly ascribed to the investment and
financing behaviour of some of the more publicised entrepreneurs of the
1980s. As this story unfolds, it reveals that the corporate cowboys can do
their thing only because they had the open ranges on which to run wild.
We show that those commercial ranges have been, in many respects,
untouched for decades.

Whilst Table 1.1 reveals that Australian corporate failures in the 1980s
increased relative to the Australian company population, the number of
failures remains small. For the years 1962–1981, annual liquidations of
companies in New South Wales, for example, averaged 77.1 companies
per 10,000 companies registered. The highest rate of failure in a single
year was 104 liquidations per 10,000 companies in 1977.[3] Figures since
the late 1880s through to 1960 reveal a similar incidence of failure.[4] In
the depression following the October 1987 stock market crash, ASC
annual reports disclosed national business failure rates at levels of
0.77 per cent (1989), 0.88 per cent (1990), 0.95 per cent (1991), 1 per
cent in 1992, just over 1 per cent in 1993, and declining to less than 1 per
cent in 1994 and 1995. This relatively low failure rate is in line with US
data over the last 60 years produced by Dun and Bradstreet Corporation's *Business Failure Record.*[5]

Table 1.2 Selected corporate losses, 1990 to 1992* (Consolidated operating
and extraordinary figures, after tax, attributable to members of the holding
company for the 1990, 1991 and 1992 financial years.)

Institution	1990 $bn	1991 $bn	1992 $bn
Bond Corporation	2.250	1.066	0.310
State Bank of South Australia	–	2.180	–
State Bank of Victoria	1.978	–	–
Westpac Banking Corporation	–	–	1.670
Adelaide Steamship	–	1.358	0.049
David Jones	–	1.381	0.061
Fosters Brewing Group	1.264	0.043	0.949
Tooth and Co.	-	0.720	0.038
Bell Resources (Aust. Cons. Invest.)	0.829	0.108	0.034
National Consolidated	–	0.390	0.044
Industrial Equity	–	0.341	–
Petersville Sleigh	–	0.309	–
News Corporation	–	0.296	–
TNT	–	0.275	0.024
Barrack Mines	0.169	0.130	–
FAI Insurances Group	–	0.144	0.049
Ariadne Australia	0.067	0.019	0.103

Note: * A '–' indicates the company reported a profit for that period.

Source: Annual reports of companies for the 1990, 1991 and 1992 financial
years.

Despite the inevitable hysteria, Australian experience with corporate
failures is far from unique. Similar corporate crises also occurred in the
United Kingdom and the United States in the 1980s and during previous
decades. Moreover, official responses to the latest Australian corporate
failures fit the pattern elsewhere.

The relatively low frequency of corporate failure is likely to mask its
historical significance and commercial impact. Real resource allocation has
social consequences. One large failure, or a large number of small failures,
is an event of historic, rather than merely historical, dimensions causing
considerable hardship and often inciting outrage among shareholders,
creditors and the general public.[6] Damage done before and after the
excesses of the 1980s also has had far-reaching direct consequences:
undermining confidence in Australia's securities markets, inciting public
outrage and creating a perception by some that Australia's self-regulatory
Accounting Standards-setting process is deficient, much more so than in
Britain or the United States.[7]

Thus, following Lonrho's well-publicised 1972 liquidity crisis and
allegations of corrupt business practices, UK Prime Minister Edward
Heath labelled Tiny Rowland's actions at Lonrho 'the unpleasant and

unacceptable face of capitalism'. Apt too are the comments of a group of British Labour Party members that those actions were 'the inevitable logic of capitalism'.[8]

Note their symmetry with the comment made nearly 50 years earlier in Britain in the wake of the Royal Mail failure, that it was 'an offence [by Lord Kylsant, Chairman of the Royal Mail Steam Packet Co.] which, however innocently committed, struck deep at the roots of investment confidence and menaced the whole stability of commercial financial practice'.[9] Similar Australian sentiments were evident in the aftermath of 1960s corporate collapses – for example, this editorial comment following the H.G. Palmer failure: 'the questions raised . . . are so serious and affect so seriously the confidence felt in the conduct of our business affairs that only the most thorough inquiry can now satisfy the public';[10] and following the 1970s Minsec collapse, it 'was the biggest borrower on the Australian unofficial money markets. Its fall sparked one of the biggest money panics in Australian history . . . white-anting the whole Australian money market.'[11]

It is easy to find nearly identical comments following the belatedly-revealed 1980s excesses of Australia's failed entrepreneurs:

> . . . thanks to Spedley . . . the security blanket of audited accounts is an illusion, . . . the duties of directors are a nonsense when and if they don't know what is going on. . . . It is time, perhaps, for a rethink on how we do business [and account for it!].[12]

> The failure of the accounting profession to establish and adhere to decent standards has . . . proved that many of their figures cannot be trusted. . . . Billions of dollars of investors' funds vanished. . . . Accounts presented by the accounting profession in many cases cannot be trusted.[13]

> . . . arguably the September 1991 accounts [of Westpac] are now shown to have been grossly misleading. . . . something like two billion dollars of assets claimed in those accounts did not exist. . . . what Westpac is now shown to have done is not all that different from the central charge levelled at the so-called 'entrepreneurs' in the 1980s. That they reported assets and profits that were grossly inflated and untrue, and that those untruths were then ticked [by the auditors].[14]

> However, proprietors are entitled to ask why they were misled by their directors. The property market has not deteriorated to anywhere near the extent recorded in the Westpac figures over the last three months; it's been on a deep slide for two years.[15]

One might imagine anguish on the part of representatives of the accounting profession faced with such comments, for each is incontestable. Occasionally members have expressed horror. With members facing massive litigation claims, the official professional bodies have described the profession as being 'in crisis'.[16] Mostly, however, the

comments have evoked a flurry of attention by the professional accountancy bodies to search out someone, or more commonly 'something',
they might blame – bad management, declining business ethics and
inadequate educational resources have each had their turn.[17] Indicative
of the search for causes is the 1994 Australian study by Greatorex *et al.*,
Corporate Collapses: Lessons for the future, which surveyed Australian liquidators of 162 cases of corporate collapse and recorded their observations
on the causes of corporate failure.[18] They identified lack of CEO management skills, overreliance on debt, and the failure to have sufficient
capital for ongoing development or survival. An equally pertinent
question might have been why those who failed had shortly earlier been
reported as profitable, sometimes as highly successful.

Cult of the individual

One theme explored here is that because many of the participants in
corporate collapse are household names, the ensuing publicity has emphasised the fallen in the entrepreneurial 'cult', the individuals involved.
How families cope with their anxieties, and other personal matters, have
become fodder for the media. That diverts attention from important
social issues. Exploiting inquisitiveness, the media has focused on the
cult of the individual. This has nurtured the general ineffectiveness of
responses to our regulatory mechanisms, allowed the parts played by
accounting and auditing in exacerbating failure and its consequences to
survive more or less untouched.

Descriptions of the financial difficulties particular companies experienced (Chapters 3 to 14) are as diverse in style and substance as they are
with respect to the extent to which fraud or other illegalities influenced
the events to which they refer. Some have been the subject of official
investigations (Royal Commissions, inspectors' investigations or liquidators' analyses), others simply the subject of lay commentary. However,
most of them are far less diverse in so far as accounting and other
financial reports, subsequently found to be false, had passed the scrutiny
of auditors. Some also had passed the so-described informed and
efficient securities market in general and (many) analysts in particular.
Accounting and audit failure has continued to slip through the regulatory net, evoking the issues to be addressed here – in particular: does
the incidence of failure suggest that the securities market is uninformed;
will the more centralised and greater-resourced ASC regulatory mechanism prove more effective than its NCSC predecessor; in what practical
sense is the market supposed to be efficient; is the commercial society
getting value for money from audits of publicly listed companies; is the
role of an auditor currently feasible or are auditors engaged in a mission

impossible; are the professionally-endorsed responses of auditor rotation, an auditor disciplinary board guaranteeing swift and open hearings,
the introduction of audit committees, audit firm incorporation or
putting a cap on auditor liability, likely to be effective regulatory responses; is it necessary for a fundamental reconstruction of accounting
to be undertaken?

Underlying our analysis and speculations are the pertinent wider issues
relating to the education of professional accountants and auditors – and,
when it comes to that, the education of the regulators, their motivating
philosophy and the structure of their *modus operandi*. Professional
accountancy bodies and the regulatory bodies need to come under
scrutiny, for they have had the opportunity to restructure the *status quo*,
but generally have not done so. Interestingly, professional accountancy
bodies suggest that the remedy is more education – educate the public
on the limited utility of traditional accounting information. This
approach is a curious example of *caveat emptor*.

We concur with the paradoxical view that success and failure are
closely linked – 'success itself and the things that cause success seem very
much to contribute to decline. In order for firms to remain competitive
they must learn to master these "perils of excellence".'[19] Nearly all of the
failed companies featuring here, at least at one point in their corporate
history, were lauded as being successful, sometimes exceedingly so. In
some cases this praise occurred just prior to collapse. In some instances
that timely praise was warranted. For some, it was wishful thinking. And
for others, it was without obvious thought!

There is no dispute, for example, that in 1960s Australia, Reid Murray
was a successfully aggressive retailer. In three years it had grown, albeit
by takeover, to the fourth-largest publicly-listed company in Australia.
H.G. Palmer was Australia's largest electrical retailer by the early 1960s
with 140 branches, and Cox Brothers had been Australia's fastest growing
retailer in the late 1950s. They were eminently 'successful'. Similarly,
Minsec, formed in 1965, had within four years undeniable claims to the
position of leading money market operator in Australia. By contrast, it is
doubtful, notwithstanding their sales growth, whether Reid Murray or
H.G. Palmer were ever *truly* profitable, or whether Rothwells was ever
one of the leading merchant banks of the 1980s. With hindsight it is also
debatable whether Bond Corporation or Westmex *actually* operated
successfully from the mid-1980s. The suggestion now being raised is that
possibly Bond Corporation was in financial distress as long ago as 1984![20]
But before their declines became public, both Westmex and Bond
Corporation were lauded in the financial press as corporate high-fliers.
Their chief executives were referred to with great deference as leading
businessmen. Indeed, recall that in 1978 Alan Bond was 'Businessman

of the Year'; in 1985 he was fêted for his Castlemaine Tooheys 'Takeover of the Year' and in 1987 was awarded 'Australian of the Year'. By the end of 1989 Bond's shine had worn off. Russell Goward was described as a financial whiz kid and was awarded the 1987 'Acorn Business Award'. His Westmex was perceived as a successful conglomerate, as was John Spalvins' Adsteam. In the financial press this adulation of those chief executives continued until just prior to each company's demise. And it dissolved thereafter in the same authoritative haze as quickly as it had been achieved.

There is no disputing that these leading companies had another common factor. They all collapsed, many suddenly, seemingly unexpectedly. For many, collapse followed news releases of reportedly successful operations. Only occasionally, in advance of collapse, were those companies identified to be ailing over a period of years. Certainly they were not failing according to many in the press and some of those in the market claiming to be in-the-know. Understandably so, for those companies' financial reports failed to indicate unambiguously their impending failure. Despite claims by the 'punters' (the uninformed investors) that they are denied information apparently available to others in the market, the published financial statements are the primary source of financial information to virtually all in-the-know punters (e.g. the institutional investors) too. History demonstrates that corporate failure does not appear to have had a lengthy public incubation period. Whilst symptoms are there and some ferret them out, the financial reporting system masks them. Therein lies a major problem – matters of unquestionable public interest are able to be kept private.

Public complaint, criticism, and questioning of the role of accountants and auditors were features of the highly publicised bankruptcies and liquidations in the 1980s and early 1990s. Complaint and criticism of that kind were international phenomena.[21] Comments on the crumbled empires of Asil Nadir, Aghan Abedi and Robert Maxwell in the United Kingdom indicate that 'the crumbling of firms like Polly Peck, BCCI, and, most recently, Maxwell Communication, [occurred] all within months of getting a clean bill of health from their auditors, has raised serious questions about the usefulness of company accounts.'[22] Likewise in this assessment on the US Savings and Loans affair: '[Democratic Congressman] Wyden and others lay a large part of the blame for the S&L crisis at the door of the accounting profession. "Accountants didn't cause the S&L crisis", says Wyden. "But they could have saved taxpayers a lot of money if they did their jobs properly and set off enough warning alarms for regulators."'[23] And the similar lament in a 1993 United States Public Oversight Board Report: 'The accounting profession has suffered a serious erosion of confidence: . . . *in its standards, in the relevance of its*

work and the financial reporting process . . . [because] in some cases, not long
before an entity failed, it received an auditor's report giving no indication that the entity was in its latter days.'[24]

In Australia, public criticism was legion following the October 1987
stock market crash: 'Auditors are being called to account', 'The accounts
are a joke', 'Audit served no useful purpose', 'What makes an audit "true
and fair"?', 'Uproar on accounting proposals', 'Auditors in danger from
$2.5bn claims' and 'Accountants want to stop the carnage'.[25] Those
comments were indicative of sentiment in the financial press regarding
the state of Australian accounting and auditing. Unquestionably they
were an old refrain – a case of the 1960s and 1970s *déjà vu* – for then
similar headlines had adorned the business pages in Australia following
company crashes.[26]

Interestingly, virtually none of the commentaries attack the organisational and accounting fundamentals – virtually all imply that the
current Standards have not been applied adequately. None observe that
even if they *had* been, it would not have solved the problem. Generally,
the responses entail a push for more rules, more sanctions of the kind
already in place.

Such a strategy is curious. It has not worked in the past and there is no
compelling reason to expect that more of the same will work better in the
future. Indeed, a theme pursued in this book is that existing regulations
– in particular, current accounting prescriptions – contribute to the
collapse of many companies being so unexpected. The adverse drift in
these companies' financial affairs was not publicly disclosed, and the
evidence suggests that more of the same type of accounting prescriptions
will not facilitate the provision of useful, predictive data.

For, whereas there has been a surge in forging Accounting and Auditing
Standards, the generic defects in conventional accounting remain. Notwithstanding the increased number of Standards with which accounts
must conform, they continue to contain data which are not serviceable in
determining a company's financial position, its past financial performance, and associated trends in its wealth and progress. Certainly, particular
Standards have addressed and eliminated individual accounting infelici-
ties. But, therein is the problem. Remedial action has been cosmetic. It has
attacked the symptoms only and done little to eradicate the cause.

Anxiety spawned by the corporate collapses following the October 1987
crash produced increasing pressures on regulators to implement reforms.
There was a new Australian Corporations Law with additional sections
including those relating to loans to directors and related party
transactions, directors' duties regarding insolvent trading, aspects of
liquidations and winding-ups, and new prospectus provisions; and cen-
tralisation of the monitoring body, the ASC – resourced with nearly

$1 billion over its first five years. In conjunction with the Australian Stock Exchange, a continuous disclosure reporting system has been introduced. Overall the impact is likely to be more dramatic on Australia's forests than on the serviceability of accounting reports.

Not surprisingly in this climate the accounting profession has also perceived a need to react. Suggestions proffered have included: auditor rotation; mandatory audit committees; various proposals to limit auditor liability; initially quickening, but then stalling, of the development of a *mandatory* conceptual framework underlying accounting practice and method; renewed attempts at merging the two major professional accountancy bodies; quality assurance accreditation procedures for CPAs; and a push for professional ethics components to be given greater emphasis in university educational programmes. This is commendable action, though somewhat belated and merely increasing the tempo of an old, familiar and overplayed tune.

Underpinning those regulatory developments is a move away from general 'fuzzy law' to a more 'black-letter' (adherence to the rules) approach. This has been criticised by the Business Council of Australia and others. Yet, leading members of the accounting profession incongruously are calling for more of the same type of Accounting Standards. One objective seems to be to eliminate *totally* the qualitative *true and fair* view override criterion (see pp. 251–252) by eventually removing it from the new Corporations Law.[27] Yet the true and fair view override is a succinct general quality criterion which captures the essence of what consumer laws struggle to enshrine, has world-wide currency and is unique to accounting. It has been proposed that in view of global competition and bundling of capital in ever increasingly complex financial packaging, 'these imprecise adjectives ["true and fair"] have become increasingly meaningless' and the clause has become patently 'an anachronism'.[28] That is a peculiar analysis indeed, for historical and contemporary evidence from the autopsies of corporate failures illustrates the continuing, even increasing, need for enforcement of a qualitative, 'fuzzy' criterion, and less (even a decreasing) need for a formula-driven, prescriptive accounting system.

The need for systemic, rather than cosmetic, changes in the mechanics and function of accounting is clear, but inexplicably it is not on the professional accountancy bodies' or other regulatory agencies' agendas. The evidence adduced in this book is not new. Nor are the problems to which it relates. Lawyers appointed as inspectors in 1965 into the affairs of the Reid Murray collapse remarked: '. . . neither of us is skilled in accountancy and . . . much . . . we have said will not be acceptable by the accounting profession generally. [We use] commonsense, and commonsense has compelled us to reject a number of practices used in the group and apparently regarded as acceptable by accountants.'[29] A lament with which the financial press concurred: 'Accountants and directors also have a duty in a public company and the Reid Murray story has again brought home the realisation of the position of trust they hold for investors.'[30] The need for a 'commonsense' approach and recognition of a 'public duty' would seem to be grist to the mill for every professional. Yet, in accounting, suggestions for such a 'professional' response generally have gone unheeded.

Regulatory theatre

'Corporate governance' is one of the buzz phrases of the 1990s, fertile ground for producing reports and codes of practice. Following the 1960s failures, the Australian accountancy profession sheeted most of the blame to poor management in its white paper, *Accounting Principles and Practices Discussed in Reports on Company Failures.*[31] Analysis of the 1980s collapses has contained more of the same, blaming bad management and declining ethics. It is the same the world over. Pratten's 1991 inquiry into UK failures commissioned by The Institute of Chartered Accountants in England and Wales trots out the same rhetoric, despite recent evidence in the affairs of Polly Peck, Maxwell and BCCI of more fundamental problems in corporate governance. There has been little effective introspection despite a disturbing repetition of past behaviour.

One might have expected increased promulgation of Accounting and Auditing Standards to have been accompanied by decreased complaint and criticism. But just the opposite is the case – increased specification of accounting and auditing practices by the profession is positively correlated with increased litigation. Understandably so, we would argue, for compliance with Standards then in vogue was as likely to have contributed to creative accounting as deviation from them. Perversely, corporate regulators and the accounting profession are calling for even more Accounting and Auditing Standards.

One pervading problem in seeking to reform corporate conduct is the populace's soft attitude to corporate crime – at least until it affects them. White-collar crime occurs in a world remote to many. It appears to be so different from a mugging in the park. To many Australians, corporate offenders possibly fit neatly into the Ned Kelly syndrome; for Americans, they conjure up the inexplicable fascination with the exploits of Bonnie and Clyde, or of Butch Cassidy and the Sundance Kid; for the British, they possibly rekindle the best of the fantasies regarding Robin Hood – their boldness almost always evoking curiosity, their acts more admired for their daring rather than deplored for their offence against the rights of others, perceived as reluctantly fleecing their victims rather than callously indifferent to their welfare.

That delusion is endemic to the way financial finagling is perceived. It always has been. Accounts of John Blunt's 18th century deception underlying the collapse of the South Sea Company and of John Law's fraudulent Mississippi Scheme fit the romantic image. Lord Kylsant is misrepresented as a *victim* rather than a manipulator of the 1905 *Companies Act* (UK), as it affected his misreporting of the Royal Mail's affairs; Samuel Insull presents as a rather kindly, lonely manipulator, despite the financial misery caused by the collapse of his utilities empire at the commencement of the Great Depression; Swedish 'match king', Ivar Kreuger emerges as the financial genius of the 1920s and 1930s, duping governments and investors over a 30-year rampage; Philip Musica's masquerade, underpinning the 1930s McKesson and Robbins fraud, becomes an impish pre-war escapade; Tino de Angelis's swindles in vegetable oils appear more the actions of a lovable eccentric dabbling in the post-war aid schemes than of a corporate criminal indifferent to any hardship his actions may have imposed on others.[32] Coverage given to Michael Milken's junk bond exploits in the gutsy 1980s captures more of his daring than exposure of the glaring regulatory gaps that facilitated the investors' losses. Asil Nadir fleeing to Turkish Cyprus to avoid answering for dubious gains with his Polly Peck empire is labelled romantically as a modern Ronnie Biggs, as if that were a virtue. The financial subterfuge of BCCI's Aghan Abedi is relegated to the bottom line in favour of description of his life at the top. Germany's Jurgen Schneider's demise early in 1994 is described in *Time* magazine as 'The King Absconds'. Australian media interest in Christopher Skase, now, more fuels in some a curious admiration for his in-exile lifestyle, than deplores the climate of business adventuring which had led to his earlier widespread disdain. And, seemingly everyone gets more joy from the Catholic Church's embarrassment from Robert Calvi's Banco Ambrosiano and Vatican Bank foreign currency affair than from contemplating the defects of the national and international monetary systems facilitating it. That also is the general style of the populist coverage of the failure of the US thrifts in the 1980s.

In virtually all of those episodes, failure of the publicly-available financial information to disclose a true and fair view of companies' financial positions facilitated deception and in some cases exacerbated the losses.

Perhaps providing a glimmer of hope for our proposals addressing, then redressing, generic defects in *the system* are the comments by one of Australia's best known (albeit much maligned) regulators of the 1980s, Henry Bosch (an aggressive chairman of the NCSC from 1985 to 1990). He addresses matters pertaining to the system. He has been very active in promoting his assessment of the existing corporate regulatory mechanisms in Australia and his remedies for its ills. We challenge his understanding of the effectiveness of Accounting Standards and especially his call for more of them. His general advocacy for changing the regulatory mechanism to a more legislative-bound setting makes sense, as does his plea for regulatory mechanisms with teeth. Few should object to that. It *is* an acknowledgement that human nature cannot be changed, whereas the system can. We can gaol the individuals and they can die off, but there will always be another crop to replace them next season. Likewise, the complaint by Bosch's immediate successor at the NCSC, Tony Hartnell, of the difficulty in getting corporate offenders into court, hits at the system rather than the individuals. But notwithstanding these exceptions there is an institutional blind-spot regarding the generic defects of accounting and auditing practice. No other professional activity has enjoyed such a level of continued support and excuse in the wake of a prolonged public record of default.

What follows catalogues events leading to several notorious, often unexpected collapses, reveals repeated accounting anomalies and exposes the accounting profession's inadequate responses. It is a sorry tale, one inimical to a profession, but needing to be told. It is not a story about the personal defects of people *per se*; it does not set out to draw up who might be placed on a swindlers' list. It is about the huff-and-puff of the regulatory theatre, its rhetoric and its ineffective action, about the defects in critical elements of the regulatory environment – the inherent defects in rules and conventional practices – in which those who have made the headlines operated. Indeed, it is doubtful in respect of some matters whether some of those headline-grabbers deserve to be on a list of bad guys any more than those well-intentioned individuals who made the rules and drafted the Accounting and Auditing Standards that have proved so unserviceable in informing and protecting commercial society. In many ways, those on whom the media have focused are victims of the system, too. Without the regulatory system being as it is, many of the events of which the corporate watchdogs and the financial media have cried 'foul' might not have occurred.

Those defects and their contribution to the financial impact of corporate collapse are the subject of what follows. No doubt it will please few, enrage many, enlighten some.

TWO

Creative Accounting

'The proper object of standards is to reduce this permissiveness. It has long been said by the leaders of the profession that the diversity of accounting rules should be reduced.'

Accounting Standards Review Committee (1978, p. 62)

That would be a laudable sentiment were it to result in more truthful financial statements. Generally on the national fronts the stated aim has been to strive for less diversity. To the extent that this has been achieved it has been at the expense of creating increased opportunities for greater deception. Conventional accounting produces institutionalised window-dressing.

Vehement complaint and criticism regarding the serviceability of the end products of conventional accounting and auditing processes has accompanied corporate failures. Disbelief has followed the collapse of companies soon after they have reported profits and received clean audit reports. Whereas the 'what-the-hell-has-happened?' type of cry has been common, the fact that conventional accounting is unlikely ever to produce data serviceable for determining the wealth and progress of companies has, by and large, attracted little comment. Habitually, financial indicators such as profitability, solvency, liquidity, rate of return, asset backing, the ratio of debt to equity, and the like, are calculated in the financial press and by financial analysts from the data in the published accounts. Calculated from the annual financial statements conforming to the Accounting Standards endorsed by the accounting profession, those derived data are reasonably expected to expose, and help explain, the salient financial characteristics of firms. The problem is, generally they do not, indeed cannot.

Existing Accounting Standards have failed to match the admirable claims of the leaders of the profession – namely, that compliance with them would reduce the diversity of accounting practices and thereby provide data relevant to the making of informed financial assess-ments. Debris from unexpected failures exposes little progress on either front. Whatever progress there has been is cold comfort

17

for everybody wanting to draw inferences from published financial
statements.

Compulsory use of tax effect accounting has meant that the resulting
accounting fictions (provisions for deferred income tax debits tax and
future income tax credits) have to come into the calculation of profit and
loss and into the balance sheet, to delude.[1] *Tax effect accounting* refers to
a method mandated by the profession to report the financial effects due
to 'timing' or 'permanent' differences between actual taxation payable
and tax payable based on professional accounting treatments of transactions. Resulting deferred tax debits and credits do not have any real-
world referent. They are fictions – fictions that are legitimately the
product of applying the Standard. Fictions arise, too, through the artifacts of consolidated financial statements – goodwill and capital reserves
emerging entirely from the mechanics of consolidation, the elimination
of the effects of transactions between related companies without regard
for the actual financial outcomes and the exacerbated consolidated
impact of injecting tax effect accounting.

Another dilemma arises under foreign currency accounting – whether
to record the financial effects of beneficial foreign exchange movements
as part of operating profits or as an increment to reserves. Consider also
having to inject charges for depreciation irrespective of whether there
has been a decline in the market worth of physical assets; compulsory
valuation (in most circumstances) of saleable inventories at a variety of
costs, rather than always at market selling price; and the implied
requirement to value some physical assets by reference to hypothetical
calculations of the net present (discounted) value of the income streams
expected from their future use can do nothing but mislead the users (the
consumers) of the resulting data, which do not relate in any sensible way
to financial realities. Other dilemmas are created by capitalising
expenses as assets and through recourse to the abnormal/extraordinary
items classifications.[2] These, and many other examples, emerge below.

Paradoxically, the best-case scenario from the Standards-setters' point
of view – that there is *less* diversity in accounting practices now than in
the past – possibly has done more to reduce the usefulness of accounting
data than would have enhancing accountants' capacity to exercise their
professional judgement on how to account for, and report on, the
outcome of financial matters.

According to the corporate regulators, deviation from the prescribed
practices or the deceitful misinterpretation of the Standards produces
creative (misleading) accounting. Defying financial common sense, complying with certain practices endorsed by the accounting profession
itself, producing the standard nonsensical, fictional financial outcomes,
are not regarded by either the regulators or (so it seems) the accounting

profession to be a wilful indulgence in creative accounting. Inexplicably, the most common financial nonsense arising from complying with an endorsed accounting practice is implied to be acceptable, whereas the common sense arising from deviating from many of the endorsed practices is not.

It is no wonder that the public at large is nonplussed. Over the years, companies with strings of reported good performances and a succession of clean audit reports, some even eulogised in the financial press as the jewels in the nation's corporate crown, have suddenly gone belly-up or reported massive losses – for example, H.G. Palmer, Reid Murray, Neon Signs in the sixties; Minsec, Gollins and Cambridge Credit in the seventies; and Ariadne, Qintex, Bond, Hooker, Rothwells, Interwest, Westmex and Adsteam in the eighties.

Creative standards

In 1978 the NSW government Accounting Standards Review Committee concluded that, despite the Standards then in force, diversity in accounting practice was to the fore.[3] Earlier in the 1960s, the chairman of the 1978 Review Committee, Professor Ray Chambers, had demonstrated that there are 'A million sets of mutually exclusive rules each giving a true and fair view of a company's state of affairs and its profits! This is absurd.'[4]

Absurd, yes. But evidently not so absurd as to ensure change. Notwithstanding the addition of numerous legislatively-endorsed professional Accounting Standards to the accountants' armoury since then, that variety persists – indeed, it probably grows. There are still more than a million possible reported sets of accounting data for one company in any one period.[5]

Similar 'absurd' comments have been made for decades – for example: 'BHP's annual statement of profitability is an accountant's dream – you can produce almost any trend you want depending on which adjustments you make'[6] and under a banner 'Take your pick of accounting methods, all of them are confusing': 'Accounts and statements released in the last 48 hours by five leading companies – BHP, APM, Actrol, Clark Rubber and CRA – reveal an amazing variation in accounting practices which must be confusing all but the most qualified of analysts.'[7]

A decade later, then NCSC chairman Henry Bosch expressed similar sentiments – that accounts of some companies were being distorted by what the NCSC perceived to be unjustifiable accounting producing unfairly favourable results.[8] Bosch was perceived as a guardian of 1980s accounts and he contemplated making a test case of one of the high-fliers' accounts. Allegedly this was aborted on advice that there would be difficulty getting expert accounting opinion to support the Commission's view.

A CORRECTION FOR CREATIVE ACCOUNTANTS

Henry Bosch, NCSC Chairman (1985–1990), depicted here as the guardian of corporate accounts in the 1980s in a caption to an article by H. Killen, 'A correction for creative accountants', *Australian Financial Review*, 15 May 1987, p. 10. Courtesy of Pascal Locanto.

We demonstrate in Chapter 3 that much the same had been said in the fall-out from the 1960s company failures. One is tempted to muse that there has been little change in accounting's serviceability in the inter-regnum. Whatever changes there have been, in the form of due process in Standards-setting, tighter Standard prescriptions and limited recourse to market price information, do not appear to have substantially improved affairs.

Invariably, unexpected corporate collapses world-wide have been associated with a crisis in confidence in the accounting profession,[9] manifested primarily in calls for accountants and auditors to clean up their act. To this end, longstanding critic of the US accounting profession Abe Briloff persistently criticised accounting and auditing practices in the US Savings and Loans and other 1980s financial scandals, with little visible success.[10]

Corporate collapses, instances of takeover and other asset plays in the 1980s were the catalyst for the current calls for change to eliminate creative accounting practices in Anglo-American countries.[11] But *creative accounting* takes on many meanings. To management analyst John Argenti (in the seventies) it was a deliberate policy pursued by managers to deceive shareholders, creditors or themselves (or all three) regarding a company's wealth and progress in general and its financial difficulties in particular. That possibly captures the prevailing perception of creative accounting – practices deviating from accounting principles (Standards) underlying the preparation of financial statements. Others have drawn a more explicit bead on specific accounting practices, sometimes delineating a distinction between window-dressing, creative accounting and cooking the books.[12] Generally it is left unstated whether these accounting practices are intentionally or unintentionally used. But such a distinction is important in differentiating the deceitful (the *feral*) from the accidental, the blameworthy from the blameless. We use *feral accounting* to describe accounting creativity with the intent to deceive.

Argenti produced a list of 'creative' techniques under the heading of accounting and business practices.[13] It was developed following extensive world-wide conglomerate takeover activity by the financial 'whiz kids' – including Jim Slater, Peter Walker and James Goldsmith in the UK, James Ling and Harold Geneen in the US, whilst in Australia, amongst others, Alexander Barton and Ronald Brierley plied their trade.

However defined, 'creative accounting' generally conjures up financial permissiveness, a feature with a long history. It has been discussed by many observers, including: in the US, Ripley and Berle and Means in the 1920s; Twentieth Century Fund (1937), and Briloff (1972, 1976 and 1981); in the UK, Stamp and Marley (1970); and in Australia, Chambers (1965, 1973).[14] None of those observers was popular with the accountancy profession for 'telling it how they saw it'.

The practices to which those critical commentaries refer preceded the speculative frenzy of the so-called greedy eighties. Understandably, further catalogues of similar creative accounting techniques have appeared.[15]

Whilst a continuing fertile ground for debate, and despite their criticisms, to date little has been produced in terms of effective reforms to the general system of accounting. There has been an ever-growing list of professional Accounting and Auditing Standards in Australia. Undoubtedly they have thwarted particular misleading accounting mechanisms. But they have done little-to-nothing in respect of removing the primary generic problems of which those practices were merely contemporary methods. Thus, reported results over many years for the 1960s and 1970s failures arguably were as misleading in a generic sense as those in the 1980s. Justifiably, criticism of the serviceability of accounting data remains both within and outside the accountancy profession.

More recent analyses of creative accounting have produced a mixed assessment. Jameson advocates a theme with which we have sympathy – that creative accounting (bordering on our *feral*) refers to a practice entirely within the framework of the law and Accounting Standards, but with intention to defeat the spirit of both. It is 'essentially a process of using the rules, . . . to make financial statements look somewhat different from what was intended by the rule . . . rule-bending and loophole-seeking.'[16] Implied is the idea that such a practice is against the public good. Jameson described two insidious consequences of creative accounting: (1) Standards avoidance designed to thwart the objectives of the law-makers; and (2) opinion-shopping – the practice of asking a number of firms of auditors about their attitude to a particular accounting treatment or practice.[17]

In contrast, Griffiths sees some merit in creative accounting, arguing that creative accounting (if used *appropriately*) can result in the presentation of substance over form, 'merely *reflecting the underlying trends* in the value of the business which would not always be apparent *if the accounts were prepared and presented in accordance with a strict interpretation of the appropriate accounting rules and regulations*'.[18] Griffiths' statement, however, begs consideration of the potential danger of creative accounting being used to *support* the results of a company experiencing ongoing trading difficulties. Creative accounting can be used to offset otherwise bad news. Whilst this cannot continue in perpetuity, without resort by managers to a 'foozle' – dubious, misleading actions bordering on the illegal – or a definite fraud,[19] our cases reveal that sometimes the delusion can last for one or two decades.

In Australia, Professor Bob Walker, another critic of conventional accounting, identified at least ten legal creative accounting practices: creating 'assets' by mere bookkeeeping entries; reporting gains and losses 'above or below the line' to achieve desired results; adjustments after balance date; capitalisation of expenses; sales with options to reverse the outcome after balance date; manipulating compliance with Standards by inventive interpretations; changing accounting methods and the like.[20]

On the regulatory front, Henry Bosch was particularly concerned about the use of creative accounting (or, as he preferred, 'cosmetic accounting') to present company results in the most favourable light. His primary theme was that accounting creativity arose from deliberate manipulation of, and non-compliance with, the profession's approved

Accounting Standards – that complying with the black letter of the Standards would produce serviceable data. True to his theme, Bosch described departures from the Standards as unethical behaviour, 'which, if they became known, would damage the reputation of the profession or the market or which would be considered unfair by the great majority of market participants'.[21] His two-tier catalogue of creative practices was similar to Walker's: first tier – moving capital gains and losses, in and out of the same statement, accruing profits of related companies, off-balance sheet financing, and the transfer of assets between related companies;[22] and the second tier – arrangements to reverse transactions after balance date, pyramiding asset values through related-party transactions,[23] and general consolidation foozles.[24]

Interestingly, the practices in Walker's and (many) in Bosch's lists were and still are legally permissible. Moreover, whilst some may not be intended explicitly by the profession, many are permissible (and some required) under their Standards. On page 18 we referred to other professionally-endorsed devices not mentioned by Bosch or Walker which were used by the 1980s entrepreneurs to mask the true performance of their entities. All that suggests that the way Argenti was using the label *creative accounting*, whilst broader in its purview, was not far removed from its earlier 1960s usage, and its usage subsequently in the 1980s. Overall, the dominant theme has been to lump creative accounting with wilful deceit and intention to mislead. Our feral accounting differentiates the two.

Creative accounting – compliant, rather than deviant

There is not much on the mechanics of creative accounting from Griffiths, Jameson, Bosch or Walker with which to disagree, other than a pervading overtone that it always is with the intent to deceive, mislead or trick. No doubt much of it does have that intent. There is incontestable evidence in support of that judgement from the analyses of many of the practices of companies to be described here. There will always be cheats and tricksters. The obverse is true, too. There will always be those who, scrupulously honest, try to tell it how it is by complying with the rules. Our view is that, perversely, conventional accounting practices frequently frustrate those attempts to tell the financial truth. Whether this results in increased or decreased earnings volatility is not our main concern. The facts should be disclosed to all those operating in the market.

Contrary to the popular view, it is our proposition that compliance with the so-called *spirit* of many conventional practices and endorsed Standards produces grossly misleading data, without necessarily any intention to deceive on anybody's part. This is notwithstanding that in respect of physical assets, section 294(4) of the Corporations Law requires directors to 'take reasonable steps to find out whether the value of any non-current asset [does not exceed an] amount that would be reasonable for the company to spend to acquire the asset as at the end of the financial year.' Also, Accounting Standard AASB 1010, 'Accounting for the Revaluation of Non-current Assets', prohibits directors from reporting non-current assets that have been revalued at an amount more than their recoverable amount – that is, no more than the amounts expected to be recovered from continued use and disposal.[25] Interestingly, neither the law nor the profession's Standards prohibit either accidental or deliberate understatement of the worth of assets. Yet, understatements are equally as misleading as overstatements.

A peculiarity of the *brouhaha* surrounding corporate failures is that many of the companies in the early 1990s reporting losses appear to have fared reasonably well during the post-October 1987 reporting periods, at least according to conventional accounting. However, these good performances have been reversed through subsequent extraordinary and abnormal asset value write-offs. In the 1990/91 reporting period, for example, writing $71 million off property values pushed Raptis to its reported loss. Equitilink's $2.1 million pre-tax operating profit dipped when $40 million was written off 'management rights'. In the 1991/92 reporting period, Fay, Richwhite and Co's pre-tax bank operating profit of NZ$44.5 million was more than offset by the NZ$122.5 million goodwill on acquisition write-off. IEL's pre-tax operating profit (after interest) of $92 million was reversed by an abnormal loss of $482 million. And CRA reported an after-tax operating profit of $350 million, only to have it reduced by extraordinary write-offs of $384 million – primarily relating to its Bougainville copper mine – resulting in a net loss of $34 million! The impact of abnormals and extraordinaries continued in 1992/93; in respect of companies reporting in the half year to December 1992:

> The profit performance of the *Top 500* was buoyed by a second successive half year of lower abnormal and extraordinary losses which fell from $1.4 billion to $879 million. The losses associated with corporate collapse, write downs of asset values and losses from asset disposals have hobbled profitability during the past three years. The combined total of abnormal losses two years ago was $2.96 billion, most of which flowed from the collapse of John Spalvins' Adsteam empire.[26]

Included in the 20 'Biggest "abnormal losses" for that half year, were NAB with $126.6 million, Adsteam $107.81 million, Westpac $84.7 million, David Jones $73.74 million . . . TNT $45.89 million . . . News

Corp. $37.25 million . . . ANZ $23.80 million down to Premier Investments with $18.51 million'.[27]

Many others over this period have had their conventionally calculated *operating* results pruned by asset write-offs. In the 18 months period ending March 1991, for example, 'a total of nearly $6.2 billion was written off the net assets of the companies concerned'.[28] Bond Corporation is a case in point. Its reported 1988/89 loss of $980 million included a $453.4 million write-off of an FITB. The accounts had been injected with this item in compliance with the prescribed professional Accounting Standard on tax-effect accounting, AAS 3. Tooth & Co.'s 1990/91 $95 million operating loss was increased by a $625 million abnormal loss including a $46.6 million deferred tax benefit write-off. Reducing the value of its radio licences by $75 million primarily resulted in abnormal and extraordinary write-offs which extended Hoyts' $15.5 million pre-tax operating loss by $98 million. And in the 1990/91 financial year, a downward revaluation of some of FAI's assets pushed losses on insurance activities to a pre-tax loss of $219 million, offset partially by a deferred tax benefit of $75 million. David Jones added $1.1 billion of abnormal losses to its $147 million pre-tax operating loss. National Consolidated's $5.9 million pre-tax operating loss was increased by a $317 million charge to write off investments in the Adsteam group.

Write-downs of FITBs have been common. Adsteam had built up substantial FITBs by the early 1990s which are now the subject of proposed litigation (details in Chapter 12). In another instance, TNT wrote off $76 million as part of a reported 1992/93 loss of $133.7 million. As with the Bond Corporation's 1989 $453 million FITB write-down, it was not so much that the benefits in question had been lost, as that they never existed in the first place.

Westpac's 1992 first-half-year results reveal that directors had decided to revise the provisioning policy on its portfolio of commercial property and property-related loans. The $2.6 billion write-off produced a $2.3 billion before-tax and $1.67 billion after-tax loss, the fourth-largest reported corporate loss in the annals of corporate Australia. Westpac's rationale, according to the managing director, was to make public what was already 'well known'.[29] Whilst the share price had declined considerably in the period prior to the announcement, whether the full extent of the loss was known is arguable and, if it was 'well known', why were the write-offs not made earlier? Expressions of surprise and bewilderment following the announcement of the size of those write-downs invites the inference that Westpac's position was not as generally well known by the financial press as suggested. Not that it should have been, for its annual reports over the years had not indicated the extent of the fall in its property portfolio's worth. Reactions of market participants evident in the post-announcement stock price declines (albeit relatively minor) in the UK and Australia and the decision by rating agencies to reassess Westpac, reinforce the view that the all-wise market, influenced by the financial *cognoscenti*, was long on rhetoric, but caught rather short on performance.

Most 'depreciation' accounting mechanisms attempt to simulate what can be observed from the market. It is inexplicable why simulations are prescribed, indeed preferred to a demand that first there be recourse to the potentially more objective selling price indicators. Of course, at issue is whether there exists an unfettered and informed market, and what is the feasibility and cost of obtaining those data.

Depreciation (*de pretium*) logically is the decrease in the asset's price, not 'the allocation of the asset's cost over its useful life', as the conventional accounting rationale would have it. Amounts injected into the accounts for depreciation more than often are wide of the mark. Long after the event, that fact becomes obvious. Consider the gains and losses on the sale of fixed assets habitually reported as extraordinary items; during the 1991 and 1992 financial years of 100 companies from the top 500 listed on the ASX reported $1.9 billion and $1.05 billion respectively as catch-up adjustments when the market prices of assets entered the calculation of profits and losses on the sale or disposition of fixed assets. Clearly a large portion of that amounted to corrections to previous calculations in the compulsory depreciation simulations.

Consider the impact on the accounts of the mechanism for reporting abnormal and extraordinary items. Extraordinary items and abnormal items respectively reported by those 100 companies mentioned in the previous paragraph amounted to $7.05 billion in 1991 and $3.95 billion in 1992. Tax effect accounting by those companies alone produced balance sheet balances aggregating $12 billion in 1991 and $12.2 billion in 1992 – all potential adjustments to be made in subsequent years.

Adjustments such as those occur on much the same scale year-after-year. They are questionable enough to indicate the unreliability of the results of the previous years and the representations of the companies' financial positions. True to form, the disastrous outcomes of the write-downs and the publicity they received (Westpac's 1992 humiliation is a good example) initiate mainly *ad hoc*, knee-jerk reactions from the accountancy profession's Standards-setters. Under the new prescription in AASB 1018, extraordinary and abnormal items will now be included above the line. What good that is likely to do is far from clear. It certainly will not change the critical character of the incorrect data being adjustments to whatever had been reported in previous years. In any event, those adjustments were all too late to influence the decisions taken in the meantime and nothing will change under AASB 1018. At least by being below the line, as they were prior to AASB 1018, they were automatically highlighted, even if their positioning might have encouraged readers not to treat them as part of the ordinary scheme of things. Some analysts are already raising doubts about the new practice.[30]

No doubt the idea is to restrict flexibility in the manner in which such items are dealt with in calculating profits and losses. But, paradoxically, such fiddling with the previously reported results may be even less obvious now than it was under the old regime. Consider some of the spate of reported abnormal adjustments in the 1995 reporting season. Under the caption 'The great profit recovery', the *Australian Financial Review* reported that a huge turnaround in 1995 corporate profits – five times 1994 results – 'was obscured in bottom-line earnings, which were hit by a big rise in abnormal losses . . . more than a billion dollars in abnormal write-offs' in the companies surveyed by the AFR and the ASX.[31] Big abnormal write-offs included BHP ($318 million), MIM ($224.4 million), Gold Mines of Kalgoorlie ($334.9 million), Adelaide Brighton ($455.8 million) and Goodman Fielder's net $150 million abnormal loss caused by writing down goodwill on its European and Australian poultry operations. AWA Ltd reported abnormal losses amounting to $26.2 million, half of which related to Research and Development. Other 1995 abnormal write-offs included Westfield Holdings ($275 million), Ampol Exploration ($224 million), Pacific Dunlop ($157 million) and Coles Myer ($112 million), causing one journalist to muse (in line with our pervading theme) whether those companies' managers had been 'realistic in capitalising items in the past because the write-downs have not been in response to any sudden and unforeseeable changes in circumstances'.[32] Also correctly noted were the consequential distortions in respect of previous years' accounts.

Perhaps ironically, as in 1977, BHP's 1996 profit report has again grabbed the financial headlines: 'BHP slumps 20pc to $1.29 bn'. The commentary continues citing a $222 million abnormal write-off from its Newcastle blast furnace, probably leaving a balance around zero.[33] The hoary valuation issue and its relation to earnings management again surfaces.

The only way to fix the problem is to remove the cause (in many cases, the delayed reporting of movements in the market selling prices of companies' physical assets) simply by bringing to account changes in selling prices as they arise. This is a theme pursued throughout and discussed in detail in Chapter 16. Of primary concern are the obvious defects in the asset valuation mechanism in the current package of Standard practices.

Valuation problems in Australia with AASB 1010 have been well aired.[34] Central to the physical asset valuation problem is the muddled reasoning underlying AASB 1010's prescription that long-lived physical assets be 'valued' at amounts not exceeding their 'recoverable amount' –

the amount expected to be recovered through the net cash inflows arising from their continued use and subsequent disposal (AASB 1010, para. 13). Ordinarily the prevailing situation would have to be that an asset's 'recoverable amount' calculated in that fashion would have to exceed its current selling price. If it did not, management would sell it to optimise the return. And it would have to exceed the asset's current replacement price too, for if it did not, management would sell the asset and replace it at a lower cost. Everything we know of price theory tells us that an excess of the selling prices of such assets over their current replacement prices cannot prevail in existing imperfect markets.

Two things flow from that. First, cash inflows and outflows are anticipatory, imaginary. And if AASB 1010 is to be taken to imply that they are to be discounted (a point still in dispute), they must be considered even more problematic. Second, the anticipated cash inflows and outflows or the net present (discounted?) value thereof (for which current replacement price is commonly regarded as a surrogate) must ordinarily be greater than the asset's immediate cash value. So, compliance with AASB 1010 almost certainly will result in long-lived physical assets being stated at amounts which are not serviceable for determining a company's current capacity to meet its debts. Yet, solvency is a critical and legislatively-prescribed financial indicator that one might imagine every investor would want to have access to. Curiously, the central issue in the recent debate on AASB 1010 appears to be whether the calculation of 'recoverable amount' entails discounting anticipated future income streams. Some experts tell us that surely it does, and the debate has proceeded as if NPVs actually exist, as if they are hard data. But no company *has* the NPV of its expected future income streams. Companies (or their managements) have hopes, expectations to be sure, some of them very well founded and many equally not, but they never have the NPV *per se*. NPVs are pure fiction, mere calculations based upon what is *thought*, not what *is*, no matter how well intended, no matter how much integrity is possessed by those who do the thinking. In a true financial accountability sense, they are *non-data*. Notwithstanding, discounting has become a feature of recent Australian Standards – for example, in lease accounting (AASB 1008), debt defeasance (AASB 1014) and accounting for superannuation funds (AAS 25).

Those examples are typical. They disclose how the Standards work quite contrary to the purpose they are intended to serve, almost certainly producing misleading data, even with the best of intentions on the part of the preparers. If the data are reliable and serviceable in calculating the usual financial indicators, it is more by accident than design. Consider the impossibility of calculating periodic profits and losses with the injection of such data. Consider, too, the nature of solvency assessments, calculations of debt to equity, asset backing, and the like. How can such subjectively-based data, and non-data, lead to a reasonably reliable indication of the financial position of the enterprise at any particular time? It cannot, never could and never will.

It is sobering to reflect that many data of the NPV genre arise *not* from the manipulation of the prescribed Accounting Standards, but from compliance with them. Yet, as noted in the 1978 Accounting Standards Review Committee's Report, departure from the prescribed Accounting Standards has been targeted as the root *modus operandi* of creative accounting. Much of the rhetoric about creative accounting has been misplaced. Departure from the Standards is, as often as not, the only way to produce data likely to accord with the financial facts.

Directors of an Australian company are between a 'sword and the wall'. Under the Corporations Law they are required to ensure that the published profit and loss account and balance sheet comply with the AAS and AASB Accounting Standards *and* portray a true and fair view of their company's results for the period and its state of affairs. They also have to give a 'solvency statement' – whether the company is (in their opinion) able to pay its debts as they fall due. Even so, this is a confusing setting; for, under the Corporations Law, companies have to keep such accounts and records as will 'explain its transactions . . . and financial position'. Nowhere is it explained what the difference is between the 'state of affairs' on which the directors have to report and the 'financial position' which has to be explicable by the accounting records. All this is to be achieved against a background of the profession's dictum that complying with the Accounting Standards will achieve those ends and the empirical evidence that clearly it will not. Directors are further required to declare it if their assessment is that the accounts do not disclose the true position of the company. There are few such declarations. But when one occurs, usually the recalcitrant company is persuaded in future to conform to the Standard. Auditors also are in an invidious situation. They are to report whether the accounts conform to the Accounting Standards and show a true and fair view of the same matters on which the directors are to report and the accounting records are required to explain. It is a curious arrangement, for the previous override – that the accounts had to conform to the Standards, subject to them showing a true and fair view – has been removed from the law as a first order imperative. Company directors are on a hiding to nothing when it comes to trusting their reputations to the accounting statements for which they are responsible.[35] And for their part, auditors are on a mission impossible!

In that context the actions of directors in the early 1990s are instructive. In 1992 the actions of directors of QBE in publishing two sets of statements, one complying with the Standards and the other not complying but declared to show a true and fair view, were on the right track, though (we would argue) for the wrong reasons. Their objections were against the outcome of reporting the adjustments from the mark-to-market mechanisms prescribed in AASB 1023. Advocacy of marking-to-market is one instance where we would argue the Standard-setters are on the right track. But the motives of the directors of QBE are to be applauded. Despite our disagreement with their reasoning, the directors had followed the historically valid pursuit of informing the public at large of what they perceived to be the true and fair view of their companies' wealth and progress. As a matter of professional judgement they rejected the Standard prescriptions which they believed failed to disclose it. (Chapter 17 provides further examples.)

Compliance – for instance, with AASBs 1018–1021 – cannot (except by accident) produce data which are serviceable for the purposes stated above, for none is directed towards producing data indicative of the measurement of actual amounts of money or its equivalent. Compliance with AASB 1008, 1009, 1011, 1018 and 1022 requires money *spent* to be treated as if it were still in possession – the ultimate in the counterfactual.

For a 'self-sustaining' foreign operation, AASB 1003 prescribes converting (translating) past prices, money spent and no longer in possession, by applying the current price of the domestic currency for a foreign currency, as if everything in the foreign operations' accounts represented actual money or its equivalent. For 'integrated' foreign entities, exchange rates applicable to the time of the transactions are to be applied. Net outcomes from the former do not hit the calculation of income – they are to be excluded; whereas outcomes from the latter are to be included. AASB 1003 thereby promotes the absurdity that the prices for foreign currency can be applied to convert any number in accounts, but some of the gains and losses thereby calculated are to be accounted for as real gains and losses and others not – the ultimate in asymmetry.

How a convincing defence could be mounted that the financial data from using those Accounting Standards are generally serviceable to assess the vital financial characteristics of companies, is beyond comprehension. Equally perplexing is the current push for more Accounting Standards of the kind already failing to measure up. Instead of producing a perceived improvement in the quality of accounting data, the increase in the number of Standards is correlated positively with increased complaint, criticism, bewilderment, frustration, disbelief and, ultimately, increased litigation.

Large adjustments to asset balances to approximate their current worths divorced annual income calculation and the inferences to be drawn from the related balance sheet data from meaningful representations of a company's financial progress and its wealth. Consider the write-offs from the recorded amounts of physical assets. Consider, too, the extraordinary and abnormal adjustments to which we have just referred. Two matters are sobering. It is most unlikely, virtually impossible, that the entire changes in the worth of those assets occurred only over the year immediately prior to the write-offs. Failure to mark-(assets)-to-market progressively has meant that successive financial positions were distorted, profits of earlier years were overstated (or losses understated), and balance sheets could not possibly have been reliable indicators of the companies' periodic progress and wealth. Second, many of the write-downs appear to be approximations of current selling prices and most of the extraordinary items were adjustments to selling prices. One must wonder why accountants, and regulators seemingly, have no qualms about accepting selling prices as the relevant valuation bases for determining those companies' financial positions when they are in trouble, but not in the ordinary course of events when they are perceived to be travelling well.[36]

Scope for manipulating results legally is indicated by the response to the Australian government's 1995 Budget corporate tax rate increase from 33 per cent to 36 per cent. Tax effect balances would increase automatically – incongruously, balance sheets could look better (or worse) because companies stood to be worse off because of a tax hike. Immediately there was talk of increasing stock valuations, delaying asset write-offs, reducing the depreciation rate to shift profits into the 33 per cent tax regime currently in force and to delay inducing the losses until the 36 per cent regime commenced. Each apparently legal, each within the Standards mechanisms and each virtually impossible to forbid, for those kinds of adjustments are made irrespective of whether the tax regime changes. They exploit the rubbery rules-of-thumb and speculations built into the Standards.

Possibly the limited and non-systematic recourse to selling price data by regulators and others can be explained through a crisis theory scenario. Some Australian instances are instructive. In 1979 anguish was expressed that Ansett Ltd was withdrawing its support for its 49 per cent associated company Associated Securities Limited, in financial difficulty due to its overexposure to property and property-related loans. Immediately regulatory changes required the provision of market price data for land contained in prospectuses. Early in 1988, following the October 1987 stock market crash, NCSC Release 135 urged fuller disclosure of the basis of current valuations of assets in prospectuses, annual reports and expert reports. Similarly, the NCSC acted to require all listed companies to provide market price information on listed investments. A spate of asset write-downs and explanations resulted. Yet, it has been suggested that 'in the midst of the [early 1990s] recession many listed companies are carrying properties on their balance sheets at figures far in excess of their current resale value'.[37] Also it is clear some were and still are carrying properties at well below their current resale price. That is equally misleading, understates asset-backing, borrowing capacity, the denominator in the rate of return calculation, and the like. We might spare a thought for those who buy and sell shares under those conditions. Secret reserves, the *sine qua non* of the UK's Royal Mail saga (see Chapters 4 and 15) 60-odd years ago, are almost certainly alive and well, albeit under a new guise. Continuing the international scope in the 1990s, the tale of Sumitomo Corporation's 1996 copper losses is apposite. In announcing those losses, Sumitomo was able to disclose that they would be offset by the equivalent of over $4 billion in secret reserves. These instances represent creativity at its professionally endorsed best.

Accounting's role in analyses of corporate collapse has in the main been brushed aside. Those failures and the accounting relied upon prior to each collapse deserve closer attention to illustrate the points raised to date.

Happier times. Stanley Korman (left) and Conrad Hilton at Hawaiian Village Hotel to mark the signing of the momentous agreement between the Australian and US tourist industries, through Conrad Hilton representing the world organisation Hilton International and Stanley Korman, head of Stanhill-Chevron Group of Tourism Industry in Australia. Courtesy of News Ltd.

Stanley Korman outside Melbourne City Court. Courtesy of News Ltd.

H.G. Palmer on big game fishing boat. 14 April 1963. Courtesy of John Fairfax Holdings Ltd.

Headline and photos of Reid Murray directors, upon release of the *Inspectors' Interim Report into the affairs of the Reid Murray Group. Sydney Morning Herald*, 4 December 1963. Courtesy of John Fairfax Holdings Ltd.

GROUP FIGURES

MR O. J. O'GRADY

K. N. WILKINSON

MR R. REID

MR M. E. BATES

PART II

The 1960s

THREE

The Corporate 1960s: Dubious Credit and Tangled Webs

A true and fair view of the financial state of affairs of an entity? An impossible dream or commercial imperative?

Conventionally prepared profit and loss statements and balance sheets are not 'telling it as it is'. This position will remain until the professionally-endorsed accounting practices incorporate current market prices and periodic changes in them to report companies' financial positions and calculate their profits and losses. Thirty years ago the fundamental error of not doing that, irrespective of deliberate deceit, was aptly illustrated (Table 3.1) in the affairs of New Investments, Latec Investments, Cox Brothers, Stanhill Development Finance, Reid Murray Holdings and H.G. Palmer (Consolidated) Ltd.

Conventional practice then was exposed for ignoring the movements in the market worth of investments, resting upon the contractual amount of debts despite the decrease in the worth of the related hire purchase assets and, indeed, concerns about the collectability of the debts *per se*; in many instances hiding behind the fictional artifacts of consolidation accounting, aggregating the moneys spent to acquire land and develop it to invent its value in defiance of the evidence of its contemporary market price, and the general overall failure to match up the derived outcome of accounting procedures with evidence of the market worth of physical assets. The outcomes were exacerbated losses for investors, prosecution and, in a few instances, gaol for company officers. In retrospect it is fair to suggest perhaps a very fine line existed between deceit on the part of many corporate officers and their being bamboozled, misled or seduced by the accounting data.

In respect of the veracity of information in published financial statements, virtually nothing has changed. The proliferation of endorsed Accounting Standards since has created a climate of false security. As noted in the previous chapter, the current Standards have done no more than plug holes and eject idiosyncratic practices from the scene. They

Table 3.1   Major company failures in Australia, 1961 to 1965

Year of failure – date administrator appointed	Name of company	Basis of criticism	Actions against auditors/ officials
November 1961	New Investments *et al.*	Failure to write off investments in associates which had been trading at a loss.	n.a.
September 1962	Latec Investments	(i) Inadequate debtors provisioning; and (ii) Unearned income on debts.	n.a.
December 1962	Stanhill Development Finance	(i) Consolidation practices; (ii) Intermingling of private and public companies; and (iii) Valuation of land and shares.	Stanley Korman gaoled for six months.
April 1963	Reid Murray Holdings/ Reid Murray Acceptance	(i) Consolidation practices; (ii) Valuation of debtors; (iii) Treatment of unearned income – judicious use of Rule of 78; and (iv) Intermingling of private and public company interests.	Directors O'Grady, Wilkinson and Wolstenholme were fined £400 each; L.A. Borg, director of Paynes Properties, gaoled for nine years.
October 1965	H.G. Palmer (Consolidated) Ltd	(i) Omitting material particulars in the profit statement in a prospectus; (ii) Valuation of debtors; and (iii) Treatment of unearned income.	$1 million civil action settlement. Herbert Palmer gaoled for four years, auditor J. McBlane for three years.

Source: Expanded version of Table 7.1 from A.T. Craswell, *Auditing* (New York: Garland Publishing Inc., 1984).

have not eliminated the generic problems. Nor have they created a system providing financial data that will disclose the wealth and progress of firms with much greater certainty than in the past.

Following the 1960s, the professional bodies and regulators claimed to have tightened the rules governing accounting practices. Coupled to the impression of frenetic activity within due process to develop useful Standards, this has emerged as little more than seductive window-dressing.

Table 3.1 lists some of the criticisms of inspectors and the actions against auditors and company officers in respect of those major 1960s failures. Ineffective response by the accounting profession in respect of the issues of measurement and asset valuation exposed by the 1960s accounting practices is instructive for our analysis of the pattern of events to unfold in the 1970s and 1980s.

Professional response – *sotto voce!*

There was some response, yes; but more *sotto* than *voce*!

Fallout from those 1960s collapses was far-reaching. The Australian accounting profession was struggling to attain a professional image. Professional rule-making by accountants was in its infancy. Birkett and Walker captured the extensive 1950s debate on whether the existing role of the profession needed strengthening, its general 'confusion' and concentration on 'form rather than substance'. They noted:

> The response of *The Accountant* to dicta of Mr Justice Vaisey in the [UK] *Press Caps* case received considerable notice and approval. The judge had said:
> . . . the market value of a share quoted on the stock exchange is seriously affected by the balance sheets, which are available for inspection. If you find such an undervaluation of a most important asset, of no less than £60,000, I should have thought that threw a great deal of doubt on the sufficiency of the balance sheet as an estimate of value, and also threw doubt on the market price of the shares. . . . [1]

By 1959 the Australian accounting profession had firmed up its position. Recommendations on accounting practices had increased, and clearly more were on the way. Whether to enforce those practices had been left unresolved. Then the company failures in the early 1960s redirected attention to the role of the professional accountancy bodies. Birkett and Walker recount a public perception of the inadequacy of the existing position that emerged in the financial press:

> 'Yesterday ["Black Thursday", twelfth of December, 1963] was one of the darkest days in Australia's financial history. Six public companies, including three in the [Stanley Korman] Australian Factors group, revealed losses totalling more than [$7.2 million].' (*AFR*, 13 December 1963.)

'Latec revealed further losses of $4.6 million. Chevron Sydney Ltd reported further losses of $1 million. The Australian Factors group losses were $1 million. Neon Signs (Australasia) Ltd disclosed a loss of $0.5 million – six weeks after the company's chairman had indicated that he expected a small profit.' (*AFR*, 30 October 1963.)

[Thus] . . . public criticism began to be directed at the accounting profession. Some criticisms were cautiously expressed:

One point that does emerge clearly from these results is that several companies concerned have very misleading statements of profits in the previous year's accounts and in interim statements last year. (*AFR*, 22 January 1963.)

Others were more extravagant:

. . . there must have been collusion between directors, accountants and auditors to what amounts to fraud.

An academic was reported as describing all investment as 'gambling' in 'state of affairs'. 'No accountant or skilled investment dealer (and therefore investor) could tell from present balance sheets whether they represented the facts per se or the method of presentation.' (*AFR*, 19 March 1963.)

Stock exchange officials claimed that 'poor accounting . . . brought about these situations' (*AFR*, 22 January 1963.) A financial journalist stated that '"a ready acceptance of responsibility to the community" has been lacking in too many accounting places in the recent period of company distresses' (J.C. Horsfall, *The Bulletin*, 27 July 1963.)[2]

Following protracted debate the profession commissioned an official inquiry. A portent of all subsequent professional inquiries followed. 'Bad management' and 'non-compliance with recommended and approved accounting practices' attracted considerable blame for the 1960s corporate failures in the resulting report, *Accounting Principles and Practices Discussed in Reports on Company Failures* (1966). More official prescription of accounting procedures formulated under due process and compulsory compliance with them was the proposed remedy. Whilst the report recommended some incremental change, with few exceptions the fundamental structure and tenets of conventional accounting were left untouched – the remedy was to educate the public on the limitations of accounts as an information source. It was an old response. In the United States in the 1930s, George O. May, a spokesperson for the profession, had first used the 'limitation of accounts' defence.

Comments in the financial press in the aftermath of the 1960s boom–bust cycle suggested a widespread malaise in business practice in general and in accounting in particular. It is debatable whether the post-1980s public criticisms of accounting exceeded those in the 1960s and 1970s.[3] Many well-known companies unexpectedly collapsed in those earlier decades with drama, trauma, individual hardship for investors and creditors, and immense legal problems for their directors and auditors.

Whilst losses to investors may initially appear small, they were substantial in context and are actually very large in today's dollars. A million dollars in 1960 equates to approximately $10 million in 1996 general purchasing power terms. Understandably, then, the level of outrage, the cry for someone's blood, was as strong following those earlier episodes as it is now. Then also as now, scapegoats had to be found. Blame had to be sheeted home. Although the causes of corporate collapse are varied, there is general agreement that internal rather than external factors are the more significant. Hence, it is not surprising to hear the suggestion repeatedly that 'bad management' is the *primary cause* of the majority of company failures.[4] But this is a limp explanation. The concept is nebulous, capable of so wide a definition as to encompass any and all defects of failed companies.

What is surprising, however, is that the role of accounting has often been ignored and its significance generally denied.[5] Recent exceptions were a 1990 report by the Australian Bankers Association and Chambers' 1991 questioning of that role and the ethics of the profession refusing to acknowledge it.[6] This error applied equally in the 1960s as in the 1980s. When the opportunity came for the profession to examine accounting's role, the 1966 Report of the General Council of the Australian Society of Accountants virtually exonerated accounting – characteristically, management (or the lack of it) was identified as the main culprit:

Criticism of Accounting Principles Generally
General Council is aware that some members of the profession have expressed the view that accounting reports prepared on the basis of 'generally accepted accounting principles' do not provide the data which company management, shareholders, investors and creditors need if they are to make informed decisions.
. . . it therefore proposes that a research group and the new Accounting Research Foundation be asked to investigate and report on these wider issues.

Criticism of Financial and Management Policies
Much of the criticism levelled at the companies under investigation appears to be related not to accounting principles, but to financial policies and apparent deficiencies in management.[7]

The General Council proposed several remedial actions:

- formulation, promulgation and regular review of accounting principles by the professional bodies;
- continued adherence to generally accepted accounting principles on the part of members of the profession;
- audit of accounts required review in the areas of: (i) the responsibilities of auditors, (ii) the independence of the auditor, and (iii) the audit of the accounts of subsidiary or related companies;
- need for reconsideration of the relationship between the management and the accountant; and
- general questioning of the adequacy, form and content of published financial statements.

The General Council concluded there was little evidence that accounting played any fundamental role in company collapses. Hence, there was no need for any fundamental change to the conventional cost-based accounting practices. Inevitably the General Council's reforms mainly comprised more accounting prescriptions, administrative changes to the manner in which they were determined, and only an *ad hoc* tinkering with the historical cost-based system of accounting. Substantive changes aimed at shifting the attention from cost to market-price information, although recognised by some members of the profession as being needed, were not considered by the General Council as worthy of immediate action: 'Unless and until a sound basis is established which has the force of law, it can be expected that some companies will use the present somewhat unsatisfactory system in doubtful ways – and still remain technically within the law.'[8] It is here that there is room for debate. In this and later chapters we explore this aspect in the light of the profession's ineffectual response to company failures over the past three decades.

Those crashes highlighted the need for fundamental changes to the way accounting is practised: 'Piece-meal patching will not make a worm-eaten craft seaworthy; neither will the piece-meal tinkering of individuals, boards and committees make cost-based valuations trustworthy.'[9] Nevertheless, the substance of that has fallen on deaf ears, for, whereas the promulgated Standards that have emerged *may* have reduced diversity through compulsory compliance rules, arguably the 'permissiveness' has increased!

Despite the 1966 ASA Committee Report having noted that the 'present system is somewhat unsatisfactory', inertia has reigned supreme. Some members of the profession had argued that accounting reports can only become meaningful to users if they are based on current market values or their equivalent, but to little effect. For 30 years, virtually nothing systematic has been done by the profession to require its members to provide for the general disclosure of contemporary market prices of assets. The accounting profession remains wedded to a variant of historical cost accounting – in essence, taking into account the prices encountered in transactions when they occurred in the past and ignoring changes in the selling prices until assets are disposed of. In the 1990s there have been limited modifications incorporating market prices – the introduction of the mark-to-market approach in some Accounting Standards (for example, AASB 1023 and 1025) and recourse to valuing fixed assets at recoverable amounts in AASB 1010.

Professional intransigence on the general issue of marking-to-market is clearly evident in our accounts of selected corporate crashes in the sixties, seventies and eighties. First, we consider the *causes célèbres* of the

1960s: the rise and fall of the large retail chain, Reid Murray; followed by Stanley Korman's spinning of public and private corporate webs over Sydney Guarantee and Stanhill Consolidated; and, finally, the sorry saga of electrical and whitegoods supplier, the House of Palmer.

Those events of the 1960s (and the succeeding decade) are instructive for a considered assessment of professional ethics and business techniques, transactions, structures and accounting employed by the 1980s entrepreneurs. Fall-out covered all sectors of the community, from the financial *cognoscenti* (including the major financial institutions) to the smallest of investors. The government-imposed credit squeeze in 1960 had an impact on all industries, the greatest impact possibly being on the finance and property sectors. It was a new corporate setting for the post-war baby boomers.

FOUR

Reid Murray:
The Archetypal Failure*

'The rearrangement of Reid Murray Holdings . . . allowed
Mr R.C. Borg, a director of Payne's and later a director of
Reid Murray Holdings, so as to entangle his and his family
business affairs with those of the Reid Murray group that
they became withal partners, and in some cases competitors,
so far as profits are concerned with at any rate.'
B.L. Murray and B.J. Shaw (1963)

Reid Murray Holdings Ltd was one of the largest retailers in Australia in
the early 1960s. It was placed in receivership most unexpectedly in May
1963.

Its financial *fundamentals* had either been masked by the prevailing
accounting practices or otherwise ignored by an investing public whose
expectations had been inflated to unrealistic levels by unusually buoyant
economic conditions. The Reid Murray affair is indicative of the dilemmas
potentially created when private and public investments and financial
interests become entangled. With over 220 subsidiaries, it illustrates how
complex structures and consolidated accounting practices coalesced to
cloak the wealth and progress of the Reid Murray group. It is an exemplar
of many of the other collapses examined in this volume.

Karmel and Brunt's *The Structure of the Australian Economy*[1] listed Reid
Murray Holdings (RMH) as the fourth-largest Australian-owned company in 1961, in terms of *consolidated assets*. Only BHP, CSR and ICI were
ahead. It was in the very best of company indeed. But, little separates
success from failure, even for the largest companies and the most fêted
of entrepreneurs. Less than three years later, in May 1963, a court order
directed the winding up of the RMH group. Total losses amounted to
£23.727 million, a shortfall of approximately $450 million in equivalent
1996 dollar terms.[2]

RMH had been formed in 1957 by the merger of Robert Reid & Co.
Ltd with David Murray Holdings Ltd. The former was a long-established
warehousing and retailing company, with branches in all capital cities
and a chain of cash-order retailers in the south-eastern States. Conservatively financed and managed, DMH was the outgrowth of a series of
ventures of Oswald (Ossie) O'Grady. An accountant, he had entered the
cash order business in South Australia in 1931, extended into retail

merchandising on credit, set up a company listed on the stock exchange (to increase potential sources of funds), acquired other companies and in the mid-1950s sought to step up its credit-retailing business in other States. DMH was much less conservatively financed than RR; in October 1957 their debt to equity ratios were 4.2 and 1.7, respectively. Combining RR and DMH consolidated the finances of the group (provided a larger equity base) and enabled debt-financed expansion of the DMH style of trading.

Early in 1958 RMH raised about £1.6 million by issues of registered unsecured notes. Under the existing stock exchange listing rules these could not be listed. Reid Murray wanted its securities 'in the market', so, in true group enterprise spirit, a related company, Reid Murray Acceptance, was formed. A new issue of RMH shares for cash raised about £600,000 and newly listed RMA commenced business with an issued capital of that amount in June 1958. About that time the 5s. shares of RMH were selling at around 10s.

Until mid-1960 RMH engaged in an aggressive takeover programme (Table 4.1). By May 1960 its share price had peaked at about 20s. (Figure 4.1). No doubt the market premium made it possible to extend the operations of RMH in this way, for vendors would be acquiring listed shares with a record of appreciation. Inspectors were to note later that inclusion of pre-acquisition profits as part of the annual operating profits of the group was to prove misleading and integral to the continuation of a deceptive reported position of the group.[3] We show in Chapter 14 that nearly 30 years later a similar device was used by the Westmex group to inflate its reported profits. And in the mid-1990s there is legal and accounting dispute over what constitutes approximately the inverse case – the initiation of several gold company takeovers delayed because of the proposed accounting treatment of goodwill acquired in the takeover documents.[4]

RMA was formed as a subsidiary 'banker' for RMH, it seems, with the objective of financing the hire purchase business of all RMH subsidiaries. The initial capital of RMA (two tranches totalling £2.5 million) came from RMH purchasing shares in RMA. The public provided the source of these funds, with RMH raising additional equity capital. It was the beginning of a circuitous loop between public and private activities within the Reid Murray group, and the beginning of group enterprise rather than entity action. Effectively RMA acted as an RMH branch. Decisions of RMA were taken informally by the RMH board. According to its first prospectus offering first mortgage debenture stock, that was the 'chief function' of RMA, though it would seek 'any sound finance business available' outside the group.

'Any' indeed! Between July 1958 and May 1962, RMA issued nine prospectuses for stock issues, raising £43 million of new money (equivalent

Table 4.1 Takeovers by Reid Murray Holdings Ltd, 1958 to 1960

Date of takeovers	No. of companies	No. of 5s. shares	Cash paid £
July–Dec. 1958	11	4,611,528	166,348
Jan.–June 1959	9	501,071	342,936
July–Dec. 1959	7	191,431	926,219
Jan.–July 1960	9	1,020,900	509,816
Total	36	6,324,930	
	=	£1,581,232	£1,945,319

Source: B.L. Murray and B.J. Shaw (both QCs), *Interim Report of an Investigation . . . into the Affairs of Reid Murray Holdings Limited* (Melbourne: Victorian Government Printer, March 1965).

to approximately $800 million in current terms). The net surplus of 'new money' from those issues and retirements of stock was £3 million for the six months of 1958, £12 million in 1959, £12 million in 1960 and £2 million in 1961. At its peak late in 1959 and early 1960 the company borrowed £3 million every two months. That success in the capital market was against a background of RMH enjoying a glowing financial press in recognition of its reported outstanding financial performance over those years and the appearance in its accounts of going from financial strength to strength. The nominal amounts of most of the offerings were £1 million, but the company had reserved the right to retain oversubscriptions. The popularity and oversubscriptions of the issues made it almost obligatory to find some use for the money. Curiously, that may have contributed substantially to the sloppiness in its use. Similarities here are obvious with the capital raisings and their use at H.G. Palmer and Stanhill, described in the following chapters. Acquired companies brought into the group were allowed to run themselves, in O'Grady's belief that managers could be relied upon to run their companies efficiently. O'Grady's main concern seemed to be to keep the borrowed money coming in.

The level of capital and hence asset valuation were critical determinants of RMA's capacity to borrow and RMH's ability to invest. The first trust deed (July 1958), subject to Equity Trustees Executors and Agency Co. Limited monitoring, limited RMA borrowings to five times the shareholders' funds of RMA – the excess of tangible assets (including hire purchase and time payment debtors, less unearned income) over all liabilities (including tax and dividend provisions), as shown in the audited accounts. Clearly, the higher the asset valuation the greater the leverage for borrowing more. RMH guaranteed the stock issue. This too was curious, since RMA provided the principal financing of the group.

The security constituted by the deed depended on the value of the assets of RMA – the value of the assets of RMA depended on the book value of the assets of RMH and its subsidiaries. If RMA defaulted, and recourse was made to the guarantor, the guarantee was dependent on the assets of RMH and those of its subsidiaries which included RMA.

That Byzantine arrangement meant that the incestuous security was in fact no security. Also, the loans by RMA to RMH were unsecured. More-over, the borrowing power constraint could easily be overcome. *Groupthink* and group enterprise action began. Companies whose ordinary business was not financing could not lend to finance the purchase of their own shares. But RMA could lend, and thus could increase by a factor of five what it could borrow on the strength of new capital. RMA could issue shares to RMH, who could draw its cheque and pay it to RMA. RMA could then lend the same amount to RMH by return cheque, and then borrow forthwith five times that amount on the market. Facilitating this was resort to a now common commercial device – the cheque round robin (a circuitous routing of cheques through related companies so as to obscure the real source of the payment and legitimise its ultimate destination – often one of the entrepreneur's family companies). This group action exemplifies *groupthink* which is discussed further in Chapters 15 and 16. RMA thus became a financing innovator, for this circuitous device was to become almost an art-form by the 1980s.[5] That mechanism raised £2 million in December 1959, £0.5 million in May 1960, £1 million in August 1960 and £1 million in February 1961. It was pursued on legal advice – advice which the investigators later thought to be 'misconceived'. But pursued it was. There was a questioning of the role of the trustee's monitoring of this aspect of the deed. It will be shown below that a substantially similar unsecured financing practice and alleged ineffective trustee monitoring was to recur during the 1970s and 1980s.

At the management level the RMH board was dominated by its founding chief executive. As the inspectors noted in their 1963 Interim Report: 'There is no doubt in our minds that Mr O'Grady dominated the Board completely, but by and large, it was a Board willing, then anxious, and finally (it would seem) determined, to be dominated by him.'[6] This matter recurs in analyses of corporate collapses, yet there seems to be little learned by trustees, other board members or regulators on this score.

Figure 4.1 illustrates RMH's share price history[7] and shows what John Argenti described as a trajectory pattern of 'remarkable ascent and rapid demise' – one of three common failure trajectories he identified. This price movement at RMH was fuelled by a frenetic growth-by-acquisition policy before its weaknesses were exposed by the externally imposed government credit squeeze which commenced in November 1960 and extended into 1962.

Figure 4.1   Reid Murray Holdings Ltd – share price, March 1958 to April 1963

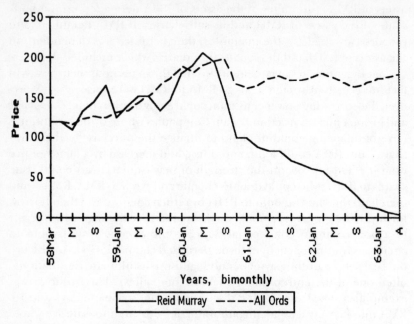

Source: Prices taken from issues of the *Sydney Stock Exchange Gazette.*

In 1959 the group had interests in wholesaling, general retailing, specialty retailing (electrical goods principally), financing and land development. It had diversified into financing land development late in the land boom of the post-war years. By the end of 1960, £7 million was invested in that direction. Diversification was facilitated by the group's capacity to borrow which, in turn, was the outcome of the financial esteem it enjoyed, augmented by what the accounts reported. The breadth of that diversification and the credit-retailing of consumer durables made the group very sensitive to shifts in economic conditions. By mid-1960 RMH was desperate for liquid funds, yet its published accounts presented a much rosier picture.

Government was already beginning to tighten credit in early 1960 and the business-crunching credit squeeze began with the announcement of Prime Minister Menzies' mini-Budget. That should not have been an outright disaster. Other finance companies, accustomed to regulating their borrowings and repayments in difficult times, seemed to be little affected. But some of the more adventurous in exploiting asset valuation to increase their apparent debenture trust deed limits, and less discriminating in what they financed, would soon collapse.

RMH had made good use of its bankers and it continued to do so. But in April 1961 the National Bank sought to draw directors' attention to the need for control over trade creditors, to exercise dividend restraint, and to sell assets or increase equity to reduce borrowing, thereby avoiding any action likely to depress the market price of the company's shares. The National Bank also sought an immediate investigation of the group's affairs on the request of the company's creditors. But apparently the complexity of the group's business and the pressure of other work necessitated abandonment of that inquiry.

The anxiety was well founded as RMH's gearing was always uncomfortably high even on the basis of its suspect asset valuations. B.L. Murray QC and B.J. Shaw QC, reporting to the Victorian Parliament in 1963 on the causes of Reid Murray's collapse, expressed concern at the parlous state of the group by 1961. Their summary is given in Table 4.2. Their analysis revealed an exceedingly high proportion of external borrowed funds relative to the group's own funds – £53 million to £13 million. This was exacerbated when the nature of some of those 'group assets' was dissected. The inspectors, for instance, were alarmed by the 'complete lack of reality' shown in the 1961 accounts:

> . . . either the published reports and accounts of the group must have been deceptive or inaccurate or that [advisers to invest in Reid Murray] were either incompetent or negligent. We do not think the latter is the case. . . . We believe that . . . the accounts of the group must have fallen short of their supposed objective – namely that of presenting *a true and fair view of the state of affairs* of the group and the results of its operations.[8]

They concluded that the defects in RMH's accounts were partly responsible for the collapse. It is interesting to note Murray's and Shaw's observations that the accounts purportedly were to present 'a true and fair view of the state of affairs' of Reid Murray's financial affairs. This tone implies a belief that *that* objective is axiomatic with respect to published financial statements. Thirty years later, essentially that axiom has been ditched by the Australian legislature as an essential quality element of primary financial statements providing investor protection (see Chapter 18).

RMH's fourth annual report, dated 31 August 1961, showed a substantial decline in consolidated net profit after tax – from £1,545,340 in 1960 to £895,892. Those 1961 accounts were given a clean audit report, notwithstanding that the auditors were acutely concerned about some features of them.

Later the inspectors were to criticise vehemently the reported results. In general, they were concerned about the overvaluation of land, the improper capitalisation of interest and the understatement of bad debt

Table 4.2 Inspector's summary of the 1961 position of Reid Murray Holdings Ltd

Group assets	£	£
Current assets	53,886,811	
Fixed assets	12,348,138	
		66,234,949
Group liabilities		
Debentures and secured borrowings –		
Due within 1 year	4,911,156	
Due after 1 year	28,128,624	
Registered and other deposits –		
Due within 1 year	1,915,707	
Due after 1 year	2,923,758	
Convertible Notes	698	
Amount due in respect of development projects –		
Due within 1 year	823,805	
Due after 1 year	2,507,634	
Bank overdrafts	5,837,647	
Trade creditors, bills payable and accrued liabilities	6,152,057	
		53,202,086

Source: B.J. Shaw, *Final Report of an Investigation . . . into the Affairs of Reid Murray Holdings Limited* (Melbourne: Victorian Government Printer, 1966), p. 71.

provisions. Within those categories there were five elements in the accounting without which the reported 1961 result would, according to the inspectors, have been a loss of £67,120:

(a) A change to the use of the Rule of 78 for the calculation of unearned income, increased the reported result by   £382,607
(b) A change in the method of calculating rental income of Radio Rentals to anticipation of the rental receipts, yielding   £136,016
(c) A change in the method of accounting for the profit on land sales by a WA subsidiary, taking 'instant' profits, and yielding   £85,084
(d) a transfer to profit of a trading stock valuation provision previously made on the acquisition of a subsidiary   £25,000
(e) An increase in a provision for doubtful debts out of reported unappropriated profits (rather than as a charge in calculating profits), yielding   £350,000

Total:	£979,707

Concern was more than warranted. But it has to be noted that each of the above accounting practices, of themselves, accorded with accepted practice then, and some even today. For example, the Rule of 78 was the accepted method of apportioning interest on term (say, hire purchase) contracts. This disguised the traditional interpretation of the accounting principle of 'matching' – the idea that the 'revenues' and 'costs' attach to one another in an artificially simulated physical sense. What the market indicated was that the current worth of the physical assets, subject to hire purchase and the actual receipt by the hirer of interest payments, was taken to be of little consequence. Consolidation practices were also questioned. And justifiably so, for there is considerable evidence that the assumptions and techniques of consolidation accounting are far from conducive to the accumulation of financial data showing the aggregate wealth and progress of related companies. On the contrary, the inherent complexities of consolidated financial statements have been an incorrigible means of deception without any intent to deceive. Arguably, by virtue of their association with corporate group failure, they have exacerbated investor losses.

Reporting real estate development projects (£9.6 million) as a current asset (as 'inventories') in the consolidated accounts was seriously questioned by the RMH investigators. That ploy exploited the different valuation rules as they applied to 'fixed' and 'current' assets and the impact of increased closing inventory valuations on the conventional profit and loss calculation. Differential valuation rules remain. If, indeed, all the physical assets were 'marked-to-market' and the changes were brought into the profit calculation, the artificial, financial effect of classification would disappear. The misleading nature of the 1961 report led to the extension of further credit to the group by trade suppliers and to the lending of more money to the group by the public (£2.6 million of new debenture money was raised, and conversions into equity of £1.2 million were made after 21 December 1961).[9] Critically, capitalisation of interest charges increased the 'book value' of the projects – a matter which recourse to the market at the time would have revealed to have been potentially false although consistent perhaps with the 'costs attach' idea.

In fact, the last two prospectuses (December 1961 and May 1962) continued to give the impression that the funds of the group were invested in 'comparatively short-term investment, mainly in hire purchase and instalment debtors', suggesting that the debts were in some sense secured. Even so, often the value of the security (under the tightened conditions) was less than the tangible assets reported. That form of disclosure masked that the bulk of the borrowings of RMA was in fact invested in unsecured debts of other companies in the group (£33 million of the £37 million 'current assets' shown in the accounts of February 1962). The proceeds of those two issues were much less than the group had become accustomed to. Desperately in need of cash from December 1961 onwards, RMA proceeded to raise money by other devices. Under its debenture trust deeds it was unable to create prior charges as security for loans. But it could sell assets (i.e. book debts) to other subsidiaries of RMH which, in turn, could borrow on their security (it sold £1.67 million of debts in this fashion, for which the group obtained loans of £916,000); and it could sell blocks of its book debts to other finance companies. During 1962 it sold £4.4 million of such debts for £2.6 million. In October 1962 the group's electrical stores in New South Wales were sold to Electronic Industries, one of the group's creditors. And the trustees (The Equity Trustees Executor and Agency Co. Ltd) had been told by O'Grady that RMH might not be able to meet the interest on debentures, £600,000 payable in December.

The 1962 accounts of the group were unavailable. In January 1963 the trustees had receivers appointed to RMA. With the acquiescence of the directors of RMH, the affairs of the group were made subject to the receivers of RMA, and on 16 May an order was made appointing liquidators to RMA and RMH. From a high of nearly 20s. in May 1960, RMH shares had fallen to 3d by 14 May 1963 and 1d by 31 May. The liquidators recommended another scheme of arrangement which eventually was accepted.

RMH's rapid expansion through exploiting physical asset valuation, without regard for other limitations on growth – in this case, especially failing to plan for peak borrowings maturities – was, and continues to be, a generic recipe for failure. With regard to debt, RMA accepted public subscriptions seemingly without discrimination. Apparently there was no plan for repayment of debentures except by further borrowings from the public.[10] Summing up the causes of the company's failure, inspectors Shaw and Murray concluded: 'The simple fact is that the business of the group was badly run. It borrowed without thought and invested without wisdom.'[11] They might equally have added that its accounts never faithfully reported its true financial position.

Borg, a director of a Reid Murray subsidiary Paynes Properties, was found guilty of fraud and sentenced to nine years' gaol. Importantly, the investigators found no evidence of fraud by other main players. Some directors were fined minor amounts for prospectus offences (see Table 3.1 in Chapter 3). O'Grady was eventually fined the sum of £400 for having made untrue statements in a debenture prospectus dated 9 May 1962 and issued on 30 May 1962. In that prospectus, which raised a total of £920,000 from the public, O'Grady had stated:

> . . . profits were lower than for the corresponding [previous] period . . . However, reorganisation . . . is being successfully carried out, and with an easier economic climate now prevailing, trade and profits should gradually improve . . . [Regarding] real estate . . . current values are substantially in excess of the book values.[12]

It is worth noting that if the accounts had incorporated the financial effects of the current market worth (value) of the real estate (and been verified as a matter of course), no such statement need have been made. More importantly, its truth or falsity would have been obvious – public knowledge for all to see and to include in their business assessments. But, as accounting stands in the 1990s, it would be no more obvious now than when O'Grady made the statement. The day after this prospectus was issued, Reid Murray Holdings made its first interest payment default.

A significant feature of this 'still-born' failure depends largely upon how one interprets two pieces of evidence: one a public datum – the company's accounts; the other anecdotal and highly subjective – the personality of O'Grady. Sykes describes Ossie O'Grady as a 'visionary',[13] a 'charming man' and a 'local hero in South Australia'.[14] While this immediately brings to mind the 'charismatic' chief executive so central to many earlier and modern failures, O'Grady was never in the same league as, say, in the 1920s: Lord Kylsant of the Royal Mail; in the 1960s: Stanley Korman; and the modern entrepreneurs: Alan Bond or Robert Maxwell. The inspector's final report concluded that O'Grady was innocent of any fraud, but was an artless victim of his own incompetence. The group's managers were adjudged as at best 'second class', whilst others 'were worse'.[15] O'Grady's 'no-management theory' was blamed for many of the group's problems, as he left full responsibility for operating the group's operating subsidiaries to others whose 'talents were insufficient for the task'.

The inspector might also have added the observation that the entirely inept practices of the (then) conventional accounting failed miserably to inform and thereby protect directors from being a financial risk to themselves and to investors. Another of the inspectors' comments highlights the seductive role of accounting in inducing investors to participate and hence exacerbating the consequences of the collapse:

> It was the spirit of the late 50s which encouraged the public (enchanted by the *spectacular growth* and *apparent profitability of the Reid Murray group as shown in the published accounts*) to pour into Reid Murray Acceptance much of the money which was subsequently lost. . . . Easy availability of huge sums of public moneys . . . and the acceptance of the view (both inside and outside the group) that such sums . . . could be indiscriminately used to construct and expand the group were necessary pre-conditions for the losses which followed . . . [16]

The importance of Reid Murray cannot be underestimated. Commentators still refer to Reid Murray, suggesting that little has changed in the way of corporate *group* business dealings and business ethics. Also, many of the modern related-party transactions, and using a subsidiary as 'group banker', share similarities with the operations of the Reid Murray

group. Partly because of the complexity and obfuscatory nature of the
group dealings, the Reid Murray receivership continues some 30 years
on and is Australia's longest corporate administration.

Many features of the Reid Murray saga were repeated soon after in the
Stanhill collapse. Commingling public and private affairs with deleterious
public consequences was even more graphically evident in Stanhill, as were
the deficiencies of group accounting coupled to accounting for related-
party transactions, and the perennial failure to mark-(assets)-to-market.

FIVE

Stanhill:
Private and Public Corporate 'Games'

What curious webs our corporates weave. The round robin
device emerges and produces 'unjust enrichment of the
Korman family [which] was effected at the expense of the
public company, SCL and indirectly at the expense of the
public company, SDF . . .'

P. Murphy (1967, p. 121)

When Polish-born Stanley Korman emigrated to Australia it was unlikely
he could have predicted that he would become a household name in his
adopted country. His commercial expertise initially lay in textiles, an area
which flourished after World War II, taking Korman and Stanhill with it.

Korman is reported to have been a man of boundless energies and
vision – 'Short and dapper in a pinstripe suit and meticulously trimmed
pencil moustache . . . an exciting, highly persuasive salesman and an
aggressive, ruthless fighter/negotiator',[1] though whether some of those
characteristics are necessarily commercially virtuous is another question.
Such a description evokes comparisons with contemporary immigrant
entrepreneurs, Alan Bond, Christopher Skase, George Herscu and the
1980s textile king Abe Goldberg; all smart enough dressers and *successes*
in their time, too.

As so often in the corporate collapses which followed, a complex
group structure provided the medium in Sydney Guarantee and Stanhill
for a bewildering array of commercial transactions, masking their
occurrence and scrambling the reporting of their financial outcomes.

Acquisitions and instant profits

Stanhill Pty Limited had been incorporated in 1945 by the Korman
brothers, Stanley and Hilel. It was to be the major private vehicle for the
Kormans' business activities. Stanhill's corporate connections are set out
in Figure 5.1. It remained a private company with all its share capital held
by the Korman family throughout the ensuing commercial drama.[2]

From the outset the Stanhill-controlled business often involved
related-party transactions. Transactions were full of intrigue – complex
almost beyond description. Below is exposure of but a small part of the

Figure 5.1 Stanhill Consolidated Ltd group structure

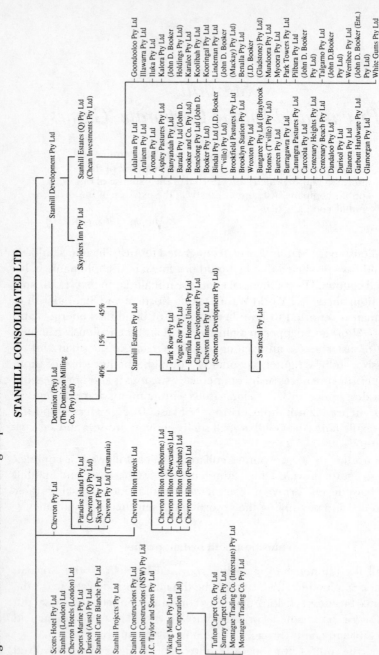

Note: All wholly owned except as shown. Former names are shown in brackets.

Source: P. Murphy, *Interim Report of an Investigation . . . into the Affairs of Stanhill Development Finance Limited . . .* (Melbourne: Victorian Government Printer, November 1964), Appendix A, at p. 82.

Table 5.1 Growth and amount of funds within Stanhill group

	Nominal capital £	Paid-up capital £	Shareholders' funds £	Long-term liabilities £	Other liabilities £	Total assets £
30 June 1956						
SCL	1,000,000	371,556	952,966	1,005,165	344,167	2,302,298
31 July 1961						
SCL	12,500,000	1,942,797	3,206,200	7,221,960	4,021,983	14,450,143
Factors	15,000,000	3,695,233	5,075,403	11,265,719	8,781,057	25,122,179
SDF	5,000,000	750,001	783,418	2,260,377	159,496	3,203,291
Chevron Sydney	10,000,000	1,500,000	1,352,211	2,587,200	3,369,449	7,308,860
Subtotal named companies	42,500,000	7,888,031	10,417,232	23,335,256	16,331,985	50,084,473
Chevron Queensland	2,000,000	987,125	1,435,906	1,653,297	204,912	3,294,115
Grand total	44,500,000	8,875,156	11,853,138	24,988,553	16,536,897	53,378,588

Source: P. Murphy, *Interim Report of an Investigation . . . into the Affairs of Stanhill Development Finance Limited . . .* (Melbourne: Victorian Government Printer, 1967), p. 1. The table is compiled from the published consolidated balance sheets of the principal companies without offsetting intercompany holdings of shares or advances by the companies to one another.

complex group dealings. During 1953 Stanhill acquired control of
Chevron Pty Limited (incorporated during 1934 to run the Chevron
Private Hotel in St Kilda). In April 1955 Park Lake Pty Limited (see Table
5.1), another Korman family private company, sold properties to
Chevron for a profit of £296,118. In October 1955 Stanhill exchanged its
shares in Chevron for shares in a new company, Stanhill Consolidated
Limited. SCL had been incorporated on 29 July 1955 with a nominal
capital of £1 million (4 million 5s. ordinary shares), for the purpose *inter
alia* of acquiring all the issued shares in the capital of Chevron Pty Ltd.
SCL did that on 23 September 1955, by issuing four SCL shares of 5s.
each for each £1 Chevron share.

The result was Korman's dominance of SCL as follows: Korman, via
private companies, Stanhill (937,000 shares) and Park Lake (24,420),
and he or his family held another 37,000 shares – a total of nearly
1 million shares or 99 per cent of SCL's issued capital.

Public funding was sought in October 1955 with a prospectus offering
£285,000 6.5 per cent registered first mortgage debenture stock (maturing 1962) and 325,000 5s. shares at par (in aggregate approximately
$10 million in current terms). Also, £213,700 debenture stock was to be
offered for private placement. Actually a private member of the Korman
corporate web, Park Lake (wholly-owned by Stanhill) put up £210,000 of
the amount – circuitously the cash had come from Chevron in payment
for the properties (known as The Town House) bought from Park Lake
in April 1955. Chevron had picked up the cash on advance, targeted for
the purpose from SCL. Not surprisingly, the prospectus was confusing –
the 'objects' of the issues were stated to be to 'raise the funds to pay the
balance, amounting to £285,000 owing by Chevron Pty Ltd, on the
purchase of The Town House', but the Additional Statutory Information
declared the £285,000 that was needed for the purchase of The Town
House exceeded reasonable approximations of its market value at the
time. Perhaps this was a hint of things to come.

The £435,000 price tag was £60,000 greater than the highest
independent valuation that had been placed upon it. Nine years later
The Town House sold for only £341,000 – £94,000 less than Park Lake
charged Chevron for it in 1955. SCL was established. So, too, was the
pattern for subsequent transactions entailing asset sales at arranged
prices (defying other market evidence) between private and public
companies within the Korman group. And, as it turned out, for many
group companies in the next two decades.

Easy money – other people's

Expansion of SCL was rapid. So was its diversification into debt factoring
– but expansion was an entrée to a cash flow. Again the antecedents of

the 1980s exploitation of 'cash-cow' companies within a corporate group are clearly visible.

Cash flow regularity is essential in business. Some wait for it. Korman went out and snared it, using Factors Limited as his vehicle. Control of Factors Limited was acquired by SCL, 'under agreement' in October 1957 between Korman and Factors' founder, Oswald, 'for a song'.[3]

To obtain one-third of the share capital of SCL, Korman made an initial part payment of £160,000 on 31 December 1957 with the residual to be paid in two equal instalments (of £240,000) over the next two years. The payments were never made. Thus, effective control had been achieved of a public company with net assets booked at over £900,000 and reported profits of £120,000 for the year ended June 1957, for only £160,000. The price was cheap enough. Not paying the instalments made it a real bargain – and a very liquid one at that. A future cash flow had been secured.

Korman could certainly put a deal together, even if the actual financial outcome was never that clear. He was decisive. Conversely, it is doubtful if anyone could be sure of why many of the deals were done or what they achieved – other than providing some benefit for the Korman family companies. Creation of Stanhill Estates was a salient example.

Stanhill Development Pty Limited had been incorporated as a wholly-owned subsidiary of SCL in December 1957. Then it joined with Stanhill and Dominion to form Stanhill Estates Pty Ltd. Again, it is unclear what actual function the companies were to serve, though real property investment looks the most likely. Not that it mattered, for the convenience they gave to moving cheques through their books in a quick and circular series of transactions was reason enough for their existence. This was service enough. In fact, the web of companies was an essential medium for it – a technique that would be repeated often in ensuing decades. Disclosures in the 1990s of the financial consequences of the complex structures of Bond, Westmex, Adsteam, Linter, Spedleys and Rothwells illustrate how this medium has developed over those 30-odd years despite all the regulatory and Standards-setting attention given to it. The dealings of the Stanhill companies at that stage were described as 'confused, and in many cases, puzzling. The general pattern emerges to show that the family companies received benefits, and they stood to make a large share of the profits if the development plans had proceeded to function.'[4]

Externalities, however, are beyond internal manipulation – though they often provide a convenient excuse for poor managerial performance. The mini-Budget and Menzies' credit restrictions of November 1960 were the kiss of death to any possibility of borrowing to develop the land in which Stanhill Estates was dealing. Interest was no longer a taxation deduction. Borrowing was no longer cheap. But, not all was lost. SCL acquired the shareholdings of Dominion and Stanhill in Stanhill

Estates, moving the possible losses from the family companies to public purses. The public arm of the Stanhill empire and the Korman family company fiefdom were indistinguishable.

Those and subsequent events in Stanhill trialled the shape of the related-party transactions of the 1970s and 1980s entrepreneurs.

SCL had acquired Scotts Hotel Pty Ltd in 1955. The hotel site was revalued, then mortgaged. The accounting and finance nexus was clear. Though trading at a loss, Scotts paid dividends to SCL out of the 'Revaluation and Re-establishment Reserve' created by revaluing assets. The hotel was sold for £480,000 in February 1958 and the business leased. Substantial sums of money were advanced by Scotts to SCL up to the lease's expiry in December 1961. Scotts soon became insolvent, with outstanding debts to trade creditors and the Commissioner of Taxation. The cause was SCL's inability to repay the outstanding £200,070 of the amount Scotts had advanced. In April 1958, SCL contracted to build Factors House in St Kilda for £418,905. Exploiting the scope for deception offered by consolidated financial statements that year also saw the 'Shuffling of Chevron Island' – a transaction that accounted characteristically for over 40 per cent of SCL's *consolidated* net profits in 1958 and 1959.[5]

Invariably asset valuation is a rogue element in the affairs of corporate groups. SCL exploited it thoroughly. It revalued Chevron's shares from 5s. to £1.12s.6d. The surplus of £155,625 was credited to an Asset Revaluation Reserve, and a 1-for-8 bonus issue was made. Similar 1-for-8 bonus issues were made out of the Asset Revaluation Reserve in July 1959 and July 1960. Expansion of SCL's capital base appears to have been a possible motive for the revaluation. In January 1959, the SCL board resolved to acquire Stanhill's shares in Factors – 3,030,210 of them – with an exchange of 5s. ordinary shares without a cash outlay. SCL would then have been large enough to qualify for SEC registration in the United States.[6] Stanhill was the largest shareholder in Factors – yet, curiously, the offer was rejected. It is not so much that the asset value is to be disputed, as recognition that the failure to mark-to-market on a continuous audited basis opens the way to the worst aspects of *ad hoc* corporate behaviour. Accounting becomes a means for all varieties of commercial legerdemain, as corporate events before and after Stanhill reveal.

Family circles

Group structures often have proven to be particularly *family-company-friendly*. Korman family companies were financially adept in acquiring land and equally adept in revaluing it and borrowing on the collateral. They proved equally profitable in disposing of such land to related *public* companies – another useful *modus operandi* to be used repeatedly in the

Table 5.2   Real estate purchases – family circles

Party to the transaction	Original vendor	Original purchase price £	Purchase price payable by Stanhill Estates £
1. From Stanhill	W.A Stoney	48,000	119,540
2. From Dominion	(i) E.B. Campbell	35,000	104,250
	(ii) F. Kay	35,000	97,125
	(iii) H. & M. McDougall	2,000	3,750
	(iv) C.F.R. Palmer	83,250	124,545
	(v) B.R. Jefferies	24,000	65,800
		179,250	395,470
3. From Stanhill Development	(i) V.I. Mitchell	114,197	430,250
	(ii) J.G. Attwood	19,800	49,000
		133,997	479,250

Source: Stanhill Final Report, p. 26, based on Schedule 3, p. 174.

ensuing decades of boom and bust. From late in 1957, Dominion, General Investments and Discounts, Stanhill, Stanhill Estates, Tufton and Stanhill Development Pty Ltd purchased land around Gladstone Park, an outer western suburb of Melbourne. Korman's plan was to develop a satellite township to be named Woodlands Estate. The pattern of transactions proved favourable to the family companies. Data in Table 5.2 show properties acquired by Stanhill and Dominion for £227,250 and sold to Stanhill Estates only months later for £515,010 – a profit of £287,760 to Stanhill and Dominion. In all but one instance, land purchased by either Stanhill or Dominion at an average of £289 per acre sold for something like £750 per acre. Milking the public companies is bad enough. Insult to injury arises through the accounting convention which would have the land valued at its 'new' purchase price – its 'historical cost' – and giving the false impression of the money's worth of the property to would-be purchasers and others. This was the *modus operandi* of the 1980s Savings and Loans 'daisy chain' land values. Much the same is possible, even permissible, under standard accounting practice in the 1990s.

Land purchases by Stanhill Development Pty Ltd (from Mitchell and Attwood) were the start of another unusual event, albeit one no doubt familiar to those 1980s entrepreneurs who engaged in related-party transactions. Stanhill Development then did business with Stanhill Estates. After Stanhill Estates had entered into an agreement to purchase the properties from Stanhill Development Pty Ltd for £479,250 (a profit to Stanhill Development Pty Ltd of £345,253) and a deposit of

£23,962.10s. had been paid, the contract was rescinded. In place of the original agreement, Stanhill Estates took up options to purchase the properties for £23,955. The arrangement was convenient for Stanhill Development. It retained the properties and hence the capacity to revalue them in its accounts. It did just that. In June 1958 the property was revalued to £281,533. Curiously, that was £197,717 short of the sales price to Stanhill Estates. What the £281,533 represented is problematic; but it does illustrate the unreliable nature of *ad hoc* revaluations among related companies. As it stood, it is questionable whether the amount stated could have informed anyone of anything serviceable in making the usual financial assessments. An amount of £137,018 was transferred to an 'Unearned Increment on Unsold Subdivisional Land Account', increasing 'tangible assets' as outlined in the trust deed covering its note issues. This manoeuvre avoided any breach of the borrowing clause in its trust deed. Though recourse to technical accounting debits of this sort – what some might describe as a 'financial foozle' – was to avoid technical breaches of trust deeds, the lessons appear to have gone unheeded. Decades later they emerged as a set-play.

Between June 1958 and July 1961 over £200,000 was expended on the Woodlands Estate project – valuation expenses, legal expenses, architects' fees, and travelling and entertainment. The project benefits failed to materialise. Stanhill Estates had capitalised costs incurred to develop much of the land it acquired, as if they increased its worth. Just another bookkeeping 'foozle' used to boost reported asset values and facilitate borrowings.

The £24,320 of expenses, deemed to be the Gladstone Park share and to be met by that family syndicate, was never paid. Nor does it appear that the syndicate was ever called upon to meet commitments.

'Profits' for the group appear to have been manipulated through book entries and accommodating related-party transactions. For example, Tufton Corporation (a subsidiary of Stanhill) faced a trading loss of £46,201 for the year ended 30 June 1958. The matter was rectified easily. Land purchased at Greenvale was sold immediately to Gladstone Park at a profit of £64,410. In the Directors' Report, Korman explained that 'an operating loss of £46,201 was converted to a profit as a result of a non-operating profit of £64,410 from the sale of land procured during the year'. It was 'a straight quick profit . . . just in and out'.[7] A useful device, especially at year-end! Nevertheless, it was quite in keeping with the pattern of land transactions between the SCL group companies and the Korman family companies or interests. Cambridge Credit Corporation nearly a decade, and others two decades, later repeated the play. Of course, no good purpose would be served by such circuitous transactions if property transferred between related parties was continually 'booked' at its market value – its current selling price in the ordinary course of business – and, most importantly, then verified by independent auditors using their accumulated professional judgement.

The Chevron Sydney episode

Stanley Korman was determined to enter the hotel business. Unhappy encounters with Scotts and Chevron Queensland and an abortive attempt to acquire Lennons Hotel Limited had not deterred him. In April 1959 the Cairo Hotel in Macleay Street, Potts Point, was targeted. It was initially conceived as a modest venture: the price was £400,000. On 15 May 1959, Chevron Sydney Limited was incorporated for the purposes of acquiring the Cairo and, under Korman's wishes, constructing a 'colossus, a mammoth structure', a luxury hotel of international class. Chevron Sydney and SCL entered into an agreement on 12 August 1959 whereby SCL was to manage the construction for a fee of 5 per cent of the capital cost of constructing and furnishing the new hotel. Chevron Sydney was to become a *de facto* subsidiary of SCL. SCL took up 2,950,000 Chevron shares, representing 49.17 per cent of the issued capital and Chevon thus, under the share criterion of control, was not a subsidiary in the terms of the *Companies Act* 1958 (Vic.). Thus consolidation of its accounts with those of SCL would not be required, or in fact permissible.

A prospectus was issued on 20 August 1959 with the object of issuing £3.5 million in notes and shares to 'provide funds for the erection of a large modern international hotel, tourist centre and airways terminal' on the Macleay Street site. Total cost of the land and buildings acquired was declared to be £766,150, so around £2,750,000 would be left to get on with the hotel construction.

The construction of stage I of the Sydney Chevron building was financially disastrous. Developing the 'hole in the ground' cost £408,873, with £110,000 being paid to SCL for its management services. Essentially, construction was on a 'cost-plus' basis. Amendments to and changes in the plans were to be achieved 'irrespective of cost' so that the Sydney Chevron could compete with potential competition from Qantas and the Hooker organisation, who intended to build luxury hotels. By August 1961 the cost of the project was already £3,170,600. Total cost to complete stage I (including the cost of the site and excavation) eventually amounted to £5,516,083. According to the Final Inspector's Report, construction of the first stage was a managerial disaster, lacking pre-planning, having no budget controls and placing undue emphasis on haste.[8]

More to the point, however, nothing in the published accounting reports reflected the 'true financial state of affairs'. In particular, there was no recourse to market value data from which the public at large would be able to assess the 'value added' (or 'lost') on the project. It demonstrated the folly of treating money spent (on the 'hole in the ground') as an asset – possessing some kind of potential benefit which might materialise in the future. That generic folly – the idea that an asset is *service potential* or embodies *future economic benefit* – remains embedded in the current Australian Accounting Standards and Concept Statements and in overseas prescriptions.

The 1959 prospectus had raised £2,835,200 by November of that year. Since approximately £770,000 was required to pay for the site and buildings, over £2 million was available to be used for the construction. Although the completion date of stage I was to be May 1960, consistent with established practice in Stanhill the money was not left idle. Between October 1959 and February 1960, £173,000 was advanced to Stanhill for its private purposes. Chevron Sydney went on a 'spending spree' and committed itself for £3 million to pay for city and country properties. It appears that Chevron Sydney's moneys were used for the purchases, because another group company, SCL, would have breached its trust deed had it incurred further obligations at the time.

In November 1959 SCL set up a Chevron Sydney Development Committee whose function was 'to form companies to promote and function as unit companies to cover proposed buildings on sites either already obtained or about to be obtained'. Presumably it was to be 'any type of development whatsoever'.[9] The initial estimate of the costs was £44 million. Of course, the purchase of the lands and the commitment made of the prospectus proceeds were, at best, a breach of trust. Murphy described it as 'a criminal breach of trust'.[10] SDF was conceived as a medium through which to divest SCL of the properties. SDF was thus incorporated on 25 September 1959 to wipe the slate clean. It had an authorised capital of £5 million in 5s. shares. Its issued capital was five 5s. shares, which was not, in fact, paid until July 1960 when a prospectus calling for £2,750,000 in shares and notes was issued. Stanley Korman was SDF's first chairman.

SDF's fundraising

SDF's July 1960 prospectus offering £750,000 in 5s. shares and £2 million in Registered Unsecured Notes was heavily oversubscribed. Over £2 million was forthcoming within the first 24 hours. The funds were to be used, according to the prospectus, for:

- providing finance for industrial undertakings to purchase properties;
- acquiring sites and erecting buildings on a lease–purchase arrangement;
- acquiring sites for subdivision;

- acquiring sites for development;
- financing unit developmental projects;
- financing suitable development projects such as regional centres;
- lending funds on mortgage; and
- underwriting development finance.

Actual disposition of the funds turned out to be somewhat different. And while that is not an accounting matter, the threading of transactions through the related companies facilitated complexity, and frustrated and discouraged inquiry – similar to that experienced at Adsteam two decades later. Advances were made to group and Korman family companies; SCL received £750,000, Chevron £73,558, J.C. Taylor and Sons Pty Ltd £20,000, Stanhill Estates £927,155, Stanhill £75,000, Park Lake £45,000, Factors £200,000 and Falco Realty (a subsidiary of Factors) £525,000 – a total of £2,615,713. No property of any kind was acquired by Stanhill Development Finance up to 31 October 1960, yet almost the entire funds of the company had been diverted into other related companies needing the cash. The cash transfers were consistent with the peculiar 'all-in-the-family' notion of a 'corporate group' justifying actions which otherwise should have been open to grave doubt. But then, and indeed now, the notion of what constitutes a group of companies for financial purposes has been contestable. Injection of the 'corporate group' notion has served to confound the financial outcomes of transactions between related companies in virtually every major corporate collapse. Groups and group (consolidated) accounts have been a major tool of financial obfuscation.

The introduction of the November 1960 economic adjustments meant the Stanhill group was in financial trouble. As with Reid Murray, a cheque round robin was to be Stanhill's saviour.

The Korman round robin

Companies stuck with properties acquired from Chevron, and the associated debt the acquisitions entailed, had to find a quick fix. The private family companies badly needed an escape route. The answer was the cheques round robin of 17 February 1961. As Peter Murphy QC, the official inspector, explained:

> It is not difficult to see why the [round robin] was negotiated by Stanley Korman in a furtive manner. It was, in effect, a refined arrangement whereby money was taken from the public company, SCL [Stanhill Consolidated Limited], and paid to Stanhill [Pty Ltd]. This unjust enrichment of the Korman family was effected at the expense of the public company, SCL, and indirectly at the expense of the public company SDF [Stanhill Development Finance]. . . . The only interest considered at the time was the Korman family companies, and it did not matter that two public companies suffered, provided that the Korman companies were to be benefited.[11]

Figure 5.2   Round robin cheques

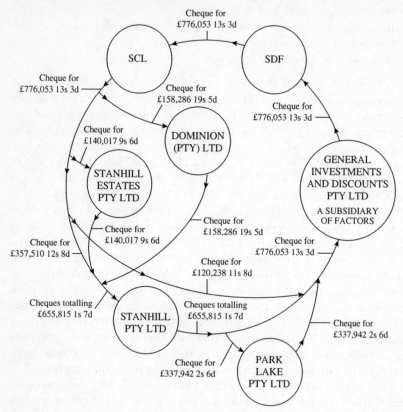

Source: P. Murphy, *Interim Report . . . into an Investigation . . . into the Affairs of Stanhill . . .* 1964, p. 41.

Its effect was to reconstruct the legal relationship of the participants. Its mechanism is depicted diagrammatically in Figure 5.2.

The round robbin effected the takeover of Dominion and Stanhill Estates by SCL. Stanhill and Park Lake thereby were able to receive in cash their profits on the sale of the land to Stanhill Estates, repay their debts to Factors, and divest themselves of further responsibility regarding the real estate owned by Stanhill Estates and Dominion. Unquestionably the transaction was designed to benefit the Korman family. The consequences were that SDF was owed £2.3 million by SCL (almost the amount raised by SDF from the public in 1960) and, most importantly, the family companies' debts had been repaid – consequences that were not publicly disclosed at the time.

Nearly two years later, on 14 February 1963, upon the trigger of a debtor's judgment for £2,113,219, a receiver was appointed to SDF, leading to the financial facts being *publicly* revealed. SDF's Statement of Affairs as at 6 December 1963 showed a deficiency of £1,902,641. The *public arm* of the Stanhill group had collapsed. SCL and its subsidiaries, Stanhill Estates and Dominion, ended in liquidation and a Victorian government inspector was appointed to examine the group's dealings; Chevron Sydney went into receivership, the hotel was sold and the other assets were distributed to claimants. Inspector Murphy QC estimated the losses of the Stanhill group to be approximately £24 million (or nearly $500 million in current terms):[12]

		£
(i)	Subscriptions for share capital, including Factors' purchase of Rockmans Ltd shares	9,168,208
(ii)	Losses by Debenture and Note Holders	6,584,748
(iii)	Creditors	7,994,513
		23,747,469

Corporate games – Korman's kindergarten?

The rise and fall of the Stanhill group contains many features similar to later Australian corporate collapses. Complex transactions between a labyrinth of private and public companies became a common technique; the ability to mask poorly performing individual companies by various group-related accounting techniques became the norm, particularly as land and other assets were shuffled around the group companies, often with profits (generally for the private companies) and losses (for the public companies) being recorded at each shuffle. It was a good *ponzi* scheme, antecedent of events in the 1970s and 1980s. A 'ponzi' scheme was named after a 1920s US market operator, Charles Ponzi. Such schemes promised high returns on risky assets and their success depended on maintaining investors' belief that the assets' prices would continue to rise forever.

That few, if any, major lessons appear to have been learned from the Stanhill saga is disturbing. Inequity and moral (arguably legal) impropriety in the round robin transaction, realising profits for the Korman private companies as well as repayment of Korman private company debt to the public companies, was a valuable lesson to be learned – seemingly it wasn't. Finally, the use of a public company 'cash-cow' (Factors) was virtually identical in method, and consistent in motive to later corporate manoeuvres – for example, the alleged 'cash-cow' role played by Bell Resources in the Bond Corporation group's desperate moves in 1989 to stave off liquidation. In both instances it is arguable that directors of a recognised group of public companies acted commercially as if there was no legal distinction between each separate company comprising it. The effects on shareholders, especially minority shareholders, and on the creditors of each separate company are potentially dramatic.

Some of Stanhill's contemporaries fell just as heavily. None hit the wall any harder than electrical and whitegoods retailer H.G. Palmer, to whom we now turn.

SIX

H.G. Palmer:
'Gilt' by Association*

'Did H.G. Palmer (Consolidated) Ltd. (receiver appointed)
ever make a profit?'

Anon (1965)

Possibly not! Or so it seems from the commercial post-mortem on the
House of Palmer. In its 15 years as a listed public company reported
profits totalled only £5.6 million before tax. In 1965 H.G. Palmer
unexpectedly reported what was then Australia's biggest-ever annual loss
of £10 million (approximately $200 million in current terms). Following
the first report of the receiver's investigation into Palmer's collapse, the
Financial Editor of the *Sydney Morning Herald*, Tom Fitzgerald, stated that,
after retrospective accounting restatements, 'H.G. Palmer has never been
a truly profitable business since it came on to the Stock Exchange in
1949.'[1] Of critical importance is why it took 16 years to find that out, for
the 'retrospective accounting restatements' could have been made
contemporaneously had accounting regulation been different.

Fitzgerald's observation begs the question as to what 'never truly
profitable' might mean. To virtually everyone (outside of the accounting
fraternity, it appears) it would mean ordinarily that the company's wealth
had decreased year after year, accumulating to the aggregative loss that
was revealed in the eventual liquidation of H.G. Palmer. The problem is,
conventional accounting does not calculate periodic profit (or loss) in
terms of an increase (decrease) in the wealth period by period. Invariably
it isn't until the end of a company's life that it becomes publicly known
how it fared financially year by year.

Palmer's collapse and the concurrent demise of Cox Brothers were two
major 1960s retail disasters. Both were rude shocks to Australia's retail
establishment.

Palmer's founder, Herbert George Palmer, was a salesman, not a financier. He learned his selling techniques during the depression,[2] successfully
hawking radio sets from door to door in Sydney's suburbs. Conventional
retailing commenced in 1932 in a rented shop space in the Sydney suburb

of Bankstown. A year later he opened his own retail store in Bankstown, thereby expanding his sales of radio and electrical equipment.

In 1938 operations expanded by opening a branch on the south coast, in Wollongong. This was the start of his big assault on the electrical retail market. 'Herbie' Palmer was switched on in a big way. There is no doubt that he was well thought of during those years: to all, he was a respectable businessman. He was the prototype of the many indigenous entrepreneurs who were to follow. Palmer possessed style. He was well known as a man-about-Bankstown, to be sure. It was reported in the press at the time of his fall from grace that Palmer 'until quite recently might have been found in the company of the most reputable men in the community'.[3]

Wartime had limited the availability of electrical products and spare parts. Thus, in the early days the Palmer business was largely restricted to repair work. After the war, supplies of stock improved. There was the inevitable period of general post-war business expansion and Palmer was there to capitalise on it. He had a 'natural' sense of opportunity, a 'nose' for where prospects lay. There also were peacetime benefits of wartime research and development being fed into the appliance market. In 1947 two companies were incorporated to conduct the Palmer retailing businesses: H.G. Palmer Pty Ltd and H.G. Palmer (Wollongong) Pty Ltd. Most sales were for cash, with the remaining hire purchase sales financed by H.G. Palmer (Finance) Pty Ltd (also formed in 1947). In 1949 Palmer incorporated Remlap Electric Pty Ltd as an avenue for the activities of installing and servicing refrigeration equipment. A refrigerator in the home was a kind of status symbol – ice-boxes were *passé*. The whitegoods boom was about to begin.

H.G. Palmer (Consolidated) Ltd was incorporated as a holding company to acquire interests in these four family companies on 7 December 1949. Clearly Palmer had an eye for the emerging business entity *par excellence* – the holding company. In this respect H.G. Palmer was a structural exemplar for failed and successful companies alike in subsequent decades – for in fact, it is difficult to find a sizeable 'success' or collapse since 1950 which has not embraced the holding company/subsidiary organisational structure.

Palmer was on a common failure trajectory from almost day one – rapid expansion by acquisition using debt finance, seeking increased sales without associated increased actual profits. The prospectus (dated 12 December) for the issue of shares in this company claimed that the aggregates of the annual profits (1947–1949 years, ending 30 June) of the four Palmer family companies since their date of incorporation were: £1,805, £8,431 and £12,215.

The disclosed aggregate book value of the prospective subsidiaries' net assets was £29,472. After deducting £3,500 preference capital, the equity of ordinary shareholders was £25,972. The consideration to be paid to H.G. Palmer and seven relatives for their shares in the four companies totalled £66,935.16s.8d. Of this, £13,435 was to be payable immediately the contract was finalised. The balance was to remain unpaid for up to ten years if so desired by the purchaser, and in return the vendors were granted an option to take up £53,501 in ordinary shares on or before 1 July 1951. The prospectus invited the public to subscribe for 34,000 5s. ordinary shares, payable in full on application. A further 66,000 5s. ordinary shares were applied for by the shareholders of the Palmer family companies under identical terms, and official listing on the Sydney Stock Exchange was granted on 5 September 1950. Palmer's move into the public arena was off and running – at full speed.

Typical of many of the other failed companies referred to here, from the day of listing until acquired by one of the largest life assurance companies (the Mutual Life Corporation Ltd in 1963), H.G. Palmer (Consolidated) expanded 'by acquisition'. Palmers swallowed a number of electrical retailing companies in its expansion phase. In 1954 it was Crooks (Auburn) Pty Ltd and Crooks (Auburn) Finance Pty Ltd; in 1955 followed acquisitions of the Manly Electric and Radio Co. Pty Ltd and Manly Television Co. Pty Ltd. In order to give the group an edge in sales tax matters, in 1956 Crooks (Auburn) Pty Ltd became H.G. Palmer (Wholesale) Pty Ltd. Other group companies also underwent name changes to generate the H.G. Palmer legend. A Canberra register was achieved through the incorporation of Music Masters (ACT) Pty Ltd in 1957. Music Masters Pty Ltd (Qld) was acquired in 1958, as was Downie Pty Ltd (Vic.); it had been reported to the Sydney Stock Exchange that the main reason for this takeover was the acquisition of a retail site.

The Palmer group did not so much add corporate value as acquire value which already existed. Growth-by-acquisition was the name of the game. It was easy and there for the taking. Downie was voluntarily wound up in 1960. Two other companies were incorporated in Victoria and the Australian Capital Territory and H.G. Palmer (Consolidated) Ltd had a total of 11 subsidiaries, all wholly-owned except for some holdings of preference shares. The group soon comprised approximately 150 retail outlets, in New South Wales, Victoria, Queensland and South Australia. Expansion had been frenetic – sensational, but unstructured, more of it by accident than by design. If there was an electrical retailer for sale, then H.G. Palmer bought it. In this respect Palmers were moving along a similar, but not identical, failure trajectory to that of Reid Murray. As it turned out, the paths proved equally slippery.[4]

Late on the afternoon of Monday, 8 April 1963, the MLC Ltd made a takeover offer for the issued ordinary capital of H.G. Palmer (Consolidated) Ltd. The MLC was then the second-largest life office in Australia.

H.G. Palmer was the largest retailer of electrical appliances in the country. Publicly it had the appearances of a perfect union. The share exchange bid was calculated to be worth 21s. for each H.G. Palmer stock unit, 5s. more than the latest market price.[5]

The bid was a 'bolt from the blue',[6] at least for many members of the public. There seemed little doubt in the minds of at least some financial commentators that H.G. Palmer was very prosperous. 'H.G. Palmer sets records.'[7] Only a few weeks earlier the reported growth of H.G. Palmer had been described as 'the most heartening . . . of the success stories of Australian retailing'.[8] Those assessments are in stark contrast to Tom Fitzgerald's referred to earlier.

That raises doubts that the market generally is in-the-know about such things. Importantly, it exposes that nothing is as seductive as reported success backed up by corroborative financial statements. At least some in the market were very much in the dark, but did not know it. By virtue of thinking that they knew all, they probably were worse off than those who were aware that they did not. That feature has been endemic of many Australian corporate failures discussed in this book.

MLC's purchase of H.G. Palmer was the first plunge by an Australian life assurance company into retailing. But the feeling in the market was that the acquisition promised to be profitable.[9] It certainly enhanced the commercial status of Palmers. Within a very short period, it failed to turn out that way. Again, many experts were wrong. Perhaps not surprisingly, for ultimately even experts are left to draw their financial inferences primarily from published financial statements chock full of creativity – as seductive to the expert as to the layman.

Financing

Successful growth in H.G. Palmer sales of electrical goods has been attributed to its reliance on borrowing.[10] And, of course, its capacity to borrow was boosted by the illusion of the group's profitability contained in its audited financial reports. Analysis of Palmer's debt and equity raising history is instructive for the insight it gives to the manner in which alternative financing resources were tapped one by one. It also points to gross misunderstanding regarding the worth of the asset cover for the accumulating debt. Conventional accounting then, as now, facilitated recourse to 'book values' – artifacts of the bookkeeping system – rather than to current selling prices of the assets pledged. As many before and many since have done, as one finance source dried up H.G. Palmer moved on to yet another. Possibly the market did not disseminate the news about the rejected lines of finance as efficiently as one might have expected. Nor apparently was the market overtly cognisant of the uselessness of 'book values' when it comes to assessing the security for debt. Both aspects are matters which contemporary market commentators ought to contemplate.

We might presume that the reliance on Palmer's perceived profitability drove the financial support it received. It is hard to imagine that, had the financial truth been known, investors would have been so forthcoming. Between incorporation in 1950 and the appointment of the receiver in 1965, the issued equity capital of H.G. Palmer increased from (approximately) £25,000 to £6,824,082. Generally, the equity issues were to 'finance the expansion of the subsidiary companies'. Acquisition of most of the subsidiaries was effected through share issues – for example, the takeovers of Music Masters Radio Pty Ltd (Brisbane) in 1958 and Manly Electric and Radio Company Pty Ltd (Sydney) in 1960. Again, none of that may have occurred had the audited accounts disclosed Palmer's true financial state. However, during the early 1960s equity issues served another role. In June 1964, 500,000 20s. 7 per cent cumulative 2nd preference shares were issued to the MLC in order to provide cash for the 'maintenance of liquidity'. During October 1964 the procedure was repeated: another 500,000 20s. cumulative 2nd preference shares were issued to the MLC. Thus, £1 million had been injected by the MLC in a space of four months. Six months later, another rescue bid was undertaken by the MLC upon the discovery, by one of its officers, of at least £2.5 million in bad debts at H.G. Palmer with possibly another £1.5 million problematic. Good money poured after bad – a fatal managerial strategy. To cover the loss, 4 million 20s. 'A' class cumulative redeemable preference shares were issued. MLC subscribed £3,625,000 and the Palmer family company, Palfam Investments Pty Ltd, put up the residual. Unfortunately the group was within six months of receivership, but nothing in the reported financial results gave indications of it (Table 6.1).

Palmer's scenario, like many others here, included accelerated growth under a charismatic leader, coupled to a quick, unexpected collapse. And further, like those others, conventional accounting practices did not get in the way – indeed, they were most accommodating, not of a kind likely to disclose Palmer's precarious financial position.

As with most financial intermediaries, prior to 1956 major debt financing came from bank overdrafts and trade credit. Palmer's first public debt raising was in August 1956.[11] Thereafter, 15 issues to the public of notes and debentures were made. Borrowing ceased with the recall of the prospectus issued on 15 January 1965 because of the alleged misstatements it contained.

As early as the 1960s the difficulties in interpreting the disclosed financial information by Australian public companies, even without management manipulation, were commonly acknowledged outside the

Table 6.1 Palmer's reported trading results, 1950 to 1965

At 30 June	Approximate turnover £	Debtors balance outstanding £	Reported profits £	Preference % Interim	Preference % Final	Ord. %
1950	214,000	84,199	6,403	–	–	10
1951	1,044,000	165,798	31,317	–	–	10
1952	1,398,000	197,807	31,729	6	–	10
1953	2,400,000	342,087	72,092	6	–	10
1954	3,400,000	1,757,842	100,676	6	–	10
1955	3,350,000	2,326,962	101,536	6	7	10
1956	3,300,000	2,378,735	96,170	6	7	10
1957	4,400,000	3,128,307	131,318	6	7	10
1958	8,400,000	4,606,832	250,147	10	–	10
1959	10,010,000	8,533,320	301,494	10	–	12
1960	13,800,000	12,291,095	413,246	10	–	12
1961	14,100,000	15,302,972	421,596	10	–	12
1962	14,300,000	18,547,916	428,746	10	–	12
1963	14,400,000	20,903,869	431,624	10	–	12
1964	13,700,000	23,920,221	408,371	10	–	12
1965	15,000,000	22,184,606	(4,350,091)	5	–	–

Source: H.G. Palmer, *Statement of Affairs.*

professional accounting ranks. Chroniclers of financial institutions Hirst and Wallace had noted:

> . . . adherence to historical cost conventions . . . means that the accounting reports of companies provide measures of periodic surplus and funds employed which are meaningless as indicators . . . [they] do not contain the information needed to convert reported profits and funds employed to current values, [hence] shareholders and investors are not able to choose between alternative avenues of investment on a rational basis.[12]

Nonetheless, in the Palmer case, choose investors did, seemingly undaunted by that general warning and warnings from many others.

Buoyed by their reputation, created, or at least corroborated, by impressive reported financials, borrowing seemingly was easy for Palmer during that period. Palmer prospectuses were issued by the banker for the group, H.G. Palmer (Consolidated) Ltd, but cross-guaranteed by all the subsidiaries when required to set up the floating charge securing the debenture issues. Oversubscriptions at this time were common and legally retained. For example, the August 1956 issue of £100,000 in fixed deposit notes (in multiples of £25) produced £2,004,642; in February 1959, £250,000 was offered and resulted in an increase in debt of

£3,763,710 (net of the proceeds required to redeem maturing debt); in June 1960 the first issue of mortgage debentures was followed closely by further offers in November of that year and April 1961; £1,500,000 was asked for and £5,684,575 had been received by June 1961. The retention pattern continued, for legislation did not prevent retention of over-subscriptions. Obviously, many in the market must have viewed H.G. Palmer favourably. Following the introduction of the 1961 *Uniform Companies Act*, oversubscription retentions were limited by the terms of the prospectus. Oversubscriptions were still common in the early 1960s raisings. Between July 1961 and June 1965, £35,181,382 had been borrowed.

When a receiver was appointed to the group on 25 October 1965, outstanding borrowings raised by prospectus issues stood at:

	£
Debentures (secured by a floating charge and the assets of H.G. Palmer (Consolidated) Ltd and subsidiaries)	41,701,270
Registered Unsecured Deposit Notes	7,316,374
Registered Fixed Deposit Notes	5,690,548

an equivalent of nearly $1 billion in current terms.

It is not surprising that continued borrowing was easy for the Palmer group. It enjoyed a more than favourable press, almost right up to the time of the appointment of the receiver. Indeed, as already indicated, the financial press was most exuberant in its praise. For example, under the 'H.G. Palmer shareholders on clover'[13] accolade sat this positive assessment:

> [In spite of the November 1960 credit squeeze] to record an increase in profit albeit small was a mark of a highly flexible merchandising technique. . . . [Palmer] may strengthen more than ever its grip on a market whose boundaries are set by replacement sales and the natural growth, because the end of the TV boom means the passing of a mushroom of 'fly-by-night' retailers.[14]

and under the caption, 'Palmer Progress': 'If Mr Menzies' credit squeeze did nothing else it did at least indicate where the *quality* lay. Among those to show out with a *nicely gilded fleece* has been H.G.P.'[15] It would seem that, like beauty, quality is in the eye of the beholder – almost certainly influenced, however, by what is being reported about the wealth and progress of the company under assessment. And, of course, all that glitters is not gold, although conventional accounting certainly injects the alchemist's touch.

Shareholders, noteholders and the like were more likely on quicksand than clover! Reputable, knowledgeable broking houses were just as eulogistic. Perhaps on the basis of their presumed superior financial knowledge, share prices rose steadily from a low of 3s. in 1952 to the end of 1963 when they stood at 22s. It seems that those presumed to be in-the-know had created H.G. Palmer a 'legend in their own mind' and were quite sanguine regarding the difficulties other retailers were experiencing. Palmer's management was perceived by many to be one of only a few who had not lost the plot.

Trading activities

Selling electrical appliances on credit terms was the major source of revenue for the group. Credit contracts were entered into mainly through H.G. Palmer Pty Ltd and H.G. Palmer (Vic.) Pty Ltd. Transactions were financed internally by H.G. Palmer Pty Ltd, Hire Purchase Securities Ltd, Mutual Acceptance Corporation Ltd and Control Securities Ltd. Record sales were the main revenue source of the Music Masters Pty Ltd stores in Queensland, reputed to have the largest business of that type in the State.

Goods sold on credit prior to 1965 accounted for approximately 90 per cent of the group's business. Those goods usually were the subject of a credit sale agreement under the *Credit Sales Act* in New South Wales and similar legislation in Victoria and Queensland. In contrast with sales under hire purchase, property in the goods legally passed to the purchaser upon entering into the agreement, which provided for not more than eight payments to be made over the period of 12 months for which credit was given. Interest rates ranged from 10 per cent for short term contracts to 12 per cent over a longer period. Presumably (as usually was the practice) the credit sale agreement entered into was designed to avoid the requirements of the *Hire Purchase Act*. Private arrangements often executed between H.G. Palmer and customers enabled payments to be made over a period longer than the 12 months specified by the *Credit Sales Act* – a good strategy for showing reported sales growth, but questionable for ensuring long-term survival. Not surprisingly, Palmers were moving the goods at a time when the other retailers in general, and whitegoods dealers in particular, were struggling.

Although many products had an H.G. Palmer brand name, Palmer companies did not manufacture. Component parts were imported in most cases and assembled under contract for H.G. Palmer (Wholesale) Pty Ltd by various Australian companies. Faith in the Palmer group's financial stability proved costly. On liquidation, Palmer's Statement of Affairs disclosed large (at the time) debts to well-known manufacturers and distributors, including:

	£
Email Limited	72,505
Kelvinator Limited	96,751
Simpson Pope Group	235,087
Kriesler Limited	38,639
Hoover (Aust.) Limited	37,920
Philips Elect. Ind. Ltd	39,266

Little difficulty was experienced by H.G. Palmer in establishing those credit facilities, which was not surprising given its sales and profit records. Nor, apparently, was there any problem raising debenture moneys from many institutional investors, possibly for the same reasons, especially so after the MLC acquisition. Money poured in from the big institutions, including the AMP who provided £825,000; National Mutual Life £405,000; the NSW GIO £500,000 and MBF of Australia £210,000. In current dollars this was approximately $40 million, but, more importantly, it was a sizeable amount at the time.

Financial measures of the volume of H.G. Palmer business are contestable. Disclosure of turnover figures did not become mandatory in Australia until the beginning of the 1970s. However, there are some clues which assist its approximation. Turnover, here, should be taken as a composite of sales of goods for cash, or credit, finance charges apportioned to the Profit and Loss account via the application of the Rule of 78 and proceeds from service contracts and maintenance services.

Employees reported that a net 3 per cent to 4 per cent profit on turnover was aimed for in budget preparation; hence this percentage could be applied to the reported profit figures to approximate turnover. Second, Sir Norman Nock, in his chairman's address at the annual general meeting for the year ended 30 June 1958, stated that 'turnover now exceeded £8 million'. The profit reported in 1958 was £250,147 which represented approximately 3 per cent of Nock's disclosure. So, it appears that the rough formula passed the test. Applying the 3 per cent, the turnover for the ten years to 1964 shows a steady trend in sales growth from approximately £3.4 million in 1955 to £14 million in 1961. The rate of growth then dropped greatly to level the turnover at approximately the £14 million to £15 million mark by 1965 – approximating $300 million in 1996 dollars.

The levelling out after 1961 could have several explanations. First, the credit squeeze of 1960/61 put a brake on the sale of consumer durables. Or second, the saturation point of television sales, which had picked up where the whitegoods left off in the mid-1950s, had been reached. And third, colour television, which Palmer expected to be the saving white knight had failed to arrive on time. Possibly there was a mixture of all three.

Yet Palmer's growth in assets, sales and debt finance, then and subsequently, was apparently premised on the belief that the market would expand forever. A familiar pattern of entrepreneurial behaviour had emerged. Similar beliefs in respect of investment in securities and real property were integral in many of the 1970s and 1980s collapses.

Returning to Palmer, signs which many in the industry were noting eluded Herbie Palmer's gaze as well as those of his admirers in the press gallery. The growth at Palmers is instructive. From 1950 onwards the number of stores opened yearly had increased; averaging four a year until 1958 when 21 were opened (NSW 7, Victoria 9, South Australia 2 and Queensland 3). The expansion continued in 1959 with 17 stores being opened, in 1960/61 (14), 1962 (25), 1963 (25) and 1964 (25). By January 1965, 146 retail outlets existed under the Palmer name, yet retailing was having a hard time.

Palmer's financial reports were out of line with the public signals of retailing's woes. It was a victory for 'accounting fiction' over 'financial facts'; fiction that was duly audited and presumably passed on to the market as if it were fact. The failure of the market to consider more closely the public signals is curious, but definitely not a one-off occurrence.

It would seem that few knew of – or if they did, heeded – the notorious 1950s deeds in the United States of Tino De Angelis, where records revealed that reported increases in De Angelis's companies' holdings of vegetable oils exceeded the US Department of Agriculture's production figures; likewise, again in the United States, when Billie Sol Estes embarked upon his 1960s grain frauds; and when the 1972 reported growth in Equity Funding's life policies meant that within the next decade it would have insured more people than currently resided in the US. The revelations in the derivatives, futures and foreign exchange trading fiascos of the 1990s (e.g. at Barings, Sumitomo and Daiwa) similarly suggest that it is too much to expect these financial lessons of history to be transmitted across countries, let alone across decades within the same country.[16]

Palmer's public, seemingly unquestioning, support is a compelling example of the apparent public preference for the representations in duly verified accounting reports, favourable press and 'gilt' associations, over other externally available information. It also points to the failure of accounting to be structured in such a way that it corresponds to the financial and the related physical facts of the market.

'Gilt' by association

Between mid-1963 and early 1965, H.G. Palmer (Consolidated) Limited issued several prospectuses strongly featuring a photograph of the MLC's head office and emphasising that H.G. Palmer was a wholly-owned subsidiary of the MLC.

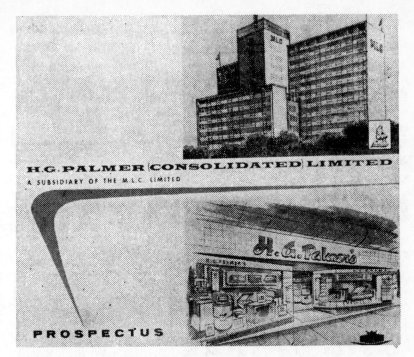

An example of an H.G. Palmer prospectus cover dated 31 July 1964.
Sydney Morning Herald, 20 November 1965. Reproduced with approval from
John Fairfax & Sons Ltd.

According to the evidence given in 1966 at the committal proceedings
against officers of H.G. Palmer, the company's liquidity problem had
been identified mid-1964. The court was told of the apparent need of
approximately £6 million at that time to meet the repayment of borrowings which were then due. The company was incurring a net outflow of
cash. Palmer was informed that the company was living beyond its means.
'The chief accountant had prepared a set of figures which showed that
[Palmers] were living at the rate of $140,000 a week over and above our
inflow. This relates purely to cash.'[17]

However, the liquidity problem was relieved by the oversubscribed July
1964 issue of 1st debenture stock. Oversubscriptions were so heavy that a
reduction of creditors was effected and the accommodating finance from
MLC Ltd was repaid prior to 30 June 1965. The remaining £1 million cash
surplus was loaned to MLC. Perhaps MLC had earned special treatment,
for Palmers were riding high on the MLC bandwagon of financial strength
and respectability. It was a case of 'gilt by association'. Some perceived
benefits of the interaction between MLC and H.G. Palmer are provided
by: 'An anonymous Newcastle widow of modest means [who] wrote to The
Sydney Morning Herald . . . "I had intended to reinvest [H.G. Palmer

debenture redemptions] elsewhere, but under the umbrella of the MLC's great strength and reputation – and strongly urged by my broker – I reinvested in H.G.P. debentures".[18] This was a view apparently shared by many. H.G. Palmer advertised in its prospectus (see p. 79 above) that MLC had a 100 per cent interest, implying that MLC would support H.G. Palmer. Consider this extract from a letter to the *Australian Financial Review* under the caption 'Palmers a good buy': 'In making the investment it is comforting to know the MLC insurance group owns the ordinary capital of Palmers.'[19] Comfort it may have been, but it was to be short-lived. The Newcastle widow's umbrella metaphorically quickly blew inside-out when Palmer collapsed suddenly.

The growth of Palmer's 'debtors' was at a greater pace than that of turnover, and any thoughts that another liquidity problem would ensue should have been anticipated, since borrowings were intended (according to the prospectus) to redeem maturing issues of like securities.

Accounting magic

Reported trading results (Table 6.1) provide a glowing account of the prosperity of the group; profits increasing nearly every year from a humble £31,317 for the year ended 30 June 1951 (the first full year of trading) to £408,371 at 30 June 1964. Particularly noteworthy is that just over a year before being placed in receivership H.G. Palmer recorded its highest reported profits of more than £431,000 (approximately $8 million in 1996 dollars).

Nobody – shareholder, debenture holder or noteholder – went short during those heady years: Table 6.1 shows that the constant stream of preference dividends of 6 per cent and 7 per cent to 1957 and 10 per cent thereafter – and 10 per cent ordinary dividend to 1958 and 12 per cent thereafter – continued to the year ended 30 June 1964.

From the date of its formation the group paid out a total of £2,472,348 in dividends. This amount exceeded the amount estimated to be available (according to the Statement of Affairs) to meet the unsecured creditors of the group at the time the receiver was appointed.

Several aspects of the preparation of the accounts and associated financing are noteworthy:

- Little credit control existed. In evidence before Mr Scarlett SM it was reported that branch managers were required to keep rejection of contract proposals down to 2 per cent of the proposals received. Credit was granted therefore, if this is to be taken as indication of the group policy, on a mathematical basis rather than by an investigation of the creditworthiness of the would-be customer.

  Estimated sales were the result of budget projections prepared by the branch manager, proven salesmen and, although each branch had an accountant, his duties were restricted to bookkeeping activities. The basis for the budgetary system was the desired 3–4 per cent net return on sales noted earlier.

Each branch manager was allocated a proportion of fixed expenses and by adding the expenses peculiar to his branch area, a total expense figure was ascertained. A gross margin of 28 per cent was required. Thus, expenses were to be approximately 24–25 per cent of the total revenues. An anticipated (in fact, essential) sales figure was then projected by multiplying the expense figure by four. Credit policy was tailored to guarantee the sales volume.

The expansion of the amount of credit extended is evidenced by the path of the growth of debtors' balances outstanding, as shown in Table 6.1.

- Hiring charges were apportioned on the basis of the Rule of 78; no allowance was made for: (a) probability of collection; or (b) a hedge against inflation.
- No provision was made for doubtful debts despite the evidence of difficulty of collection. This difficulty was referred to by Mr Davis Hughes, in a speech to the NSW Legislative Assembly on 9 September 1964, when he disclosed that of 26,000 actions in the Bankstown Small Debts Court in 1963, 18,000 were at the suit of H.G. Palmer Pty Ltd.

Board of directors' reports had not mentioned the bad debts to that point. However, in 1965 the chairman had reported: 'Bad Debts which are proved have been progressively written off from year to year. Reported Loss for the Year Ended 30 June 1965 was £4,350,091. The reported 1965 loss was the result of adverse trading as reported by the Chairman in his address and the writing off of £1,258,876 "bad debts" and the provision for £2,741,124 anticipated to prove "bad".' The write-off and provision followed an investigation initiated by MLC Ltd on the H.G. Palmer group debtors' ledgers on 4 March 1964, before the takeover. This investigation was carried out by MLC Ltd in response to information received and the general rumour of 'bad debts' in H.G. Palmer Pty Ltd. Rumour was rife at the time in the city, but presumably it did not discourage the many investors trading in H.G. Palmer securities or those recommending them. Subsequently a report was issued on 11 March 1964 by H.G. Palmer, suggesting that £2.5 million should be written off debts in the 'black-ledger' immediately and a further £1.5 million provided for further bad debts. The 'black-ledger', said to have been removed when earlier investigators had arrived to look at the debtors' ledger, subsequently was found located at the Bankstown headquarters in a toilet – not an altogether inappropriate place for it. The write-offs were financed by the preference issue (mainly) to MLC Ltd.

At the end of September 1965 the preliminary accounts for the year ended 30 June 1965 were released. It was apparent by the end of October

1965 that a substantial breach of the borrowing ratio of the trust deed
had occurred. The MLC board acted swiftly. It moved to write off its
entire investment in H.G. Palmer – $8.7 million. Then it requested the
trustee for the debenture holders, Permanent Trustee Company of New
South Wales, to appoint a receiver, Mr C.H.R. Jackson. Institutional
investors at the Circular Quay end of Pitt Street, Sydney, were staggered;
elsewhere, thousands of H.G. Palmer's customers settled back with
gratitude to watch the hottest household wonder – monochrome TV.

Doubtful debts and a true and fair view

Of significance for accountants in the H.G. Palmer failure is the
similarity with the issues that had arisen over three decades earlier in the
United Kingdom in the Royal Mail affair. As Lord Jowitt had so succinctly
summed up: 'If the documents convey to a reasonably intelligent person
a false impression, all the technical rules of accountancy may be
observed and at the same time the accountants' profession has failed to
carry out its primary and obvious duty . . . to ensure that in the documents which are produced a true and accurate account of the affairs of
the company is given.'[20]

Sentencing Herbert Palmer and the auditor John McBlane, Lee J.
observed: 'Investment by the public in companies plays an important
part in the commercial life of the community and it is of the utmost
importance that prospectuses . . . should be true and accurate in the
statements they contain.'[21] Those comments ring somewhat hollow
against the current downgrading of the *true and fair* override clause from
Australia's Corporations Law. Somewhere along the way since the Palmer
debacle the ethos enunciated by Lee J. has been crudely abandoned. We
have more to say on this in Chapter 18.

There was ample evidence of H.G. Palmer's compliance, in some
instances, to the 'technical rules of accountancy' – for example, the use
of the Rule of 78 to recognise income hiring charges accrued but not yet
paid and (say) mechanical debtors' write-offs without periodic recourse
to their separate money's worth. The reality was that H.G. Palmer had
not made an actual profit in any year since incorporation, let alone the
record profit levels for 1963 and 1964. A headline in the press captured
the perceived deception: 'H.G. Palmer gets 4 years . . . auditor 3 years –
Prospectuses should be true and accurate'. Indeed, *all* public accounting
information should be.

The issue of what represents 'a true and accurate (fair) view' of an
entity's state of affairs was to bedevil the accounting profession for the next
three decades. It is likely to be the subject of several court cases in the latter
part of the nineties, and perhaps judicial directives might emerge.[22]

Two of ASL's 'white knights',
Sir Henry Bolte and Sir
Reginald Ansett. *National
Times*, 10 March 1979, p. 23.
Courtesy of John Fairfax
Holdings Ltd.

Kenneth McMahon after
having charges dismissed
against him over a Minsec
profit statement. Courtesy
of News Ltd.

THE MINSEC AFFAIR:
NAILING THE COFFIN SHUT

Battles rage as liquidator fights for time

JOHN BYRNE concludes his series on the crash that cost 8,000 investors $45 million.

J.H. Jamison (left) had been provisional liquidator for only one week when the then Prime Minister, John Gorton, met in Sydney with Minsec's major creditors in an abortive attempt to have them pool their security. *The Australian*, 28 April 1973, p. 12. Courtesy of News Ltd.

PART III

The 1970s

SEVEN

Going for Broke in the 1970s

'If, . . . due to the optional accounting rules available to
them, company managers and directors are able to conceal
the drift [in financial position] shareholders and creditors
will continue to support, and support with new money,
companies which are weaker than their accounts represent
them to be.'

R.J. Chambers (1973b, p. 166)

At last in the 1970s there was an apparent regulatory response. It was to
prove an opportunity lost.

As in the sixties, notable Australian collapses in the early seventies
prompted extensive public concern. This resulted in the NSW government forming the Accounting Standards Review Committee chaired by
Professor R.J. Chambers, conventional accounting's most trenchant
critic, 'to examine the accounting standards . . . promulgated . . . or at
the exposure draft stage . . . and to consider any other standards . . .
which should be considered in the interest of parties who use published
accounting information.'[1] The Review Committee's May 1978 Report was
extremely critical of the existing system of accounting. NSW Attorney
General Frank Walker threatened state intervention in the Accounting
Standards-setting process unless the accountancy profession issued
sensible and enforceable directives. For whatever reason, little direct
action resulted from this committee's report and those threats. Despite
the committee's strong criticism of conventional accounting practices,
the pervading public concern of the regulators – government and the
accounting profession – was the extent of non-compliance with practices
prescribed by the profession. Non-compliance was perceived in all cases
to be deviant professional behaviour. The underlying cost-based accounting practices were not deemed the major problem.

Between 1975 and 1977 the NSW Corporate Affairs Commission had
reviewed annually 249, 535 and 250 accounts of companies. This revealed
62, 253 and 211 instances of non-compliance, respectively. Monitoring
continued after the release of the Accounting Standards Review
Committee Report, with an analysis of 8,699 companies between 1978 and
1982 revealing non-compliance with one or more accounting standards
occurring in 3,428 (41 per cent) of companies. Whereas that result was

presented as a serious threat to the disclosure of necessary financial information, it is argued here that just the opposite was equally likely. So many of the non-compliances related to prescribed practices that were counterfactual – providing for depreciation on buildings when the overall market price of property (including the buildings) was increasing; providing for future income tax and booking future income tax benefits without the immediate existence of or any *definite* prospect that the *supposed* liabilities or assets would materialise, for example. Of course, any subsequent change in tax rates will affect, often materially, the amount of reported asset or liability balances. This was highlighted with the proposed reductions from 36 per cent to 33 per cent in the prevailing corporate tax rates announced in 1993.

A Potter Warburg study disclosed that the likely effect on the already 'reported' asset and liability balances of certain public companies would be to 'boost BHP's net profit after abnormals by more than $200 million . . . [and] CRA Ltd [by] $93 million. . . . [whilst] companies which have previously reported significant losses are likely to show high write downs of the [previously reported] tax benefits'.[2] Earlier we referred to the similar potential being seized upon following the corporate tax rate changes in the 1995 federal Budget.

Failure to report the money's worth of physical assets has been shown to be a pervading accounting problem. This is especially so under conventional practice which frequently prescribes the treatment of money spent as if it were still in the hands of the spender – a particular problem when the expenditure is on speculative ventures in, say, mining and property which have had top-billing in a number of Australia's 1970s collapses. Exploration holes and high-rise office blocks have more in common than might at first appear. Both cost a lot before any revenue rolls in. Until it does, they may amount to a financial loss.

Precipitating the formation of the 1978 Chambers Committee were the mining-cum-investment and property financial dilemmas of the 1970s, aftermaths of the mining boom of the late 1960s and the property boom of the early 1970s. These included: investment traders, Mineral Securities Australia Ltd and Patrick Partners; construction group, Mainline; property-cum-financier, Cambridge Credit Corporation Ltd; the conglomerate, Gollins Holdings Ltd; and, for example, the finance-cum-property development company, Associated Securities Ltd (Table 7.1).

Like their counterparts in the 1960s, these unexpected (to many) major corporate collapses in the 1970s created public pressure on regulators to reassess the utility of existing regulatory mechanisms – in particular, the utility of existing professional accounting and auditing practices. For example, Gollins collapsed in 1975 shortly after an interim six-monthly report had revealed a reported *profit* of $835,192. Inquiries

Table 7.1 Major company failures in Australia, 1970 to 1979

Year of failure – date administrator appointed	Name of company	Basis of criticism	Actions against auditors/officials
February 1971	Mineral Securities Australia Ltd (Minsec)	Profit had been created by dealings between related group companies.	Directors of Minsec were charged over matters relating to a published 'consolidated' profit figure. All charges were dismissed
August 1974	Mainline Corporation	(i) Borrowing short and investing long in construction projects. (ii) Overgeared.	n.a.
September 1974	Cambridge Credit Corporation	(i) Consolidation practices; (ii) Intermingling of private and public companies; and (iii) Valuation of land and shares.	'Class action'-type civil proceedings against the auditors by the debenture holders resulted in an out-of-court settlement of approximately $20 million. Criminal actions against directors dismissed.
June 1976	Gollins Holdings Ltd	Reported *profit* statement of $835,192 was subsequently restated as a *loss* of $10,776,606. This was due to: (i) inadequate inventory valuation procedures; and (ii) failure to recognise losses in overseas affiliate.	Civil actions against auditors produced a $6 million out-of-court settlement. Criminal actions against directors saw two gaoled – Gale for 13 years and Glenister for 12 years.
February 1979	Associated Securities Ltd (ASL)	(i) Real estate property valuations; (ii) Capitalising interest costs; (iii) Recognition of income; (iv) Use of equity-accounted profits; and (v) Lack of assistance from controlling company when associate was in financial difficulty.	n.a.

Source: Expanded version of Table 7.1 of A.T. Craswell, *Auditing* (New York: Garland Publishing Inc, 1984).

by an official inspector resulted in it being adjusted to a *loss* of $10,776,606.[3] Construction heavyweight Mainline had also suddenly gone belly-up a year earlier. Apt examples – familiar scenarios which are further revealed in the telling analyses of collapses at Minsec, Cambridge Credit and ASL.

Setting up the Chambers Committee was a 'politically' shrewd response given the public outcry. Ignoring its recommendations was 'politically' correct given the profession's public opposition to the committee's recommendations. That nothing came of its report is indicative of the gap between public rhetoric and the private and professional intransigence. That intransigence is inexcusable against a background of the accounting disclosures examined in the following chapters.

EIGHT

Minsec:
Decline of a Share Trader*

'Mineral Securities Australia Ltd had started slowly enough
but once the accelerator went down there was no stopping
it.'

G. Souter (1971, p. 7)

That observation captured the flavour of Minsec's meteoric rise. 'Ken
[McMahon] and Tom [Nestel] . . . moved like the wind. They never
made a wrong move until the end.'[1] Minsec's lifetime operations
occupied just over five years – another 'still-born' failure, but one also
illustrative of how extreme success can presage failure.[2] As the Rae
Senate Select Committee on Securities and Exchange Report noted: 'No
company in Australia has had a more spectacular rise and fall than
Mineral Securities Australia Ltd'.[3] Subsequent collapses in the eighties
at Westmex and Compass Airlines would be worthy contenders for that
title.

Mineral Securities of Australia Ltd was incorporated as an unlisted
company in May 1965 with an authorised capital of $500,000. Its object
was to engage in share trading and investment activities as an offshoot of
mining consultants and advisers Kenneth McMahon and Partners.
McMahon and Tom Nestel dominated the affairs of the company as the
chairman and the managing director, respectively.[4] Minsec was listed in
1967 to take advantage of the share market boom of the late 1960s.

Minsec achieved rapid growth, using share trading profits to acquire
control of several companies. Minsec and Patrick Partners were reported
to be 'the two great success stories . . . [of Australia's] financial markets
. . . of the late 1960s'.[5] Quickly this adulation would fade.

By June 1970, capital of Minsec was reported to be $10.2 million and
the profit for the 1969/70 financial year was $12.7 million (Tables 8.1
and 8.2). Minsec had acquired a significant position in mineral
developments in tin, wolfram, rutile, uranium and iron ore. Its share
trading activities were of staggering proportions for the Australian
market. In 1970 Minsec had purchased $107 million and sold $47 million
worth of shares. The Rae Committee placed this in perspective by

91

Table 8.1   Mineral Securities Australia Ltd, Minsec Investments Pty Ltd and
Norausam Pty Ltd – balance sheet as at 30 June and 31 December 1970

30 June 1970		31 December 1970	
$m	Issued Capital	$m	$m
4.5	Ordinary	4.5	
5.7	Preference	5.7	10.2
	Capital Reserves		
13.4	Share Premium	13.4	
2.0	Capital Profits	2.0	15.4
	Revenue Reserves		
–	Tax Exempt		–
10.1	Unappropriated Profits		13.2*
35.7	Share Capital and Reserves		$38.8
	Represented by:–		
23.7	Current Liabilities – less than 12 months		86.4
	Less		
3.8	Current Assets		23.9
19.9	Net Short-term Indebtedness		62.5
–	Liabilities – after 12 months		–
19.9	TOTAL Net Indebtedness		62.5
52.2	Investments		97.7*
3.6	Convertible Loan to Robe River Limited		3.6
$35.7			$38.8

Note: *Subject to subsequent reduction of $6.8 million in 'Unappropriated
profits' and in 'Investments', upon correction of half-yearly profit statement.
Source: Rae Report (1974), Table 14–9, p. 14.87.

indicating that the trading volume that year of the AMP Society – by far
the largest life assurance company in Australia – involved purchases of
$40 million and sales of $8 million. Minsec's share trading activity certainly was on a grand scale. It was claimed to be 'the heaviest share trader
that Australia has known'.[6] But this also presented Minsec with a potential problem, as it ran the risk of being unable to liquidate a holding
without causing a run on the market in that stock.

Growing pains

Understandably, Minsec's growth plans required a continuation of
favourable annual net profit reports – $1.9 million in 1968; $1.4 million
in 1969 and $12.7 million in 1970. However, the share market boom had
begun to wane in late 1969 and into early 1970. Indeed, Minsec's
managers decided in February not to buy any further trading stock, new
issues, placements below market prices and shares involving rights issues.
By the end of May the trading portfolio was reduced to three stocks

Table 8.2 Mineral Securities Australia Ltd – summary of consolidated profit items and dividends, 1965/66 to 1969/70 (to nearest $000)

	1965/66	1966/67	1967/68	1968/69	1969/70
Share trading profits	21,000	161,000	1,887,000	1,946,000	12,418,000
Mining profits (*before* deducting outside interests)	–	–	–	–	7,659,000
Mining profits (*after* deducting outside interests, approximate)	–	–	–	–	2,400,000
Interest and dividends received	6,000	28,000	46,000	124,000	415,000
Outside minority interests in group profits	–	–	303,000	523,000	7,220,000
Taxation provision	7,000	–	–	–	61,000
Consolidated net profit	21,000	161,000	1,584,000	1,423,000	12,707,000
Dividends paid					
Preference	–	–	–	61,000	215,000
Ordinary	–	33,000	91,000	221,000	555,000

Source: Rae Report (1974), p. 14.20.

costing $101,000 and possessing a market value of $92,000. Although conditions did not warrant it, the decision was reversed and by 30 June the trading portfolio had increased to 132 stocks costing $13.1 million and possessing a market value of $12.3 million. One stock, Poseidon, cost approximately $4.5 million.

Poseidon was the most notorious of the speculative mining (nickel) stocks during the 1968–1972 mining boom. Its share price was on a roller-coaster ride in 1969, increasing from $0.80 on 31 July 1969 to $280 on 12 February 1970, falling back to $178 on 31 March, $73 on 30 April and $44 on 31 December 1970. Primarily these variations were driven by what turned out to be 'over-optimistic' reports of geological surveys of 'nickel reserves'.[7] The market had peaked in early 1970 and in the downturn Minsec and its wholly-owned subsidiaries sustained realised losses of $3.1 million and $1.6 million in July and August 1970, respectively.

In order to retrieve its position, Minsec initiated a number of policies having accounting consequences. Subsequent scrutiny by the Rae Committee and the inspectors appointed by the NSW government exposed three practices arguably contravening convention: (1) the back-dating of share trading losses – principally incurred on Poseidon shares; (2) group dealings in Robe River shares, including back-to-back loans; and (3) 'opportunistic' accounting treatment of its investments in Queensland Mines, Kathleen Investments and Thiess Holdings.

Australian accounting practice had never required securities to be marked-to-market in the primary accounts.[8] Accordingly, Minsec back-dated some of the losses on sales related to share trading after 30 June 1970 to the previous year. This was achieved by writing off an amount of $2.1 million from the trading portfolio as at 30 June 1970. Of that amount, $1.3 million was attributable to the mining investment darling of the period, Poseidon. This policy was disclosed (but without quan-tifying the effect) in Note 10 to the accounts, declaring: 'Market value of the investments of the group has been calculated on the basis of the last sale price of each stock on 30 June 1970, with the exception of one stock which has been further written down in the light of post-balance events to the realised value.' The stock was Poseidon. This adjustment was reflected in the internal accounts for Minsec and its wholly-owned subsidiaries for the month of September wherein the total losses of $4.1 million from share trading incurred up to 28 September were reduced by that $2.1 million figure.

Later, the Rae Committee was extremely critical of this approach, stating: 'If this statement [in Note 10] was referring to the Poseidon transactions it was uninformative or misleading in several ways. It gave no indication of the amount involved in the adjustment, nor any indication of the bearing, if any, that the adjustment had on the declared profits, and it would be taken by readers to apply to stocks actually held at 30 June, and not to any stocks that might have been bought after that date and subsequently sold at a loss.'[9] However, the inspectors stated that 'the action taken was adequately explained in a note to and forming part of the accounts for 1970'.[10] They might also have said that compulsorily done, on a continuous basis, it made more sense and better informed shareholders of the current position than the existing method did.

That general rubric remains. Moves in the 1990s by the Australian accounting profession to have securities accounted for on a marked-to-market basis by financial institutions (ED 59, 'Accounting for Financial Instruments', 1993) met vehement objection from those in the industry as being too costly, too subjective, too unreliable, too volatile, too prone to change, too different from the inclusion in 'Notes'. Similar objections greeted the requirements of AASB 1023, 'Financial Reporting of General

Figure 8.1 Mineral Securities Australia Ltd – major investments as at 30 June 1970

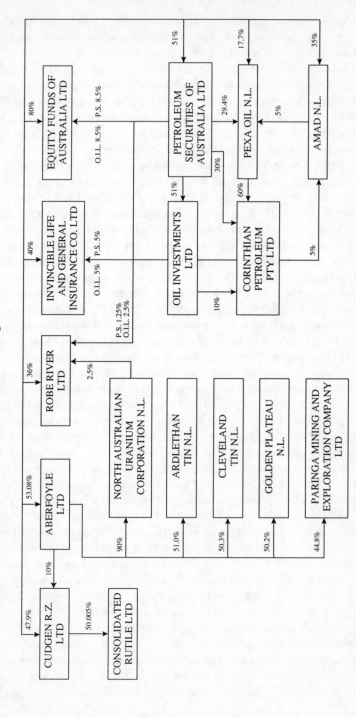

Source: Inspectors' Report, Vol. 1 (1977), p. 229.

Insurance Activities', that investments of insurance companies, akin to their inventory, be marked-to-market. Marking-to-market is for many a valuation method, it seems, too close to the truth.

In a one-step-forward, two-steps-back routine, Minsec turned to consolidation accounting to legitimise a shuffling of Robe River shares to side-step investment losses. Control of Robe was purchased, *on-sold* to a friendly intermediary, then *bought back* by Minsec entities to retrieve control. The fancy footwork with which the film *Strictly Ballroom* delighted is an apt metaphor for the tempo of 1960s Australian commerce.

The shuffle was a ploy to side-step losses on share trading. Minsec had subscribed to the issue of Robe River Ltd in early 1970, taking up 14.4 million shares at $1 par value. It also had contributed a $3.6 million interest-free convertible loan to Robe River. Effectively, as at 30 June 1970 Minsec had achieved control of Robe River, which meant it was a subsidiary of the Minsec group. The price of Robe's shares on the market was substantially above par – largely due to the buying by members of the group (Table 8.3). Minsec resolved to realise these paper profits. During October–December 400,000 shares were sold to external parties at a profit of nearly $250,000, reducing Minsec's equity in Robe River to around 40 per cent. During the following month Minsec then acquired another 10 per cent of Robe River – thereby giving it more than 50 per cent and hence, again, formal control. According to the *Companies Act* at the time, this made Robe River a subsidiary of Minsec for accounting purposes; and its profits, which were consolidated, helped to disguise Minsec's share trading losses for 1970. All this was within the law, though as we demonstrate in Chapter 16 it amounted to financial nonsense.

Perversely, superior financial disclosure being promoted as a virtue of consolidation accounting was having precisely the opposite effect. Again, this was an example of professionally and legislatively sanctioned creativity, at least in the accounts of the individual companies.

Minsec's dabbling in the mysteries of consolidation accounting involved it and Petroleum Securities of Australia Limited, one of Minsec's subsidiaries, in selling Robe River shares to the group's brokers, Hattersley & Maxwell. Hattersley & Maxwell then on-sold to wholly-owned subsidiaries of the Minsec group, Minsec Investments Pty Ltd and Petsec Investments Pty Ltd. Over the last three-month period of 1970 the Minsec group dealt with 6.175 million shares in this manner and 'realised' a profit of $6.6 million. The intention was to circumvent the conventional consolidation accounting rule that profits and losses on intra-group transactions are to be eliminated, deemed fictitious, in determining the *group's* income or loss. Hattersley & Maxwell were placed as intermediaries in the deal so that the transactions would not fall foul of the intra-group company elimination rule and the resulting profits thereby could be included in the

Table 8.3 Minsec intra-group dealings, October to December 1970

Month	Profit from share trading $	Robe River shares sold $	Profit from Robe River shares $	Profit (loss) excluding Robe River $
October	4,305,874	3,103,000	3,776,947	528,927
November	1,579,090	1,207,800	1,580,548	(1,458)
December	1,055,205	946,000	1,256,223	(201,018)

Source: Inspectors' Report, Vol. 1 (1977), p. 20.

published consolidated results. At best it is a clumsy rule, inviting smart tactics like the Robe River shuffle. It is to be noted that if assets were marked-to-market continuously, manipulations – under- or overstatements of the money's worth of assets – could not go undetected. There would be no need then to assume that all intra-group transactions entail manipulations and the Minsec–PSAL drama need not have arisen.

The figures in Table 8.3 disclose the impact of the policies of asset valuations and share trading. Ultimately the reported outcome of the deal was reversed, after considerable dispute – inexplicably not over what the shares were worth in the market, but whether the transaction was 'intra-group' and thus caught by the consolidation intra-group transaction elimination rule. It was almost as if the financial truth of the outcome was irrelevant – but, then, it was an accounting issue where financial reality so often, it seems, is given a back seat.

Minsec's shuffling of assets, profits and losses was, to a major extent, facilitated by the holding/subsidiary company organisational structure, the endorsed accounting practice of valuing physical assets at historical cost and consolidating the financial data of group companies. It entailed the compulsory elimination of the financial effect of intra-group transactions. That combination has been a recurrent feature of Australia's post-World War II failures – obscuring financial reality. Shuffling and relocating assets, injecting the aggregated data with fictional assets and equities, reversing the trends in the separate accounts of the constituent companies, and plugging the accounts on consolidation with artifacts of the consolidation process, have contributed significantly to the confusion and have cost some investors dearly.

Twenty-five years after the Robe River affair the position remains unaltered.[11] Neither the concept of a 'group' comprising a holding company and subsidiaries, nor the provision of consolidated financial statements have assisted the securities market to achieve greater confidence or orderliness. Retention of conventional consolidated financial statements in the accounting bag-of-tricks is as unjustified as it is avoidable.

Financial obfuscation was facilitated also by intra-group and back-to-back loans. Under its debenture trust deed, Robe River was forbidden to lend in excess of 5 per cent of its *total* tangible assets to related companies without the consent of the debenture trustee. Again, asset valuation looms as a major factor. Clearly, as we show here and in other cases, this is an unworkable covenant to monitor or to regulate unless the audited market selling prices of physical assets are disclosed continually. But accounting practice did not require assets to be reported at their market prices then, nor do the current set of Accounting Standards require it universally. If they did, all those *extraordinaries* and *abnormals* discussed in Chapter 2 would be less dramatic when they are reported.

Between 30 June 1970 and 31 December 1970 the borrowing limit of Robe River was approximately $1.5 million.[12] Robe was able to circumvent the limit by back-to-back loans.[13] It would lend funds to an intermediary (on occasions, reputable houses such as King & Yuill Investments or Ord-BT), which would then lend an identical amount to Minsec. The Rae Committee stated that at the end of January 1971 this form of indebtedness was $3 million; at November 1970 it was $4 million, a week earlier $3.5 million, a week later $5.8 million.[14] The committee also stated: 'A knowledge of the financial condition in which Minsec stood then leaves no room for doubt that the loans obtained surreptitiously from Robe helped materially to finance the process by which Robe became a subsidiary of Minsec, or that Robe River was being placed at risk in making such loans to Minsec at the time.'

Interestingly, those back-to-back financing practices were apparently occurring world-wide, if Charles Raw's account of the way the Vatican Bank and the Banco Ambrosiano defied monetary regulations in shuffling funds in and out of Italy is to be believed.[15] And the Bond Corporation manoeuvres described in Chapter 13 imply that they have contemporary currency.

During this crucial period Minsec embarked upon other investments. Between September and December 1970 significant stakes in Queensland Mines, Kathleen Investments and Thiess were purchased. In total these investments cost $30 million – $16.6 million in QM, $10.9 million in KI and $2.5 million in Thiess. These stocks were initially classified as trading stock in Minsec's internal activity reports. In the November 1970 internal activity report the market gain on all trading stocks was shown as $513,000, including a gain on QM and KI of approximately $1.5 million. At 31 December 1970 the internally recorded losses on QM, KI and Thiess were $3.15 million, $2.15 million and $205,000, respectively. At the end of December, fortuitously, the three stocks were 'reclassified' as long-term investments and therefore not required to be reported with other trading stocks, under the 'lower of cost or market rule'[16] – a variety of bases complying with accountants' conservatism doctrine (which implies it is more prudent to understate the current worth of an asset than overstate it). The inspectors thought the reclassification problematical. Without it Minsec would almost certainly have had to report a trading loss rather than a profit for the six-month period ending 31 December.

It should be noted that the variant valuation rules for trading stocks and investments existing then effectively remain today. So does the general thrust of the conservatism rule – though how one can continue to justify deliberate understatement any more than deliberate overstatement defies logic. Virtue would appear to lie only in 'telling it how it is'.

Note also the similarity between this impact of classification on the valuation basis to be applied to the asset and the earlier use of classification of property by Reid Murray as a current asset which facilitated not having to inject the profit and loss account with amortisation changes. Clearly it is nonsense to claim that assets are worth more or less, have greater or less value, according to how directors classify them.

Unfulfilled ambitions of a share trader

Despite the difficulties encountered from the falling share market, Minsec did not seek to retreat and strengthen its position. Thirty million dollars had been spent acquiring a position in QM, KI and Thiess. It also had spent a net $7 million expanding its Robe River holding. Minsec's financial positions at 30 June 1970 and 31 December 1970 reveal how these acquisitions were financed (Table 8.1). At 30 June, current liabilities stood at $23.9 million and current assets at $3.8 million. At 31 December, current liabilities had jumped to $86.4 million and current assets were only $23.9 million. Of the current liabilities, $20.9 million was at call, nearly all unsecured, whilst a further $31 million comprised short-term obligations – a familiar, precarious strategy of borrowing short and investing long.

In summary, many factors coalesced to threaten Minsec's future. First, the downturn in the prices of QM and KI was a result of suspicions that the Nabarlek ore bodies were not as rich as earlier geological announcements had indicated. Minsec's share price fell to $10 compared with its $23 peak during the previous six-month period. Second, Minsec had received a report from Hill Samuel, its merchant bankers, indicating that significant restructuring would be required if Minsec were to survive. The report continued: 'to form a syndicate to provide additional facilities for MSAL . . . would be a distinct danger, . . . it will be necessary to reveal full information regarding MSAL's current position and commitments, its very great temporary dependence on the market might become widely known and discussed, with the effect that its own operation in this

area could be prejudiced.'[17] Third, confidence was further damaged by
the disclosure in Minsec's takeover documents showing that the cost of
its share portfolio had increased by $34.6 million but was financed with
outside borrowings to the extent of $31.2 million. Further, Minsec's loans
secured by shares required additional collateral as the share prices fell,
which in turn limited Minsec's ability to raise fresh secured loans.

Minsec's main hope of overcoming its liquidity problems lay in
being able to report a favourable profit. On 25 January 1971, Minsec
announced:

> The consolidated net profit, subject to audit, from both mining operations
> and share trading of MSAL and its subsidiaries for the 6 months ended 31st
> December, 1970, was in excess of $3.5 million after deducting the minority
> shareholders' interests, provision for tax and writing down the share trading
> portfolio to the lower of cost or market value.[18]

Reporting a profit was dependent upon the three policies discussed
earlier – in particular, on the contribution from the dealings in Robe
River shares, without which the reported group profit of $3.5 million
would become a reported loss of over $3.2 million. In a nutshell, the
main issue for the accountants and regulators was not whether the
separate subsidiary companies involved had realised a profit on the back-
to-back share deals – the inspectors, the judge and common sense would
dictate that a profit existed on these transactions; the real issue was
whether under conventional consolidation accounting, a *consolidated
profit* could be reported. The conventional treatment of subsidiary profits
generated from group transactions would be to eliminate those profits.
Whilst not accepted in Mr Justice Taylor's initial 1976 judgment, this view
prevailed later on appeal – a most peculiar outcome.

As we noted earlier, the adjudication turned not on what the securities
were worth in the market, but upon whether the parties to the transactions were related. They were deemed on appeal to be related – so
what was profit when they were thought unrelated, turned into a loss
when they were deemed to be related, irrespective of what the market
disclosed.[19] It would appear that it was important not to let the actual and
observable financial outcomes of the deal get in the way of assessing the
accounting profit or loss. And that is an interesting outcome, bearing in
mind the obsession in the accountancy profession with advocating the
'substance' and not the 'form' of transactions in determining how to
account for them. Accounting convention in the 1990s would imply in
the Minsec case that no profit was earned, simply because the parties
were related. Unless, that is, the parties had been banks, in which case
the securities would be marked-to-market in accordance with ED 59 and
the actual financial outcomes would prevail.

So, it is likely that exactly the same result would emerge if facts similar to this case were to be heard today. Despite all the *substance over form* rhetoric, when it comes to unravelling the financial effects of transactions between related companies, the form often prevails no matter what the financial substance happens to be.

In addition to its other activities, Minsec established two mutual funds – the First Australian Growth and Income Fund and the Second Australian Growth and Income Fund – early in 1970. Minsec subscribed $1 million and $2.5 million to the FAGIF and the SAGIF respectively. The funds' prospectuses, as noted in the *Rae Report*, confirmed that each fund: 'will be of a "general" investment type. . . . MSAL has now substantially reduced its long-term investments in companies in which it does not have management control . . . it is intended that the Fund will direct its activities to long-term portfolio investment not associated with management control. . . .'[20] Despite those assurances, the *Rae Report* concluded that the funds concentrated the majority of their long-term investment funds in the Minsec group and associated companies.[21]

Minsec also utilised the funds as a source of short-term finance, for Minsec was not an approved money market borrower. Again adopting a 'group' perspective, this was not a problem – as at Stanhill, it was merely a hazard to be overcome. It was circumvented by the use of intermediaries, Minsec's brokers, principally King & Yuill Investments. The Rae Committee stated that 'the combined back-to-back loans from the two Funds passing through King & Yuill Investments to Minsec reached a peak of $7.8 million in mid-June 1970.'[22] Minsec's reported financial position had been obfuscated again by the use of related-party transactions through intermediaries within a group setting.

An unexpected collapse

On 2 February 1971 Minsec was advised by its legal counsel that the profit on the Robe River share transactions should be excluded from the calculation of income for the preceding six-month period ending 31 December 1970. On 3 February Minsec redeemed its shares in FAGIF and SAGIF, realising $2.87 million. Payment was based on valuations of the funds' assets as at that date. Allegedly, Minsec was aware by then of the difficulties it was in and of the probable impact on the Funds of the impending announcement of the profit reversal.[23] Clearly this would have had a significant effect on the value of the funds' investments in the group and the redemption value of its shares. Indeed, the collapse of Minsec brought an immediate suspension of redemptions for investors in the funds and losses in excess of $5.5 million on shares which the funds had bought. Redemptions did not recommence until 20 months later.

The next day, 4 February, directors of Minsec issued this statement:

> The directors wish to withdraw the statement made in the Company's circular of 25th January 1971 . . . directors were advised by senior counsel that 5,193,400 of the Robe River shares purchased by Minsec Investment P/L must be treated as having been purchased from the Company. Accepted account-ancy practice requires that profits derived from a sale by a parent company to its subsidiary should be eliminated from the consolidated profit and loss accounts . . . the profit of $6.63 million earned by the Company on the sale of these shares is to be eliminated from the consolidated profit and loss account, so that the results for the six months will appear as a loss of approximately $3.283 million.[24]

Events moved quickly. Minsec's demise matched its rise. Dealing in Minsec shares was suspended on all exchanges at the company's request. Creditors petitioned the NSW Supreme Court for the winding up of Minsec and Jim Jamison was appointed liquidator on 11 February 1971.

Aftermath – money market dominoes

Minsec's collapse illustrates the inevitable spread of trouble as the financial fallout from a large collapse settles. Minsec owed significant amounts in the official short-term money market and the intercompany market. In Minsec's fall there was the potential for severe economic repercussions. A company domino effect could have developed – companies with significant loans to Minsec failing and falling, with the impact spreading to other related companies. The likelihood of such a flow-on is evident in the reported reaction of businessmen and politicians who met to consider the possible repercussions for the Australian money market.[25] It might have been amusing to see those captains of finance wringing their hands in despair at Sydney's Kirribilli House. Again we might ponder their thoughts regarding the advice over the years from those in-the-know. There is no better place to plan damage control than Kirribilli's bush gardens and softening harbour views – Australia's political leaders have been doing it there for years.

Damage control no doubt was necessary. In the longer term it would have been more effective had there been a proposal to discuss how the accounting and other regulatory frameworks had meshed to veil Minsec's financial position so effectively.

Those events ring familiar. There were counterparts in late 1973 in the United Kingdom, with the Bank of England's 'lifeboat' rescue of Britain's secondary banks in the aftermath of their ill-fated exposures to property,[26] and in the United States in the 1980s with the salvage package by the US government for the Savings and Loans industry. Again in the UK, in 1991/92, the Bank of England secretly propped up the major banks in response to the potential crisis from their exposure to declining property values and poor performing loan portfolios. On each of these occasions a possible domino effect has been used to justify intervention by committed free-market governments. On each of these occasions, too, accounting data have been remiss in failing to warn insiders and outsiders of an impending crisis.

With Minsec the domino effect was avoided through a consortium of trading banks and other large Australian organisations. A line of credit of $35 million was offered to the liquidator of Minsec. Jamison did not accept it, but the fact that it was made restored confidence until other satisfactory arrangements were made.

Charges

Kenneth McMahon, Tom Nestel and other directors of Minsec were charged in relation to its collapse. The charges mainly related to the publication of the 25 January profit figure. They were prosecuted under section 176 of the *Crimes Act* which covers the publication of any written statement of account knowing it to be false in any material particular with intent to deceive any shareholders or attempting to induce any person to become a shareholder; under section 73 of the *Securities Industry Act* – which covers the dissemination of any information which at the time it is made or disseminated that person knows or has reasonable grounds for knowing is false or misleading in any material particular; and under section 47 of the *Companies Act* – which covers untrue statements or wilful non-disclosure in a prospectus. Similar legal issues were described in respect of the *H.G. Palmer* and *Royal Mail* cases.

On this occasion, however, all charges were subsequently dismissed. The trial judge, Mr Justice Taylor, stated, *inter alia*: '. . . if MSAL sold shares, for which it paid a dollar, to Hattersley & Maxwell at $2.50, then in fact and in law, in my opinion, it made a profit. . . . if the Crown wishes to establish that this profit statement is false, then it might be expected that they would have produced from an account what they say is *a* true statement. . . . there is no evidence fit to go to the jury to consider that this profit statement is false.'[27] A strong point. Indeed, if conventional practices were drawn upon it is unlikely that any such 'true statement' could have been prepared. In many respects the characteristics of conventional accounting facilitated the calculations of profit to which the charges referred. That position substantially prevails today. It would be very interesting to witness a case being made that compliance with the current batch of Accounting Standards could give *a* 'true statement' of a company's wealth and financial progress. Mr Justice Taylor's challenge for *a* 'true statement' would have exciting consequences today.

The Crown appealed the decision, not over the acquittals, but to clarify a number of points of law. The NSW Court of Appeal handed down its judgment in June 1979. It found that Mr Justice Taylor 'Fell in error in determining as a matter of fact that the dealings were not sham transactions instead of leaving that question to the jury'.[28] This issue would not have been in question had accounting practice been competent to deal with the situation. It was not. And remains so in the 1990s.

Minsec's rise and fall again highlights the difficulties of properly accounting for profits, losses and asset balances when group transactions are involved. Most of those would not exist if assets were marked-to-market periodically and verified. Minsec's financial problems also evidence the post-balance date dilemma facing accountants and auditors, exacerbated further by the realisation of profit issue. Much of the anguish is due to reliance on cost-based valuations and conventional consolidation procedures. Minsec's virtual control of share trading on the Australian share market created another hitch. Marking-to-market could thus encounter problems of obtaining the externally verifiable market prices of shares to which auditors could refer to corroborate the data presented by directors. Against that it could be argued that this is where the role of the professional would have been significant – the use of judgement based upon the accumulated professional judgement would have been an imperative.

Finally, Minsec provides another instance of a large, publicly-listed company disclosing a large reported profit figure, just weeks prior to being placed in the hands of a liquidator. The effectiveness of accounting and auditing, even though within the ambit of existing professional practices and the law, clearly was found wanting.

Four years later, events surrounding the collapse of the Cambridge Credit Corporation group were in many respects of the same genre, a familiar scenario. Plans there for building a financial empire relied primarily on property investment, without sound financial foundations.

NINE

Cambridge Credit:
Other People's Money*

Q. Inspector: 'Did you regard Cambridge as a one man
show?'
A. Hutcheson (Director): 'In my opinion most large
companies are dominated by one man, and if that's a
one-man show, well Cambridge is a one-man show.'
Inspectors' 1st Report (1977, p. 24)

Hutcheson's assessment raises difficulties in a public company context.
Clearly, Cambridge Credit Corporation Ltd was a 'one-man show', under
the direction of R.E.M. (Mort) Hutcheson. He had qualified as an
accountant in 1940, receiving his early training in a finance company,
and formed R.E.M. Hutcheson Pty Ltd, later renamed Unilateral
Services Pty Ltd, to set up and manage a number of small businesses for
individual investors. For these services a management fee and a share of
the profits were received.

Newcastle Acceptance Company Ltd was incorporated in 1950 with an
authorised capital of $200,000. Prior to commencing trading in November
1950 the company took over the Hutchesons' father and son partnership
as a going concern. Management was vested in the Hutcheson family
company, Unilateral Services Pty Ltd. This arrangement was formalised in
June 1957 by a 25-year service agreement, providing extensive management powers, including the right to hire and fire employees. The remuneration for the services consisted of reimbursement of all costs, a commission of 5 per cent of audited net profit before tax, and $3,000 per
annum (added later). Whilst this was not unusual it was fraught with
temptation. And it bore a similarity to the contingency basis which
determined Lord Kylsant's remuneration from his ill-fated Royal Mail
company in the 1920s.

Initially the main business involved hire purchase financing for all
types of durable goods and money-lending in Newcastle and surrounding districts and the large country cities of Tamworth and Wollongong.
A name change to Cambridge Credit Corporation Ltd was registered in
September 1955, by which time it was one of some 100 private and public
companies financing hire purchase agreements managed by the
Hutchesons.

Table 9.1   Cambridge Credit Corporation Ltd and subsidiaries –
paid-up capital, borrowings and reported total assets, selected years,
1957 to 1974

Year end 30 June	Paid-up capital $**	Borrowings* $**	Total assets $**	Gearing: borrowings/ total assets %
1957	320,000	387,210	961,444	40.3
1960	1,015,000	7,964,818	9,363,880	85.1
1962	2,362,678	21,558,124	25,429,322	84.8
1965	3,386,000	26,191,000	31,874,000	82.2
1967	3,778,000	30,073,000	36,215,000	83.4
1969	6,365,000	50,148,000	59,564,000	84.2
1970	8,865,000	76,027,000	89,215,000	85.2
1971	10,800,000	88,361,000	104,135,000	84.9
1972	11,800,000	103,288,000	120,934,000	85.4
1973	12,400,000	149,363,000	174,097,000	85.8
1974	12,400,000	188,004,975	215,007,835	87.4

Notes: * Excluding bank overdraft.
   ** Dollar figures in this table represent a 2:1 conversion of reported
   £ amounts prior to 1966 and the actual reported $ amounts thereafter.
Source: Sydney Stock Exchange Investment Service, C129 (1974).

After June 1956, several of these companies were acquired by Cambridge, consideration being shares and debenture stock. By June 1957, issued and paid-up capital was $320,000, first mortgage debenture stock totalled $150,000 and deposits with Cambridge amounted to $237,210. Around this time the business emphasis shifted to real estate, home financing, property investment and land development.

Official listing on the Sydney and Newcastle stock exchanges was effected in November 1957, with the first public issue of debenture stock in July 1958. Subsequent expansion was rapid, primarily as financier and principal engaged in property trading, land subdivision and lease rental. Despite an increase in debenture borrowings from $2,510,000 to $7,890,726, the group survived the November 1960 credit squeeze – it even achieved an increase in paid-up capital from $1,015,000 to $1,565,000 during the year ended 30 June 1961. Reported consolidated earnings for the financial years 1959/60 to 1961/62 represented 18.7, 18.1, and 19.42 per cent, respectively, on average ordinary capital employed.[1] Cambridge was an *apparent* success even through those difficult economic times.

Data in Table 9.1 illustrate the group's expansion. The nature of the business medium is revealing. Sometimes unsecured loans were granted to the acquired companies, which in turn built up a substantial equity in Cambridge. On other occasions, joint ventures were undertaken using finance and administrative services provided by Cambridge. Hutcheson's group entity perspective was clearly evident from the outset. Undoubtedly so, for it was an 'accounting way' of arranging business.

Byzantine family structures

From 1966 onwards Cambridge advanced substantial amounts to subsidiaries or joint venture companies for investment in large areas of undeveloped land with a view to long-term subdivision and sale, often in working-class outer suburbs of the eastern States' capital cities. Generation of sufficient cash flows to service the projects and the borrowings proved difficult, Cambridge having to rely increasingly on further borrowings. Undoubtedly the ability to borrow largely depended on reporting satisfactory trading profits, meeting interest, loan redemptions and other obligations, maintaining its share price and *reporting* that it was preserving a capital structure within the limits imposed by the various trust deeds – a tall order, typifying the normal accounting, finance and management bind perennially facing business. But Cambridge managed to sustain an illusion of prosperity for over a decade following its heady start.

By 1962 the company was increasingly enmeshed with private companies substantially owned or controlled by the Hutcheson family. Thus, at Cambridge, the prevailing network of subsidiary and associated companies and joint venture arrangements[2] was woven into the affairs of a complex group structure and accordingly complex financing arrangements (Figure 9.1) – a familiar refrain. Cambridge's complexity mirrors the conglomerate structure at Adsteam in the 1980s, and the complex structures in the 1920s at Insull Utilities in the United States and at the Royal Mail Steam Packet Company in the United Kingdom. Time changes little, it seems, in conducting big business, especially the inadequacy of accountability checks on large, complex organisations.

Apart from the Hutchesons and Davis-Raiss, none of the directors at Cambridge had formal training in accounting or business management. It is not surprising that, in keeping with conventional wisdom, the inspectors reported: 'Mr Hutcheson was the dominant personality in . . . the company and the way in which the Cambridge group evolved was the result of his personal ambition and initiative.'[3] Further, 'Mr Davis-Raiss was the only member of the Board apart from Mr Hutcheson who had any real ability but he, too, was dominated by Mr Hutcheson . . . had a loyalty to him which infringed upon any independence of approach . . . Accounting practices adopted by the group we believe to have been of his devising and initiative.'[4]

Figure 9.1 Hutcheson Conglomerate as at 30 June 1973

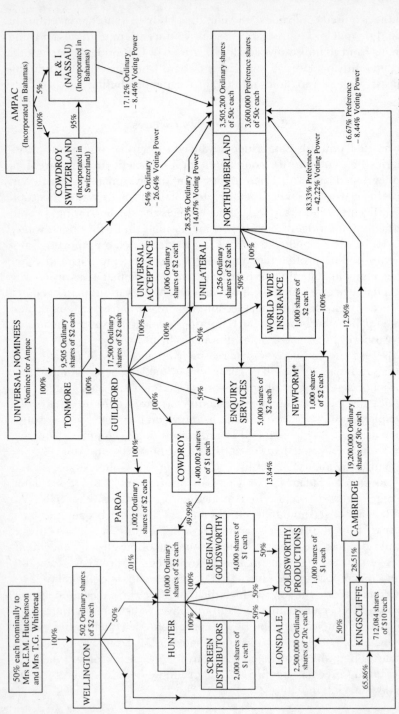

Note: * An additional 1,000 shares were recorded by Newform as allotted to Paroa Investments Pty Ltd on 29 June 1973. This allotment was never taken up, paid for or recognised as an investment by that company.

Hutcheson, in response to an inspector's question concerning the appointment of outside directors, replied: 'I had the ambition . . . to make my own name in the city and didn't want an outside director, whoever or however prestigious he may be, because it was my determination to build Cambridge up into a large successful company. . . . In my opinion most large companies are dominated by one man and if that's a one-man show, well Cambridge is a one-man show'.[5]

That was a fair enough comment and one which might have been made of most of the companies discussed here – certainly of Bond Corporation, Qintex, Hooker Corporation, Adsteam and Westmex – and of many successful ongoing companies. The difficulty for outsiders and insiders is differentiating the public from the private affairs.

Private and public operations

Throughout Cambridge's history there was a close relationship between the Cambridge group and an 'amorphous group of private companies' substantially owned or controlled by Hutcheson. The government-appointed inspectors formed the view that:

> The conglomerate comprised the two publicly recognised operating groups, Cambridge and Northumberland, each ostensibly independent . . . and the Hutcheson family companies. The latter companies were used to disguise the true nature and profitability of both . . . the extent to which public investment by way of debentures and unsecured notes (in the case of Cambridge) and insurance premiums (in the case of Northumberland) had been used to cover undisclosed losses, and to hold assets for the potential benefit of the Hutcheson family. The conglomerate members can be conveniently categorised as:
>
> (i)   Cambridge and its recognised subsidiaries.
>
> (ii) Companies associated with [and dependent on] . . . Cambridge, used by its management to carry on activities or hold assets on its behalf. . . . primarily comprised Hunter and Wellington . . . various joint venture companies where the original joint venture partner had ceased to be involved as a result of Cambridge's initiative, or because of insolvency or takeover. . . .
>
> (iii) Northumberland and its recognised subsidiaries.
>
> (iv) Companies associated with Northumberland . . . used by its management to carry on activities or hold assets on its behalf. . . .
>
> (v) Companies used for the personal benefit of the Hutcheson family to control –
>
>   (a) The relatively inconsiderable ($200,000 approximate total book value) private Hutcheson family assets which were in no way connected with the main operating groups. . . .
>
>   (b) The ownership of the equity in Cambridge and Northumberland to the extent it was not held by cross-investment between those groups or by the external shareholders of Cambridge. . . .
>
>   (c) The management of Cambridge [by] Unilateral Services Pty Limited (Unilateral).[6]

Northumberland and Hunter

Between October 1963 and October 1969 Hutcheson's direct and indirect ordinary shareholdings in Cambridge increased from 18.2 per cent to 60.25 per cent. Almost all the additional shares issued by Cambridge were purchased by Northumberland Insurance Co. Ltd and Cowdroy Investments Pty Ltd, the latter being used from June 1967 when Cambridge was in danger of becoming a subsidiary of Northumberland.[7]

Northumberland had been formed in 1955 to provide insurance services to Cambridge's hire purchase customers. Newcastle folklore has it that staff scoured the daily papers for details of accidents and the like in which Cambridge-financed and Northumberland-insured property – motor vehicles, in particular – might have been involved. A good-sized car pile-up might have proven disastrous for Northumberland, so shallow allegedly were its actual financial foundations. By 31 December 1969, 95.5 per cent of the 2,505,200 issued ordinary 50 cent shares in Northumberland were held effectively by the Hutcheson family interests. Cambridge held 3,600,000 10 per cent cumulative redeemable non-participating 50 cent preference shares, the contention being that such a financing arrangement avoided consolidation of Northumberland in Cambridge's accounts. Critically, Northumberland had operated at a loss for some time, financing its operations from funds originating with Cambridge and channelled through other companies of the group. Using non-disclosed transactions through related parties, from 1971 to 1974 Cambridge management channelled approximately $2.5 million of income to offset Northumberland's accumulated losses.[8] Fortuitously, Northumberland also picked up the insurance of the hire purchase goods Cambridge financed. It was a matter of business convenience and financial necessity.

Hunter, a private company within the Cambridge group, was critical to the saga. Incorporated on 19 December 1955, but inactive from 1961 to 1966, Hunter was 'revived to extricate Cambridge from an embarrassing situation which had developed in its Brisbane branch'.[9] The inspectors were concerned that Hunter was used to quarantine bad debts of Cambridge. The original $2 shareholders of Hunter were Cambridge and Mort Hutcheson. Such an arrangement should raise questions for accountants and auditors, both then and now; in particular, in Hunter's case was it a subsidiary of Cambridge? Although Hunter was passed off as an independent Hutcheson family company, the beneficial ownership of its shares during the relevant period is difficult to determine because of the use of nominees. Notwithstanding this difficulty, the inspectors concluded that 'Hunter was managed and wholly financed by Cambridge and was no more than a device for holding undisclosed Cambridge losses and conducting undisclosed Cambridge business. . . . if Hunter was not a subsidiary of Cambridge it was nothing more than an agent of Cambridge or a bare trustee for Cambridge.'[10] For all practical purposes it would have performed as effectively as a Cambridge branch.

That, even today, aptly describes the usual roles for many subsidiaries, especially those that are wholly owned: 'Such was Cambridge's involvement with Hunter that . . . , as in the case of Wellington [another family company], Cambridge's published accounts could not show a true and fair view of its affairs without incorporating the underlying assets and liabilities of Hunter on a line-by-line basis or consolidating Hunter's accounts as a subsidiary.'[11] The former might have added clarification, whilst the latter, contrary to the inspectors' beliefs, almost certainly would have provided further obfuscation.

Accounting practices

Inspectors alleged that the Hutcheson family companies were vehicles used to manipulate the profits of Cambridge so as to preserve borrowing rights. Capital structures were devised to avoid consolidation as Cambridge subsidiaries, yet they operated on funds originating in Cambridge.[12] Eventually group profits were achieved primarily from profits on 'front-end' sales and non-recognition by Cambridge of bad debts in loans to its subsidiaries.

'Front-end sales' – when is a sale really a sale?

One would think it reasonable to presume a sale when property in the goods passes (or the services have been received). A distinction has to be drawn between a gain or loss on the transfer of property and a gain or loss on extending credit to the purchaser. Cambridge made the former, but not the latter.

The generally incisive observations of the inspectors on the matter of 'front-end sales' appear, however, to miss the market price issues:

4.2 Real estate development projects . . . generally passed through three stages . . . As a project passed from one stage to the next, it would be 'on-sold' at a price which would show a front end profit to the vendor. A typical first stage joint venture situation was financed wholly by Cambridge and the only cash flow outwards was in respect of option fees or deposits paid in respect of conditional contracts to acquire the site in question, and agents' and consultants' fees and similar items.

4.3 [In] the second stage . . . Cambridge was able to negotiate a loan . . . in its own name on behalf of a new joint venture in which Cambridge and the original co-venturer either participated on different terms or into which a new co-venturer was introduced. . . . *In the second stage joint venture Cambridge normally remained the sole proprietor of the property with sole liability under the mortgage to the outside financier again on behalf of the joint venture. . . .*

4.4 [In] the third and final stage . . . *Cambridge and its original joint venture partners remained partners in the third stage joint venture and as such accepted liability to guarantee secured loans made to the purchaser by the outside financier as capital partner [taking over] the financing role [previously] performed by Cambridge in the first and second stage joint ventures.* Any front end profit on the sale between the two joint ventures was brought into account in the same way as in 4.3 above. [Effectively] . . . Cambridge received full repayment of its advances to the earlier stage joint ventures and depending on the terms . . . would receive all or part of its share of any front end profit in cash. . . .. in marked contrast to any profit taken at the stage of a sale by a first stage venture, which sale was entirely financed by Cambridge.[13]

Two features of the front-end sale mechanism are worth noting. Both have counterparts in contemporary commercial arrangements. First, the calculation of profit or loss rests there on the historical cost maxim that what is paid for an asset is what it is worth – *good* buys and *bad* buys are not differentiated, even though prevailing market prices might indicate that they should be. Second, Cambridge's joint ventures employed the 50-odd-year-old tactic of *asset pyramiding* – used by, among others, Samuel Insull to build his US utilities empire in the 1920s. Then, as now, consolidation accounting is intended to frustrate pyramiding – it does, but does nothing towards having the accounting figures for assets correspond to their market worths. So consolidation accounting can have exactly the opposite effect to what is intended in so far as it requires the elimination of data, even when they are moving the booked values for assets closer to their prevailing market prices.

From 1970, a significant proportion of the reported trading profits of the Cambridge group was derived from sales of undeveloped land (by companies in which Cambridge had an equity interest) to joint ventures (in which Cambridge also had an equity interest). It was the practice for Cambridge's published accounts to include its full share of the vendor's profits from front-end sales without allowances for, or disclosure of, the proportion attributable to Cambridge's interest in the purchaser.[14] Often, Cambridge had lent the purchaser the necessary finance for the transaction in the first place.

Considerable unease was reported to be occurring within the firm auditing Cambridge regarding inclusion of front-end profits. Specifically, 'it does not seem right for a profit to be "engineered" simply by moving a small percentage of a project ownership to another party so that it can be said that an actual cash profit has emerged which can be taken in as income in the accounts of one of the original parties to the full extent of the percentage ownership in the project when a major portion of the ownership is still actually retained'.[15] The practice was not limited to Australia.

In 1965 a similar concern had been expressed in the United States by the Securities and Exchange Commission, Accounting Series Release No. 95,[16] and was reiterated in 1975 in Accounting Series Release No. 173.[17] Specified criteria had to be met before the front-end sale could be booked.

Inspectors into Cambridge's operations reported that the national audit partner at Cambridge was particularly eager that the accounting treatment of such profits be disclosed by way of notes to the accounts.[18] Inclusion of approximately $8 million profit arising from front-end sales during the financial years 1973 and 1974 was challenged by the Cambridge inspectors largely on the basis that the actual transactions were a sham – they lacked substance.[19] Legitimately one might ask, when *is* a sale?

Profit recognition remains one of the many difficult issues related to accounting for real estate. External bodies, like the ASX's Statex service and private financial advisory services, attempt to restate (standardise) the raw accounting data of publicly-listed companies to facilitate comparability in financial analyses undertaken by investors or creditors. Transactions of the Cambridge variety, however, are likely to be privy only to the managers and auditors and therefore unlikely to be the subject of any public adjustments. It is an area which lends itself to increased scope for management manipulation and places auditors at risk. Not marking physical assets 'to market' facilitates misleading data at best and, at worst, outright deceit. Not surprisingly, anomalies in the methods of accounting for real estate are a recurrent theme in this book.

Non-recognition by CCC of bad debts in loans to subsidiaries

Around June 1961, Northumberland commenced to underwrite Cambridge's hire purchase debtors and losses on investments, whatever their variety. In this manner the Cambridge public group used a technique whereby a loss situation could be carried forward as a claim against an associated company whose results it was not required to bring to account. To 30 June 1966, according to the inspectors, $415,623 had been debited to Northumberland in this manner. Around 1963–1964, managerial concern was expressed about credit controls in the group's hire purchase businesses at Wagga and Brisbane. The Wagga office was closed and in May 1966 Hunter was used to take over several Brisbane electrical retail businesses. Their indebtedness to Cambridge amounted to almost $1 million. Its significance is clear. By June 1966, Cambridge's shareholders' funds amounted to $4,168,568 under conventional accounting, and group profits before tax were reported to be $650,778 for the year.

Another feature of the operations was the level of advances made to joint venture and associated companies within the conglomerate. By

1969 the auditors were uneasy regarding the recoverability of $7 million advanced to the family companies, Hunter, Austral and Carbir, in view of their accumulated losses totalling some $4 million. The problem was easily fixed – the debts were eliminated by the intra-group transfer of profits from Cambridge between 1971 and 1973.[20]

Collectability of a $9 million accumulated debt as at 30 June 1971 owing by Hunter to Cambridge eventually was the subject of protracted litigation. Mr Justice Rogers provided an interim ruling on an application by the plaintiffs (Cambridge) that had the auditors done their duty, shareholders' funds should have been written down or a large provision made for bad debts. The indebtedness of Hunter had increased from $5,129,000 in 1966 to $7,830,000 by June 1970 as a result of repeated trading losses. In an effort to recover some of these losses, Cambridge poured money into Hunter to support investments in production and share trading activities. Both ventures were financial disasters.[21] Rogers J. ruled on 27 June 1983, that 'an auditor acting reasonably should have been satisfied that the security and cover for the Hunter debt was doubtful at least in part. An auditor acting with reasonable prudence would have considered it necessary to call for provision against the Hunter debt to the extent of $4,600,000, that being the extent to which repayment was doubtful'.[22] The significance of the Hunter debt is clearly evident from an analysis of the reported undistributed profits and reserves of the Cambridge group for the relevant period: only $780,000 in 1966, $870,000 in 1967, $1,080,000 in 1968, $1,226,000 in 1969, $1,330,000 in 1970 and $1,470,000 in 1971.[23] Writing off the Hunter debt would have just about extinguished Cambridge's reported profits from 1967 onwards.

It was a similar scenario to H.G. Palmer. Had Cambridge ever made a profit since 1967? The inspectors concluded it had not. Although giving the above interim ruling, on 16 September 1983 Rogers J. ruled that the plaintiffs, the auditors of Cambridge, were not liable for damages.[24] In a later 1985 judgment the auditors were ruled liable and damages awarded at $145 million, resulting in an out-of-court settlement.

How accounting hinders

Financial consequences of those accounting practices were particularly disadvantageous for creditors and debenture holders. Especially notable was the regulatory ineffectiveness of the group accounting practices. Cambridge's dealings with Northumberland bear witness to that.

In 1971, Northumberland was in default over the payment of preference dividends to Cambridge. Consequently, these shares attracted voting rights, which it has been asserted meant that Northumberland

Table 9.2 Accumulated shareholders' funds, selected years, 1966 to 1973

Year ended 30 June	Reported $	Adjusted $
1966	4,168,658	1,649,846
1971	12,270,104	(2,209,680)
1973	15,672,055	127,623

Source: Inspectors' 2nd Report (1979), p. 278.

Table 9.3 Debenture profile, 1966 to 1973

Prospectus no. – date	Cambridge share/funds adjusted to exclude overstatement, etc. $	Five times Cambridge shareholders' funds as adjusted $	Debentures in issue $	Excess debentures in issue $
15 – 21/9/66	3,095,019	15,475,095	19,912,082	4,436,987
17 – 2/10/67	3,254,114	16,270,570	22,587,952	6,317,382
19 – 11/10/68	2,629,389	13,146,945	27,512,615	14,365,670
21 – 10/10/69	2,973,965	14,869,825	36,287,969	21,418,144
24 – 6/11/70	4,129,143	20,645,715	46,525,378	25,879,663
26 – 1/11/71	3,046,453	15,232,265	56,016,482	40,784,217
28 – 20/11/72	4,225,753	21,128,765	66,352,471	45,223,706
30 – 12/11/73	6,256,692	31,283,460	69,359,105	38,075,645

Source: Inspectors' 2nd Report (1979), p. 278.

had become a subsidiary of Cambridge. Share transfers to another family company avoided consolidation, though the total preference shareholding remained booked as a Cambridge investment asset.

Table 9.2 summarises the inspectors' calculation of the conventional accounting effect of Cambridge avoiding consolidation. The inspectors show that as a gross default on Cambridge's part. Whereas the inspectors' assessment of Cambridge's connivance to avoid consolidation may be correct, we would disagree with the implication that consolidated statements were a 'virtue avoided'. Cambridge's asset valuation and income measurement would most likely have been no more reliable and in accord with financial facts with consolidation than they were without it – though, indisputably, they would have been different!

The continuing survival of the group depended on Cambridge's ability to borrow from the public, which in turn depended on reporting

Table 9.4 Cambridge Credit Corporation Ltd – effect of overstatement of assets on various prospectus documents issued during the period 30 June 1966 to 30 September 1974

Prospectus number	15	17	19	21	24	26	28	30	31	Total
Prospectus date	21/9/66	2/10/67	11/10/68	10/10/69	6/11/70	1/11/71	20/11/72	12/11/73	6/5/74	
Details per auditors' report										
Last balance date	30/6/66	30/6/67	30/6/68	30/6/69	30/6/70	30/6/71	30/6/72	30/6/73	31/12/73	
Cambridge shareholders' funds	4,132,028	4,619,387	5,682,660	7,591,784	10,195,509	12,270,104	13,650,797	15,548,634	15,542,206	
Cambridge profits before tax for the										
full year	413,920	434,067	661,345	750,670	674,121	1,534,614	2,387,688	1,864,837	–	
half year									1,435,258	
Overstatement Cambridge profit and Cambridge shareholders' funds –										
Amount due from Hunter –										
Accumulated losses at 30 June 1966 and subsequent losses	1,037,013	326,764	1,291,936	810,467	(981,580)	48,499	(914,148)	(152,819)	–	1,466,132
Issued capital at 30 June 1966 and subsequent increases	(4)	–	(19,996)	–	–	–	–	–	–	(20,000)
Overstatement of investment in listed shares	–	–	–	–	1,367,584	1,939,415	(1,180,141)	(2,126,858)	–	–
Overstatement of investment in film companies	–	1,500	226,689	506,515	587,649	154,511	(3,629)	(1,196,835)	(276,400)	–
Assets not taken up by Cambridge	–	–	–	–	–	–	–	–	171,096	171,096
Amounts written off by Cambridge	–	–	–	–	–	–	–	(1,342,228)	(275,000)	(1,617,228)
	1,037,009	328,264	1,498,629	1,316,982	973,653	2,142,425	(2,097,918)	(4,818,740)	(380,304)	–
Amounts due from Garbir and Town and Country	–	–	189,369	247,566	199,894	(85,140)	(551,689)	–	–	–
Mark-up over cost of Kingscliffe and Surfers shares and Burleigh Garden Heights land	–	–	–	–	275,000	1,100,000	2,251,000	482,400	–	4,108,400

Bad debts capitalised as interest-free loan	–	–	–	–	–	–	–	600,000	–	600,000
Front-end profits –										
IRPD	–	–	–	–	–	–	–	640,255	–	640,255
Others	–	–	–	–	–	–	–	2,684,185	3,627,718	6,311,903
Subsidiary company cost of shares reduced by amount finally recognised in the 1973–1974 Cambridge draft accounts	–	–	–	–	–	–	–	878,798	–	878,798
Profit on sale of land to Loftus	–	–	–	–	–	–	–	–	284,973	284,973
Interest income on advance to Elbrook	–	–	–	–	–	–	–	–	40,000	40,000
Overstatement of Cambridge profit	1,037,009	328,264	1,687,998	1,564,548	1,448,547	3,157,285	201,393	(133,102)	3,627,387	12,864,329
Cumulative balance carried forward	–	1,037,009	1,365,273	3,053,271	4,617,819	6,066,366	9,223,651	9,425,044	9,291,942	–
Overstatement of Cambridge shareholders' funds	1,037,009	1,365,273	3,053,271	4,617,819	6,066,366	9,223,651	9,425,044	9,291,942	12,864,329	12,864,329
Adjusted Cambridge shareholders' funds	3,095,019	3,254,114	2,629,389	2,973,965	4,129,143	3,046,453	4,225,753	6,256,692	2,677,877	
Five times adjusted Cambridge shareholders' funds	15,475,095	16,270,570	13,146,945	14,869,825	20,645,715	15,232,265	21,128,765	31,283,460	13,389,385	
Cambridge debentures in issue	19,912,082	22,587,952	27,512,615	36,287,969	46,525,378	56,016,482	66,352,471	69,359,105	77,247,060	
Debentures not capable of issue	4,436,987	6,317,382	14,365,670	21,418,144	25,879,663	40,784,217	45,223,706	38,075,645	63,857,675	

Source: Inspectors' 2nd Report (1979), pp. 330–331.

satisfactory group profits and maintaining the capital structure pre-scribed in the trust deeds. Both the debenture stock trust deed and the unsecured notes trust deed (as amended) limited borrowings to the lesser amount of five times the value of shareholders' funds or three-quarters of liquid assets. A similar constraint had been faced by H.G. Palmer. Precise terminology and relevant accounting data are imperatives in ensuring that those financial constraints are workable. The point was not lost on the inspectors of Cambridge: '[B]ecause of faulty practices and principles . . . , coupled with the failure of the Board and the auditors to perform adequately their respective duties, [a mis-leading] *outward appearance of viability and growth of assets and profits was presented to the investing public generally.*'[25]

By reason of the alleged overstatement of profits and shareholders' funds after 30 June 1966, the inspectors concluded that Cambridge thereafter had exceeded its borrowing powers. It is to be remembered, too, that the inspectors were still travelling the conventional accountant's route. Had the true market worths of the physical assets been injected, the calculation might have produced an outcome considerably worse than the inspectors claimed – and predictably closer to what the liquid-ators discovered – as summarised in Table 9.3 and detailed in Table 9.4.

That analysis indicates Cambridge's high-risk heavy reliance on debt capital to finance long-term investment projects and its need to realise adequate returns to fund the cost of debt and report acceptable profits. Dividends and company taxation paid on dubious profits further de-pleted the cash resources of the group; these two outflows perhaps were being financed from capital. It was a complex situation requiring tight regulatory mechanisms to ensure investor protection, which neither the holding company/subsidiary structure nor the consolidation accounting for it could have delivered. That regulatory ineffectiveness remains.

In the opinion of the inspectors, five companies, viz. Bremer, Burhead, Dunnoch, Mount Warren and Southern Pacific, were incorrectly treated as guarantor subsidiaries for the purposes of the last two prospectuses. Cam-bridge's reported profit of $1,970,697 after tax for the six months ended 31 December 1973 was deemed to have been overstated by $3,952,691.[26]

Cambridge's advances to its joint ventures, $88 million as at 31 December 1973 and $102 million as at 30 June 1974, were described in its accounts as 'mortgages and other receivables' and counted as 'liquid assets' in determining borrowing limitations under Cambridge's trust deeds. That was contested – though more in respect to the labels attached to assets than to their financial substance.

From 1969, explanatory notes were included in the accounts, viz. 'Included in "mortgages and other receivables when charges not written in" are secured loans to joint ventures.' At issue was the legal interpreta-

Table 9.5   Cash flow and debt analysis, 1964 to 1973

Year ended 30 June	Gross retained cash inflows $000	Total asset expenditure $000	Deficiency (cols 2–3) $000	Borrowings at 30 June $000	Capital at 30 June $000
1964	201	2,281	2,080	26,200	3,386
1965	212	1,056	844	27,800	3,386
1966	176	1,103	927	27,200	3,386
1967	172	3,537	3,365	31,500	3,778
1968	217	6,206	5,989	37,300	4,700
1969	237	9,924	9,687	52,000	6,365
1970	342	18,970	18,628	79,000	8,865
1971	481	11,573	11,092	91,000	10,800
1972	636	10,798	10,162	107,000	11,800
1973	1,344	47,227	45,883	158,400	12,400

Sources: Sydney Stock Exchange Statex Service and *Sydney Stock Exchange Investment Service*, C129 (1973).

tion of definitions contained in the trust deeds. The inspectors observed that, if judgment did not uphold the inclusion of all such advances as 'liquid assets', the company was without borrowing power from around 1969 when the joint ventures commenced.[27]

The Cambridge group's dependency on borrowings to finance expanding investments in projects is apparent from the large and (mostly) increasing deficiency between gross retained cash inflows from trading and increases in total asset expenditure. This short-fall, together with borrowing repayments, was financed from increased debt and/or equity capital. The maturity schedule of 'receivables and borrowings due' confirms the parlous cash position of the group.[28] Basic financial prudence was absent – irrespective of how the assets and liabilities were labelled.

If the receivables analysis undertaken by Statex had not recognised 'amounts due from joint ventures' to be receivables possibly due within two or five years or some time later, rather than as 'liquid assets', then the actual situation as disclosed in that table would deteriorate markedly.

Incorrect profit figures, bad debts and diversion of irrecoverable funds to associated companies compound the resulting error.

Default – beginning of the end

Similar to the events immediately preceding the Minsec and Gollins collapses, around 12 March 1974 Cambridge issued a press release reporting a 99.9 per cent increase in 'net audited profit' for the six months ended 31 December 1973 ($986,547 to $1,970,697), a high renewal of maturing borrowings and a 'high degree of liquidity'.[29]

Within a few months the group was admitting to serious liquidity problems, intensifying to a crisis by August 1974. Existing financial supporters were unwilling, or unable, to renew loans. Internal evaluation of the liquidity position in October that year indicated an estimated deficiency amounting to $3.5 million if interest and proposed dividends were to be paid. Contracted development costs threatened an accumulated $10.8 million cash deficiency to July 1975.[30]

Incongruously, despite the obvious cash crisis, on 16 September 1974 an unqualified audited statement implied a healthy picture by announcing a profit increase of 33.2 per cent for the year ended 30 June 1974. Strapped for cash, directors of Cambridge held meetings on 25 and 26 September with the Sydney Committee of the Australian Finance Conference (of which Cambridge was not a member) seeking support. It was refused. Not to be denied, the Reserve Bank was notified and Cambridge directors commenced negotiations for overseas borrowings. Borrowings had always done the trick in the past! On this occasion the required lifeline, from either private institutions or public authorities, did not eventuate. On 27 September the shares dropped from 48 cents to 10 cents on the Sydney Stock Exchange, prompting a request from the Exchange 'for information'. Cambridge failed to reply and immediately its shares were suspended. Within minutes the trustee delivered a letter to the company requesting evidence of ability to meet interest commitments due on 30 September. Receipt of a reply on 30 September, indicating the company's inability to meet the payments, necessitated the trustee to appoint a receiver, C.H.R. Jackson of Hungerford, Spooner and Kirkhope.

Receivership and litigation

Cambridge's annual report for the year ended 30 June 1975 was eventually completed on 10 April 1979. Therein directors referred to the extraordinary losses incurred under receivership as due to mortgages and other secured liabilities which became immediately due and payable, and from a need for the receiver, 'in the course of their duties, having to dispose of assets of the group at a time when, by virtue of the prevailing economic conditions, the market was in a state of deep depression'. By 1982 accumulated losses exceeded $212 million, leaving a deficiency of nearly $199 million. The receivership continues into the mid-1990s, losses accumulating. Interestingly, for the financial years 1967 to 1973, approximately $4,618,000 was paid in company tax and $5,184,000 distributed as dividends from *reported* 'profits before tax' totalling some $11,517,000. Inspectors claimed that overstatement of profits for 1966–1973 was approximately $9.3 million.[31]

The Cambridge affair proved to be a breakthrough for aggrieved investors, perversely for directors and auditors, too. It spawned a new approach to corporate litigation in Australia – the class action. In a letter to debenture holders, receivers advised of a statement of claim issued by the company (through the Receivers and the trustee for debenture holders), seeking damages against the directors who held office between April 1971 and September 1974 and the auditors. Also forwarded was a notice from the Corporate Affairs Commission containing details of advice given in a judgment regarding individual stockholder's rights to take action as a class against the company and its former directors and auditors.

This was to be the first of several similar class actions taken by regulatory authorities on behalf of many debenture holders in the following two decades, including in 1994 the ASC's $340 million claim against the auditor and some of the directors of Adsteam. A decade after Cambridge collapsed, Rogers J. awarded the receivers $145 million in special damages against the auditors Fell & Starkey – holding that breaches of their duty were a substantial cause of the collapse at Cambridge. Whilst this judgment was overturned by the Court of Appeal (2–1) in July 1987, the High Court subsequently followed the judgment of Rogers J. Eventually an out-of-court settlement (believed to be approximately $20 million) was paid to the receivers by the insurers of Cambridge.

Action initiated by the regulatory authorities in the case was the start of a new ball-game between officers of failed companies, investors and regulators. But regulatory action had been protracted – a point not lost on subsequent regulators such as Henry Bosch, who complained bitterly of his difficulty (as NCSC chief) in getting directors into court in the 1980s.[32] By the mid-1990s several 1980s entrepreneurs had been put on trial and some convicted.[33] For others, the inordinate prosecution delays continued.

Cambridge's failure conforms in many respects to a familiar pattern – dominant personality (Hutcheson) in the management of the company seeking to build an empire to satisfy personal ambitions, the company expanding rapidly with substantial short-term borrowings to finance long-term high-risk investments, compounding cash problems by reliance on rolling over its borrowings when due by reporting satisfactory short-term profits and paying tax and dividends thereon, and maintaining the price of the shares on the stock market. That is, keeping the outward (public) signs looking relatively good (certainly not a loss!) for as long as possible. The interaction of an economic downturn precipitated what was to many (though mainly with hindsight) an inevitable failure. Mr Justice Rogers aptly captured the interacting factors: 'Cambridge was *destined* to collapse because financial gearing . . . was unable to sustain the aggregate demands . . . once the abnormal boom conditions abated. . . . *low equity*, . . . *servicing large borrowings and . . . maintaining the myriad of money losing satellites imposed a strain which . . .* made Cambridge's financial position insupportable.'[34] Arguably Rogers J. misses a critical point – everybody is entitled to make errors of judgement, including errors of financial prudence. There can be no doubt that Hutcheson and his fellow directors wanted the group to be a financial success. They had everything to gain by it. More to the point, along with the privilege to make bad decisions, it is everybody's right to expect accounting to 'tell it how it is', rather than mask the financial facts with the 'jiggery-pokery' of the kind which conventional accounting passes off as sophisticated (though mysterious) financial representation. Cambridge's financial position was, in hindsight, 'insupportable', but no more so than the accounting practices used to account for it.

Conflicts between personal and company interests are inevitable in operations using pooled group finance to facilitate related-party trans- actions between private and public companies. This was clearly the case in the *Reid Murray, Stanhill* and other cases. Rules imposed to regulate such conduct are invariably broken or bent. Conventional accounting and auditing practices, by their very nature, provided a vehicle for public deception. Consolidation practices, asset valuation, income realisation and periodic determination, asset and transaction classification, accoun- ting for (and disclosure of) associated interests and relationships and audit practices are some of the accounting and auditing matters indi- cated in the Cambridge failure to warrant reform. The frequency with which these matters continue to arise in episodes of corporate collapse since Cambridge is explicable, but unacceptable. 'Explicable', by virtue of the prevailing regulatory and accounting orthodoxy and inertia; regulatory mechanisms in vogue, accounting practices in particular, do not ensure a continuous flow of contemporary information on com- panies' financial affairs. Consumers of published financial information which conforms to the conventional and compulsory pattern put them- selves at grave financial risk, a result that is unacceptable, given the frequency of the message.

TEN

*Uncoordinated Financial Strategies at Associated Securities Ltd**

A lethal mix – the lack of lender-of-last-resort finance,
unplanned hedging, mismatched maturities on receivables
and borrowings, and an inability of accounting data to
inform in a timely manner.

'What in hell's name happened?'[1] This lament appeared as a caption on a letter to the editor of the *Australian Financial Review* in the wake of the Associated Securities collapse. Such expressions of disbelief by investors are par for the course upon the sudden, unexpected collapse of a large financial institution.[2] With ASL such despair was more than justified. Its financial reports had not clearly and unambiguously warned investors of imminent financial disaster.

One account of ASL's problems, published immediately after its collapse, claimed the crash arose because of 'bad property investments . . . , exchange losses on Swiss borrowings, and the high interest rate structure, far higher than its competitors'.[3] Undeniably these were major factors, but there are other facets of ASL's property incursions which warrant close attention. Five factors are critical:

- The shortening of the maturities structure of ASL's borrowings.
- ASL's failure to match borrowings and receivables.
- The inability of ASL's board, from the late 1950s until the mid-1970s, to obtain lender-of-last-resort facility from a local bank.
- The exacerbation of the financial consequences of those three factors by the unplanned hedging operations in real property.
- And, perhaps the strongest factor of all – the failure of conventional accounting to produce *public* data indicative of ASL's declining wealth, deleterious drifts in its financial position, declining capacity to service and meet its debts, and the paradoxical capacity of conventional accounting to portray precisely the opposite.

At the time the receivers were appointed (8 February 1979), ASL was a mixed bag – a financier, realtor and underwriter of property development. It was the largest non bank-affiliated finance company in Australia. Assets (at cost or some other variety of book value) totalled $292.5 million. The Statement of Affairs (March 1979) revealed a deficiency of approximately $12 million in the cover for unsecured ASL creditors. Consequently, there was little likelihood of any return to the shareholders.

The story begins some 50-odd years earlier.

Australian Securities Ltd (the name of ASL was adopted in 1946) had been incorporated in Sydney in 1926 with an issued capital of £158,498 (396,245 8s. shares). Prior to 1956, its major activity, consumer finance, was conducted almost exclusively in the Sydney metropolitan area. In November 1956 the directors authorised ASL's first public debenture issue of £500,000. Including oversubscriptions, it raised £726,008. The 1960s cases revealed that this form of corporate capital raising was novel in Australia but that it soon gained avant-garde status and was to be the main source of ASL's finance.[4]

By 1960 ASL had begun to diversify and expand its operations across Australia. It was providing consumer finance, finance for transport, mortgage finance, operating finance for sections of industry and finance for capital expenditure, and also debt factoring. At year-end the directors announced the diversification into the financing of real estate.

Those diversifications involved three subsidiaries and nine branches across Australia. ASL appeared resilient, as Table 10.1 shows that the major economic event of the early 1960s, the November 1960 credit squeeze, failed to slow down ASL's reported improved performance, asset and debt financing growth.

Exceptional growth was claimed between 1966 and 1974. ASL's assets (at book value) increased by over $300 million and were financed almost entirely from external borrowing. Outstanding liabilities at the end of June 1974 were $347 million. Through a now familiar policy of acquisition and incorporation, ASL had become a diversified company having 22 wholly-owned, and one 95 per cent-owned, subsidiaries. Activities now included finance (general, leasing and real estate advances), real estate development, real estate investment, investments in securities, trading in securities and general insurances. The apogee occurred in 1974.

But the salient features of ASL's management and financial structures had potentially put it on a path to failure that would be replicated at Bond Corporation a decade on. Relieved of the accounting subtleties, ASL was in financial difficulties for several years before it finally collapsed.

Dominant management and finance

ASL's management performance is best examined over three distinct periods: 1946–1963, 1964–1974 and 1975–1979. From the late 1940s to 1963, D.H. Currie (chairman) and C.J. Perry (managing director)

Table 10.1 Associated Securities Ltd – details of performance, growth and financing, 30 June 1956 to 30 June 1978

Year ended 30 June	Net profit[1] $000	Dividend percentage %	Total assets[2] $000	Share capital[3] $000	Borrowed funds[4] $000
1956	210	15	4,123	1,030	2,057
1957	243	15	5,336	1,030	3,176
1958	291	15	9,419	1,030	6,805
1959	362	15	16,155	1,233	12,787
1960	468	16	29,824	2,686	21,646
1961	861	16	40,250	2,636	28,524
1962	947	16	47,567	3,358	36,700
1963	1,003	16	59,962	3,358	47,436
1964	1,161	16	67,494	4,314	52,309
1965	1,411	16	74,138	4,814	59,196
1966	1,534	16	78,215	4,814	62,641
1967	1,765	16	95,861	6,017	76,384
1968	2,236	16	123,649	7,025	96,443
1969	2,705	16	149,774	9,025	119,078
1970	3,306	16	173,475	12,073	133,706
1971	4,027	16	203,785	13,983	158,699
1972	5,239	16	255,503	18,999	195,013
1973	6,365	16	328,106	21,410	256,812
1974	7,378	10	369,549	25,026	290,667
1975	2,507	8	317,504	25,026	241,728
1976	(5,415)	–	279,253	25,026	214,350
1977	(16,630)	–	235,933	25,026	189,718
1978	178	–	283,942	32,026	226,915

Notes: (1) Net profit after tax, abnormal and extraordinary items; (2) Total assets, excluding unearned income; (3) Share capital – subscribed ordinary capital plus, in 1978, $7 million in preference capital; (4) Borrowed funds consist of first charge debenture stock, second charge debenture stock, term deposits, commercial bills of exchange and bank facilities.
Source: Annual Reports, 1956–1978, on a consolidated basis.

dominated the operations. They 'guided the company's fortunes with a simple but effective philosophy. Remarkably they believed in profits first and foremost, profits before size and growth (although they were not averse to these).'[5] This is supported by data in Table 10.1. Currie and Perry confined ASL's activities almost entirely to motor vehicle finance. From 1946 to 1963 they steered annual reported net profits from approximately $10,000 to $500,000, and total assets increased from $410,000 to $33 million. During this period the traditional form of finance, hire purchase, was encouraged. By 1963, it accounted for $48 million, or 76 per cent, of ASL's gross receivables.

With a change in management in 1964 came a change in the direction of ASL's investments, especially into real estate. Moreover, patterns of real estate investment vacillated between home units and land subdivision, often with 'little hope of being rezoned for residential purposes this century, if ever'.[6] Daly recounts the diversity and extent of these real estate incursions, as ASL 'followed the home unit craze' in Sydney, and 'was planning an entire new suburb on 2,308 hectares (in Melbourne). . . . even though it was zoned non-urban' and notwithstanding that some of the land 'was resaleable only in 12-hectare lots'.[7]

Perry disapproved of the diversification of the company's resources into real estate financing and ultimately into real estate development. Such a move, however, had the support of Reginald Shanahan (who became managing director of ASL after the death of Currie) as well as the members of the board – in particular, John Darling: '[He] and Reg Shanahan were not the only financiers who believed that property values could not go down.'[8] And, of course, property financiers' accounts generally reflected that view.

In March 1974, Shanahan retired as managing director and was replaced by Eric Upton. His arrival coincided with an emerging liquidity crisis arising from ASL's increasing involvement in real estate investment. In 1976 this was exacerbated when the Royal Bank of Scotland severed a 16-year association with ASL by selling its ASL shares to Ansett. This action, however, heralded the entry of the 'white knights'[9] of Australia's corporate finance to the board of ASL. At the time they all held directorships with Ansett.

The financial consequences of the change in management personnel and their policies post-1963 were immediate and startling.

The book value of ASL's assets base and its borrowings both grew by 500 per cent in the period from 1964 to 1974. Analysis of the individual components of the assets and the maturity schedules of ASL's assets and borrowings provides valuable insights into the implications of that growth – increased financial instability and increased risk of failure.

Considerable variability in the composition of ASL's gross receivables prevailed. Prior to 1967, hire purchase agreements and personal loans represented over half of the total (gross) receivables. Increased investment in real estate in each subsequent year until 1975 reduced hire purchase and personal loans to only 26 per cent. Then a management rationalisation policy resurrected consumer finance, and by 1978 the proportion was 46 per cent. On the other hand, real estate mortgage finance[10] fell in relative terms from 34 per cent in 1960 to approximately 20 per cent in the mid-1960s, hovered around 25 per cent during the period 1969–1971, and then sharply declined to 14 per cent just prior to the receivership.

Table 10.2 Percentage of leasing/
gross receivables, selected financial years,
1957/58 to 1977/78[11]

Financial year	ASL	AFC
1957/58	–	0.1
1969/70	14.4	11.6
1974/75	9.4	15.6
1977/78	5.0	25.1

Sources: ASL and AFC *Annual Reports.*

Variability of the components of ASL's receivables is evident in the pattern of the leasing and development projects. Although only introduced in 1964, by 1969 lease finance had grown to 15 per cent of ASL's gross receivables, peaking at 15.2 per cent in 1971 (Table 10.2). Out of favour in the 1970s, it constituted less than 5 per cent by 1978. This trend in the latter years differed from that of other large finance companies operating in Australia.

Diversification peaked in 1974. ASL had attempted to offset its declining leasing activity with investment in real estate 'development projects' as *principal* (rather than financier). Included under the label 'development projects' were lands for subdivision, domestic and commercial construction, and undeveloped lands held for sale. This form of investment began in 1966 (as part of ASL's diversification policy) and was undertaken by a wholly-owned subsidiary, ASL Finance Pty Ltd. In a decade, development project finance had grown to nearly 20 per cent of ASL's gross receivables.

The first public signs of ASL's overextension and imminent liquidity problems surfaced in 1973. It is obvious from the share market's response that year that ASL was perceived as not performing well, but that was ten years since it had started its diversification strategy.[12] To forestall ASL's immediate collapse, the directors publicly advocated rationalising its assets – in particular, selling its real estate development projects. But the real estate market had bottomed out, and even by 1978 this rationalisation policy had been only partially completed.

Capital structure and borrowings pressure

Finance companies rely on equity capital and retained profits to a greater extent than other financial intermediaries. Over the ten years to 1973, the average of shareholders' funds to total capital of Australian Finance Conference member companies was 14 per cent – a figure which ASL

Table 10.3   Percentage of borrowed funds/
total capital, selected years, 1965 to 1978

Year	ASL	AFC
1965	78.0	–
1970	77.0	82.6
1974	76.0	84.6
1978	79.5	76.2

Sources: Derived from ASL and AFC *Annual Reports.*

consistently matched. Notwithstanding this shareholder finance base, the majority of finance companies' operations are financed by public borrowing (varying classes of debentures, notes and deposits). To this extent they have to be more careful in their investment strategies than perhaps when capital gearing is lower. While ASL's proportion of public issues to total capital relative to AFC member companies had been lower for a considerable period, by 1978 it marginally exceeded the average of AFC member companies (Table 10.3).

Of course, the validity of those data is contestable. Indeed the prevailing focus in this book is just that. Gearing ratios of this type depend upon the 'valuation' of the assets taken into account to calculate the denominator. Without injecting current market prices through an audited mark-to-market rule, the serviceability of the data is anybody's guess. It is doubtful whether the financial significance of data such as those in Table 10.3 is capable of being unravelled properly. Nonetheless, they were the only available data for making comparisons between the ASL and AFC averages.

One consequence of ASL's adoption of a gearing policy commensurate with other AFC members (albeit slightly lower) during the latter part of the 1970s was the need, between 1974 and 1978, to recover over $20 million annually through its operations (or through successive debenture issues) to meet interest payments.

From 1964, overdraft finance represented between 0.5 and 1 per cent of ASL's total capital requirements, while for the AFC it was between 0.3 and 1 per cent. During the troublesome period of 1973/74, ASL increased its overdraft from $1 million to $10 million – 3 per cent of total capital (AFC: 2 per cent), its highest level since 1964. To overcome the liquidity crisis in July 1974, ASL raised $20 million in the Eurodollar markets with the aid of the Royal Bank of Scotland's guarantee. Bank standby facilities of $50 million were also arranged.[13] That *facility* and the booked values of the assets, no doubt made ASL look financially sound. With hindsight it appears not to have been.

And therein lies another peculiarity of conventional accounting. In hindsight the data provide insight into what the position was *not*; a curious outcome for an activity whose products are used habitually to assess what the position is at the time and to predict what it might possibly be in the future.

Asymmetrical maturities of receivables and borrowings

Table 10.1 shows the aggregated assets (at book value) and aggregated borrowings of ASL. The maturity profile of ASL's assets and borrowings illustrates the group's financial difficulties more vividly – especially the maturities schedules of ASL's borrowings and receivables from 1964 to 1978, detailed in Table 10.4.

Several points emerge from analysis of Table 10.4.

- The proportion of ASL's aggregate borrowed funds to receivables was increasing, whereas other AFC member companies were experiencing a small decline in that ratio.
- During the 1970s, AFC members experienced a shortening of the average maturity structure of borrowings. For ASL it was more pronounced over this period than for the other companies. The percentage of ASL's borrowings greater than five years dropped from 27 per cent in 1965 (AFC: 20 per cent) to 7 per cent in 1974 (AFC: 8 per cent) and 1 per cent in 1978 (AFC: 1 per cent); while receivables greater than five years remained steady at around 8–10 per cent from 1964 to 1973 (AFC: 7–9 per cent); with a ballooning out to 14 per cent, 15 per cent and 13 per cent in 1974, 1975 and 1976, respectively (AFC: 10, 9 and 8 per cent). Reinforcing ASL's seemingly 'above average' liquidity problem, the proportions of its borrowings due within two years increased from 43 per cent in 1964 (AFC n.a.) to 83 per cent in 1977 (AFC: 70 per cent); while the proportion due within one year increased from 31 per cent in 1964 to 49 per cent in 1974 to a peak of 54 per cent in 1977.
- In the less-than-two-years category, the ratio of borrowings of finance companies relative to aggregate receivables was increasing steadily from 1964 to 1974, whereas for AFC members the relative increase was significantly slower. In contrast, although for the two-to-five-years category the proportion was decreasing for AFC member companies, for ASL it was the opposite. This mismatching characteristic in respect of the financing and investment strategies of ASL and finance companies in general was described as a 'dangerous convergence' by one scribe.[14]

Although finance companies, generally, were having trouble financing their operations,[15] ASL's position (relative to AFC member companies)

Table 10.4 Amount and percentage of borrowings/receivables of ASL and AFC members, selected years, 1965 to 1978

Financial year	ASL Total		AFC Total		ASL < 2 Years		AFC < 2 Years		ASL 2–5 Years		AFC 2–5 Years	
	$m	%	$m	%	$m	%	$m	%	$m	%	$m	%
1965	62/83	76	958/1,429	67	28/61	46	440/1,059	42	17/15	113	328/264	124
1970	142/205	69	1,989/2,901	69	75/133	56	1,000/2,079	48	37/56	66	661/614	108
1974	314/377	83	4,704/6,964	68	212/239	89	2,876/4,832	60	80/85	94	1,460/1,419	103
1978	238/285	84	7,976/12,170	66	129/166	77	5,404/7,887	68	102/90	113	2,449/3,162	77

Source: Based on data in F.L. Clarke and G.W. Dean, *Working Paper* (1987).

was parlous – particularly so in respect to matching maturities of borrowings and receivables due within two years. Liquidity problems were inevitable unless the group could find access to its own banker.

ASL was not Robinson Crusoe in that respect. The inability of ASL to match properly liquid assets' and borrowings' maturities was a common feature of both Australian finance companies and the comparable overseas financial intermediaries involved in the national property booms of the early 1970s (the Secondary Banks in the United Kingdom and Real Estate Investment Trusts in the United States).[16] As such, it is worth contemplating whether ASL's directors were merely following a path of seeking higher returns (in boom conditions) while recognising the higher risks they were taking. If that were so, is it appropriate to criticise their actions with hindsight? But all that begs the question as to whether accounting information provided to directors enabled a proper assessment of the risks. Matching borrowings and receivables maturities was incontestable – straight comparisons of actual amounts of money. If property had been marked-to-market (and verified), related total asset backing, collateral and the like, liquidity and solvency assessments would have been more transparent.

Without knowledge of the contemporary movements in the market prices of ASL's property, the diagnosis that 'bad property investments' were a major factor in the demise of ASL is impossible to confirm or refute on financial grounds. In contrast, the behavioural aspect of ASL's investment policies is a different matter.

Functional transmutation – diversification into real property

Longstanding ideas characterising business activity rest firmly on the proposition that companies are 'going concerns'. Going concern is a firmly entrenched fundamental convention of accounting. Auditors have a primary duty to attest to that going concern status – essentially, whether firms have the financial capacity to continue to do what they are currently doing. Yet the history of business enterprise militates strongly against that. The very use of 'enterprise' evokes the strongest awareness of the function of continual adaptation, speculation, strategic change in operations, expansion or contraction of operations at the margin, as parts of managements' armouries. Frequently, operational changes escape immediate attention by virtue of euphemisms such as 'expansion', 'conglomeration', 'rationalisation' and 'diversification'. At the same time, those euphemisms tend to disguise the altered direction of business activity. More importantly, managers' use of euphemisms often masks the necessity of adapting other strategic aspects of their enterprise, marketing techniques, advertising practices, public relations exercises, and in particular, operating and financing techniques, to the new circumstances. There is some evidence to support the suspicion that ASL's management may have laboured behind the protection of such screens to hide the reality of things.

The ASL group's increased investment in real estate in general and property development in particular should not be viewed as unusual. It was not atypical managerial action *per se*, nor was it atypical action by a member of the AFC. The gradual transmutation of ASL from a regular financier of consumer durables to the financing and underwriting of property development was nothing remarkable. In contrast with many companies, ASL's functional change could be considered quite conservative. Irrespective of size, financial structure, market participation, being a price leader or price taker, or public or private status, periodic transmutations of corporate functions are ordinary, everyday events; the essence of going concerns. That is the antithesis of the idea embedded in managerial and financial accounting practices, and underlying a considerable corpus of commercial practices, that firms continue doing the same things throughout their existence. Interestingly, had ASL's move proved successful it would have been attributed to a highly developed business acumen.

Nor was ASL's behaviour different in that respect from the actions of other members of the AFC and by some non-member financial institutions as well. Growth in those companies' assets, in their receivables in particular, was indicative of a common involvement in real property. According to Daly, the property boom was the most significant influence on growth of finance companies' assets between 1968 and 1973.[17] Using Daly's data, real estate assets alone of those companies rose from a

reported book value of $684 million to $2,689 million. We would assume
that in the rising market the 'book value' was closer to cost than the
higher selling price, though it cannot be known for certain on a case-by-
case basis. In contrast, the amount of the related debt is unequivocal. Not
unexpectedly, the receivables portfolios of finance companies reflected
most of the increase. But whereas leasing of real estate was a growth
activity during that period, finance companies acting directly as the
bankers for developers was more significant, by far. Over the same
period, Australian Bureau of Statistics data calculate the 129.7 per cent
growth in net receivables of the finance companies to have outstripped
that of the trading banks (92.8 per cent), the savings banks (66.1 per
cent) and the life offices (25 per cent). Only the building societies'
increase of 435 per cent bettered them. But it is noteworthy that the
finance companies' net receivables of $5,307 million more than doubled
those held by the building societies ($2,510 million), even though the
latter clearly held a distinct comparative market advantage in the real
estate area.

In contrast, the entry of the finance companies in general and ASL in
particular into that market was a maverick action, according to the
pervading conception of continuity of business activity. The implications
are important for an understanding of the crash. Gottliebsen *et al.*'s post-
mortem and conclusion of 'bad property investments'[18] is representative
of the view at the time of the ASL receivership. For example, Daly is quick
to indicate the significance of 'the movement out of consumer durables'
and a critical shortfall in 'managerial skills in the property area'.[19]

But in what sense were those investments necessarily bad, when
property was the growth asset at the time and when the banks, life offices
and building societies were each competing for as large a share of the
action as possible? Nowhere is it explained in those analyses why
investments in property by ASL were bad, when similar investments by
others who did not fail were (presumably) good. Nor is it shown that
ASL's management was generally inferior to that of other members of
the Finance Conference, or inferior in particular when it came to
property management. In fact, there are some indications that on a
number of counts ASL's management was rather conservative relative to
others. Not that we would suggest conservatism is a good management
trait, though 1990s popular wisdom would appear to rank it above the
more risky cowboyish behaviour.

Prima facie, for a significant time ASL's reported capital gearing was
somewhat lower than the AFC average. Irresponsible programmes of rapid
and continuous growth in gearing have featured in virtually all the major
company failures experienced in Australia since World War II. Many of
those companies featured in the expansion of consumer credit in Australia

and so have something in common with ASL. Cambridge's adventure into property development forges an even closer link. Moreover, the growth in ASL's share of consumer credit over the period from 1960 to 1970 (2.8 per cent) was on a similar scale to that of a number of other AFC members and considerably lower than some – for example, Finance Corporation of Australia's move from 2.6 per cent to 7.6 per cent.[20]

Unplanned hedging and unserviceable debt – the role of accounting

More relevant to the peculiar circumstances of ASL's performance and independent of subjective evaluations of the propriety of the move into property financing is the examination of how it fared in the real estate market. Whereas holding real estate is an attractive long-term financial proposition during inflationary periods, such as those between the mid-1960s, the late 1970s and the mid-1980s, it clearly has numerous pitfalls. It is a paradox that the primary source of the financial attraction is a major contributor to the most hostile of the problems which beset developers during periods of price instability.

Inflation has always been the catalyst for the flight from liquidity and the corresponding investment in physical assets (*Sachwerte*, as the Germans labelled it in the hyperinflation of 1923)[21] to exploit possible disproportionate rises in their selling prices, relative to the increase in the general price level. In nearly every extended inflationary period encountered by Western countries this century, investment in real property has found strong support. The fortunes of European industrialists and financiers following World War I were founded on that strategy.[22] Fleeing liquidity and investing in those assets with the greatest differential increases in their prices compared to the inflation rate was the normal means. It was good business. Sustained upward movement in Australian real property prices, ahead of inflation, more than justified ASL's transmutation. It also exposed ASL and its fellow travellers to the snare of being seduced into holding property as a hedge against inflation, rather than pursuing their chosen role of profit takers.

In that context, corporate property holders and developers should be distinguished from the individuals who feature in the Bresciani-Turroni[23] and Guttmann and Meehan[24] descriptions of loss mitigation and profit seeking during inflation. Almost without exception, profitable exploitation of differential price increases has been by wealthy individuals who purchased property outright, or under conditions in which revenues offset repairs and fiscal charges, including financing costs. No significant penalty accrues if the property inventory turns over slowly. Probably it is financially better to hold the property than to sell it, for the increase in selling prices of properties outstrips the decline in general purchasing power of money and more than compensates for having to meet interest and other period charges. Such investors virtually become their own bankers.

Hedging necessitates self-financing, or at least a near-to-positive cash inflow. In contrast, under a planned profit-making operation, a negative cash inflow is of little consequence, provided the gestation period is short. Those in the AFC who had banking affiliates, guaranteed financial back-up, stood in a similar position to individuals holding property as a hedge. In contrast, ASL lacked the financial support of a local bank affiliate. Financial backing from the Royal Bank of Scotland proved insufficient. Unless property could be disposed of relatively quickly, the cash drain would be too great to service. Property development is a time-consuming and costly operation. According to temporal criteria, developers have similar characteristics to those in property as a hedge against inflation. During the late 1960s and early 1970s the property market favoured buyers. And in any case, ASL was heavily involved in development schemes. Perhaps unwittingly, it was forced to adopt the hedging stance.

Without the expectation of a back-up banking facility, ASL was unlikely to have ever engineered itself into a position of being able to service its debt portfolio. Sir Reginald Ansett alluded to the critical need for ASL to have the lender-of-last-resort type of facility that only its own bank could ensure: 'ASL has a magnificent future . . . We'll either marry a bank or we (Ansett Transport Industries) will buy the lot. That should fix it like a shot out of a gun, for once it is wholly owned (by Ansett) there is an enormous amount of freedom to solve the problems.'[25]

Such a statement came far too late to have had any significant impact on ASL's destiny. It now is well known that a portion of the reported growth in ASL's assets was the product of capitalising period costs of holding and developing real estate – a variation on the historical cost theme that money spent on acquiring and holding physical assets necessarily adds wealth. Even when the downturn in property prices came during 1974/75, there was no about-face in the method of valuing ASL assets until a 1976 $12 million write-down following the takeover of the group by Ansett and the $18 million it pumped into ASL during the doomed rescue bid mounted during 1977–1979.

Prior to 1974, ASL appeared to be well placed to hedge the growing inflation with its growing property and property-related loan portfolios. The market perceived it so with its share price at above-average levels. Over 50 per cent of the book value of its assets comprised real estate and real estate-linked receivables. The 30 per cent shareholding held by the Royal Bank of Scotland perhaps implied that help was nearby if cash were required quickly. Some of that expectation materialised in 1974 when $20 million was raised on the Eurodollar market. A $2.5 million reported annual profit, the illusion of the strong real estate hedge against inflation and the trust that the Scottish bank would stand behind the group implied stability – in hindsight, all were pious hopes.

The Stock Exchange's Statex Service recalculated the 1974 $2.5 million reported profit to have been more like a $218,000 loss, and the disclosed losses from 1975 to 1978 amounting to $22 million to have been closer to $25 million. One of the problems with those kinds of analyses is the general practice of recalculating by recourse to conventional accounting methods.

Accordingly, often those going on attack cast doubt on the appropriateness of the uncommon accounting practices which perversely make more sense than many of those enjoying the common approbation. Consider the following analysis of one such accounting method used at ASL – equity accounting (the practice of injecting an investor's profit and loss statement and balance sheet with the proportion of the periodic income or loss of another company over which it exercises a 'significant influence' on the latter's activities) – and other techniques to boost reported profits in the 1976/77 and 1977/78 financial years: 'The financial year 1976–77 saw a skimpy net profit of $51,000. . . . $874,000 for unrealised foreign-exchange losses. . . . was offset only by $666,000 in profits from associated companies brought in through equity accounting' and '[I]n the December half of 1977–78, the adoption of equity accounting increased the group's pre-tax profits by $274,000. If equity accounting had not been used the group would have reported a loss, probably somewhere around $170,000 . . . Further, the results were inflated by at least one dubious transaction. In December 1977 ASL sold land . . . to a joint venture for $1.6m. on a deposit of $50,000.'[26] The sale generated a profit of over $500,000 and without it ASL would have recorded a $200,000 loss for the year.

Reporting increased profits is certainly desirable, but keeping out of the red is seemingly a commercial imperative. One is reminded of the desperate manoeuvres of Korman, Reid Murray, Minsec, Cambridge Credit and Gollins several years earlier, and Ariadne, Rothwells, Adsteam, Westmex and the Bond Corporation over a decade later. However, more germane is that equity accounting is a surrogate, though a poor surrogate, for marking-investments-to-market. The criticism quoted above is contestable.

Paradoxically, some aspects of equity accounting, combined with recognising changes in market prices of physical assets as they occur, have considerable merit. Equity accounting is, in principle, merely a second-best mechanism for assessing the underlying worth of a shareholding. Obviously the best mechanism would be to use the investment's market selling price, were it available. If equity accounting were applied in respect of the affairs of related companies whose profits and losses were based on changes in the money's worth of the underlying net assets, the likelihood is

'Ansett bales out of ASL', *The Australian*, 12 February 1979, p. 8.
Courtesy of Larry Pickering.

that the outcome would be much more reliable than either the practice of
investment valuation in ASL's time or the practice now. And in respect to
the land sale, surely the real issue is not the terms upon which the
transaction is effected but how it is reflected in the accounts. If the land
were marked-to-market in the joint venture, ASL's share in the joint
venture would have been adjusted accordingly. That would have brought
only a change in the structure of ASL's assets, not their worth.

When Ansett 'baled out' from ASL on 8 February 1979, the trustee for
the debenture holders, Perpetual Trustees Company, appointed Gary
Warhurst and Tony Koshin of Hungerfords as receivers.

Overdoing a good thing

The real estate vehicle ASL Developments was nowhere near being either
financed or geared to be an effective hedging medium. As a relatively
short-term profit seeker, it had engaged in nearly every conceivable
structural error. Its link with the Royal Bank of Scotland,[27] ASL's sole
remaining hope, was sacrificed in the Ansett takeover – ironically
designed as a rescue mission!

Contrary to many of the press reports and other commentaries on
ASL, the group's property incursion was neither unusual, nor worthy
necessarily of the 'bad investment' epitaph. With the onset of inflation
and strong expectations of even greater price rises to come, ASL's

transmutation conformed to a traditional, historically precedented and often successful business strategy. As it turned out, price movements in 1980/81 somewhat justified those expectations. It is far from clear that the ASL management was inefficient in that respect. Nor is it clear that the management was any less efficient in handling the finance available to it. The difference which the access to bank back-up could have made when ASL was trapped into an unplanned hedge is clear, as is the impossibility of survival in the borrowing conditions at the time, as declining property values restricted the capacity to service current debt, meet maturing principal or negotiate roll-over refinancing. It is a pity that the accounting did not disclose that.

ASL's woes invite conclusions which are *indicative*, rather than definitive. Already we have shown that corporate collapse invariably involves complex arrangements. Autopsies cannot exploit the privilege of working through a catalogue of established, universally agreed, proven, fatal conditions in the manner enjoyed by medical examiners. Nonetheless, failed and non-failed companies often have common characteristics.[28] Painted with a broad brush they present the same public picture. Published financial data relating to both often report a positive picture, reinforcing that common image.

Notwithstanding that disclaimer, the analysis of ASL revealed aspects of its operations which help to explain critical circumstances of the collapse. The rapid escalation in assets, debt and reported profits in the late 1960s and early 1970s, and the prolonged period of languishing (1974–1979) is a familiar scenario.

Dangerous shortening of the maturity structure of ASL's borrowings was coupled to the failure to match borrowings and receivables. The inability of the board to secure lender-of-last-resort support from a local bank placed ASL under extreme pressure in its unplanned hedging operations in real property. More than likely, those features in isolation would not be fatal. The performance and survival of other AFC companies implies that. Together, and in the absence of a system of accounting serviceable for exposing their cumulative financial effects, they are a recipe for disaster. Commingled, as they were in ASL, they become a potent mixture – and ASL overdosed.

'Bid to keep Goward bankrupt' – caption adorning this caricature of Russell Goward as he faced perjury charges. *Australian Financial Review*, 15 December 1993, p. 13. Courtesy of David Rowe

'Adsteam sinks $3.7 billion into red under Spalvins' leadership.' *Sydney Morning Herald*, 29 March 1991, p. 17. Courtesy of Rocco Fazzari.

John Spalvins addresses Tooth & Co. meeting, November 1990. Courtesy of John Fairfax Holdings Ltd.

Ron Brierley and Russell Goward have a beer at the Windsor Hotel, Melbourne. *Age*, 30 November 1983. Courtesy of John Fairfax Holdings Ltd.

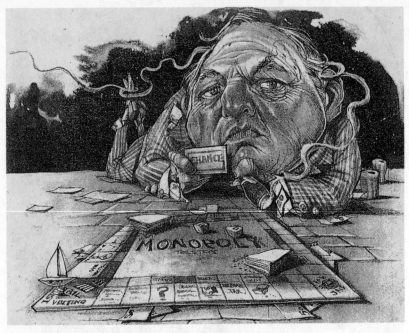

Caricature of Alan Bond. *Australian Financial Review*, 16 January 1995, p. 14.
Courtesy of David Rowe.

Alan Bond flies over Sydney (12 June 1986) in his new airship on its maiden voyage.
Couresty of News Ltd.

PART IV

The 1980s

ELEVEN

The 1980s: Decade of the Deal?

> 'Inter-company shareholdings and transactions have given
> cover to fraudulent dealings and to legally less serious but
> financially no less deceptive mis-statements of results and
> position.'
>
> *R.J. Chambers (1973, p. 225)*

The 1980s in Australia has been described as a decade of dreams – 'the dreamtime casino',[1] a time when the financial system went crazy, when the nation was wooed by the 'decade of the deal', by the call that 'greed was good'.[2] Yet, the collapses that occurred in the 1980s were simply repeats of earlier experiences. The chapter headnote is as apt for the eighties as it was in describing commercial practices of the sixties and seventies.

More of the same it certainly was. But the scale was different. Financial hangovers on the morning-after demonstrate that without doubt the 1980s hosted a corporate party to remember. Many have, but not fondly. Receiverships and liquidations of publicly-listed companies were at record levels, with nearly 500 companies delisted because of the appointment of a liquidator or receiver during the period 1986 to 1995, approximately equal to the total number of such delistings over the previous three decades.

Capturing the flavour of those corporate excesses and the paranoia regarding them was the assessment: 'So what went wrong in Australia . . . ? Close your eyes! In reality, that is what went wrong. . . . Everyone [bankers, lawyers, accountants, regulators and directors] had their eyes closed. . . . Some directors fraudulently abused their trust. . . . Some directors negligently or *even innocently abused their trust*. . . . Unfortunately, . . . some honest directors . . . closed their eyes and slept.'[3]

The problem is, the paranoia clouded the focus of the corporate observers, blinded *them* to the real issues, and generally let the regulators and the accountancy profession off the hook. 'Bankers, lawyers, accountants and directors', the dishonest and the innocent alike, have been judged through the false perception that most regulatory mechanisms were apt.

Table 11.1 Progress report on the ASC's 1991/92 '16 National Priority' investigations

Company	Official under scrutiny	Action
1. Bond Group	Alan Bond was charged over an alleged dishonesty matter relating to Rothwells. Subsequently, different charges were laid against Bond and other directors pertaining to transactions between Bell Resources and other BCH group companies. All are awaiting trial on this matter: In July 1994, committal hearings on another matter began with Alan Bond charged with breaching his duties as a director, furnishing false information to fellow directors and providing misleading information to auditors over the *La Promenade* art purchase and its 1988 sale, contiguous with BCH's acquisition from Sotheby's of Van Gogh's *Irises*.	Alan Bond was gaoled for a year on the Rothwells charges but released after three months on appeal. He was acquitted on the retrial. In 1996 Alan Bond was found guilty of fraud charges relating to the *La Promenade* transactions. He was sentenced to two years' gaol on one count and one year on another. Bond, Antony Oates and Peter Mitchell committed for trial on charges related to the Bell Resources matter.
2. Budget Group	Directors Robert Ansett and Stanley Hamley and two others were committed in November 1994 to stand trial. The two other officials had charges dismissed in October 1994.	All were charged over information in a 1989 Budget Corporation Ltd prospectus. The trial of Ansett and Hamley is scheduled to be heard in 1997.
3. Duke Group	Proceedings brought by liquidator over experts' report in respect of the reverse takeover of the Duke Group in June 1988 by Kia Ora Gold Corporation. ASC concerned over possible criminal matters, ultimately resulting in three directors being charged in 1993 for allegedly failing to act honestly under sections 229(1)(b) and 129 of the former Companies Code.	Three former directors charged by ASC with allegedly breaching duties under section 229(1)(b); two directors charged with breaching section 129, involving Duke Group Ltd financing dealings in its own shares. In December 1994 all parties were committed for trial.
4. Entity Group	Directors Gary Carter, Dennis Vickery, Christopher Blaxland were investigated by ASC and briefs sent to the DPP.	Charges laid against Carter, Vickery and Blaxland in 1991 who were committed for trial in May 1992. Carter subsequently was gaoled for four years. In July 1993, Entity's auditors appeared in court charged with making false or misleading statements in an Investigating Accountants' report – in August 1994 those charges were dismissed.

5. Equiticorp	Concern over alleged transfer of funds out of the group by former chairman of Equity House Limited, Allan Hawkins.	In June 1993, Hawkins was charged but the case was dropped upon his release from six years' imprisonment in New Zealand on another matter.
6. Estate Mortgage	Concern over alleged misleading advertising. Also concern over a possible secret commission payment.	Multiple charges. Richard Lew is gaoled for two years (15 months suspended). Carl Davis was gaoled for eight months; Reuben Lew was gaoled for three years (suspended sentence for two years), and a valuer received a suspended one-year sentence.
7. Girvan Corp.	ASC sought appointment of liquidator to preserve assets.	No charges laid.
8. Golden Bounty Resources	Investigation into suspected market manipulation by Golden Bounty – civil action initiated by the ASC.	Court found that defendants 'ramped' share price and ordered that the shares be forfeited.
9. Hallwood (Hooker) Corporation	Analysis of circumstances surrounding failure.	No basis for criminal or civil action. On another matter, managing director George Herscu was gaoled for five years in respect of a secret commission.
10. Independent Resources	Directors Michael Fuller and Joseph Cummins were alleged to have made improper use of their position in three IRL Group companies.	13 charges against directors and intervention by ASC in a series of civil actions.
11. Interwest Group	Concern over the group's collapse at the end of 1989 after reporting excellent profits and proposing a healthy dividend.	15 charges. Criminal prosecutions started against chief executive John Avram in May 1994, and chairman, Stanley Schneider and Interwest shareholder, P. Jordan, relating to placement of 25 million Interwest shares.

Continued

Table 11.1 Continued

Company	Official under scrutiny	Action
12. Linter Group	Warrants issued in respect of alleged *window dressing* using related party transactions authorised allegedly by former chairman Abe Goldberg who is currently in Poland, a country with whom Australia does not have an extradition treaty covering a Polish citizen.	Goldberg charged with breaches of director's duties, engaging in fraudulent transactions and issuing misleading statements. Also the former company secretary and finance director, Katy Boskovitz, was charged on 11 counts relating to related party transactions between the 'banker' company and other Linter satellites.
13. Metrogrowth Property Trust	Several matters investigated.	DPP did not pursue matters raised. Records of interviews released to assist civil litigation.
14. Qintex Group	Criminal charges against former Chairman Christopher Skase for allegedly 'improperly' using his position involving $10 million of company funds.	Criminal prosecutions initiated. Extradition application to bring Skase from Spain was initially granted in September 1994 but then overturned on appeal in December 1994.
15. Rothwells	Directors Laurie Connell and Peter Lucas and the auditor, Louis Carter, were suspected of conspiracy to defraud.	105 charges laid; 63 were laid against Laurie Connell. Connell died during the proceedings in 1996 – proceedings against the other parties continue.
16. Spedley Securities	Brian Yuill investigated by ASC over alleged misuse of position to transfer $17 million from Spedley Securities to his family company.	Criminal prosecutions resulted in 16 charges laid. Yuill was found guilty and sentenced to three years and nine months imprisonment. Another former Spedley's director, James Craven, was gaoled for nine months.

Sources: Summarised primarily from data disclosed in the 1991–92 *ASC Annual Report*, pp. 40–41. 'Of the 13 matters referred [in Table 11.1] to the DPP for possible criminal charges [several] have resulted in the commencement of criminal prosecutions. One matter was successfully resolved by civil action undertaken directly by the ASC (Golden Bounty). In the Duke Group matter the ASC was given leave to appear in a civil action which was subsequently settled ... In the Hooker Corporation matter the ASC decided there was no basis for further action. Seven of the 16 matters [as of June 1992] involved civil action as well as investigation of possible criminal conduct (Bond Group, Girvan, Independent Resources, Duke Group, Rothwells, Spedley Securities and Golden Bounty' (pp. 5–6, ASC *Annual Report*); amended on the basis of information reported in subsequent ASC *Annual Reports*, the latest being the 1994–95 *Report*.

Entrepreneurs such as Bond, Skase, Goward, Ansett, Connell, Parry, Judge, Hawkins, Goldberg, Yuill, Herscu and Spalvins were at one time described as the heroes, the icons, of our financial system. The aftermath of the 1980s boom produced public inquiries into the actions of many of those financial icons (see Table 11.1). In some cases their business reputations were irreparably tarnished, some exposed to be inept, some were deemed outright villains – though perhaps equally victims of the financial reporting systems guiding their actions.

The 1980s were significant also for public acknowledgement of the extent of complex corporate structures and related-party transactions. Of course such disclosures were not new. They had existed informally, and some were more of a kind publicly noted in previous decades. But the 1980s revealed more publicly than before the extent of those structures and transactions and their scope for corporate devilment. A commingling of Australian public companies was further facilitated by the actions of a corporate vehicle, Australia 2000 Pty Ltd, formed by a group of business-men to prevent the takeover of some of Australia's oldest blue chip companies. A 'white knight' cross-shareholding strategy was employed to defend those companies. That further blurred the notion of a separate legal entity. Whilst the aim may have been laudable the consequences of similar related party arrangements proved dramatic, as revealed in the accounts of several 1980s cases below.

During this period, 'substance over form' became the buzz phrase of regulators – in particular, of the Accounting Standards-setters. While compulsory Statements of Accounting Standards were intended to provide 'authoritative guidance' on matters of accounting measurement and disclosure, the necessary exercise of professional judgement appeared to take a back seat to the cookbook of rules. In this setting, paragraph four of AAS 6, 'Accounting Policies: Determination, Application and Disclosure', acknowledges the substance over form concept as being one of five overriding criteria to be considered in choosing appropriate accounting policies.[4] The difficulties of identifying the substance of transactions, either with or without legal form, have been evident in the earlier accounts of events preceding failure in the 1960s and 1970s. It is demonstrated further in the following 1980s *causes célèbres*. However, it is difficult to contemplate the usefulness of accounting for the substance of a transaction without there being legal form.

Public experience with Reid Murray, H.G. Palmer, Stanhill, ASL, Cambridge, Minsec, and the like should dispel the suggestions that the 1980s experiences were unusual. In respect of many matters pertinent to commercial practice and corporate failure it was definitely more of the same. Mixing the financial affairs of public and private companies within complex group structures facilitated share transactions, property dealings and other asset transfers via extensive use of related-party, often round robin, transactions.

Our conventional standard accounting practices were unable to cope with the complexities. Primarily they failed because of their *ad hoc*, one-off, orientation – methods drummed-up as a *quick fix* for a current anomaly, the current object of complaint, the subject of current pressure on the accounting, irrespective of whether they meshed or conflicted with other practices or financial common sense. Whereas the 1980s was the 'decade of the deal' for the entrepreneurs, it was the 'decade of the quick fix' for the Accounting Standards-setters. Attraction to the quick fix continues. In the mid-1990s, professional bodies world-wide have set in place Urgent Issues Groups (UIGs) to come up with a speedy fix to urgent accounting problems. It is an interesting approach to the systemic defects of current practice – the old reductionist process and its one-off 'solutions' continues, and with as little hope of success in improving accounting data generally as the well-intentioned efforts in the past.

The Australian UIG's capacity for ad hocery and quick fixing is indisputable. Its 1996 handling of Pacific Dunlop's use of the inverse-sum-of-the-years'-digits method to amortise goodwill (more slowly than the straight line method) clearly illustrates that. Unable to muster convincing argument why the ISOYD method was 'wrong', the UIG went straight for the jugular of the complaints levelled at Pacific Dunlop: it declared the method unacceptable, implied it was wrong, but then let bygones-be-bygones and allowed the company's past practice to stand, although it prohibited it in respect of future transactions. That was a strange outcome. If the ISOYD method was wrong, then the UIG should have required the PacDun's accounts to be recast; and if the ISOYD's method was acceptable (not wrong by implication) in the past, then it ought not to have been outlawed in the future. The episode suggests that the UIG engages in a very peculiar practice, indeed.

In the 1980s, misleading or untrue statements caused by balance date adjustments, market rigging or insider trading were sometimes facilitated by the judicious use of financial window-dressing – misleading accounting.

Again, complex business structures and questionable group accounting practices were to the fore, and the sudden, unexpected collapses of public companies continued. Take Ariadne Australia Limited, for instance. For the year ended 30 June 1987, Ariadne had announced a record profit of $142 million. Incredibly, a year later, Ariadne reported it was in financial difficulty, having announced what was then a record Australian corporate loss of $640 million.[5] Interwest was another, as it reported a record operating profit of $25 million in September 1989, only to be placed in receivership three months later. Similarly, in the aftermath of Rothwells' 1988 collapse, 'according to an estimate by Deloitte Ross Tohmatsu, Rothwells made a loss each year instead of the profit it had reported. In 1987 it declared a profit of $28 million, when its actual result was a loss of $107 million.'[6]

Whereas criticism has not been confined to Australia,[7] concern over the way Australian accounting and auditing function is more than justified.

Contrary to the pervading rhetoric, during the 1980s the form of transactions ruled over the financial substance in accounting's depiction of certain entities' financial affairs.[8]

Evidence of transactions, some without intent to deceive, others allegedly contrived or sham in the extreme, produced reported profit figures and related asset balances subsequently expunged from entities' financial statements. Some of this has been due to the suspect techniques described immediately above. Some has been the outcome of compliance with professionally and legally endorsed Standards. These include:

(a) questionable asset balance items, such as the ubiquitous FITB, clearly demonstrated, for instance, in Bond Corporation's 1988 half a billion dollars write-off; and the proposed Adsteam litigation involving asset amounts of hundreds of millions of dollars being questioned;

(b) interest expenditure being capitalised – amounts exceeding tens of millions of dollars have subsequently been written off in one period;

(c) formation expenditure being treated as an asset. In (for example) Compass Airline's 1990 accounts, 'formation expenditure' represented over 40 per cent of the total *assets* of the company;

(d) other types of expenses capitalised and then, several years later, written off to the Profit and Loss account as a one-off charge;

(e) terminological difficulties ('self-sustaining' or 'integrated, dependent subsidiary', etc.) driving the accounting for foreign-held assets and liabilities and periodic transactions involving foreign exchange;

(f) ambiguities regarding whether convertible notes are 'debt' or 'equity'. Again, Bond Corporation's accounts are instructive. In 1987/88, convertible notes classified as equity lowered substantially the debt to equity ratio; and,

(g) the related-party (often round robin) transaction was a device used by many 1980s entrepreneurs. In evidence adduced in court cases at Spedley, Rothwells and Linter, round robin transactions are alleged to have been a medium for masking the true state of those entities' affairs at balance date.

Raking over the particulars of the 'accounting' rise and fall of three 1980s collapses, Adelaide Steamship, Bond Corporation and Westmex, shows that many of the financing, accounting and commercial practices of the 1980s were really repeat performances of what were so well rehearsed in the 1960s and 1970s. In each 1980s case the directors and auditors either have been the subject of, or are currently subject to, civil litigation. We make no assessments on those matters. Our analyses are based on the publicly available material and thus, necessarily, are not commentaries on specific matters being litigated.

TWELVE

Adsteam on the Rocks

The complexity in Samuel Insull's *top-heavy pyramid* in
1920s USA is more than matched by the outcome of the
cross-shareholdings within the Adelaide Steamship
(Adsteam) group of companies in 1980s Australia.

'Adsteam a humiliation for the accounting profession' – 'Adsteam's
$4.49 billion loss is biggest ever.'[1] Those headlines captured the impor-
tance of the saga associated with the scuttling of the monolithic Adsteam
group comprising numerous less-than-majority-owned (albeit effectively-
controlled) companies.

At the time of its partial breaking-up, Adsteam was arguably Australia's
biggest and certainly the most complex conglomerate (Figure 12.1). In
March 1991, Adelaide Steamship Company Limited (the parent
company) was placed under an informal receivership-style scheme of
arrangement at the behest of a syndicate of banks. It took action to restructure, to simplify the cross-shareholding-based conglomerate structure and to pare the Adsteam group's mountain of debt. By the end of
1993, debt within the group had been reduced to around $1.5 billion,
but post-1990 group losses had accumulated to nearly $3 billion.[2]

December 1994 saw a class action, initiated by the ASC on behalf of
Adsteam, against its 1990 auditor and several of its directors, including
the former chairman and managing director, John Spalvins. Adsteam
sought damages of $340 million related to an alleged $518 million overstatement of its 1990 reported profit and the consequential alleged
improper payment of dividends.

Adsteam's former auditor challenged the validity of the ASC to initiate
this action under section 50 of the ASC law. In April 1996 the appeal was
upheld by Justice Lindgren, but the ASC then successfully appealed that
judgment.

Financial data of the flagship, The Adelaide Steamship Company
Limited (Tables 12.1 and 12.2), offer insight into the changing fortunes of
the Adsteam group during the 1980s. Undoubtedly these reported figures
portray an incomplete picture of Adsteam's financial affairs, an aspect
explored below.

150

Figure 12.1   Adsteam group structure as at 30 September 1990, holdings under 5% not included

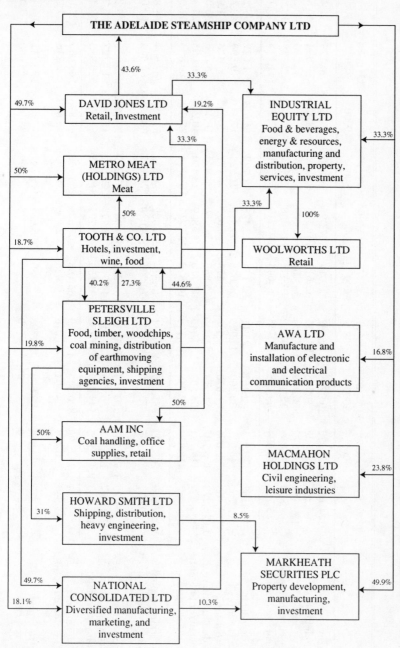

Source: *Australian Financial Review*, 8 November 1990, p. 18.

Table 12.1 The Adelaide Steamship Company Ltd – Statex balance sheet summary, ratios and profit and loss data, 30 June 1982 to 30 June 1991

	30/6/91 $000	30/6/90 $000	30/6/89 $000	30/6/88 $000	30/6/87 $000	30/6/86 $000	30/6/85 $000	30/6/84 $000	30/6/83 $000	30/6/82 $000
Cash and liquids	174,165	273,072	394,748	181,892	8,017	67,326	59,697	18,998	20,175	51,454
Trade debtors	66,284	156,825	94,948	103,255	45,615	131,306	53,234	48,438	39,034	40,849
Stocks	139,484	135,872	56,959	117,834	54,461	65,129	57,507	52,745	59,896	60,266
Other current assets	108,850	20,855	12,473	39,752	19,552	148,458	5,303	9,273	22,038	18,229
Total current assets	488,783	586,624	559,128	442,733	127,645	412,219	175,741	129,454	141,143	170,798
Bank overdraft	68,162	3,921	2,467	2,911	2,154	2,438	1,722	1,454	1,622	8,262
Trade creditors	19,761	43,011	29,390	44,925	38,638	55,313	21,928	17,116	19,890	40,353
Tax provisions	35,165	2,099	1,076	633	475	6,677	171	353	428	1,918
Debt due in one year	1,078,279	153,707	31,914	37,638	25,852	55,930	28,840	18,464	35,296	36,025
Other current liabilities	44,685	115,781	163,101	59,045	41,710	35,859	48,450	40,218	29,603	25,364
Current liabilities	1,246,052	318,519	227,948	145,152	108,829	156,217	101,111	77,668	86,839	111,922
Net working capital	-757,269	268,105	331,180	297,581	18,816	256,002	74,630	51,786	54,304	58,876
Net plant and property	50,872	57,195	75,170	102,030	70,301	68,040	70,192	89,186	86,503	69,605
Investments	596,493	1,992,727	1,619,984	907,759	767,317	639,982	637,259	424,696	385,939	355,230
Deferred assets	211,667	129,912	118,075	132,114	144,716	28,773	29,012	15,887	10,227	5,746
Total invested capital	101,763	2,447,939	2,144,409	1,439,484	1,001,150	992,797	811,093	581,555	536,973	489,457
Long-term debt	4	743,390	826,345	417,619	165,186	407,594	266,406	147,876	148,895	125,602
Other deferred liabilities	34,347	6,479	3,701	4,218	3,945	2,685	2,169	2,608	2,118	1,997
Minority interest	-75	43,254	29,600	25,798	359	76,604	117,243	117,677	100,811	106,479
Preferred capital	0	0	0	0	0	0	3,000	3,000	3,000	5,000

Ordinary equity	67,487	1,654,816	1,284,763	991,849	831,660	505,914	422,275	310,394	282,149	250,379
Total invested funds	101,763	2,447,939	2,144,409	1,439,484	1,001,150	992,797	811,093	581,555	536,973	489,457
Total tangible assets	1,347,815	2,766,458	2,372,357	1,584,636	1,109,979	1,149,014	912,204	659,223	623,812	601,379
Intangibles	9	55	871	18,416	125	145	166	187	208	105
Total assets	1,347,824	2,766,513	2,373,228	1,603,052	1,110,104	1,149,159	912,370	659,410	624,020	601,484
Balance sheet ratios										
Liquid ratio	0.29	1.43	2.22	2.28	0.68	2.25	1.18	1.00	0.95	1.06
Current ratio	0.39	1.84	2.45	3.05	1.17	2.63	1.73	1.66	1.62	1.52
Shareholders' interest	5.0	61.4	55.4	64.2	75.0	50.7	59.5	65.4	61.9	60.2
% Market/Bk listed inv.	59.3	94.1	101.8	100.0	135.8	168.6	128.4	109.2	138.6	108.6
Net assets/share (adj.)	1.01	4.65	4.83	4.49	3.00	2.28	1.92	1.45	1.34	1.20
Dilution factor used	1.00	1.00	0.72	0.60	0.53	0.42	0.34	0.34	0.34	0.34
Long-term debt/equity	0.0	44.9	64.3	42.1	19.8	80.5	63.0	47.6	52.7	50.1
Short-term debt/equity	1698.7	9.5	2.6	4.0	3.3	11.5	7.2	6.4	13.0	17.6
Profit after tax, after minority interest (000)										
As per Adel. Steamship Co. accounts	(1,358.21)	220.33	200.85	160.71	64.14	117.22	60.19	41.60	32.69	24.03
As per Statex	(1,358.21)	220.33	200.85	160.71	64.14	117.22	60.19	41.60	32.69	23.08
Sales (000)	312,320	136,738	409,325	388,525	.473,324	365,473	244,372	392,695	447,664	354,290

Source: Stock Exchange Research Pty Ltd, *Statex Service*, Adsteam (A2) run on 7 November 1991.

The Adelaide Steamship Company Limited, one of Australia's oldest surviving industrial companies, had operated passenger and cargo ships since 1875. By 1996, several years of large reported group losses and its sagging share price indicated it was only just maintaining that position. Downturns in its initial core activities in the 1960s and 1970s pre-empted a metamorphosis in the company, especially from 1977 under John Spalvins' leadership. Major shipping interests, except towage and port services, were disposed of and a process of extensive diversification begun. The stated goal of Spalvins' leadership was to acquire between 40 to 50 per cent of a target company and hence secure effective control.

Numero uno acquisitions

Changes in Adsteam's share price over the Spalvins era are revealing. Rises occurred in each year from around $1 in 1982 to over $5 in 1987. Dropping to around $4 after the October 1987 crash, Adsteam surged to a high of over $8 in 1989 before declining to between 10 and 20 cents in 1991 and 1992. It remained low into the mid-1990s, as disposal of the empire's assets continued. Adsteam, it must be recalled, was regarded as one of the most active of the 1980s entrepreneurial companies. Publicly maintaining a strategy of being in basic businesses such as food, ship towage, building and retailing, Adsteam acquired major shareholdings in numerous companies throughout the 1980s. Coincidentally, Table 12.1 discloses a similar pattern of increases in reported profits over that period.

Spalvins' philosophy was to retain only those companies that were an industry's *numero uno*, or at worst number two – a strategy which diverges greatly from that followed by that other leading 1980s entrepreneurial company, Westmex Ltd.

Adsteam's run began with the acquisition of 'controlling' (though less than 50 per cent) shareholdings in Tooths and David Jones in 1982. Major investments in H.C. Sleigh and the National Consolidated group followed. It culminated in the late 1989 joint venture acquisition by Dextran Pty Ltd of Industrial Equity Limited. Dextran comprised equal investments by Adsteam's 'public' arms, David Jones, Tooth and Co. and Adelaide Steamship. Acquisition of IEL was possibly a fatal mistake, for it left Sir Ronald Brierley a wounded adversary. He would return at a crucial time in 1990, just when Spalvins needed a breathing space.

Adsteam was the very-model-of-a-model-conglomerate. Industries penetrated included retailing (David Jones and Clark Rubber), food, meat, wine and smallgoods (Tooth & Co., Petersville Sleigh and Metro Meat Holdings), real estate and property investment (Pioneer Property, W.A. Realty and Markheath Securities Plc), its traditional activities of towage and port services (Adelaide Steamship and Petersville Sleigh) and manufacturing (National Consolidated and Ajax Cooke). If diversity gave strength, Adsteam ought to have been a Goliath. Then again, perhaps it was.

Acquisition strategy resulted in an extremely complicated cross-shareholding-based structure. This facilitated loans to subsidiary companies, the recording of interest receivable from those subsidiaries, the inclusion of the ubiquitous company *debit* – the future income tax benefit. It also presented a nightmare for auditors in attesting the worth of the investments in related companies and the collateral underlying Adsteam's loans to them. Adsteam's structure was the seminal example of auditors' worst nightmares.

The maximum amount of shareholdings of any company in other group entities was kept below 50 per cent. That practice, perhaps, is an excellent instance of how the rule-book approach to consolidation accounting imposed by the law and the Accounting Standards *at the time* determined managerial actions. It also, of course, thereby determined asset valuation bases and the 'group' profit calculation at Adsteam. And it created difficulty for anyone trying to unravel the financial significance of transactions between the related companies.

At that time percentage shareholding essentially determined whether control existed and hence whether companies' accounts were to be consolidated, and with that the injection of the consolidation accounting artifacts. Now, under AASB 1024, arguably a broader criterion of 'control' determines whether a company is a subsidiary of another. But the point remains – curiously, how the financial outcomes are reported depends upon the relationship between the companies, not upon the financial facts. Adsteam's cross-shareholding strategy meant that consolidated financial statements were not required, though Adsteam officers publicly provided different reasons for the complex shareholding arrangements. Closing off possible takeover opportunities against Adsteam group companies was advanced, as was the need to use shelf companies to buy and sell shares of Adsteam group companies. To that end, between 1984 and 1987 shelf companies issued preference shares to other Adsteam companies who were then, under the complex arrangement, entitled to all realised profits on the share deals. It was the epitome of group enterprise action.

Whereas many analysts and financial institutions were wary of the resulting conglomerate, untangling it appeared to be beyond virtually everyone. It is far from clear whether Adsteam's management and accountants could do so themselves. Certainly, if they employed something akin to consolidation accounting practices to obtain a clue or two, they were bound to be more in the dark than when they started.

Table 12.2 Summary financial statistics of the operations of The Adelaide Steamship Company Ltd, 30 June 1982 to 30 June 1991

Year end 30 June	Sales (other revenue) $m	After-tax profits $m	Total assets $m	Total debt $m
1982	354	24	601	139
1983	448	33	624	238
1984	393	42	659	228
1985	244	60	912	368
1986	365	117	1,149	566
1987	473	64	1,110	277
1988	389	160	1,603	567
1989	409	201	2,373	1,058
1990	137	220	2,767	1,068
1991	312	(1,358)	1,348	1,280

Source: Sydney Stock Exchange Statex Service, A2 run on 7 November 1991 (reproduced as Table 12.1).

Most of the Adsteam group companies' shares were cross-held, as shown in Figure 12.1. It is understandable that only two or three institutional shareholders appeared in the top 20 Adsteam shareholders between 1986 and 1990. Whatever the institutional view of Adsteam, the cross-shareholding strategy would have kept them out.

Spalvins' management strategy was on the one hand praised, and on the other equally criticised. As with Palmer, Reid Murray, Cambridge Credit and the like, Adsteam was reported in the financial press on numerous occasions as a corporate *success* story. Consider this early 1987 assessment: 'Adelaide Steamship, with its group of companies stands out in the stockmarket as an entrepreneurial company with the best management, backed up with a stringent, highly disciplined reporting system. The credit belongs to John Spalvins.'[3] Table 12.2 supports this view as it reveals increasing profits nearly every year from 1982 to 1990. Another Icarus paradox example suggesting that extreme success is a portent for impending failure? Or, as suggested previously, is it more the case that *reportedly* successful companies relying on creative accounting should be considered likely candidates for failure?

Twenty-five years before, almost identical comments and certainly the same sentiments had been expressed regarding the business acumen of Herbie Palmer. Perhaps it was a foreboding of Adsteam's fate. And then in 1988: 'Spalvins has the market guessing. . . . Adsteam is basically a strong group with good operating businesses, but the cream on its earnings has come from takeovers and dealing, and Spalvins undoubtedly wants to generate more such cream.'[4]

Producing 'cream' was proving difficult by 1989. But Spalvins went for two ambitious investment plays. One was a miscalculated greenmail investment in Bell Resources at the time of Bond Corporation's move on Bell's cash-box. By the time the Adsteam investment had been secured, the now notorious $1.2 billion 'loan' (see Chapter 13) from Bell to several Bond group companies appears to have been sealed. The cash-box emptied, Adsteam's investment in Bell was looking bad. Spalvins tried several moves to claw back funds into Bell Resources from the Bond group. They proved futile. The second poor investment in 1989 was the IEL acquisition, using Dextran. A syndicate of banks provided the $900 million required. Spalvins apparently was keen to edge out an old adversary, Sir Ronald Brierley.

Adsteam had certainly achieved conglomerate status with this 1989 acquisition. It now had a large finger in many industries – food, retailing, real estate and property, meat, wine, manufacturing, and shipping and towage. Whether because of bad luck or simply the poor investments Spalvins had made to crank up the conglomerate, Adsteam was perceived by its backers to lack collateral. Its plates were cracking – Adsteam had begun to 'take in' water.

Contiguously, regulatory interest occurred on two fronts. The Australian Taxation Office and the ASC became interested in certain aspects of Adsteam's Byzantine operations. Adsteam's public image was particularly dented by the long-running legal battle with the ATO over disputes involving millions of dollars of tax assessed on capital profits on intra-group share deals by those shelf companies. Adsteam ultimately settled this matter, paying the ATO over $250 million in March 1991.

On the other front, the ASC investigated several transactions between Adsteam and related companies during the 1989/90 period, as well as the propriety of certain asset valuations. This eventually resulted in December 1994 in the ASC launching its class action in the Federal Court against the Adsteam auditor and several of its directors on behalf of Adsteam.[5]

The ASC alleged that related-party transactions (loans, investments, sales with put options, etc.) between Adsteam, several subsidiaries and related other parties were used in order to present the financial state of affairs of the Adsteam group in a better light than it really was. Specifically, it was alleged that the directors of Adsteam should not have permitted payment of the interim dividend of $131,488,000 and the $97,313,000 final dividend for the financial year ending 30 June 1990. They should have been aware that 'Adsteam's profit for the six months ending 31 December 1989 was overstated in the 1990 interim accounts at least by the sum of $449,985,498', and that 'Adsteam's profits for the year ended 30 June 1990 were overstated in the Adsteam's accounts at least by an amount of $518,981,000'.

Several reasons were advanced by the ASC to support its contentions. ASC's claim suggested that loan asset balances should have been written down and FITB balances written off, and that asset revaluations were selective and not in accord with approved Accounting Standards. The ASC's argument drew upon the proposition that those related-party transactions masked the true state of the financial affairs of Adsteam as at 30 June 1990. We would argue that no FITB balance ought to be raised in the first place, physical asset valuation under the Standards is always selective, and related-party transactions do not so much 'mask' as does the conventional accounting for them. The successful appeal by the auditors against the validity of the ASC bringing the class action was overturned on a further appeal by the ASC.

Based on the assessments of some commentators, and certainly with hindsight, by the end of 1989 the nadir for this corporate monolith was nigh.

Adsteam's and Spalvins' critics

By April 1989, respected financial writers had contradictory assessments of Spalvins and Adsteam. Discussing an *Australian Ratings* report on Adsteam, Sykes noted: 'The carefully separated accounts of Adelaide Steamship and its associates have only ever shown parts of the picture. The whole doesn't look so pretty. . . . Investors are suspicious of the group's incestuous interlocking shareholdings.'[6] In contrast, a week later Gottliebsen, referring to Spalvins as 'the king of cross-ownership', claimed: 'While [Spalvins] has been lambasted by his critics and ignored by the sharemarket, Adsteam's chief has been building his billions.'[7] Adsteam's 1988/89 financial statements disclosed total tangible assets of $2.372 billion. But, of course, the more you have, the more there is to lose. In December 1989 Spalvins predicted that Adsteam's interim profits would exceed $100 million, which they duly did, coming in at $131.448 million in February 1990. However, as we noted, this has been questioned by the ASC.

Early in 1990, bearish sentiment followed publication of *Australian Ratings*' negative assessment of Adsteam's liquidity and interest rate cover. News reports of the assessment by stockbroker analyst Viktor Shvets (rated by *Australian Business* as the best financial analyst in 1991) certainly did not help – 'under certain conditions, the cash flow of the Adsteam group as a global entity would be deficient by as much as $250 million following the group's takeover of Industrial Equity Ltd'.[8] He also revealed that a large proportion of Adsteam's reported assets were in fact 'non-assets' in many people's reasoning – for example, the questionable FITB item. Adsteam's share price plunged. Spalvins followed a popular strategy when under attack, his bellicose remarks aimed directly at those who doubted the financial strength and viability of Adsteam.[9] But this proved to no avail.

Even towards the end of 1990 the board, in reporting to the ASX Adsteam's preliminary unaudited results, still projected an optimistic outlook for 1990/91: 'For the last fourteen years the Company has recorded a regular improvement in profit for the benefit of share-holders. We recognise that 1990/91 is going to be another challenge, but believe that the strength of our core businesses and the quality and depth of our management will ensure another good result in the year ahead.'

It was not to be. Table 12.1 discloses that a loss of over $1.35 billion was posted for 1990/91. So much for relying on managerial forecasts!

Commenting after Spalvins' fall from grace, Gottliebsen recalled that 'Spalvins was worshipped by bankers who scrambled to lend him money unsecured . . . [and] he believed the [conglomerate] game could go on forever'.[10] Interestingly, those loans were accompanied by negative pledges and corporate cross guarantees. These proved to be of little benefit to many unsecured group creditors here and in other cases, a matter about which we have more to say in Chapter 15.

Possibly the *coup de grâce* was dealt by the archetype investor-cum-entrepreneur, the wounded Sir Ronald Brierley. Spalvins had not satis-fied the essential condition if one sets out to 'kill a king' – you 'have to get him with the first shot'. Brierley's compelling negative assessment of Adsteam's financial prospects appeared in September 1990 under this caption: 'Brierley effect puts Adsteam into a freefall'.[11] Brierley's assess-ment was based on his recast Adsteam's accounts, by applying conven-tional consolidation practices.

By the end of October the tone of some analysts suggested that the financial position of Adsteam was becoming desperate. Chanticleer noted in the *Australian Financial Review*: 'The major outstanding issue [facing Adsteam's board] is the rationalisation of the convoluted and incestuous group structure. . . . Many other [than tax losses] valuable assets are held in artificial 50–50 joint ventures that will be very difficult to unravel. It is a process that will take years to complete and at the end of it there may or may not be any real equity left. I doubt that even John Spalvins knows what he will end up with.'[12]

Spalvins on profits

Critical commentaries about Adsteam's accounts appeared in the press: 'Adsteam's accounts are mysterious. Even the most diligent analysts have to admit that this labyrinth of inter-company and local and overseas off-balance sheet complexity defies full analysis.'[13] Particularly interesting

was the overwhelming allusion in the financial press to Adsteam's
strategy of denying the market the perceived benefits of consolidated
financial statements. 'The consolation is that economic entity consolidation [under AASB 1024] might make any future Adsteams easier
for analysts and investors to recognise in their infancy.'[14] One wonders
how preparing consolidated accounts of such a complex conglomerate
would have made anyone the wiser? Conventional consolidation techniques are fraught with problems and anomalies. Despite the push for
consolidated financial statements generally towards the end of the 1980s,
and more specifically in commentaries on the Adsteam case, perversely
the financial public were almost certainly better off without the additional complications consolidation brings.

Under attack, Spalvins aimed criticism of his own at members of the
accounting profession for their shifting position on differentiating
'extraordinary' and 'operating profits'. Reportedly the position he took
was 'that what matters is a company's creation of wealth by income and
asset appreciation jointly. This includes property and asset revaluations
whether they are called "profit" or not'.[15] The crucial issue in this regard
is how to determine an asset and its worth.

Undoubtedly this becomes an extremely difficult problem for auditors
and directors when related parties, especially wholly-owned subsidiaries
and private companies, become enmeshed in transactions with publicly-
listed parent companies. It was reported that in one financial period, 'an
analysis of the trading of the [Adsteam] group showed that an average of
70 per cent of the stock being traded was accounted for by associates of
Adsteam'.[16] It is perhaps a little premature to claim that accounting
numbers can be signed off as 'true and fair' even though those numbers
may not 'bear any relationship with the health of the operating business.
In Adsteam all this was done *quite legally.*'[17] Whether it occurs *legally* is
contestable. Curiously, the same commentator earlier had berated
Adsteam for not preparing consolidated statements (see note 14) – the
most notorious vehicle of misleading accounting data. A recurrent
theme throughout this book is that if many conventional accounting data
were ever extensively tested for financial truth, common sense and fairness in a court, they would fail miserably.

Within months of Spalvins' counter-attack, with Adsteam's share price
around $4, it was reported: 'How quickly times change. Just eight months
ago John Spalvins was being fêted as Australia's most dynamic entrepreneur, having snatched Industrial Equity Ltd from under its management's nose in a cleverly executed lightning raid. [The investment
proved disastrous and] . . . today the Adelaide Steamship Co. chief is
fighting to keep the share prices of his empire afloat as he buys time to
restructure.'[18]

A year later, Spalvins had departed the boards of all Adsteam companies. Corporate success had immediately presaged failure.

In a perverse twist, Spalvins, in his outpouring on what represents corporate profits, was closer to the mark than many of the pundits of the accounting profession. His comment there struck at the heart of the problem with conventional accounting practice – that it is not directed at measuring the 'wealth and progress' of a company in meaningful, real financial terms. Wealth certainly does comprise the market worth of all assets; income (increase in wealth) has to include all realised and unrealised financial gains and losses; and asset appreciation (*a pretium* – increase in price) has to be included (even if unrealised), as does depreciation (*de pretium* – a decrease in price, equally unrealised). Realisation does not create or consume wealth, it merely changes its form – a physical asset into cash, cash into a physical asset, and the like.

History has the uncanny habit of being repeated. In the United States over 65 years earlier, Samuel Insull had taken on the accounting profession in defence of his depreciation accounting policies which conflicted with the profession's wisdom. Insull only brought to account a decrease in the worth of the assets when it was evidenced in the market. He rejected the idea that regular charges for depreciation created a replacement fund as the conventional wisdom was promoting (much the same as it more-or-less does today). A charge for depreciation when the market price of the asset is constant or increasing deliberately understates profits or overstates losses, as the case may be. Like Spalvins, Insull made more financial sense on that than the accountants.

Of course Insull's views were rubbished, particularly by the accounting profession, as were Spalvins'. Even more coincidental is the correspondence in their respective corporate structures. Insull's main tilt at the profession centred on his utility maze of several holding and sub-holding companies and hundreds of subsidiaries, without consolidation accounting being employed. Insull, too, left his empire unceremoniously in the end. Several years later he was found without identification, alone and dead on a Paris Metro station with only a five centime piece in his overcoat pocket. Such might be the unjust fate of accounting reformers!

Insull's complex group structure, labelled as a 'top-heavy pyramid', is illustrated in Figure 12.2. He had imposed layers of hundreds of holding and subsidiary companies over the utility operating companies with a series of trusts at the apex. As with Adsteam, such a complex structure is likely to engender uncertainty on the part of prospective shareholders as to whose interests are being served by intra-group transactions.

Unjustly, few are likely to acknowledge, or even be aware of, Insull's or Spalvins' efforts to inject the conventional accounting of their times with some financial common sense.

Figure 12.2 Samuel Insull's 'top-heavy pyramid' (extract)

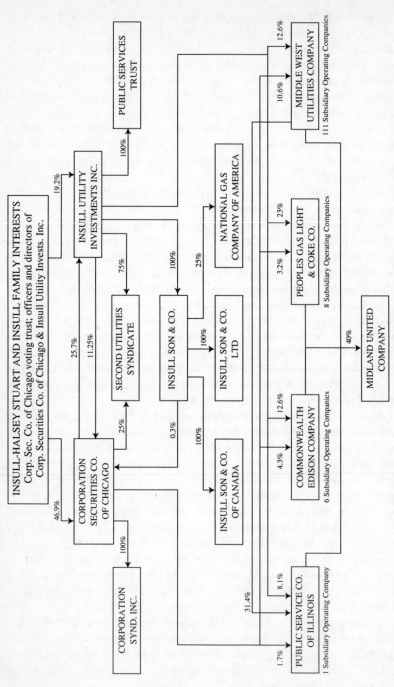

Note: Insull Utility Investments and Corporation Securities Co. of Chicago were trusts. Percentages as at end of 1929.
Source: United States Congressional Record – Senate (1935), p. 8499.

ADSTEAM 163

Returning to the Adsteam saga, a plethora of charges and counter-charges over accounting practices accompanied Adsteam's collapse. They involve several contentious matters, including whether the accounts of various entities comprising the complex Adsteam empire ought to have been consolidated. Eventually, changes to the ASX listing requirements and Accounting Standards and the post-October 1987 legislative developments mandated the production of consolidated financials for situations pertaining in the Adsteam group. The proposed charges contained in the 1994 ASC claim of presenting misleading data in the Adsteam accounts, if eventually heard in court, would make for fascinating argument. It would likely reveal if there were any substantive matters, previously not disclosed, in respect of the actual financial affairs of Adsteam prior to its major disinvestments under the informal 1990s receivership.

A lay jury drawing upon ordinary financial common sense may well be at odds with the accounting profession on whether Spalvins' views on asset appreciation and depreciation, and the merits of consolidation, were so ill-founded. Certainly it would be embarrassing to the accounting profession and the regulators if virtue in any of Adsteam's accounting practices was to be exposed by the amateurs. Like Minsec in the 1970s (and Insull some 60-odd years before), some of Adsteam's *publicly disclosed* accounting appears closer to financial common sense than the outcomes likely from using the professionally endorsed practices – consolidation, arbitrary depreciation calculations and FITBs, in particular. In accounting, recourse to financial 'common sense', casual but careful observation of financial affairs, and compliance with the rubrics of monetary calculation are uncommon practices.

We now turn to the Bond Corporation affair, aspects of which evoke similar convictions.

THIRTEEN

Bond Corporation Holdings Ltd (Group): Entrepreneurial Rise and Fall

'What has been is what will be, and what has been done is
what will be done; there is nothing new under the sun.'
Attributed to King Solomon, Ecclesiastes, 1:9

This account of the saga at the Bond Corporation group is partial –
an instalment. Much more is likely to emerge following the public
revelations from criminal and civil cases and the numerous regulatory
investigations previously undertaken and those currently in progress.[1]
Those matters are unlikely to be completed until the end of the 1990s.

Whilst an orderly, but informal liquidation of the Bond group of
companies probably began in about 1991, formally the group continued
to trade under a scheme of arrangement from the beginning of 1993
under the name of Southern Equities Corporation Ltd. That administration was to comprise two phases – initially a debt moratorium, followed
by the transformation of creditors' claims into ordinary and preference
shares, redeemable periodically until 31 December 1995. The appointment of a liquidator on 23 December 1993 halted those plans.[2]

Some of what follows is based on disclosed information, whilst other
matters are necessarily interpretative and conjectural.

The early life of the group's founder, Alan Bond – signwriter turned
multi-millionaire-cum-bankrupt – is told by Paul Barry:[3] 'Smiling, loud-
mouthed, uncomplicated, almost always cheerful, Alan Bond was a rags-
to-riches success, a role model for young Australians.' In 1985, 'Bondy'
(as Bob Hawke, the Australian Prime Minister, as well as many others,
referred to him) had already been awarded (in 1978) 'Businessman of
the Year'. He had received an Order of Australia in 1984 for services to
'yachting . . . [being] team captain of the successful America's Cup
challenge in 1983'. Then followed an 'Australian of the Year' award in
1987. He was, prior to the aftermath of the October 1987 share market
crash, presented as the epitome of Australian entrepreneurial spirit and
business acumen – a true success story. Within five years the sweetness of
success had soured. Alan Bond was declared bankrupt in April 1992,
imprisoned in 1993, then released six months later. In 1996, Bond was

164

gaoled over the *La Promenade* purchase and in 1997 faces further court charges over another matter described below; the auditor of the parent company of the Bond group is being sued over its handling of the company's 1988 audit.[4] The submissions, legal argument and outcomes of those matters should make fascinating reading, even though nearly a decade has elapsed since the main events.

Bond provides another instance of the Icarus paradox.[5] Success had quickly turned to failure. Adulation turned to derision, some claiming that the reported figures underpinning that adulation were illusory – perhaps even that the decline of the Bond group of companies may have begun as early as 1984.[6] A 'poor immigrant made good' tag draped comfortably on 'Bondy' in those heady days of the 1980s. Already he had become a multi-millionaire. His meteoric rise began with the 1956 signwriting company Nu Signs Pty Ltd. But the story of the Bond of recent fame begins with the 1967 formation of Bond Corporation Pty Ltd (Bond Corporation, the head of the Bond group), which he chaired from beginning to near its end. A reverse takeover in 1969 of Western Australian hardware merchant W. Drabble Ltd (renamed Amalgamated Industries Ltd) was the back-door means by which Bond Corporation achieved a stock exchange listing. The world, fame and fortune, public awards, national honours, the America's Cup victory, adulation, corporate collapse, bankruptcy, imprisonment and release, a heart attack, memory losses, liquidator's hearings, another imprisonment and other trials, all lay before its chairman, Alan Bond. It was a crowded agenda.

Growth by acquisition

Bond's *modus operandi* meshed real estate transactions and inter-group dealings. The following is only a slice of all BCH's investments and divestments occurring over 20 years.

The early 1970s witnessed an oft-repeated technique involving Alan Bond's group of public and private companies. Yanchep Estates Pty Ltd, a wholly-owned subsidiary of Bond Corporation, sold its half-interest in 1,450 lots of land in the Yanchep Sun City development project (near Perth) to a Bond Corporation-controlled company, W.A. Land Holdings; the half-interest was then resold to a company within the Bond group. W.A. Land Holdings then concentrated on diversifying its operations by acquiring Shield Life Assurance Ltd and the Savoy Corporation group of companies. In 1973 Bond Corporation acquired (on instalment) a 46 per cent interest in Robe River Ltd from the liquidator of the collapsed Mineral Securities (Australia) Ltd for $19.6 million.[7]

Each of the related companies within the Bond group owned a piece of the major action of the others whilst doing its own unique thing on the side. Individual company and group actions were inextricably intertwined. This was convenient, but as revealed in several of the other failures (for example, H.G. Palmer, Reid Murray, Cambridge, Adsteam, and the like), the Byzantine configuration had the potential of a house-of-cards. And it would prove a nightmare for creditors, judges and administrators when the pack imploded.

Nineteen seventy-four proved interesting. The Yanchep Sun City project was transferred from Yanchep Estates Pty Ltd to a new joint venture company, Yanchep Sun City Pty Ltd, owned by both the Tokyo Corporation of Japan and Bond Corporation. Eventually, Bond Corporation sold its interest to Tokyo Corporation. During 1974 a liquidity crisis emerged. Given the Australian wages and interest blow-out of 1974, Bond Corporation's debt-based expansion had overreached, as was the fate of other large property and construction companies at that time, including Mainline and Cambridge Credit. We have seen how placing the latter in receivership on 30 September 1974 created a panic in financial markets, which did not help Bond Corporation.

On 17 October 1974 the Perth Stock Exchange queried Bond Corporation's and home builder Landall Holdings' financial viability. Bond Corporation survived the scrutiny.

Recourse to another feature of Bond's operations (and, more recently, Rupert Murdoch's) then occurred – calling the banker's bluff, to forestall the banks 'calling in their chips'. According to Barry,[8] a frontal attack on the press and the bankers was used. With Spalvins' and Adsteam's critics the manoeuvre failed. With Alan Bond and Murdoch, it worked. Financial breathing space was achieved and Bond, after this period of expansion, merged Bond Corporation with W.A. Land Holdings. W.A. Land Holdings, the parent company, was renamed Bond Corporation Holdings Ltd on 12 June 1975. For this, another recurring technique was used – commingling private (family) company dealings with other public Bond group companies. Bond's family company, Dallhold Investments Pty Ltd, sold all its shares in Bond Corporation to W.A. Land Holdings for $17.6 million. Through a combination of direct and indirect means, Alan Bond remained the largest shareholder in BCH.

Contiguously, BCH reported a loss of $8.95 million for the 1975 financial year, claimed by the *Financial Review* to be 'one of the biggest ever by a local company'.[9] How quickly the 1960s failures had been forgotten!

Towards the end of the 1970s the Bond group changed its investment strategy. Interests in the Savoy Group of companies were disposed of. In May 1978 BCH acquired a 24 per cent shareholding in Endeavour Resources Ltd, and in August 1978 a consortium headed by BCH purchased Burmah Australia Exploration from Burmah Oil Australia for

$36 million, and changed its name to Bond Mining and Exploration Pty Ltd.[10] Its principal assets were shareholdings in Basin Oil N.L., Reef Oil N.L. and Santos Ltd, a Cooper Basin oil and gas field operator. The next two years produced continued buying and selling of corporate investments. The Santos investment proved one of BCH's most successful asset plays. By the end of 1979, BCH had achieved a paper profit of nearly $60 million on this investment.

Diversification and divestment – the name of the BCH game

Retail diversification was the portfolio play in 1981, as BCH acquired a 43 per cent interest in Waltons. Although Waltons Bond was heralded as a 'street-wise' smart move, this diversification proved to be an enormous longer-term financial drain on the group. But adulation is enjoyable and success contagious. Bond was on a deceptive roll. Everybody, it seems, was happy to be his friend and felt deprived if they were not.

We have drawn attention to conglomerate structures involving family and public companies being a recurring feature of Australian corporate failures. Growth has been through acquisition using share scrip as the consideration. Extreme diversity in operations is almost inevitable. Frequently, too, top management has neither the experience nor the capacity to control the labyrinths which they find themselves managing. It has been a common recipe for disaster which the flurry of takeover activity and hubris disguised, and in respect of which the obscurities of accounting erected a beguiling façade of success.

Whereas Adsteam's operations demonstrated that the true conglomerate has a finger in every industrial pie, BCH was still short of achieving that. Hence, forays into petroleum exploration were extended, primarily through the licensed area in Western Australia, WA-192P, complemented with further exploration acquisitions in the mid-1980s.

Acquisitions of diverse companies continued in 1982. In July Waltons Bond A.C.T. acquired all the issued capital in Norman Ross Discounts Ltd, with BCH and Waltons Bond each having a 50 per cent interest in Waltons Bond A.C.T. During 1982, BCH acquired all of the issued capital in The Swan Brewery Company Ltd (Western Australia's only brewer) for a total cost of $163 million. In turn, investments in Santos, Reef and Basin were disposed of for around $180 million. Deck-chairs were repositioned, but was the game proving profitable? At Santos – yes. With many others – no. Endeavour Resources Ltd also acquired Northern Mining Corporation N.L. in 1982. Meanwhile, on the retail front, BCH acquired just under 20 per cent of Grace Brothers. But there wasn't any sentiment. Subsequently, Myer Emporium's offer for Grace Brothers was accepted by shareholders, including both BCH and Waltons Bond A.C.T.

Mining investment dominated again in 1983. Northern Mining N.L. and Samcentre Pty Ltd were acquired from Endeavour Resources. This acquisition afforded BCH total direct ownership of the Rhonda Collieries in Queensland. Northern Mining's interest in the Argyle Diamond Mining venture was to prove controversial. BCH sold Northern Mining's 5 per cent interest in the Argyle Diamond Mines to the Western Australian government for $42 million. Poor performances continued to plague the operations of Waltons Bond; the conglomerate needed a 'cash cow', but Waltons was turning into a 'corporate dog'.

In August 1983 BCH increased its interest in Pacific Copper to over 90 per cent and also purchased a 31 per cent interest in Austmark International, a listed property developer. The Austmark acquisition was risky: it needed a reconstruction and revitalisation achieved through a cash issue in which BCH stood as principal underwriter.

Indeed, not all was rosy in the BCH group. Acquisition brings growth, but it does not necessarily generate property, increase wealth or ensure ongoing profits. Around this time *Australian Ratings* publicly expressed concerns about BCH's financial viability and re-examined its rating.

Waltons Bond's financial drain continued – it reported losses of $199.2 million in 1982/1983, while Austmark losses totalled $30.9 million that year. It was then that the America's Cup victory put a glow back into the conglomerate for some observers, even if only temporarily. Group reported profits in 1983 were $6.84 million (see Table 13.2 on p. 179). But any feeling of satisfaction was temporary as the next two years produced losses of $13.59 million and $6.99 million (on sales of $365.3 million and $517.8 million, respectively). Whilst financial prudence dictated that this reported performance trend could not continue, the acquisition policy did!

BCH entered the media by purchasing an interest in the Swan Television and Radio Broadcasters Ltd, operating in Western Australia. In early 1984, BCH expressed interest in, and not long after had control of, Winthrop Investments Limited, a company which owned various business properties in Victoria, the North Kalgurli gold mines and the hydro-carbons explorer Petro Energy, and had a controlling interest in Mid-East Minerals (which ran the Greenvale nickel mine).

By then Bond's blimp, synonymous with BCH, slow-moving with whirring engines, was a well-known sight, especially over the northern suburbs of Sydney. Residents of some of Sydney's prime suburbs in the executive belt, Wahroonga and Turramurra, objected to the snail-like observation platform sliding over their roof tops, interrupting their pool parties. Nonetheless, the blimp did conjure up the image of property and prosperity – evidence of conspicuous consumption – and whereas the locals may not have been in love with the noise, perhaps they regarded its promoter with some affection. It was no surprise when in October 1984 BCH increased its interest in Airship Industries to 82 per cent. Under an agreement with Nissan in Japan, BCH could manufacture (under licence) and sell airships in Australasia. This was to prove one of BCH's poorer investments. Airship Industries reported losses in financial years 1987 to 1989 of $5.2 million, $3.7 million and over $15 million, respectively. BCH eventually sold its interest in Airship Industries in 1991, incurring a substantial book loss.

In January 1985 BCH acquired Queensland Television (the operators of Channel Nine, Brisbane), increased expenditure ($75 million) on the Harnett offshore oilfield near Barrow Island, and in February sold its 6.7 per cent stake in Hooker for a profit of about $2 million. Rearrangement of the deck-chairs continued.

January 1985 also produced an example of a significant related-party transaction: 'Millions of dollars were tucked into private companies such as Shield Enterprises. . . . Shield came to public attention in the mid-1980s [for] receiving $8 million in tax-free profits when another [Bond group] company, Lapstone, with its subsidiary Bond Oil, were sold to Shield for just $100 in January 1985.'[11] Similar asset transfers were facilitated by setting up a legal web of trustee companies and trusts, for the benefit of Alan Bond's family. This type of manoeuvre upsets many observers, yet Australian governments over several decades have been aware of the tactic but have not prevented it. It is an apt instance of regulatory failure.

A 5 per cent stake in Arnott's was purchased in January, followed by a $400 million takeover offer. This was thwarted by the 10 per cent holding gained by Campbell's Soup Company, eventually to gain control of Arnott's in 1992. Then in June 1985 the interest in Waltons Bond A.C.T. was sold to Waltons Bond.

Alan Bond's *magic* did not insulate BCH from the need to meet the necessary conditions for ultimate financial success. BCH was buying existing assets, often companies, at a breathtaking rate, revaluing them and, on the basis of the revalued collateral, borrowing further to stake-up in order to repeat the process with another acquisition. This resembled the 'daisy chain' method so prevalent in US Savings and Loans' operations throughout the early 1980s: on-selling through related companies at ever increasing prices, booking profits on the way, and edging up the capacity to borrow on the security of the higher book value of the assets. It is similar also to Samuel Insull's utilities asset pyramiding mechanisms in 1920s pre-depression America. Without an externally verifiable, continuous, marked-to-market asset valuation practice, it was bound to have much the same result.

A critical link in a growth-by-acquisition strategy using borrowed funds is the market veracity of the valuations of assets pledged as collateral. In that respect, from the mid-1980s onwards some of Bond's companies, like the more-or-less contemporary Adsteam, and H.G. Palmer two decades earlier, were using cross guarantees and negative pledges (covenants protecting existing lenders' security) as part of their standard loan agreements. The need for verified, continual up-to-date asset valuations was clear, but there are doubts about delivery.

None of those technicalities dampened the pace of the acquisitions. During July 1985 BCH acquired all the issued capital of Castlemaine Tooheys at a cost of $1.2 billion; in February 1986 the US regional brewer, Pittsburgh Brewing Company, was acquired for US$29.8 million; in April, the Screen Entertainment Division of Thorn EMI, was purchased for £125 million and soon after sold to Cannon (UK) for £175 million. Judicious use of Jersey's tax haven status and subsidiary company dealings produced zero taxes on that deal for British coffers. Barry claims the ploy was repeated many times in the 1980s, often using the Cook Islands tax haven.[12]

Arguably that is good business, just like Bond's legal use of trusts, though commentators seem to want to take the *moral commercial high ground* in respect of it. What is missing in that moral maze is the immorality of fuelling the exercise with asset valuations at odds with the market. Whilst everybody is entitled to arrange their affairs legally to minimise their tax, our view is that nobody can justify asset valuations which market evidence refutes.

During 1986 BCH effectively acquired nearly all of the property owned by its associate, Waltons Bond. Disposals by BCH also occurred during that year, including the sale of Southern Cross Beverages Pty Ltd (a soft drinks business) for $107 million and of British Vitamin Products Ltd (a former investment of Castlemaine Tooheys), and also the disposal of various hotels, which previously had been owned by Castlemaine Tooheys and Swan Brewery, to the Austotel Trust for $326 million.

Next came BCH's move into Australia's fastest growing export industry – education. Bond University, the first private university in Australia, was the vehicle. That possibly was a landmark for BCH too, for here something was created, not just acquired. Figure 13.1 illustrates BCH's complex operations at this time.

The scale of the acquisitions was beyond anything previously experienced in Australia. Their timing also is important. The 1986/87 and 1987/88 financial years resulted in the greatest scrutiny of the accounting practices of BCH. During 1987 the acquisition binge continued.

BCH spent more than $5 billion on acquisitions – the $1 billion purchase of the Nine Network from Kerry Packer, a US$262 million stake in the Chile telephone company Componia de Telefonos de Chile, an investment in Chilean gold mines and, in September 1987, the

Figure 13.1 Bond Corporation Holdings Ltd group structure as at 30 June 1985

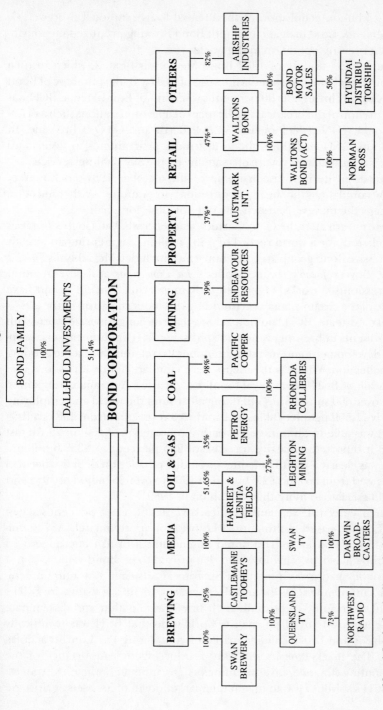

Note: * Includes indirect holdings.
Source: Australian Business, 13 November 1985, p. 18.

US$1.3 billion acquisition of the ill-fated fourth largest US brewer, G. Heileman & Co. Amalgamation with Bond Brewing produced the fourth-largest brewing operation in the world.

During the middle of 1987 Bond Media was floated, which in turn acquired the remaining media interests of BCH with the purchase of Bond Television. Through its 50 per cent ownership of Bond Media, BCH was able to control the broadcasting licences of television stations such as TCN 9 Sydney, GTV 9 Melbourne, STW 9 Perth and QTQ 9 Brisbane. In addition, BCH had the right to distribute programmes to hotels and motels Australia-wide via use of a satellite on the Sky Channel service.

Not even the unforeseen blimp of the October 1987 stock market crash could halt the heady acquisition programme. With hindsight, perhaps the massive *ponzi* scheme did not allow for a halt.

One month after the October stock market crash, Van Gogh's *Irises* was 'purchased' for a world record of A$61 million, augmenting an already impressive Bond group art collection which included McCubbin's *Finding Time*, Boyd's *Jacob's Dream*, Monet's *La Promenade* and several other Impressionists' works.[13] One can only muse what Vincent would have made of the circumstances surrounding this modern patron of the arts.

Like Adsteam, BCH had now achieved a true conglomerate status, with investments in brewing, wine and spirits, media, communications, property development and investment, minerals, retailing and a burgeoning art collection. Whereas the tactics were familiar, Figure 13.1 shows that the scale of BCH was atypical for all except a few Australian companies, with over 600 subsidiaries operating all around the world and employing nearly 11,500 people. Tables 13.2 and 13.3 reveal that from 1987 to 1989 BCH was able to announce increasing reported profits – on 22 August 1988 it reported a massive increase of 255 per cent to $355.6 million. This was clearly a useful outcome given that reliance on debt finance had increased from around $2.6 billion in 1986 to over $6 billion in 1988 and would escalate to more than $9 billion in 1989.

Then, early in 1988, came a critical investment, a 19.8 per cent stake in the London-based multinational Lonrho for approximately A$700 million. Bond's tilt at Lonrho pitted him against a British buccaneer and Lonrho chairman, Tiny Rowland. He proved to be Bond's nemesis, just as Brierley had proved to be for Spalvins at Adsteam. Rowland immediately commanded his financial executives to find a chink in BCH's financial armour – reportedly their brief was to gather and disseminate evidence to financial journalists world-wide that BCH was technically insolvent and financially incapable of completing the Lonrho acquisition. The market *cognoscenti* were reinforcing the importance of the accounting/finance/investment nexus, for, ultimately, the only true test of BCH's solvency was to match the market worth of its assets against the amount of its liabilities. What BCH had *paid* for its assets in various takeover plays was and always would be irrelevant in that assessment.

Interestingly, in the Lonrho joust 76 million of the 95 million Lonrho shares were not bought by a wholly-owned company within the BCH group, but by a subsidiary of Bell Resources at a cost of A$623 million. This was evidence again of group enterprise, not entity action in operation, for it must be recognised that Bell Resources was at the time a majority-owned subsidiary of BCH. The intertwining of the interests of the two separate, publicly-listed companies would prove controversial in subsequent years, as had similar practices in the Sydney Guarantee Ltd – Stanhill Consolidated Ltd link in the 1960s. BCH effectively was able to bypass the Bell Resources shareholders, who were not even given the opportunity to voice an opinion concerning the purchase. This arrangement benefited BCH as it left relatively little impact on BCH's balance sheet. At issue is the potential for conflict of interest when the affairs of two public companies whose boards include common directors are so intertwined.

On another front, the aborted rescue of the late Laurie Connell's Rothwells Limited added to BCH's woes.

Rothwells rescue – what are friends for?

When Laurie Connell's investment company Rothwells teetered on the brink of collapse in the wake of the October 1987 stock market crash, it was Alan Bond who engineered and led the rescue effort. Reportedly, together with Western Australian Premier Brian Burke, Bond hired James Yonge of Wardleys to approach various entrepreneurs for funds. An amount of $380 million was raised, and coupled to an additional sum of $150 million provided by the National Australia Bank. NAB, however, claimed that its advance was covered by a WA government guarantee.[14] Late in 1993 this dispute was settled out of court, reportedly in favour of the bank.

Rothwells' rescue plan entailed the WA government using the State Government Insurance Commission to buy 20 per cent of the Bell group from a Holmes à Court-owned company. BCH likewise was required to purchase a 20 per cent share. In this way, it has been reported that the two entities would have control of Bell Resources and its $2 billion in cash, in return for a relatively small outlay of $130 million each. The Bell Resources cash would then be used to purchase Petrochemical Industries Corporation Ltd from Connell for $400 million. After paying $50 million to his partner, Connell would have $350 million to pay off his poorly performing debts to Rothwells, thereby relieving the WA government of its purported guarantee to the NAB.[15] It had been described as a win–win situation for all. However, arguably there were also negative financial consequences for certain shareholders and creditors, not to mention employees.

BCH director Peter Beckwith reportedly suggested that the SGIC and BCH had in reality acted in unison. Giving an insight into the nature of the transaction relating to the shareholding in Bell Resources, he explained:

> The Government's involvement in PIL and its shareholding via the SGIC in the Bell Group were from day one enmeshed. The Government, having acquired the stake in Bell Group, proposed to this company [BCH] that the cash strength of Bell Resources be used to buy what was then PIL for a sum sufficient to enable Mr Connell to fund Rothwells to retire the Government guarantee before the Government faced the electorate. From that point forward, the Government continued to invite and induce our participation in this project.[16]

It appears unlikely that the plant was worth $400 million. Indeed, the value of the site is estimated to have been worth varying amounts to a low of $10 million.

A contentious aspect of this manoeuvre to gain control of Bell Resources and its 'pot' of cash was the $1.2 billion which Bell Resources subsequently 'lent' downstream within the BCH group, via a supposed 'deposit' being paid by Bell Resources for the brewing assets of Bond Brewing Holdings. In January 1995 criminal fraud charges were laid against Alan Bond and two other BCH directors over this transaction. Begun in 1996, the trial is scheduled to reconvene in April 1997. Whilst not commenting on the propriety of the transaction, the shuffling of funds in that manner arguably strikes at the heart of a fundamental principle of English law, the separate legal entity principle, of which we have more to say in Chapters 15 and 16.

On investigation the NCSC perceived the substance of the arrangement to involve associated groups buying 40 per cent of Bell group without making a full bid. It was the decision of the NCSC to ignore the technical (legal) form, which ensured that the two purchases would not be linked. The NCSC ruled that BCH had to put up $520 million for 80 per cent of the Bell group, in effect forcing the company to make a full bid, while excluding the 20 per cent the SGIC would continue to hold. This meant that the survival of BCH had become entangled with the liquidation of Bell, the Rothwells rescue and the value of PIL and, most importantly, the concurrent battle at Lonrho.

Confluence of these and other matters, such as the battles with the Australian Broadcasting Tribunal over whether Alan Bond was a 'fit and proper person' to hold a TV licence and the Channel Nine settlement, meant BCH's battle-front was expanding. Financial strains meant that the beginning of an unofficial liquidation of BCH was imminent.

BCH asset sales were frenetic during the 1988/89 and 1989/90 financial years as part of that unofficial liquidation. Substantial creditors' repayments were crucial to the survival of the group. Bankers demanded that debt be pared. Assets previously held by the Bell Group and Bell Resources were sold for approximately $1.8 billion, including the Lonrho investment at a loss of £110 million. Other major group asset sales were negotiated: $170 million for BCH's Harriet Oil stake; $140 million for the holding in ITC Entertainment; $25.5 million from selling the 10 per cent stake in TV-AM; a 50 per cent stake in the Hong Kong Bond Centre to joint venture partner EIE Development (International) Ltd for HK$1.3 billion; St Moritz Hotel (N.Y.) to creditor FAI Insurances Ltd; a half interest in the R&I Bank Building for $108 million; the remaining half share in the St George's hospital site in London for about $100 million; and the Australian coal mining operations to FAI for $199 million.

This was restructuring on a massive scale. As always, creditors' obligations had to be satisfied with cash or its equivalent. All the mythical book values and the artifacts of conventional accounting – the FITBs and other 'deferred' bookkeeping debits – would count for nothing in that exercise.

Unfortunately, the desirable impact of the 1988/89 asset disposals was mitigated somewhat by several significant purchases during the same period. A 56.25 per cent interest in that notorious Western Australian petrochemical plant consumed $225 million. Another $182 million was spent on a further stake in the Chilean telephone company, and $40 million on purchasing a number of coal mines from BHP. But divestment of the Chilean venture in 1990 yielded an estimated profit of A$90 million. Outflows continued as a controlling stake in J.N. Taylor Holdings Ltd was achieved with an additional share purchase for $39 million late in 1988. And the outcome, as Nolan notes: dealings between J.N. Taylor Holdings Ltd (the 'cash box') and related companies of the BCH group, especially the Bond family company, Dallhold Investments Pty Ltd, which are the subject of legal action and regulatory investigation.[17] More is certain to unfold on this aspect as the investigations and legal actions are completed and eventually disclosed to the public.

Exacerbating matters for BCH, the Lonrho misadventure was just around the corner.

Lonrho – tears of death

Table 13.1 shows that towards the end of 1988, BCH's share price began to slide. That proved irreversible. However, BCH continued to spearhead a takeover of the international trading house, Lonrho. The *raison d'être* was familiar. The plan was to use the cash and asset power of Lonrho to

Table 13.1 Bond Corporation Holdings Ltd selected last trade daily share prices, 1985/86 to 1989/90

| Year | Month beginning | | | | | |
	1 July $	1 Sept. $	1 Nov. $	1 Jan. $	1 Mar. $	1 May $
1985–86	1.23	1.80	2.20	1.80	2.50	3.85
1986–87	3.38	3.25	2.82	2.56	2.70	2.60
1987–88	2.49	2.75	1.50	1.80	1.65	1.85
1988–89	2.28	1.95	1.86	1.85	1.58	1.19
1989–90	0.92	0.47	0.29	0.13	n.a.	n.a.

Source: Sydney Stock Exchange Investment Review Service, Bond Corporation Holdings Ltd, B191.

buy the British brewer Allied-Lyons and use the latter's cash flow to venture into the field of telecommunications. This strategy had worked for BCH in the past.

Emerging in 1985 from a critical period of market pessimism, the share price moved along steadily with the general market upsurge in 1986 and 1987. Whilst suffering initially from the October 1987 crash, the price stabilised between $1.50 and $2.00. Downward pressure increased in early 1989 with further institutional selling of BCH stock. A manoeuvre was hatched and the counter-attack on Lonrho was mounted, causing the share price to rally temporarily. Directors of BCH, one suspects especially Alan Bond, clearly had not properly predicted Tiny Rowland's response. Rowland vigorously and publicly questioned BCH's financial credibility, to such an extent that, ultimately, BCH retreated.[18]

The Lonrho joust is instructive. As well as illustrating BCH's penchant for enterprise rather than entity action, it illustrates a certain style of decision making at BCH, especially in the latter stage of its life. Some have alleged that the BCH board ratified decisions of the three-man executive committee *ex post facto*, that there was little documentation backing some major investment decisions, and that there was an inadequate mechanism for communicating information about them to lower operational managers.[19] Decision making in respect of Lonrho prompted this comment by Mr Justice Sir Nicholas Brown-Wilkinson in assessing the 'need-to-know' philosophy of the three-man executive running BCH: 'It is a very remarkable phenomenon when you have a company that had by that stage invested 360 million pounds-odd (now $A781 million) that not a single piece of paper is available supporting that fact.'[20]

That comment is *déjà vu* for those familiar with the international dealings over 60 years earlier of another corporate buccaneer, the Swedish match-king Ivar Kreuger. He is reputed to have kept most of the financial details of his multinational conglomerate, Kreuger and Toll Inc. and its international match empire, in his head![21] This of course made auditing that colossus a difficult exercise. Whenever information is released only on a 'need-to-know' basis, a similar difficulty arises.

Back to BCH. The 93-page financial document, 'The Bond Group of Companies: A Financial Analysis by Lonrho Plc', selectively released world-wide on 28 November 1988, contained criticisms of BCH's accounting and managerial practices. It concluded that BCH was 'technically insolvent'. It was circulated to financial houses and bankers around the world – corporate dirty-tricks at its best. Yet, despite its apparent financial sophistication, its analysis is problematic to the extent that it relied on conventional historical cost data.[22] However, it has been suggested that without the tenacity and resources of a Tiny Rowland, it is unlikely that the extent of the BCH group's complex intra-group arrangements would eventually have been revealed to the public.[23] If true, placed with the obfuscation previously noted (at, for example, Adsteam), such a state of affairs is surely cause for concern, as it strikes a body-blow to claims of market efficiency and the adequacy of regulatory checks and balances. We return to this aspect of 'the system' in the final four chapters.

Lonrho's document produced, amongst the overseas community of investment analysts, a general consensus that the looseness of Australia's Accounting Standards was to be blamed for allowing BCH to deviate and engage in creative accounting, a line of reasoning that appears in respect of several major publicly-disclosed transactions to have been unfounded.

Clearly, the implication of that consensus was that tighter enforcement rules would have saved the day. In reality, being able to depart from the Standards or to interpret them idiosyncratically is potentially a force for the good. Contrary to general belief, with respect to several instances of misleading data and contested interpretation, the evidence is that BCH generally complied with the Accounting Standards and legal accounting requirements rather than deviated or departed from them.

Irrespective of whether the Lonrho document was accurate in depicting BCH's financial state, the convergence of several factors and Rowland's attack was fatal. BCH's share price fell rapidly during the latter part of 1989. Those other contributive factors were varied. In the first week of May 1989, *Australian Ratings* announced that BCH would be downgraded from a B credit rating to CCC, signifying 'poor debt protection levels'. BCH responded to this news by selling a major asset, its remaining half share in the Bond Centre in Hong Kong. It also began a buy-back plan of its shares in an effort to prop up its share price. Further bad news occurred when the Australian Broadcasting Tribunal announced its findings on 26 June that Alan Bond was not a 'fit and proper person' to hold a TV licence. And the ASX suspended trading in Bell Resources. A triple whammy had hit the Bond empire.

The extent of the damage was implicit in the 1989 Chairman's Report: 'Over the period spanning the 1985 to 1988 financial years total group assets grew more than seven fold and operating revenue grew eight fold ... substantially financed by debt' (p. 2). Such debt-financed growth was unsustainable even if the assets were worth their book values. Conjecture continues as to why the banks had maintained financing for it. The relationship between Alan Bond and BCH's bankers has become legend.[24] Apparently, normal prudential limits were by-passed, and this was further exacerbated in the early 1980s by Alan Bond's introduction to Michael Milken and BCH's dubious financing trifecta: negative pledges, cross guarantees and junk-bond financing.[25]

That fateful day on which the public at large was to read of Bond's collapse in the *Financial Review* had arrived. Shortly thereafter, on 29 December 1989, trading in BCH securities was suspended following the appointment of a receiver to Bond Brewing Holdings Ltd. The receiver was removed three months later, but liquidation was looking ever more likely.

During 1990 BCH staggered towards a formal liquidation. Then, in early 1991, Alan Bond resigned as chairman, with the group's creditors effectively administering BCH's affairs. Initially, under an informal arrangement, a formal scheme commenced in August 1991 and, finally, a liquidator was appointed in December 1993.

BCH's *ponzi* scheme had run out of acquisition options. At every turn in this commercial saga the BCH numbers men and the practices of accounting had played their vital role.

Accounting's temporary survival kit

BCH relied primarily on debt to engineer its earliest investments. Even after the October 1987 stock market crash BCH was able to go on a multi-million-dollar investment spree. It was revealed that BCH continued to finance acquisitions with debt (Table 13.2). Not surprisingly, the largest of international bankers and financiers, all presumably part of the 'informed' financial market, were caught when BCH finally went under, including Hongkong and Shanghai Bank, American Express Bank, Standard Chartered Bank, Salomon Bros, Midlands Bank, Drexel Burnham Lambert's clients, Barclays Bank, First National Bank of Boston and the local banks, NAB and Westpac.[26]

Following the October 1987 stock market crash other entrepreneurial companies were winding back their operations, yet BCH was expanding.

Table 13.2   Summary financial statistics of the operations of Bond
Corporation Holdings Ltd (consolidated data), 1982 to 1991

Year	Sales (other revenue) $m	Statex adjusted profits $m	Total assets $m	Total debt $m
1982	244.1	4.3	447.2	237.3
1983	308.7	6.8	531.1	276.7
1984	365.3	(13.6)	700.4	473.9
1985	517.8	(7.0)	1,221.2	874.1
1986	1,600.7	76.7	2,771.7	2,190.2
1987	2,281.9	104.7	4,115.6	2,690.4[2]
1988	4,616.9	338.6	9.015.3[1]	6,387.2[2]
1989	7,666.1	(834.7)	11,703.8[1]	9,168.9
1990	9,073.9	(1,069.0)	2,215.9[1]	2,594.8
1991[3]	339.3	(642.5)	526.8	1,822.9

Notes: 1 Intangible items were negligible before 1985; thereafter they were
$486.9 million (1986), $486.5 million (1987), $2,460 million (1988),
$2,897.5 million (1989) and $396.1 million (1990).
2 Total debt excludes Convertible Notes amounting to $457.5 million (1987)
and $707.5 million (1988).
3 For nine months' operations only.
Source: Based on *Sydney Stock Exchange Statex Service* B191, run on 16 December
1991 (reproduced as Table 13.3).

Questioned on the incongruity of it all, Bond responded that BCH had
a solid 'cash flow' to see it through the difficult times. Such queries
continued throughout the latter part of the 1980s. Some in the market
clearly were concerned. The share price of BCH declined to around
$1.80 from its $3 pre-October 1987 price. It levelled off in 1988, peaked
early in 1989 at $1.86 and then slipped further in the aftermath of the
Lonrho affair. By September 1989 it had fallen to 47 cents per share,
nearly half its July price. Obviously the market was nurturing major
reservations about the viability of BCH by this stage. For BCH to survive,
drastic surgery to its debt levels was necessary. Sale of the brewing assets
was essential. But the sale dragged on over many months. Uncertainty
and unease over the group's prospects increased.

BCH's growth strategy has many parallels with Reid Murray and
Stanhill in the 1960s, the Cambridge Credit Corporation and Gollins
sagas, and many others in the 1970s and 1980s. Borrowings growth
needed to finance BCH's *ponzi*-type investments relied on its public
image of wealth and progress, on its ability to report increased profits
and growth in net assets. Clearly the role of accounting was crucial.
Accounting Standards did not force the reporting of continuous, rather
than *ad hoc*, audited market values of physical assets. To a substantial

Table 13.3 Bond Corporation Holdings Ltd – Statex balance sheet summary and ratios, 30 June 1982 to 30 June 1991

	30/6/91 $000	05/10/90 $000	30/6/89 $000	30/6/88 $000	30/6/87 $000	30/6/86 $000	30/6/85 $000	30/6/84 $000	30/6/83 $000	30/6/82 $000
Cash and liquids	11,845	43,700	609,100	473,500	288,501	192,641	196,559	55,528	56,344	12,499
Trade debtors	1,791	63,400	451,600	486,600	117,126	113,096	31,055	21,702	15,141	22,420
Stocks	33,349	93,100	380,300	254,500	164,066	100,364	37,251	26,738	22,029	17,894
Other current assets	53,965	229,400	544,500	900,200	793,933	502,831	163,855	64,998	18,300	11,640
Total current assets	100,950	429,600	1,985,500	2,114,800	1,363,626	908,932	428,720	168,966	111,814	64,453
Bank overdraft	5,534	9,500	82,300	50,700	24,906	28,559	8,435	2,984	6,295	5,187
Trade creditors	9,834	77,500	695,900	481,800	150,812	201,431	87,222	39,624	25,430	28,611
Tax provisions	38,886	32,000	423,000	41,300	28,105	141,768	29,469	19,033	5,354	8,670
Debt due in one year	1,535,357	2,101,800	2,811,200	1,505,700	402,610	490,174	103,547	68,251	78,596	61,077
Other current liabilities	210,914	289,500	461,100	231,100	58,923	67,378	62,399	18,670	8,061	10,295
Current liabilities	1,800,525	2,510,300	4,092,800	2,310,600	665,356	929,310	291,072	148,562	123,736	113,840
Net working capital	-1,699,575	-2,080,700	-2,107,300	-195,800	698,270	-20,378	137,648	20,404	-11,922	-49,387
Net plant and property	122,956	540,000	3,639,300	1,889,600	760,459	372,913	189,219	141,253	133,031	135,485
Investments	229,926	670,800	1,870,600	1,219,300	1,073,060	474,512	274,237	209,118	160,242	186,343
Deferred assets	73,008	179,400	1,310,900	1,331,500	431,924	528,456	321,895	166,933	121,376	59,345
Total invested capital	-1,273,685	-690,500	4,713,500	4,244,600	2,963,713	1,355,503	922,999	537,708	402,727	331,786
Long-term debt	7	84,500	4,900,800	3,619,800	1,911,603	1,247,929	575,397	321,263	148,336	122,479
Other deferred liability	22,367	-315,100	175,300	456,800	113,482	12,990	7,649	4,116	4,603	990
Minority interest	0	89,700	1,908,500	1,029,400	220,924	100,143	80,134	11,745	13,706	414
Preferred capital	0	0	0	0	0	0	49,103	49,103	49,103	0
Ordinary equity	-1,296,059	-549,600	-2,271,100	-861,400	717,704	-5,559	210,716	151,481	186,979	207,903
Total invested funds	-1,273,685	-690,500	4,713,500	4,244,600	2,963,713	1,355,503	922,999	537,708	402,727	331,786

Total tangible assets	526,840	1,819,800	8,806,300	6,555,200	3,629,069	2,284,813	1,214,071	686,270	526,463	445,626
Intangibles	0	396,100	2,897,500	2,460,100	486,548	486,898	7,152	14,145	4,601	1,621
Total assets	526,840	2,215,900	11,703,800	9,015,300	4,115,617	2,771,711	1,221,223	700,415	531,064	447,247
Balance sheet ratios										
Liquid ratio	0.03	0.13	0.40	0.82	1.87	0.89	1.38	0.97	0.76	0.42
Current ratio	0.05	0.17	0.48	0.91	2.04	0.97	1.47	1.13	0.90	0.56
Shareholders' interest	245.9	25.2	4.0	2.6	25.9	4.1	28.0	30.9	47.4	46.7
% Market/book listed inv.	123.4	103.6	98.6	83.5	91.3	131.9	86.1	76.7	57.6	70.8
Net assets/share (adj.)	−2.01	−0.85	−3.40	−1.28	1.23	−0.01	0.62	0.65	0.80	0.89
Dilution factor used	1.00	1.00	1.00	1.00	1.00	0.69	0.48	0.30	0.30	0.30
Long-term debt/equity	0.0	−15.3	−215.7	−420.2	266.3	−22,448.8	273.0	212.0	79.3	58.9
Short-term debt/equity	−118.1	−384.1	−127.4	−180.6	59.5	−9,331.4	53.1	47.0	45.4	31.8
Profit after tax, after minority interest (000)										
As per Bond Corporation Holdings Limited	(642,491)	(1,065,900)	(814,100)	354,700	117,720	86,611	(5,647)	(13,585)	6,837	4,299
As per Statex	(642,491)	(1,069,000)	(834,700)	338,600	104,649	76,684	(6,990)	(13,585)	6,837	4,299
Sales (000)	339,269	9,073,900	7,666,100	4,616,900	2,281,932	1,600,710	517,815	365,270	308,653	244,091

Source: Sydney Stock Exchange Statex Service, BCH (B191), run on 16 December 1991; data are on a consolidated basis.

extent the application of many Standards prevented it. Reinforcement of the significance of the holding company/subsidiary structure, and the validation of consolidation accounting and injection of accounting artifacts thickened the financial morass. Singularly and collectively the Standards ensured that the generic defects of conventional accounting differed little from the positions prevailing in respect to similar matters decades earlier. In some senses the importance of that role may have been exacerbated inadvertently; the existence of the increasing number of Accounting Standards perhaps created a sense of false security for the investing public – a façade of protection from the generic problems.

Tables 13.2, 13.3 and the following analysis of specific practices during the period 1986–1988 disclose the significance of chosen accounting treatments publicly disclosed by BCH. Interestingly the forthcoming audit litigation is in respect of this period. Our account is based on the public information revealed at the time this volume went to print. Not being privy to the detailed matters outlined in the claim against BCH's auditor, what follows passes no comment on them. But we await with interest to see whether new material particulars are revealed as a result of that action.

Financial statements for 1986/87 and 1987/88

BCH's financials received mixed assessments from financial observers. Early in 1987 financial journalists Meagher and Chong had made this assessment: 'Bond's two biggest moves – the Castlemaine Tooheys purchase and Packer buyout – have collected prime assets and cash flow that leave the group in a comfortable position.'[27] Following the October 1987 crash, Philip Rennie was having a bet each way in this assessment: 'At any other time of share market crises in the past 15 years Bond Corporation would have been one of the first companies subject to disaster rumours. Yet there are none after the worst stock market crash in history. Some property companies that were put into receivership in 1974 were rumoured to be more solvent than Bond Corporation.'[28] A somewhat more sombre assessment appeared early in 1988 by Accounting professor Bob Walker, who exposes the perverse nature of accounting:

> . . . one could not expect to find many gains or losses from the sale of businesses treated as extraordinary items because Bond Corp specifies that the 'primary operations' . . . include 'the disposition of assets acquired during the period or held for trading purposes from prior years'.
> . . . 'normal operations of the group, . . . include operations . . . of material once only transactions'. Readers are advised that 'while relatively few of these transactions may be completed in any one year, their effect on the group's results is not regarded as being abnormal nor outside the principal operations of the group'. . . . extraordinary items which to Bond Corp are just ordinary items.[29]

Terminological niceties were used to veil what was really occurring, all under the rubric of compliance.

Two weeks later, under the caption 'Window dressing at Bond Corporation', Walker this time commented on two other technical accounting matters – one relating to tax effect accounting, and the second relating to the treatment of convertible bonds. Both these items were accounted for in a manner which, according to Walker, maximised 'the impression of growth and liquidity'.[30] Another accounting treatment having a further positive effect on BCH's financial outcome related to foreign currency. These three treatments and their effects on the 1986/87 and 1987/88 accounts are of great significance, for they invited inferences regarding BCH's financial stability from the only publicly available financial information at the time – BCH's published financial statements. They provided valuable insights into the role of accounting information and, in particular, with respect to the matter of compliance with Australia's Accounting Standards.

Reminiscent of the reliance placed upon usual or standard practice in the 1920s Royal Mail accounting saga in the United Kingdom, there was no categorical claim that BCH had not complied with the Standards. Certainly the accounts were duly audited as such. No doubt they would be claimed to offend 'the spirit' of the Standards – but 'the spirit' resides as much in the opportunity for alternative interpretations, the looseness of and omissions in the Standards, as in what they state. With H.G. Palmer the court also revealed 'omission of material particulars' – specifically, failure to make adequate *provision for bad and doubtful debts*, which produced a reported profit of £408,371 in 1964 and a year earlier a profit of £431,624. Whether accounting at BCH was creative or feral, whether material particulars were omitted from the accounts, whether parties are brought to book for any actions, may be determined by the courts in the late 1990s.

On the matter of BCH's 'cheques in the drawer'

BCH's 1986/87 financial statements reported the proceeds from $457 million in convertible bonds as having been received prior to the balance date. On this matter the use of *notes* to the accounts is instructive. They were 'noted' to have been approved by shareholders at an extraordinary general meeting on 26 June 1987 and the proceeds (amounting to US$200 million and £80 million) not to have been received until 9 July 1987.[31] The convertible bonds transactions thereby qualified as a significant 'post-balance date event'. Such a treatment was actually applied in the 1986/87 accounts in respect of the issue of A$250 million worth of convertible bonds to Monstrot Pty Ltd, a company in which Alan Bond had 'a substantial financial interest'.[32] These treatments appear to have complied with Accounting Standards, at least to the auditor's satisfaction.

Professor Walker has argued that there is a parallel between BCH's treatment of its post-balance date convertible bonds receipts and the more common commercial problem of the 'cheques in the drawer'.[33] Possibly this difference of opinion says as much about the looseness of Accounting Standards as the use BCH made of them. BCH's subsequent treatment of those convertible bonds drew upon 'assumption' rather than fact. Boom periods allow a company's directors to argue that its convertible bonds should be counted as part of equity capital, *in anticipation* that subsequently they would be converted into shares. Quite curiously, many Accounting Standards explicitly countenance the injection of the products of directors' conjectures into the accounts.

When the market crashed in October 1987 the exercise price of BCH's convertible bonds sat well above the company's share price and the probability of their conversion into shares became remote. Arguably, by 1987/88, it would have been more realistic to treat the convertible bonds as a form of debt to be redeemed at the option of the holder, for the only chance that the bonds had of being converted into ordinary shares was if BCH's share price recovered to above the conversion price of $2.89.[34] During 1986 and 1987, conversion was a possibility, since the conversion price of the bonds was marginally above the market price of the shares. However, during 1988, bondholders were faced with a substantial premium if they decided to convert their bonds into shares. Financial common sense would have dictated that the convertible bonds would not have been converted into shares. An even more common-sense approach would have been to 'tell it like it is' and not impute private conjecture which was unable to be corroborated by public fact.

The effect of that imputation was to artificially strengthen the 1986/87 balance sheet in two ways. First, it decreased the ratio of total liabilities to total shareholders' equity – by treating convertible bonds as part of shareholders' equity, this succeeded in increasing shareholders' equity and decreasing liabilities for 30 June 1987. During 1986/87, the debt to equity ratio was noticeably strengthened ('liabilities' fell from approximately 3 times to double shareholders' equity). Second, the balance sheet also looked better by virtue of doubling the current ratio. BCH applied the yet-to-be-received proceeds of the issue to 'repay certain term advances' with only the balance augmenting the amount of receivables. Thus, current liabilities were decreased by $299.9 million, while current assets (receivables and other current assets) were increased by the residual, $157.5 million.[35] This method contrasts with the usual, but not mandatory, treatment of convertible bonds being reported as a liability, which has a relatively small impact on the current ratio, since both current assets and non-current liabilities are increased, effectively off-setting one another.

Preparation of the 1987/88 accounts was subject to a new Schedule 7, and to the protestations of the NCSC that it would be scrutinising company accounts even more closely. The revised Schedule 7 prescribed mandatory treatment of convertible bonds (and other debt securities which could be converted into shares) by specifying that they had to be shown as long-term borrowings in the accounts, come what may.[36]

Recasting the 1987/88 accounts in accord with the new Schedule 7 requirements would have resulted in BCH's shareholders' equity being reported at $1.92 billion, rather than the $2.63 billion. Conversely, total liabilities would have risen from $6.39 billion to $7.10 billion, producing at 30 June 1988 a ratio of total liabilities to shareholders' equity of 3.69, rather than the figure of 2.43 – a substantial blow-out.

BCH reported convertible bonds as a separate line item, between liabilities and capital. Terminological concerns bring back memories of the notorious omnibus classification evident in the account of the Royal Mail saga some 60 years earlier: 'Balance for the year, including dividends on shares in allied and other companies, adjustment of taxation, reserves less depreciation on fleet, &c.' Classification uncertainty had been cleverly exploited by Lord Kylsant in those Royal Mail accounts. Aggregated figures were used to hide transfers from secret reserves, thereby masking current period losses, to in fact imply current profits.

The classification of the convertible bonds was changed in BCH's 1988/89 accounts, with directors stating that it was their expectation that conversion of these bonds into ordinary shares would be unlikely. Convertible bonds were reported as part of non-current liabilities. Overall a use of creative accounting at its best!

The 'benefits' of tax effect accounting

BCH, like many other companies, used the deferral method in accounting for its tax obligations, in accord with Australian Accounting Standard AAS 3, 'Accounting for Income Tax (Tax-Effect Accounting)'. However, in the 1986/87 financial year, there was a change in accounting policies involving the 'provision of group tax relief'. Significantly, it appears that in neither the notes themselves, nor in any other part of the accounts, was there disclosure of the rationale for this change in accounting policy. Walker has argued that this change in accounting policy apparently referred to the adoption of section 80G of the *Income Tax Assessment Act* 1936, thereby allowing BCH to set off losses from its wholly-owned Australian subsidiaries against the profits accruing to its other subsidiaries.

Notes to the 1986/87 BCH accounts disclosed the reduction of future income tax benefits (asset) and deferred income taxes (liability) by $156 million each during 1986/87. Further, the notes disclosed that had this accounting policy change been applied in 1985/86, the above two items in that year would each have been reduced by $59.6 million. BCH was an effective user of tax credits. And while these accounting policy changes were not hidden, being disclosed in the notes, their overall effect is not easy to determine, as Walker demonstrated:

> Some $156 million was taken from the liability item, provision for taxation, and also from the asset item, future income tax benefits. . . . it is not clear how $96.4 million of the $156 million arose during 1986–87, and how this would affect the balance of future income tax benefits. What is apparent is that the change reduces a current liability (provision for income tax) with a corresponding change in a non-current asset (future income tax benefits).[37]

In fact the reported tax position was even more contestable than that. BCH had reduced the liability with amounts drawn from 'tax-effect' balances which are mere artifacts, fictions from the bookkeeping mechanism described earlier in Chapter 2. None of that could have occurred had the FITB not been raised in accord with AAS 3. Compliance meant that a balance with financial substance was reduced by an amount without any substance at all. Thus one effect on the 1986/87 BCH accounts of the convertible notes and tax effect accounting treatments was to portray a current ratio at 2:1, instead of 1:1, a far less impressive indicator of liquidity.[38]

The illusory nature of the 'tax-effect' debits and credits was evident in the write-offs made in the 1988/89 annual reports. With either the greater attention to detail prevailing in the 1988/89 financials, or changed circumstances, BCH's reported 1988/89 loss of $980 million included a $453.4 million write-off of a future income tax benefit. The FITB recorded in compliance with the prescribed professional Accounting Standard on tax accounting was now unceremoniously dumped, again in accordance with the Standard! One might justifiably claim this to have been, substantially, a seminal example of *compulsory creativity*.

Forex accounting – compliance was more help than hazard

In the 1987/88 accounts, the treatment of foreign exchange translations was significant in determining the reported profitability of BCH – with 38 per cent of the operating profit being foreign exchange gains. Accountants and others were obliged to comply with ASRB 1012, 'Foreign Currency Translation', on this matter. And of course they did.

BCH's 1987/88 financial statements contained a change in accounting treatment of long-term monetary items with fixed or ascertainable lives, in order to comply with the new currency translation requirements of ASRB 1012. Therefore, in addition to short-term monetary items and forward exchange contracts, gains or losses on long-term monetary items were now brought to account in the profit and loss account as they arose. Again BCH would appear to have complied and, as a result, legitimately ceased to recognise any exchange fluctuations as extraordinary items. Hence, the 1987/88 profits included a $149.9 million foreign exchange gain, a figure substantially more than the one recorded in 1986/87.

However, $59.2 million of that total foreign exchange gain was attributable to the conversion of the above convertible bonds into Australian currency. Whilst recognised, since the directors had stated in the 1986/87 accounts that a fixed exchange rate would be adhered to, a provision was offset against this gain. In addition, BCH also had $3,208.6 million worth of foreign currency borrowings which would have benefited from the appreciation in the Australian dollar in the period ending 30 June 1988 (comprising $611.4 million worth of current liabilities and $2,597.2 million worth of non-current liabilities). When these loans were converted into Australian currency, the resulting 'gains' were included in the reported profit figure. In BCH's previous year's financial statements, by following AAS 20, these gains had been amortised (spread over a number of accounting periods). Again much of the backing-and-filling in BCH's profit figures was the result of following the professionally or legally-prescribed Standards, through which clearly it is difficult to discern the financial truth of the matter. At about the same time, Tiny Rowland distributed that notorious financial analysis document.[39]

Others also dissected BCH's 1987/88 accounts. Sentiments were far from positive. Journalistic attention centred on a windfall gain of $88.2 million in terms of post-extraordinary equity-accounted after-tax profits, which was possible since restatement flowed from Bond being 'one of the fullest reporters in Australia'.[40] The comment reinforced how Bond Corporation's profits were delivered by complying with the Accounting Standards, though that point was lost in rehashing the conventional equity-accounting debate.

More analysis of that kind was forthcoming. Investigatory work by the Australian Broadcasting Corporation's *Four Corners* national TV team led to some further contentions regarding the 1987/88 accounts. Specific queries related to the alleged 'overstated profit figure' from inclusion of profits on two asset 'sales': the Porta di Roma land deal and the Hilton Hotel sale. Questions surfaced over Arthur Andersen's unqualified 'true and fair' audit report.[41] Barry notes: 'The Institute of Chartered Accountants in Australia had been less than impressed with Arthur Andersen's work. Following the *Four Corners* report, the institute had asked a senior non-practising accountant to investigate whether Bond's 1988 accounts complied with Australian Accounting Standards; his conclusion was that they did not.'[42] Perhaps the courts may have an opportunity to examine this aspect thoroughly. We suspect it is likely that the Standards provided the opening – an accounting window of opportunity – for innovative, some might allege *feral*, accounting, just as it had done years earlier in the Minsec Robe River shares affair.

Despite reportedly to be 'looking increasingly like a basket case',[43] the chairman of BCH was still ebullient. Even the release of the 1988/89 financial accounts could not dampen his optimism. These accounts were scrutinised closely both prior to and after their late release. They disclosed at that time the largest ever corporate loss in Australia of nearly $1 billion. Alan Bond reportedly suggested that the loss was largely made up of non-cash items, in particular:

> . . . 330 million depreciation, future income benefits [$454 million] . . . the write down in shares included $200 million in non-cash. Foreign currency adjustments of $120 million were non-cash. . . . We have been writing our brewing assets down at $950 million book value, the difference between the real value and book value of $1.5 billion, which belongs to the shareholders . . . We are not insolvent because we have a huge net worth. The Chile Telephone company is written down at $250 million less than its worth and our properties have not been revalued – they are worth $250 million.[44]

Perversely, it had been increases in non-cash items that had been so heavily relied upon in generating BCH's profit figures as collateral for borrowings for several years. That, too, seems to have been lost on many commentators, as was the linkage between the vagaries of conventional accounting practice – especially its artifacts – and the failure to disclose generally for all physical assets their market worths (continuously updated and duly audited), and the significance of verified up-to-date asset valuation in financing expansion.

The half-a-billion dollar question was: 'What do Bond's words, "real value" and "worth", mean?' Unless they mean current money's worth – that is, what the assets could be sold for – then the numbers reported were of limited use for those making financial assessments, especially Tiny Rowland's insolvency claim.

Much has been written about the rise and fall of BCH. Most often it has examined Bond's personal fortunes and misfortunes. But the real sting in the BCH tale is its similarity with many of the previously described failures and the associated regulatory, accounting and ethical deficiencies. Some financial warnings were there, as the comments of several financial commentators above clearly indicate. However, the use of accepted accounting techniques in the context of *enterprise* action masked the true failure path which BCH was travelling. Further, our overview of selected publicly-disclosed accounting treatments, in respect of foreign currency, deferred tax and convertible notes, suggests considerable compliance with the specifics of individual Accounting Standards.

What is yet to be examined publicly is whether there was, as in the UK *Royal Mail* case (and others), a failure to disclose to investors any material particulars, and if so – to what extent not doing so was due as much to compliance with the Standards as to deviation from them.

How serviceable was BCH's accounting compliance, especially in producing the 1987 and 1988 consolidated accounting data? The complex BCH corporate structure, with over 600 subsidiaries, many registered overseas, facilitating dealings with related parties including family companies of the founder, again raises the question of whether society is well served by such structures and the conventional, standard accounting for them.

There are myriad examples of transactions similar to those at BCH – albeit, perhaps not on that scale, but generically identical – in the annals of corporate failure both in Australia and overseas. Likely as not in respect of corporate success, too!

Ultimately, virtually none of the pumped-up financial outcomes of BCH's actions would have gone undetected for as long had assets been marked-to-market continuously and been duly audited as a matter of what one might reasonably expect to be ordinary accounting and auditing best practice.

FOURTEEN

Westmex Ltd:
The Security Façade of Cross Guarantees

'[The rationale of an indemnity or cross guarantee is] that
the interests of creditors would be protected if the holding
company and the "relieved" subsidiaries entered into a Deed
of indemnity and, in the event of insolvency of any company
party to the Deed, the creditors could look to the assets of
the other companies party to the Deed.'

Mr Justice McLelland (1992)

How convenient it would be were deeds of cross guarantee to give that
protection in practice. However, they do not. In the aftermath of many
group liquidations in the early 1990s came the cry for reform of the
system governing borrowing arrangements that had exacerbated many
of the 1980s' excesses. One area of interest relevant to our theme is
whether groups and consolidation accounting, meshed with negative
pledge, cross guarantee and (sometimes) junk-bond financing, provided
an effective means of operating and informing investors. This issue
underpins this analysis of the rise and fall of Westmex.

Westmex began life on 30 June 1969 as a base metal explorer in
Western Australia. When mineral operations waned during the mid-
1970s, Westmex became a cash-box. Diversification into real estate and
share trading was followed by moves into earthmoving contracting in
1976 and 1977. It was back to resource exploration, as the resources
boom of the late 1970s and early 1980s came, then went. By the mid-
1980s Westmex's investments had been directed mainly in option and
share trading, with its mining investments concentrated on gold.

Events surrounding the collapse at Westmex reveal a dramatically
changed set of operations following the arrival of the new CEO, Russell
Goward, in 1986. During his time at Industrial Equity Limited, Goward
had been described as a 'miracle of technology with his year-round tan
and permed hair [whose] charm and enthusiasm were infectious [*sic*]'.[1]

Early in 1986 a young Russell Goward, then CEO at Sir Ronald
Brierley's IEL, seized an opportunity. He acquired a controlling stake in
Westmex Limited, reorganised it and re-listed in March 1986 on the
industrial board. Westmex, post-1986, comprised a substantially different
group of entities, under the influence of Goward's dominance and
charismatic appeal, and the group's dramatic asset growth increase.
Deceptively, it seemed he had the Midas touch.

Quick to perceive a quality performer, the financial press described Goward, one of the youngest of the 1980s Australian 'entrepreneurs', as a 'magician', a 'whiz kid', 'a curly-haired investment genius'. That acclamation proved premature. Subsequent to the equally fast descent of the Westmex empire during 1989, the fickle press penned less favourable nomenclatures – 'failed tycoon', 'bankrupt businessman' and 'grounded high-flier'.

Perhaps the acclamation was undeserved from the start. Recent accounts of Goward's days at the helm of IEL are equally less sanguine. It now is claimed that even his mentor, Sir Ronald Brierley, was said to have grown tired of Goward's desire to claim the attention of the press, and that IEL's investments under Goward proved to be less than raging successes.[2]

The right time for an idea

Goward's seizure changed the direction at Westmex, resulting in an enlarged capital base (see Table 14.2). Investments were now in entrepreneurial entities, primarily in Australia and the United Kingdom. Perhaps Goward felt this was one of those times right for a new idea. In the United States Michael Milken had already perceived the eighties to be the right time for his junk-bond financing.

In Australia the stock market was booming, entrepreneurial stocks were fashionable, bank finance was readily available, and negative pledge and cross guarantee arrangements were common in group financing, though why that should have engendered great optimism and comfort for creditors and some financial commentators is questionable. Twenty-five years earlier, cross guarantees of a similar sort did not help H.G. Palmer's creditors by providing an adequate security.

Westmex's first major investment, in June 1986, was a 52.3 per cent stake in the ailing listed UK company, Charterhall Plc. Several of Westmex's directors were appointed to its board. The venture into Charterhall enabled Westmex to springboard into the UK and the US. Charterhall's operations were transformed from that of an independent exploration and production company in the North Sea into a specialised investment group.

Although Westmex had begun corporate life as a mineral explorer, by 1986 it had been transformed into a specialised investment group, primarily a retailing and exploration venture. In the six months prior to Westmex's acquisition, Charterhall had posted a loss of £6.248 million. Within six months of Russell Goward being at the helm, Charterhall had returned to the black. Three years later, a six-monthly profit of £4.587 million was reported. Profits, assets and debt growth are summarised in Table 14.1 and detailed in Table 14.2.

Table 14.1   Westmex Ltd – reported growth in profits, 30 June 1986 to 30 June 1989

Year ended 30 June	Reported profits $	Revenue $	Dividends cents/share
1986	355,550	717,000	n.a.
1987	9,952,402	47,232,000	5.0
1988	17,448,168	192,224,000	10.5
1989	27,015,417	377,344,000	12.5

Source: Sydney Stock Exchange Statex Service, Westmex Ltd, W190, run on 31 December 1989 (reproduced herein as Table 14.2).

By 30 June 1988, Westmex's investments comprised two main operating groups, under the umbrella of CAL Resources (formerly Charterhall Australia) and Charterhall Plc in the UK. CAL Resources had petroleum interests, including Australian Petroleum Fund (Auspet), Pancontinental Petroleum Ltd (100 per cent) and IOL Petroleum. In the UK, Charterhall Plc had investments in retailing (80 per cent footwear) and petroleum.

The aura of success was promoted, and accounting again had its role to play.

The large financial institutions certainly did not miss the opportunity to be on the ride. Undoubtedly they did not foresee it was to be on a roller coaster destined to crash. So, when Westmex was placed in liquidation in early 1990 the list of creditors in the Statement of Affairs included major Australian banks, some overseas banks and many of the other major Australian financial houses. The *cognoscenti* had been caught again. Of course, it could be claimed that they had priced their exposure according to the high risk involved. However, Westmex's accounts gave their usual impression of truth and fairness, undoubtedly masking the *higher* level of financial risk involved.

Goward's 'whiz kid' appeal, aided by impressive reported growth in profits and assets, undoubtedly drew the small punters to Westmex, with 9,000 individual shareholders on the register at 30 June 1987. The next year this grew by 27 per cent to 11,500. A large multinational group had been formed with over 50 companies. A 'closed group'[3] of 36 companies indemnified under a cross guarantee instrument was interposed within that structure. The implications of that arrangement may be gleaned from the extent of transactions within the 'closed group', illustrated in Figure 14.1.[4]

Figure 14.1 Inter-company commercial dealings between Westmex 'closed group' companies ($000)

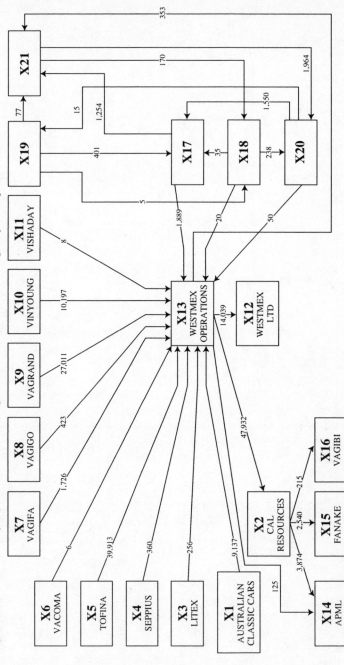

Notes: Xn = company number as in Table 14.3. Direction of arrow indicates the amount of inter-company debt from company Xi to company Xj (e.g. X1 owes X13 $9,137,000).
Source: Reconstructed from data provided in the Liquidators' Affidavit to the NSW Supreme Court, in *Westmex Ltd (in liq.)* ... February 1992.

Table 14.2 Westmex Ltd – Statex balance sheet summary and ratios, 30 June 1983 to 30 June 1989

	30/6/89 $000	30/6/88 $000	30/6/87 $000	30/6/86 $000	30/6/85 $000	30/6/84 $000	30/6/83 $000
Cash and liquids	35,698	38,416	5,833	2,257	1,532	0	1,750
Trade debtors	30,137	4,627	139	41	37	59	19
Stocks	67,833	9,382	0	0	0	0	0
Other current assets	39,107	22,231	26	970	1,417	2,086	0
Total current assets	172,775	74,656	5,998	3,268	2,986	2,145	1,769
Bank overdraft	14,057	4,314	179	115	0	2	34
Trade creditors	27,503	2,229	2,378	1,728	338	1	13
Tax provisions	0	0	0	9	50	19	109
Debt due in one year	78,038	48,512	18,674	0	0	94	0
Other current liabilities	78,780	16,531	0	0	11	71	5
Current liabilities	198,377	71,586	21,230	1,852	399	187	161
Net working capital	−25,602	3,070	−15,233*	1,417*	2,587	1,958	1,607*
Net plant and property	66,433	11,987	237	123	0	0	0
Investments	82,659	80,607	93,591	3,560	0	0	0
Deferred assets	21,003	6,479	308	195	195	433	564
Total invested capital	144,493	102,144	78,903	5,295	2,782	2,391	2,171
Long-term debt	224,082	49,244	0	0	0	0	0
Other deferred liabilities	2,893	834	0	0	0	0	0
Minority interest	70,001	15,237	0	0	0	0	0
Preferred capital	0	0	0	0	0	0	0
Ordinary equity	−152,483	36,829	78,903	5,295	2,782	2,391	2,171
Total invested funds	144,493	102,144	78,903	5,295	2,782	2,391	2,171

Total tangible assets	342,870	173,730	100,133	7,146	3,181	2,578	2,333
Intangibles	239,497	18,307	0	0	0	50	50
Total assets	582,367	192,037	100,133	7,146	3,181	2,628	2,383
Equivalent fully paid shares	172,566	113,900	91,178	59,285	12,735	12,735	12,735
Balance sheet ratios							
Liquid ratio	0.56	0.97	0.28	1.88	7.48	11.57	13.88
Current ratio	0.87	1.04	0.28	1.76	7.48	11.45	10.96
Shareholders' interest	24.0	30.0	78.8	74.1	87.5	92.7	93.1
% Mark/book list inv.	59.6	100.0	100.0	100.0	100.0	100.8	0.0
Net assets/share (adj)	−0.70	0.23	0.48	0.18	0.03	0.03	0.02
Dilution factor used	0.84	0.66	0.53	0.36	0.16	0.16	0.16
Long-term debt/equity	−146.9	133.7	0.0	0.0	0.0	0.0	0.0
Short-term debt/equity	−60.3	143.4	23.8	2.1	0.0	4.0	1.5
Profit after tax, after Minority interest (000)							
As per Westmex accounts	27,015	17,645	7,294	355	163	45	126
As per Statex	27,015	17,645	7,294	355	163	45	126
Sales (000)	312,064	79,540	8,203	n.a.	n.a.	n.a.	n.a.

Note: *Rounding errors; figures as per original.

Source: Stock Exchange Research Pty Ltd, *The Statex Service*, Westmex Ltd (W190), run on 16 December 1991; data are on a consolidated basis.

On a roller coaster

Westmex's fast descent followed seductive increases in reported profits
and asset growth from its newly acquired world-wide corporate empire.

In the 30 June 1989 Chairman's Report the exponential-like growth in
reported profits and revenues was well exploited by CEO Goward:

> Your company's continued prosperity during these adverse times is evidenced
> in the Accounts by the record 1988/89 profits (the fourth consecutive record
> year) and the substantial increase in the underlying value of the Group's core
> businesses. . . .
> Westmex's achievements over the past few years were recognised by two inde-
> pendent bodies.
> 1. Australian Business magazine gave Westmex its 'Acorn Award' for
>   outstanding new entrant to its list of Australia's Top 500 Companies.
> 2. The Australian Stock Exchange Research Department ranked Westmex as
>   the No. 1 performing company in Australia over the past five years. . . .
> 'Institutional' shareholders increased their ownership of Westmex from 22%
> one year ago to 31% today.[5]

As with Alan Bond's assessment of Bond Corporation's fortunes near
its nadir, it all depends on what is meant by Goward's words 'profits' and
'value'.

Many analysts during the mid-to-late eighties certainly thought
Westmex was a good investment. If luck lasted, its 'diversified investor'
investment strategy would soon find its way into the DIY recipe-books
of management gurus – another management fad to join the long list
which includes diversification, decentralisation, stick-to-the-core operations, just-in-time, EVA, downsizing, zero-based budgeting, total quality
control, benchmarking and then total quality management, theory X,
theory Y and finally, perhaps, theory Z.[6]

'Diversified investor' aptly described Westmex's operations. According
to Goward, Westmex was 'an investment company, a divestment company
and an operator of businesses'.[7] Westmex's disclosed corporate objective
captured its investment philosophy:

> To optimise long term returns to shareholders . . . by maximising the dividends
> paid and the wealth created . . . through the identification, acquisition and
> development of well managed operating businesses in chosen industries with
> the potential to show outstanding returns (operating profits plus increases in
> business value) . . . *where* those businesses can be acquired at an immediate
> discount on underlying business value and on-sold when they reach their full
> potential.[8]

'Where' indeed! Many of Westmex's investments were in unlisted companies. Unfashionable, fragmented industries were sought for acquisition. The purported rationale was that companies in those industries

could be acquired on a far lower price–earnings ratio and therefore offered scope for the greatest gain. This was possibly true, but it also carried the risk of the greatest loss.

Usually the companies acquired became subsidiaries, often wholly-owned. Whilst primarily in shoe retailing in Britain via the Charterhall group, and stationery in Australia, the diversification strategy thrust Westmex also into textiles in the UK. Petroleum, printing, classic car production and other miscellaneous industries were targeted in Australia. At a time when the prevailing management rhetoric suggested a move towards 'sticking to the basics', or 'sticking to one's knitting', Goward was steering the opposite course. Some analysts observed that Goward's 'counter-cyclical conglomerate investment acquisition approach' created 'an interesting and possibly unique company. . . . [whilst] many investors remain unconvinced that the conglomerate concept can achieve lasting success. Westmex is dedicated to disproving that.'[9] Such conjectures are grist for those suggesting there is no theory of management.

Regarding reported profits, it appeared that Goward had Westmex proving to be the exception to the rule. He was receiving a better than good financial press: 'Russell Goward's Westmex Ltd was another company that emerged from the chaos of last year's [October 1987] sharemarket crash in fine shape. Profit for the latest half-year was up $13.5 million, to $15.4 million';[10] 'Goward's magical P/E formula: since Black Tuesday the market was impressed, first with the jump in profit [for the six months to December 1988] from $1.1 million to $7.9 million, and second with the fact that Westmex, although expressed as an entrepreneurial stock, had seen the crash coming and reduced its exposures';[11] 'Westmex: Acorn award – outstanding new entrant: According to the Stock Exchange Research Department Westmex has been the best-performing investment among the larger stocks over the past five years and the sixth best performer during calendar 1988. It would be hard to argue that Westmex is not an appropriate winner of the Acorn Award for Outstanding New Entrant.'[12] Hard indeed, given the audited evidence. And those are the same types of sentiments expressed in favour of others previously, when H.G. Palmer, for example, was reporting performances contradicting those being experienced by its peers in the wake of the November 1960 credit squeeze.

Not all financial observers were as impressed with Westmex's performance. Just prior to the October 1987 crash, Henry Bosch was one who was publicly critical of the way Westmex Limited calculated its profits. Bosch is reported to have said the 1987 Westmex report was 'more akin to a public relations exercise than to the presentation of a true and fair view of the company's financial affairs'.[13] But then a cynic would suggest generally that this is not all that different from most annual reports and no different from the calculation of profits virtually everywhere, then and now! Specifically, it would appear that Bosch's concerns were, at least publicly, that, in respect of companies taken over, Westmex had inflated profits by including an incremental value attributed to acquisitions over their cost. In his defence, Goward insisted that he was simply applying accounting practices used previously at IEL under the direction of Sir Ronald Brierley.

That is an interesting observation in itself. It seems that Goward learned some tricks-of-the-takeover-trade, though it would be unwise to pin too much on his explanation of where his school was. Wherever it was and whether by accident or design, Goward's idea of bringing to book incremental changes to the worth of assets is spot-on, provided he was referring to their independently verifiable changes in selling prices. But of course we would argue that this should be done annually and, without exception, that it must be subject to an audit in the usual manner.

We would expect that Bosch's complaint was directed at unrealised profits being brought into account, for that is not in accord with conventional practice's *realisation principle*. But conventional practice runs counter to common sense on this point, for, at the same time, it compels approximations of decreases in selling prices (depreciation) to be brought to account, even though they are unrealised too. Goward (and it seems his mentors at IEL) all (unwittingly, we suspect) made significant contributions to accounting thought through these tilts at conventional practice. Whatever their motives, on that score they were talking more common sense than their critics, in much the same way as had Samuel Insull and John Spalvins.

Eventually Westmex changed its incremental valuing practice. Pointing to a much wider problem with the accounts, Westmex's auditors, Mann Judd (after resigning from the audit in 1987), are reported to have described Westmex accounts as 'bordering on the fictional'.[14] Whether it was only the *realisation* issue that they regarded as fictional, and if so why, has never been publicly stated. The action by the auditors is exceptional, for it appears to be the only (at least publicly acknowledged) case in the 1980s where an auditor from one of the major auditing firms resigned when a dispute between the auditor and directors of a publicly-listed company could not be settled. An alternative explanation is that all such matters were mutually agreed.

Interestingly, in 1996 two events occurred that might eventually shed light on Westmex's 1988/89 accounts. First, the Companies Auditors Liquidation Board suspended the 1988/89 auditor of Westmex for five years.[15] Then, Bankers Trust and several shareholders sued for $60 million damages under the *Trade Practices Act* 1974 against the auditor and his partners at the time of Westmex's liquidation. The claim was made under section 52, claiming negligence, and misleading and deceptive conduct.[16] Whether and, if so how, these accounts were 'fictional' may be revealed in this action.

Westmex's annual reports for the years 1987–1989 (Table 14.2) contain many contentious accounting practices, each of which had the effect of increasing Westmex's reported profits or assets, even if only in the short run. These included on a consolidated basis (1988 financial year) capitalisation of expenses for intangibles (goodwill) of $5.6 million; other expenditure of $19.12 million made up of exploration expenditure $2.87 million, future income tax benefit, $2.48 million, and trade and brand names, $11.6 million. But, as with many of the accounting practices at Bond Corporation Holdings and others, those individual practices seemed to be in accord with the Accounting Standards. Whether they, in conjunction with other accounting practices, accorded with the *Companies Act*'s 'true and fair' view override, *in toto*, is debatable. One financial commentator has described Westmex's accounts as 'a castle of sand almost from the start, based on elaborate sale and lease-back arrangements, with vast sums set aside for the goodwill of the companies purchased, and with cash flow dependent on selling things off; $28 million of the company's $38 million "profit" [before tax] in its last year of operations [1989] was from the sale of assets, leaving $10 million to service $300 million worth of debt. "In the end he [Goward] just ran out of things to sell", says a UK analyst.'[17]

This account provides an interesting contrast with the final months at Bond Corporation. BCH was financially incapable of maintaining asset purchases. Cash purchases and on-selling to related companies, rather than sales to outsiders, were critical in maintaining BCH's *ponzi* scheme.

All of this has to be balanced against the detail contained in the Westmex Ltd annual reports for 1987–1989. As with Bond Corporation the level of disclosure was extensive – detailed notes to the accounts, segmental reporting, extensive disclosure of accounting policies – all the good Standard stuff, but seemingly not serviceable one iota.

Similar to many other collapses, the latter stages of Westmex's demise occurred suddenly.

In September 1989 Russell Goward had provided a positive assessment of Westmex's prospects in his Chairman's Report. The share price was around $1.20, and net assets of the company (including intangibles) were reported at $87.014 million, or approximately 50 cents per share (Table 14.2). Fortunes nosedived. Around this time the AMP insurance company off-loaded 6 million shares with predictable effect. Westmex's share price plummeted – to 80 cents by November, then in late December to 30 cents. It was now in free-fall. By January it hovered around 15 cents. Throughout this period Goward was an aggressive

Table 14.3 Westmex Ltd 'closed group' particulars

Exhibit 1: Assets and liabilities of companies subject to Westmex Class Orders (in $000s)

Company identifier	Company name	Est. realisable value	Inter-company debtors	Total assets	Secured creditors	External creditors	Inter-company creditors	Third party guarantees	Total liabilities
X1	Aust. Classic Cars	150		150		–1,015	–9,137		–10,152
X2	CAL Resources		47,932				–6,629	–17,893	–24,522
X3	Litex						–256	–12,517	–12,773
X4	Seppius						–360		–360
X5	Tofina						–39,913		–39,913
X6	Vacoma						–6		–6
X7	Vagifa	1,090		1,090			–1,726		–1,726
X8	Vagigo						–423		–423
X9	Vagrand	9,733		9,733			–27,011		–27,011
X10	Vinyoung	6,051		6,051			–10,917		–10,917
X11	Vishaday						–8		–8
X12	Westmex Ltd		14,039		–12,517	–175,804		–86,783	–275,104
X13	Westmex Ops	439	91,726	439		–116,764	–62,449		–179,213
X14	APML		3,999						
X15	Fanake		2,540						
X16	Vagibi		215						
X17	Miscell. 1		1,986				–3,143		–3,143
X18	Miscell. 2	3	175	3			–294		–294
X19	Miscell. 3	307	15	307		–2	–483		–485
X20	Miscell. 4	661	2,203	661		–8	–1,625		–1,633
X21	Miscell. 5	1,668	1,684	1,668		–418	–2,134		–2,552
		20,102	166,514	20,102	–12,517*	–294,011*	–166,514*	–117,193	–590,235

Note: *External creditors total $294,011,000, third party guarantees plus secured creditors $129,710,000, hence the 'total' liabilities of closed group companies ($590,235,000) comprise these two amounts added to the $166,514,000 of inter-group company creditors.

acquirer of Westmex stock, but to no avail. In February 1990 the Westmex group was placed in provisional liquidation. Goward was declared bankrupt on 2 January 1991. The parlous position of the creditors of the Westmex group, especially the 'closed group' subject to cross guarantees, is shown in Table 14.3.

Deregulation and cross guarantees – a security façade?

Following the NCSC's mid-1980s deregulatory push under Henry Bosch, Westmex was one of many publicly-listed companies to take advantage of the NCSC Class Order Deed of Indemnity. This guarantee arrangement was claimed to be the NCSC's major deregulatory administrative initiative, purportedly providing cost savings to business by granting parent company relief from the accounting and auditing requirements of their wholly-owned subsidiaries.[18]

To achieve this, under the covenants of the deed the parent company and the relevant subsidiaries within the 'closed group' agreed 'to severally, unconditionally and irrevocably' guarantee each other's debts. Additionally, directors provided attestations of solvency in respect of relieved companies. To the officials of the NCSC these arrangements were perceived to be a means of improving the efficiency of the market mechanism. Effects on equity for various 'closed group' creditors has proved less certain. The full effects are being determined in the outcomes of 1990s court cases and compromises or schemes of arrangements applied to several 'closed group' administrations. They include J.N. Taylor, Halwood Corporation (formerly Hooker Corporation), Westmex, Equiticorp, Adsteam, Tricontinental, Brash Holdings and Linter.

Westmex and 36 of its wholly-owned subsidiaries covenanted to produce the Westmex 'closed group' under NCSC Class Orders 613 and 633 during 1988/89. A characteristic of those deeds is to limit investors' and creditors' access to public sources of the financial data relating to subsidiaries comprising a 'closed group'. Without access to the subsidiary companies' accounts, the consolidated data of Westmex became the public bulwark for creditors of any of the 'closed group' companies seeking financial information pertaining to the security of their loans. How this informed those creditors is anybody's guess.

Of course, creditors have the opportunity to seek out whatever information is necessary from any source at their command – itself a function of the relative bargaining powers of these contracting parties. But this begs the question as to whether the law should countenance certain creditors being privy to differential data in respect of a legislatively created corporation.

Westmex Ltd's 1987–1989 consolidated accounts, prior to the appointment of the liquidator in February 1990, disclosed the sensational 1986/87 reported growth in assets – $7.146 million to $100.133 million. Short-term debt had increased from $1.8 million to $21.23 million without any recourse to long-term debt. By 1988 the total book value of assets had increased to $192.037 million and current liabilities were now $71.586 million, but this time with a significant increase in long-term debt to $49.244 million. Westmex presented as a truly outstanding performer. It was this type of performance which attracted the 1989 Acorn Award for outstanding new entrant to its list of Australia's Top 500 Companies by *Australian Business*, as well as the Australian Stock Exchange Research Department's ranking of Westmex as the No. 1 performing company (on a share price return basis) in Australia over the past five years based on an annual compound return to shareholders of 113 per cent. Such evaluations invite anxiety regarding the capacity of the analysts and the financial community to withstand the seduction of conventional accounting data. Repeatedly it appears that few can.

However, the quicker and higher the rise, the further and harder the fall.

Naively one might have thought that the conventionally calculated consolidated asset cover for those debts in the financial year ended 30 June 1989 (an excess of $87 million, including intangibles, but excluding minority interest) would have been adequate. Final audited financial statements appeared in September 1989. And quickly, any perception of such security was to be shown to be unwarranted. Within four months of those statements, all companies within the Westmex 'closed group' had been placed in liquidation – an exemplary group domino effect.

Summary data provided by the liquidator in affidavits before the courts (Table 14.3) disclosed an alarming discrepancy between the publicly-reported consolidated financial position of the Westmex 'closed group' of companies and that revealed on liquidation. All companies within the 'closed group' were insolvent and the group deficiency was around $280 million. Recall that the last financials had disclosed an excess of $87 million! And all that within the space of four months? Well, probably not!

Recent court decisions regarding 'closed group' liquidations have cast doubt on the efficacy of the cross-guarantee arrangements in group liquidations subject to NCSC-approved Deeds of Indemnity. Mr Justice Debelle's judgment in the South Australian Supreme Court case, *Re J.N. Taylor Holdings Ltd (In liq.) (No. 7)*,[19] that the indemnity arrangements did not apply when all companies were insolvent, was a portent that the purported protection afforded to creditors may be illusory.

In October 1991 a compromise scheme of arrangement was put to creditors at Hooker Corporation based, one imagines, on reservations of the Debelle J.-type. It was suggested to creditors to avoid crystallising the guarantee. Whither creditor protection based on *ex-ante* certainty of outcome?[20]

Our analysis suggests that Westmex's rise and unexpected demise was a seminal example of regulatory and accounting failure. Westmex exposed the fragility of accounting's most complex bag-of-tricks, consolidated financial statements and other conventional practices. And there is still the possibility that more on that will emerge as the audit litigation progresses.

Curiously, the accounting profession would most likely regard consolidation accounting to be one of its, if not *the*, most sophisticated mechanisms for showing the wealth and progress of companies. Complex – yes. Sophisticated – doubtful; informative – rarely; illusory – virtually always! Accounting Standards-setters appear impatient with history. Few appear to heed the persistent way in which collapse is accompanied by consolidated accounting. Perhaps they view the correlation as spurious. Apparently a major shift in thinking is needed. In particular, there needs to be a reconsideration by regulators of the way corporate business is conducted through webs of parent companies and the companies related to them, and how conventional consolidation accounting is incapable of portraying financial outcomes.

PART V

Regulatory Reforms

FIFTEEN

Groupthink:
*Byzantine Corporate Structures**

'. . . almost any economic goal that can be achieved by the
creation of a wholly owned subsidiary can be equally well-
achieved by the creation of a division.'

M.A. *Eisenberg (1992, p. 4)*

Paradoxically, accounting's grandest invention to achieve financial
clarification is its greatest medium for deception. From its beginning,
giving special status to a *group* of related companies and the methods of
consolidating its accounts has facilitated financial deception. Equally
paradoxical, rather than abandoning it, both the regulatory bodies and
the accounting profession have preferred patching-up consolidation
accounting. Indeed, there is no evidence that proscribing the group structure and consolidated financial statements has ever been considered
possibilities by them.

Big business in Australia is done primarily through groups of companies related to one another through shareholding, common directors
or managers, and other controlling or influencing mechanisms. For
decades corporate groups, with their complex structures and their idiosyncratic consolidation accounting, have been the somewhat protected
vehicles for obscuring corporate misbehaviour and the means of public
deception, often unintentional, sometimes deliberate.

Connecting many companies to create a financial empire certainly
appealed as much to the 1980s entrepreneurs as it had throughout the
1960s, the 1970s and earlier years. And the attraction continues in the
1990s, if the well-publicised Coles Myer–Yannon transaction is any
indication.

Financial commentary on corporate collapse often refers to the
simultaneous failure of a number of related companies – the corporate
domino effect. Prized for the managerial synergism they promise, groups
of holding, subsidiary and associated companies have proven to be a
mechanism of financial obfuscation in many of the cases referred to in this
volume. Yet, curiously, the Corporations Law, even now, does not define a
corporate group, other than in terms of itself – circumlocutiously as a

structure, rather than as an entity with specific financial, economic and social dimensions. It remains a vague conception, the exact function of which is equally indeterminate. Judicial dicta, for example, Mason J. in *Walker v. Wimborne* and Murray J. in *Re Enterprise Gold Mines NL* suggest that 'corporate groups' comprise 'two or more corporations that are affiliated in a manner that depends in significant part on stock ownership . . . an affiliation . . . typically structural and not so easily terminated'.[1]

In reality a multiplicity of factors underpin the development of corporate groups, as Eisenberg explains: 'unlike many or most business structures they frequently do not represent an adaptation to economic forces'[2] and 'almost any economic goal that can be achieved by the creation of a wholly owned subsidiary can be equally well-achieved by the creation of a division.'[3]

Nonetheless, most corporate business is done through groups – holding companies and their subsidiaries – extremely complex group structures at that. Apart from being such a useful device for financial deception, one is virtually at a loss to identify any other necessary purpose for them (excluding taxation considerations, applicable mainly in the past) other than to exploit a divisionalisation of the limited liability privilege corporations enjoy.

Anglo-American financial history is replete with organisations having complex group structures, often comprising hundreds of subsidiaries, many wholly-owned. Governing legal rules are varied, but ultimately they are always geared to enable the collective entities to take on the appearance of, and act as, a single company. And that potentially is at the peril of those dealing with it.

Beneath the veil

Whereas commentators have suggested that financial markets are becoming more complex and sophisticated,[4] the late 1980s and the 1990s have been little different from the 1960s and 1970s (even 1890s Australia) when it comes to avenues for exploiting group structures and their accounting. Perhaps the increasing complexity of financial instruments has exacerbated the exploitation.

Essentially the technique has been common. Assets have been threaded through the web of related companies – backwards and forwards, round and about, the origins of the transactions in many instances being almost impossible to trace. Bond Corporation's dealings with the Porta di Roma land and others – for instance, one Bond Corporation transaction reportedly involved 25 companies – the Rothwells, Linter related-party transactions, Spedley Securities' round robin and Adsteam's intercompany share and loan transactions all bear witness to that. So too did

Stanhill's land sales, Minsec's dealings with Robe River shares and Cambridge Credit Corporation's myriad international company deals, decades earlier.[5] In the 1990s that practice continues and, human nature being what it is, will into the future as long as the existing group structure is permitted. Development and the standardisation of consolidation techniques have not removed the capacity to obscure financial consequences of group transactions – to the contrary, they have given them an undeserved legitimacy.

Contrary to the view held by some that the changed 1990s regulatory environment has provided adequate checks and balances, private entities have continued to be the intermediaries through which money is funnelled and then used to purchase shares in or otherwise trade with the prime public company. Transactions in 1990 between Coles Myer Ltd and related entities are indicative of the way in which there is the perception that, as noted in the headnote to the 1960s *Reid Murray* case, private and public interests may become entangled. It has been alleged that the so-called Yannon transaction meant Coles Myer was in effect providing a guarantee for share purchases by a C.S. First Boston shelf company, Yannon Ltd, which 'in effect, relieved [the family company of the chairman of Coles Myer] of a financial obligation to another party, FAI Insurances'.[6] According to this account, private company losses were to be guaranteed by Coles Myer.[7]

Granted, particulars of some 1980s cases may have been slightly novel due to the use of put and call options on asset transfers and a greater use of trusts registered in overseas tax havens. However, the generic principle – the lack of public disclosure – underlying the concerns is not novel.[8] Ultimately group structures and the idiosyncratic consolidation accounting for them have been perennial vehicles for masking corporate misbehaviour, the archetypal means of public deception (see note 15 in Chapter 16).[9]

Despite the image of size and solidarity generated by large corporate groups, history shows that once one of the related companies topples, the rest may fall like a wall of dominoes. Westmex was a seminal example. But it also is possible for any solvent company within a group to walk from the obligations of the insolvent if they *legally* can, as occurred with the MLC at H.G. Palmer and as Ansett did at ASL. Corporate solidarity is a financial and legal myth. Sentiment does not get in the way of corporate business. That is a major reason why corporate cross guarantees generally, and the ASC Deed of Cross Guarantee specifically, came into existence.

Modern group commercial arrangements have a long international lineage. Complex trust-based administrative and financial arrangements in the United States in the early 1900s, the group structures and the

Figure 15.1 Royal Mail global trade routes

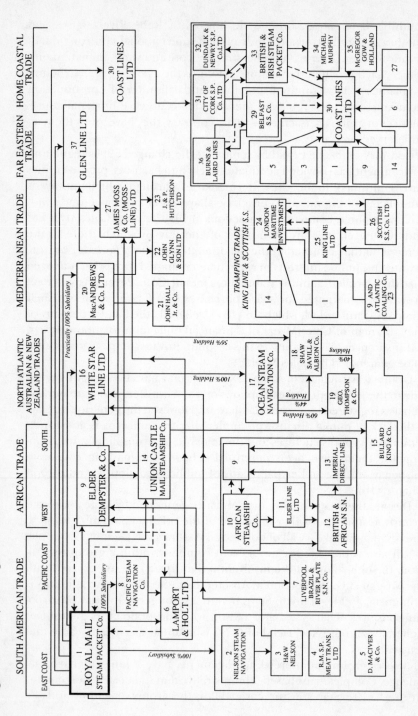

Note: Numbers in the diagram refer to Royal Mail related companies operating on various trade routes. Full details appear in *The Economist*, 5 March 1932, p. 525.

special methods of accounting for them, were fellow travellers. So were utility and other investment trust companies in the 1920s. Samuel Insull's inverted pyramid of gas and electric light companies, Ivar Kreuger's complex international match empire, and Lord Kylsant's secret reserve manoeuvres through the Royal Mail subsidiaries in the United Kingdom, for instance, are notorious examples of the exploitation of corporate groups for purposes of obfuscation.

The significance of the aggregation of assets through the complex group structure at RMSP – the biggest shipping group in the world in the 1920s – (Figure 15.1) is appositely summed up as being 'the facility it offered for maintaining in power men who had . . . become mere personal money-spinners, their personal position and gain being secured to them'.[10] That comment aptly captures the essence of *groupthink*. It has a virtual timeless applicability, being applicable equally to the complex arrangements in Britain's and Australia's 1890s land and mining boom vehicles, to the 1920s US investment trust combines, pre-World War II Japanese *zaibatsus* and post-war *keiretzus*, and to the intertwined corporate webs facilitating round-robin transactions in 1980s corporate Australia.

The issue of groupthink is integral to the 1995/96 Rothwells conspiracy case, where it was alleged by the prosecution that round robin transactions at balance date between a private company, L.R. Connell and Partners, and the two public companies, Spedley Securities and Rothwells Limited, were used to mask the true state of the financial affairs at Rothwells.

Entanglements of companies have featured in the most notorious of Australian collapses discussed above. Consider also the publicly-disclosed outcome of such entanglements in the 1990 complex loan arrangements under cross guarantee at Hooker Corporation. Figure 15.2 illustrates only the *internal* debt relationships – importantly there were more than a billion dollars of external debts also to be unravelled at Hooker. Administrators took several years to unscramble this financial morass and determine the amounts creditors were entitled to, and from which companies. And then, this was only achieved through compromise, relying on *ad hoc* methods and ignoring the cross guarantees!

Even with modern-day computer power it is virtually an impossibility to track through those types of corporate mazes, let alone determine unambiguously the financial implications of transactions within them. An essential feature of groupthink is that only the parties to the trans-action really know, and believe only they need to know, the intricacies. Consolidation accounting, in many ways, helps to obscure them to outsiders and, we suggest, perhaps to most of the insiders too.

The 1990s WA Inc. Royal Commission examining the 1989 Rothwells collapse provides ample testimony of this. There were more than 44,000 pages of transcript. Regarding Rothwells alone, 80,000 exhibits were

Figure 15.2 Internal loans between the Hooker Corporation 'closed group' companies as at date of provisional liquidation

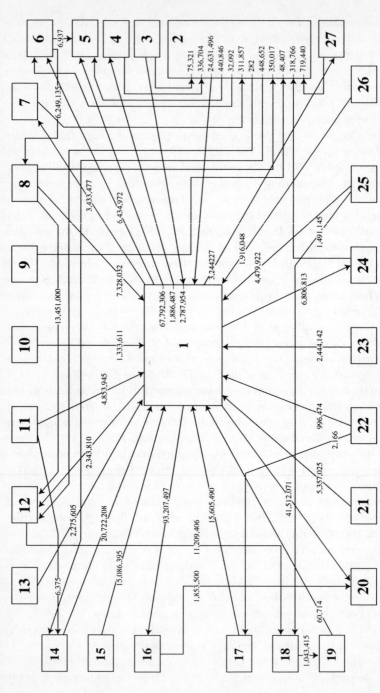

Note: The above arrows and amounts depict outstanding loan balances between subsidiary companies within the Hooker Corporation 'closed group' at the time of the Hooker Scheme of Arrangement in 1991.

Source: Based on Hooker *Statement of Affairs*, 30 June 1990.

prepared by investigators and a summary investigators' report 'commissioned to piece together Rothwells' accounts' amounted to a staggering 2,500 pages. Consider the difficulty facing those attempting to untangle numerous related-party transactions in the 1995–1996 Rothwells conspiracy case. There, over 29,000 financial exhibits were computer imaged to assist in that task. Similarly, the complexity of the transactions pertinent to the Linter Group case was revealed with the disclosure that 120,000 pages of documents had been computer imaged for ease of access in the proposed hearings.[11] Clearly, financial analysis for ongoing or collapsed firms was never meant to be easy. In the Linter case, parties were spared the possible embarrassment of publicly trying to unravel this matter when it was settled out of court. Notwithstanding Laurie Connell's death, the Rothwells conspiracy case continues, creating headaches for those trying to understand what happened.

As noted in this volume, even more disturbing is the problem of assessing which of the transactions between related companies are genuine and which are not. For ongoing companies, conventional consolidated accounting techniques purportedly make that easy – the consolidation elimination rules pertaining to related party transactions have only to be applied without letting the financial truth of the transactions get in the way. Under consolidation procedures, all within-group transactions are assumed 'from an economic group perspective' to be shams. It is mandatory that data relating to those transactions are eliminated from calculation of 'group' profits and losses, and 'group' financial position. But that is as useless a way of getting at the financial truth as assuming that they were all genuine simply because there was normal documentation. What is needed is an accounting mechanism by which the actual financial results of the transactions are truthfully presented, irrespective of whether collusion occurred.

At the heart of the matter is the fictional notion of 'the group'. Taking a contrary view, group trading has caused many to question the separate legal entity principle which underlies corporate identity and commercial practice. There is a suggestion within legal circles that it be supplanted by the group enterprise model in which the related companies become an identifiable enterprise (Blumberg, 1983; Collins, 1990; Tuebner, 1990; Pittard and McCallum, 1993; and Fisse and Braithwaite, 1993).[12] In issue is the divergence between the traditional legal treatment of groups and purported commercial reality.

Some lawyers have asserted that 'there is evidence of a general tendency [on the part of the judiciary] to ignore the separate legal entities of various companies within a group, and instead to look at the economic entity of the whole group'[13] – (as Lord Denning said) to 'draw aside the [corporate] veil', to 'pull off the mask'.[14] However, Professor

Bob Baxt has observed that, generally speaking, the courts are reluctant
to ignore the corporate veil in order to ascertain the 'true' financial or
commercial position.[15] This is a view shared by others.[16] At best, the
commercial position is confusing.

Divergence between commercial practice and legal dicta has created
increasing pressures for change. So much so that Rogers C.J. of the
Commercial Division recommended 'that the whole issue of the separate-
ness of the corporate entity be re-examined in the context of the modern
commercial contract'.[17] Further challenging the conventional wisdom,
Rogers C.J. has noted: '[I]t may be desirable for Parliament to consider
whether this distinction between the law and commercial practice should
be continued.'[18] This was not the first time he had found the distinction
troublesome. In 1989 he had referred to the law's 'scant regard to the
commercial reality'[19] – a similar judicial comment to that which had
appeared in the UK context even earlier.[20] Analysis of the regulation of
corporate groups in Australia perhaps justifies a similar stance.[21] But
disagreement over what that commercial reality is underlies all such
comments, for the essence of groupthink being touted as commercial
reality seems to be anything but that. Groups are being presented as
commercial reality. Yet virtually every aspect of the financial, social and
legal setting in which groups operate clearly indicates they are not.

A push for reassessment is evident in the 1992 changes to Australian
insolvency administration procedures. Changes to the Corporations Law
require directors of a parent company to be held liable for any debts that a
subsidiary company incurs from trading when insolvent.[22] Also, in certain
cases, sections 588v–x deem the holding company liable for debts
incurred by a subsidiary when it was already insolvent or the directors of
the holding company would have expected it to become insolvent.

Emphasis on solvency and its accounting measure have become of
primary importance to directors in their general administration of
companies. The solvency statements they have to make each year under
the Corporations Law (section 301(5)) place them at considerable risk if
the data upon which they rely for that purpose are not indicative of their
company's capacity to meet its debts. Clearly, directors face a
considerable risk in respect of individual companies and an exacerbated
risk in respect of 'closed groups' of related companies where cross
guarantees are in place.

Cross guarantees and 'closed group' accounting relief

Unease in that confused setting has spawned the avant-garde, encouraged regulatory bodies and, with recent changes to the Corporations
Law, the legislature, effectively to circumvent the separate legal entity

Table 15.1   Wholly-owned subsidiaries' class orders, 1986/87 to 1993/94[24]

Financial year	No. of deeds	No. of subsidiaries granted relief	Estimated incremental p.a. company savings $m
1986/87	219	1,155	3.5–4*
1987/88	244	1,525	4
1988/89	299	1,737	5
1989/90	306	1,700	5
1990/91	220	1,650	4
1991/92	208	2,674	5
1992/93	273	2,488	5
1993/94	89	808	2

Note: *NCSC estimate; later years are extrapolated estimates.
Source: Prepared by the authors from copies of original deeds supplied by officers of the ASC.

principle. This is most explicit in the way that commercial arrangements have been formalised by NCSC and ASC Class Orders for standard-form, regulatory-approved indemnity or cross guarantees between a holding company (chief or parent entity) and its wholly-owned subsidiaries (controlled entities). As noted in the previous chapter, initially under an NCSC Class Order Deed relief from the accounting and audit reporting requirements was granted to wholly-owned subsidiaries, so long as there was compliance with certain deed-imposed constraints. The purported security *quid pro quo* was that parent and subsidiary companies enter into indemnity arrangements – to 'severally, unconditionally and irrevocably' guarantee each other's debts. In contrast no such guarantee existed *between* the subsidiaries of the 'closed group'.

But relief was conditional upon the directors of the holding company including in the Directors' Statement a liquidity or solvency assessment 'as to whether there are reasonable grounds to believe that the guarantor company will be able to meet any obligations or liabilities to which it is, or may become, subject by virtue of the deed'.[23]

Those arrangements initially proved very popular (Table 15.1), although post-1991 anecdotal comment suggested a decline in their use. However, subsequent empirical work indicates that the initial popularity has been maintained.

Undeniably there was an initial, temporary drop in popularity of the ASC Cross Guarantee Deed from the achieved level of the NCSC Indemnity Deed. This should come as no surprise. The Deed of Cross Guarantee was more restrictive and therefore, in some respects, presumably less attractive relative to the Indemnity Deed. Also the new deed made revocation more difficult when a company within a 'closed group' had become financially insecure. Arguably, it also placed an extra burden on directors to vouch for the financial integrity of the subsidiaries whose accounts were not being reported.

When introducing the indemnity (cross guarantee) and relief arrangements in 1985 the NCSC claimed that there would be very large savings to business, especially the thousands of wholly-owned Australian subsidiaries. This would be achieved without sacrificing investor protection where the holding company was prepared to guarantee the debts of those subsidiaries.[25] An ASC rationale for extending the creditor cross claim indemnity to a cross guarantee by all companies within the 'closed group' was to ensure that a wholly-owned subsidiary effectively 'pools its assets and liabilities with its holding company' when a winding-up occurs.[26] The ASC also stated that consolidated accounting data would provide investors and creditors with the most useful data in respect of a 'closed group'.

Faith in the virtue of consolidation accounting seems unrelenting. Both the accounting profession and the legislature have sought to tighten the rules relating to consolidation accounting. Yet neither appears to have canvassed the idea of dumping consolidation practices. The Corporations Law (sections 295 and 296) and the Accounting Standard AASB 1024 have broadened the base of the 'economic entity' to which consolidation accounting applies – every parent entity that is a reporting entity and controls one or more companies or business entities is required to prepare a consolidated balance sheet, consolidated income and consolidated cash flow statements. However, what such an entity actually comprises is far from definitive, as aptly demonstrated in a 1993 dispute between Washington H. Soul Pattinson, the Australian Stock Exchange and the ASC over whether the 49.84 per cent share of Brickworks Ltd gave Soul Pattinson control and hence should be consolidated. Reportedly the directors agreed to the ASC's request to consolidate Brickworks' accounts with WHSP, adding the disclaimer that 'such a consolidation inflates the profit and net tangible assets of WHSP so as to be misleading to its shareholders and to potential investors in WHSP . . . [Accordingly, the directors] disclaim any responsibility to shareholders and/or investors who may suffer loss as a result of relying on such misleading information, the responsibility for which rests wholly with the ASC.'[27] This was a strange twist to the general principle of *caveat emptor* and similar disclaimer clauses. One must wait with interest to see the outcome of the first test case.

Other forms of group accounting reporting are no longer permitted. The prior companies legislation permitted a variety of combinations of the separate statements of constituent companies and consolidated statements. But the basic tenet of consolidation, that it is a means of ignoring the separate legal entity by accounting for the 'economic group', has been retained. Retained too are the basic consolidation procedures, which have been in vogue since about the 1930s following the appearance in the United Kingdom of Garnsey's celebrated 1923 *Holding Companies and their Published Accounts: Limitations of a Balance Sheet.*[28] And retained also it is suggested is the potential for obfuscation regarding subsidiaries' activities: 'The . . . extra corporate layer reduces the likelihood that someone will even detect the wrongdoing, much less bring suit to correct it. . . . [R]eporting requirements . . . demand little disclosure of subsidiary activity. The parent . . . may consolidate information about the financial performance and condition of the subsidiary into its own financial statements.'[29]

Debate concerning creditors' rights in group liquidations (especially in 'closed-group' liquidations) exemplifies the incorrigible entanglements which consolidation accounting helps to mask. There, it is crucial for directors to be able to assess the solvency of each company within a corporate group. Enter the wonder-world of consolidation accounting!

SIXTEEN

Groupthink – Group Therapy: Consolidation Accounting

> 'It is . . . misleading to imply that a group can have a state of affairs or can earn profits . . . no set of consolidated accounts can give a "true and fair view" of anything.'
>
> *Accounting Standards Review Committee (1978, pp. 128–129)*

Whether consolidation accounting practices should be tolerated is contestable. Accounting data are reasonably expected to reflect financial reality in its legal, social and economic contexts. And whereas reality might be less than transparent, consolidated financial data cannot by any stroke of the imagination be considered a realistic reflection of the aggregative wealth and progress of the related companies, being as they are aggregations of their separate conventional accounting data – some as they appear in the originals, some adjusted to accommodate presumed, often counterfactual, characteristics of the transactions between them.

Continued support for consolidation proceeds more by default than design. Perhaps misunderstanding within both the accounting and legal professions of the nature and financial significance of information in consolidated statements is the primary contributor to that default. Specifically, it is contestable whether the ASC's assertion that 'consolidated accounts . . . [provide] more meaningful information for users of the accounts' is sustainable. Equally contestable is the claim that enforcement of these 'new requirements' by the accounting profession will ensure that 'most of the major and well-used opportunities for the manipulation . . . under the previous Companies Code will disappear'.[1]

In supporting a mandatory legislative requirement to prepare consolidated accounts, some of the judiciary and members of the accounting profession have claimed that consolidated data best reflect group operations as a single economic or business entity. That is claimed to be the substance of the transactions between the related companies. Though supported by critics who wish to reduce conformity with the separate legal entity principle,[2] consolidation might also be contested against a background of corporate strategies which bestowed considerable advantage through exploiting that practice. At the heart of these allegiances lies the differential accounting outcomes which emerge. Yet, despite the rhetoric, a 'group' of companies is neither a single entity under the present general interpretation of the law, nor (usually) is it reasonably identifiable as a separate economic unit. Thus aggregative representations of the outcome of group operations and the financial position of the group are a financial nonsense. Contrary to what is claimed, consolidated financial statements are the product of relying on the purported economic form, rather than the legal form and financial substance.

For corporate groups it is assumed (but not evidenced) that consolidated reporting gives interested persons information on the overall financial status and current financial performance of group companies. Distinguished legal opinion, for instance from Professor Gower, explains that the UK legislature has:

> recognised at least since the Companies Act 1948 . . . where there is a relationship between companies such that one, the parent or holding company, controls the others, the subsidiary or sub-subsidiary companies, then, for certain purposes, including *especially presentation of financial statements*, all must be treated as one. . . . *The most important of these [qualifications to the separate entity principle] relate to accounts . . . .*[3]

Judicial dicta support this view. Lord Denning M.R. declined to treat a wholly-owned subsidiary, Fork Manufacturing Co. Ltd, as a separate legal entity.[4] And his dicta in *D.H.N. Ltd v. Tower Hamlets* explained: 'We all know that in many respects a *group* of companies are treated *together* for the purpose of general accounts, balance sheet and profit and loss account. They are treated as one *concern*.'[5] And Mason J., in *Industrial Equity Ltd v. Blackburn*, whilst rejecting Gower's proposition and championing the separate legal entity principle noted (in *obiter*) that the purpose of consolidation is to 'ensure that the members of, and for that matter persons dealing with, a holding company are provided with accurate information as to the profit and loss and state of affairs of that company and its subsidiaries within the group'.[6]

The 'group' was endorsed recently in an ASC Media Release, *Public Hearing: Accounting Relief for Wholly-Owned Subsidiaries*. On the basis of a presumed commonality of interests of all 'closed-group' companies, it was suggested that 'consolidated accounts would more accurately reflect commercial realities'.[7] *How* was not disclosed. Though, from these observations it would be reasonable for the lay person to expect properly constructed consolidated statements to contain an aggregation only of the data in the separate companies' accounts, perhaps adjusted to avoid double counting. They would not expect inclusion of data which are not sourced in those accounts nor the exclusion of data which are. Whether reasonable or not, that is far from the reality. Consolidation accounting does both.

Groupthink is virulent, and consolidated financial statements are the group therapy being prescribed. But there is good reason for concern over the serviceability of consolidated financial statements. The 1992 Royal Commission inquiring into the $2.2 billion bail-out of the State Bank of South Australia alluded to its doubt on the matter in referring to 'the different accounting practices which can be applied to consolidated, group, equity and aggregated accounting'.[8]

It is not only a problem of variant accounting practices. More fundamentally, the proposition that group accounts are prepared to reflect accurately the operations of the group as a single economic or business unit runs contrary to the historical development of consolidated accounting. Any allusion to consolidations being the product of an evolutionary refinement is quite wrong. Equally questionable is the proposition that consolidated or group accounts can 'ensure that the members of, and for that matter persons dealing with, a holding company are provided with accurate information as to the profit and loss and "state of affairs" of that company and its subsidiaries within the group'.[9] On several occasions we note that if the group is representative neither of a legal nor of an economic entity, how can it be said to have a state of affairs?[10] Critical to that issue is what is meant by 'state of affairs', particularly as it applies to related companies, their members and their creditors. Money is the primary concern to all parties. Legally, one of the imports of the separate legal entity principle has been to isolate the fund which belongs to the company from the fund which belongs to its members. The company fund is liable for the company's debts and the members' fund is liable for the members' debts. In that setting, consolidated accounts are more likely to be a source of deception than illumination, for the users of accounts in general and for the creditors and those dealing with the separate companies in particular.

Fuzzy financials

It is far from universally agreed what function consolidation or group accounting serves. In Australian consolidation prescriptions, AASB 1024 and the relevant sections of the Corporations Law, it is presumed that the function is to 'depict the affairs of an economic entity or group' of companies. AASB 1024 broadens the base of the consolidation process. However, Walker's (1976) comprehensive history of consolidated accounting exposes that initially numerous functions were posited, few supporting the current rationale being offered:

[In the 1920s, UK] consolidated statements were not regarded as primary reports. Nor were they thought of as depicting the affairs of an 'economic entity' or of a 'group' of companies... In the 1920's, consolidated statements were regarded as *supplementary remedial reports* (p. 77)

... U.K. accountants were concerned with *amplifying* the reports of holding companies and to *overcome the limitations* of conventional cost-based methods of accounting for inter corporate investments. (p. 353, emphasis added)[11]

Consolidating the separate financial statements of related companies lifts the corporate veil and consolidates (aggregates) the accounts of each as if they were the mere branches of one. Aggregated data are thereby claimed to be more informative than disaggregated data. This is a curious proposition. Virtually everywhere else in human endeavour, disaggregation or deconstruction is being proposed as the window on enlightenment. Idiosyncratic mechanics in the preparation of consolidated financial statements make those *aggregations* even less capable of meaningful interpretation than their components are in the separate financial statements of the controlled entities.

Conformity with other Australian Accounting Standards in the consolidation process exacerbates that effect by requiring specific adjustments of the data originating in the separate financial statements of the constituent companies. Those Standards create artifacts of their own – compulsory amortisation of the price paid for fixed assets, creation of tax-effect balances, and the carry-forwards of various types are examples. Some data appearing in the accounts of the separate companies are expunged from the consolidated financial statements, others are modified in a variety of ways, once the same Standards are applied to the aggregative data under the consolidation rubric.

Conformity with the Standard on deferred taxes in relation to eliminated profits and losses on intra-group transactions, for example, injects consolidated financial statements with data which did not appear in the accounts of any of the constituent companies. Superimposed is the impact of consolidation techniques which create data exclusively the province of consolidated statements, goodwill on consolidation, premium or capital reserves on consolidation, adjustments to consolidated fair values, consolidated assets and equities, creation of future tax benefits, and provisions for deferred income tax not in, or opposite to, those in the constituent companies, and the like. These are mere artifacts of the consolidation process. Through applying AASB 1024 and the relevant sections of the Corporations Law, consolidated balance sheets contain data for which no corresponding amount appears in the constituents' balance sheets. Using the lower of cost-or-market rule to book inventories may (in the aggregate) not correspond with the prevailing outcome of complying with the rule by the constituents.

Many of the resulting account balances do not have any counterpart elsewhere in the framework of conventional accounting. Nor do they

necessarily have any relevance to the financial assessments and evaluations habitually made in commerce. Further, the financial impact of
genuine transactions between companies within the group is eliminated
irrespective of the validity of the data. That contrasts with the legitimate
elimination of the cost of the investment in subsidiaries in the consolidation process to avoid double counting. The outcome is most curious –
artifactual data generated by the consolidation process only are inserted
in the consolidated statements, whereas genuine transaction data are
excluded. Consolidation processes manage to nurture the worst of both
sides of creative accounting.

Consider the general proposition driving consolidation techniques –
the notion of a group comprising the parent (chief) entity and its
subsidiaries or controlled entities. So much of the debate underlying
(and deemed to support) Australia's AASB 1024 and the new sections on
consolidation accounting in the Corporations Law address superficial
niceties regarding the artificial group entity to which the consolidated
statements refer (how to identify a parent company or a subsidiary; how
to eliminate the 'effect' of intra-group transactions, and the like), rather
than group superficiality *per se*.

Consolidated statements report on a fictitious structure, the group,
which lacks legal capacity generally to exercise property rights, sue or be
sued, incur physical or financial damage or impose it upon others; the
statements contradict the legal, social and financial essence which their
constituent corporations enjoy. By virtue of legal incapacity, *group* assets
and *group* liabilities are an impossibility unless the legislature intervenes,
for instance by introducing covenants such as apply under a Class Order
Deed of Cross Guarantee, or through the courts resolving liquidation
disputes by ordering *ex-post* a pooling of group assets. Recourse to the
group notion does, however, facilitate the labyrinths which have proven
so friendly to corporate finagling. Despite being paraded under the
'accounting politically correct' substance-over-form banner, consolidated
data are not user-friendly.

The substance-over-form safe harbour is an accounting fetish, with a
history dating from the 1920s. In essence, the objective is to prescribe
that accounting captures the financial substance of transactions. But, in
the context of consolidated statements, the substance-over-form criterion
offers no shelter. For the legal (and hence financial) substance is that the
assets and liabilities included in the consolidated balance sheet are those
owned and owed by the constituent companies, whereas the form is that
they are presented to be assets and liabilities of the mythical group entity.
Consolidated income or loss is the adjusted aggregate of the separate
companies' profits and losses. Consolidated statements are a particular
instance where, contrary to the profession's dictum, the form is forced
upon accountants in preference to the legal substance.

Elimination of the financial impact of legally binding transactions (e.g. sales and purchases) between group companies is a prescribed mechanism in the aggregation-cum-elimination process in consolidation accounting. Similarly, legally determined profits and losses made by the separate companies by virtue of transactions with other group companies are deemed to be fictitious, not at 'arm's length', *from the group point of view*. It is implicit in the claims made that, under the new legislative prescriptions, the consolidation process negates the possibility of assets being shuffled around group companies at ever increasing prices.[12] This is debatable. In consolidation under historical cost accounting, the purchasing company would report the asset at its cost and the selling company book its profit (or loss) on the sale; both are presumed fictitious in the group context and hence adjusted in the consolidation process. Of course, both the sale and consequently the purchase may be contracted on a genuine and commercial basis. Assets are 'worth' what they can be sold for, not what they cost to purchase. A 'view from the market' would dispose of the 'arm's length' problem. A 'view from the group' cannot.

Counterfactual reasoning encourages *corporate groupthink*. For the purposes of consolidation accounting, separate companies are deemed to be *de facto* branches of the parent company. In certain accounting texts, early consolidation procedures were, in fact, labelled the 'branching of profits and losses . . . depicting the affairs of a holding company and its subsidiaries *as if* they were a single organization or *as if* the subsidiaries were merely *branches* of the parent'.[13]

Dispensing with the legal status of the constituent companies is mischievous, in that it tampers with commercial and financial reality. The separate companies have an unquestionable separate legal status bestowed upon them by virtue of incorporation, and nothing short of liquidation can deprive them of it.

Consolidation techniques entail recourse to the counterfactual: presumptions that the profits and losses of the separate entities will filter ultimately (through dividend payments) into the parent entity, that the parent entity's assets will be applied to make good the losses of the subsidiaries, and that those of the subsidiaries will be applied to make good the debts of the parent. If that were *really* the case, then the cross guarantees would not be necessary. Expositions of accounting procedures usually present consolidation techniques as mathematical formulae applied to the separate data of the group companies to achieve the level of aggregation required. Notions of a distributive flow of wealth from subsidiaries to the parent entity, with leakages to shareholders with a non-controlling shareholding, are embedded in those formulae, though they are rarely disclosed to be what they are. In a structure of a parent entity and a string of subsidiaries and sub-subsidiaries, the amount of profits or losses of each is calculated as if to flow from the controlled entities up through the structures to the ultimate parent entity, as if the subsidiaries were *de facto* its branches. That evokes an obvious question: If the desire is to report the activities of the separate (especially wholly-owned subsidiary) companies as if, from the group point of view, they were mere branches of the controlling company, why not operate them as branches and not as separate companies in the first place?

An answer is less obvious. Eisenberg has noted that economic grounds were not driving the formation of most, if any, corporate groups. And there cannot be any accounting argument in favour of the holding/ subsidiary company structure. For if a branch structure were to be employed, the outcome would agree in broad objective – data aggregation. Idiosyncrasies of the legislatively prescribed reporting requirements of the Corporations Law and relevant Accounting Standards promote the substantial differences in the reported data that emerge. But, whereas the defects of historical cost accounting would remain, the aggregation of the branches' data would not entail the fabrication of accounting artifacts as occurs in the professionally and legally prescribed consolidation process.

Consolidated data are accounting's fabrications *par excellence*. The aggregates for the assets, equities, revenues and expenses of the constituents are virtually certain to vary from those in the consolidated balance sheet or income statement. Consolidated income or loss will vary even further from the aggregate of the constituents' results by virtue of compliance with processing Standards requiring the amortisation of the excess of the cost of the investment over the proportionate amount of the subsidiaries' equities acquired. Supposed indications of the solvency of the group, debt-to-asset cover, asset backing and other ratios conventionally calculated, are almost certain not to correspond to the aggregation of those which exist in respect of the separate companies. By virtue of the compulsory elimination technique, neither aggregate sales revenue nor aggregate expenses (by class or in total) necessarily equal the total of those of the separate companies.

These anomalies are exacerbated by applying tax effect accounting in the consolidation process. *Future income tax benefit* balances appear in the consolidated balance sheet by virtue of the compulsory elimination of any profit component in asset balances arising from intra-group transactions. Conversely, *provision for deferred income tax* balances arise in respect to the elimination of any loss component. Yet, it may well be that none of the related companies has either future income tax benefit or provision for deferred income tax balances in their separate balance sheets; or if they do, then the aggregate balances of each differ from the consolidated data; or, the net of the aggregates in respect of the separate

balance sheets differs or is in the opposite direction to that in the consolidated balance sheet. The point is, it is almost certain that the
consolidated balance sheet data will be substantially different from what
one would elicit from the balance sheets of the separate companies.

It is doubtful if anybody can make financial sense of such outcomes.
Certainly they defy common sense. Unbundling them in a group
comprising hundreds of related companies is nigh impossible. Yet it is all
done purportedly in the name of disclosure and clarification.

It is a matter of chance rather than design. Data so contrived, so
removed from real-world referents are unlikely to inform anybody of the
wealth and progress of the constituent companies, either individually or
collectively. Despite the financial obfuscation they facilitate, their counterfactual footings and the resulting artifacts, surprisingly consolidated
financial statements are perceived by legislative draftsmen, many legal
practitioners, the courts and many accountants to be a means for lifting
the corporate veil. To the contrary, they appear to achieve precisely the
opposite.

It is futile to expect progress by tinkering with the Standard on
preparing consolidated accounts. The reasoning for this view has a long
history and has been detailed elsewhere.[14] Perhaps what is required is a
Gestalt shift, a recourse to lateral solutions – either (i) proscribe wholly-
owned subsidiary companies and account for the decentralised operations *as if* they were branches; or, failing that, (ii) require an aggregation
of group assets based on the market prices of assets. Each promises data
more serviceable than any in conventionally-preferred consolidated
statements.

Alternatives to consolidation accounting

*Proscribe wholly-owned subsidiaries with recourse to branch operations and
branch accounting*

There always have been alternatives to the preparation of historical cost-
based forms of consolidation accounting. An extreme approach, for a
group comprising a parent company and wholly-owned or 'effectively'
wholly-owned subsidiaries, is to proscribe the latter's existence.[15]

The consequences of the financial chicanery recently revealed within
Robert Maxwell's public/private company combine provide an extreme
illustration of the need for radical reform. Again, difficulties arose due to
dealings between the private and public arms of the Maxwell empire –
groupthink prevailed. Over 3,000 creditors lent to this corporate monolith comprising over 400 public companies intertwined with some 400
Maxwell private companies, further complicated by their incorporation
across several national jurisdictions (Figure 16.1).

Figure 16.1 Maxwell group structure

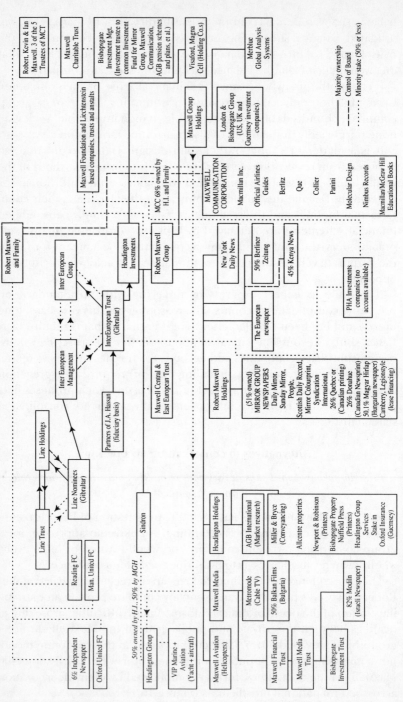

Source: Bronwen Maddox, *Financial Times*, 6 November 1991.

Interestingly, a joint report in 1995 prepared by international regulators in the banking, securities and insurance fields, *Supervision of Financial Conglomerates*, noted that where company structures are so complex as to impede effective supervision, power should be given to regulators to prohibit those structures. This is a similar response to that following revelations about the US utility holding/subsidiary company abuses in the 1920s (see note 15) and the perceived abuses in respect of the major Japanese *zaibatsus* resulting in their enforced break-up by US authorities after 1945. Such a response is long overdue in the general corporate arena.

Earlier we noted recent amendments to Australia's Corporations Law addressing abuses related to insolvent subsidiary trading. Having to lift the veil and step past the separate legal entity principle on occasions of financial stress invites the inference that the holding company/wholly-owned-subsidiary structure is failing the 'net-benefit-to-society' test. A legislative lifting of the veil would be unnecessary if subsidiary companies were prohibited.

Corporate abuses through group structures are evident in the fallout from corporate failures and dilemmas repeated each decade in Australia since World War II.[16] Erosion of public confidence in the Australian capital markets resulting from the large 'group' collapses in the 1960s and 1970s was repeated in the 1980s. Commenting on the 1960s and early 1970s collapses, it was noted that 'inter-company shareholdings and transactions have given cover to fraudulent dealing and to legally less serious but financially no less deceptive mis-statements of results and position'.[17] That observation equally describes events in the 1980s and 1990s.

Related-party transactions, especially round robins, were reportedly used by many well-known 1980s Australian entrepreneurs – in particular, the reported deals prior to Rothwells' collapse and then also in its ill-fated rescue; deals between a Spedley Holdings shelf company, P152, and a related public company, GPI Leisure Ltd;[18] and deals involving intermingled private and public companies within the Linter[19] and APA/Unity groups, respectively. The holding/subsidiary company structure certainly appears to have facilitated more than hindered those deals. It also effectively shielded them from the public gaze and scrutiny.[20]

Similarities with events at Stanhill Consolidated, Reid Murray Holdings and at Cambridge Credit Corporation decades earlier are all too clear. Commercial practices such as these have a disorderly, sometimes chaotic, effect on confidence in the securities market in particular and the capitalist system in general. More recently in the United Kingdom, echoes of Prime Minister Heath's 1970s lament can be heard clearly in the aftermath of reported shuffling of assets within the Maxwell empire prior to its collapse, to the detriment of thousands of pensioners dependent on the Maxwell pension funds.

It is highly doubtful that consolidated accounting data are serviceable for indicating the financial characteristics of either the parent company and its subsidiaries as an economic whole, or of them as separate legal entities. In many cases it is demonstrable that they can be a mechanism for manipulation.[21]

If wholly-owned subsidiaries are in effect *de facto* branches, and if consolidation accounting is intended to simulate branch accounting, an attractive proposition emerges. Make them branches, proscribe wholly-owned subsidiaries, and be done with it. Additionally, this would avoid the confusion generated by the regulatory imposition of the avant-garde ASC Class Order Deed of Cross Guarantee.

A similar hard-line approach is equally appropriate with part-owned *subsidiaries*, in so far as the *subsidiary* status attracts special accounting rules for the investment. Possibly that would be too radical for the corporate sector. But investments in the shares of other companies have the same nature irrespective of the differential power of control or other privileges they might bestow. It is difficult to identify any good reason why they should be accounted for differently. The defects and financial solecisms of consolidated statements are no less evident in respect of part-owned subsidiaries than they are for the wholly-owned.

Distinguishing between investments according to the degree of control exercised over the investment is no justification for differentiating the basis for its valuation, though it might well justify differences between their market prices. Whether there is control would have an impact on the prices the respective shareholdings would fetch in the market. The market might reasonably be expected to unravel that. Accordingly, investments in the shares of other companies ought to be reported at their current market prices, too. In our proposal, the financial affairs (assets, equities, revenues and expenses) of what now are known as wholly-owned subsidiaries would be absorbed completely as the financial activities of 'branches' of the primary company. Shares in what are now part-owned subsidiaries would be accounted for as investments in securities and would be stated at their current market prices. As such, the accounting for them would be identical with the accounting for all shareholdings in all other companies to which no controlling significance attaches. If the market does not accord the investment any market worth, then the accounts ought to report just that! It would seem reasonable to produce schedules of assets and liabilities of the partly-owned subsidiaries, as outlined in a later section discussing an alternative market-based system of accounting for wholly-owned subsidiaries.

That contrasts with accountants' and the legislatures' attempts to restructure corporate relations to alleviate the effects of commercial abuses worked through holding/subsidiary company structures. Patching up reporting by groups has kept many busy for a long time, possibly at considerable cost – but ultimately the outcomes appear to have fostered (or at least left untouched) the precise irregularities they were intended to remove.

Market price accounting for groups

Markets are never perfect. Information is never complete. But the market prices of items are as objective an evaluation of their contemporary money's worth, of their current contribution to the wealth of their owners, as can be found. The better the information, the better should be the evaluation, the financial assessments, and the decisions to invest and disinvest. Properly informed securities markets require accurate information of the current wealth and past financial progress of companies. Share prices might reasonably be expected to capture not only their companies' current financial position and an understanding of how it arose, but also impound all the expectations and fears for the future that the information might evoke. A rational economic perspective would suggest that.

Even if wholly-owned subsidiaries were proscribed, as suggested in the previous section, the great problem of accounting for investments in shareholdings remains. If wholly-owned subsidiaries remain, the problem is exacerbated. Whatever the case, it seems critical for an orderly securities market that all shareholdings be accounted for on the same basis. Differences in circumstances attaching to the shares – giving or not giving control as the case may be – would be impounded in their prices. If that were so in properly informed markets, perceptions of the relative degree of control and other advantages or disadvantages attaching to a particular shareholding would be transparent.

There are good grounds to suggest that all shareholdings should be reported in the owner's balance sheet at their approximate current market prices, as indicated by the current published details of stock market trading. Even though the trading data may not relate to parcels of the size held by the reporting company, extrapolation to fit the circumstances would effect as best an approximation as possible. Arguments of the likely impact of parcel size related to the trading data and to the holding being reported are countervailing and unlikely to diminish the validity of the process of approximation. So, we might safely invoke a general rule that the current market prices of all shareholdings be reported as primary data in the balance sheet, with no distinction between the reporting for shareholdings which give control and those which do not.

But we specify a necessary condition for the share price to be useful: the market must be informed with accurate financial information of the

wealth and financial progress of the companies in which the shares are
held. Currently, the market is uninformed or misinformed to the extent
that conventional income statement and balance sheet data are drawn
on to assess financial position. Periodic income statements and balance
sheets need, therefore, to simulate properly the only kind of calculation
that can determine the outcome of a business venture over its entire life
– a comparison between the sum of money with which it commenced
and (in like terms) the sum of money or its equivalent with which it
finishes – for that is only what periodic financial statements can
reasonably achieve. It is the function that they properly can be expected
to serve.

That prescription entails an accounting mechanism in which periodic
balance sheets contain data from which aggregations of the money and
the money's worth (selling prices) of the physical assets and the amount
of the liabilities can be determined and articulated income statements
produced. Adjusted for changes in the purchasing power of money,
income or loss then becomes, quite properly, the approximate increase
or decrease for the period in the company's general purchasing power.
Conventional accounting complying with the Accounting Standards falls
far short of that. Consolidation procedures inject their own fictions into
the conventional accounting system, exacerbating the information short-
fall. In the end a necessary condition to reporting share prices data
entails a restructuring of accounting.

If that were to be so, the reporting for share investments in unlisted
companies, for wholly-owned subsidiaries and for other unlisted companies falls into place. A reasonable surrogate for a company's non-
existent listed share price would be the proportion of its assets and
liabilities (accounted for as above). At least those data are indicative of
what underlies the shareholding, irrespective of whether it amounts to a
controlling interest or to the merest of a minority interest. If subsidiaries
were to remain, or if for substantial shareholdings disaggregated data
were deemed necessary, they could easily be provided in supporting
schedules of the various classes of assets and liabilities of the companies
in which the investments were held. Intercompany indebtedness between
related companies, intercompany sales and purchases, expenses and the
like, and the double counting they may entail in bland aggregations of
those data, can be disclosed in easily constructed schedules. In
consolidations, the veil is drawn over such information by the elimination rule, precisely the opposite to what is intended.

That approach partly accords with the view that 'The larger and the
more diverse the group, the greater is the need for the disaggregation of
consolidated accounts to show the performance and worth of operating
subsidiaries, entities or divisions within the group'.[22]

Importantly, reporting the selling prices for physical assets automatically would correct in the balance sheet of the purchaser. Irrespective of the prices at which assets had been transferred between the related companies, they automatically would be marked up, or down, to accord with the observable prevailing prices in the market. Whether these transactions were at arm's length would be irrelevant. Related companies could trade assets at whatever prices they chose and, separately, properly report the consequential profits and losses. Such data avoid the financial solecisms in consolidated financial statements, avoid the counterfactual assumptions underlying consolidation procedures, eliminate the complex and contradictory calculation endemic to the consolidation process as part of conventional accounting practice, and provide all the necessary aggregated and disaggregated data which it is said consolidated financial statements are to give – but which they fail to deliver.

Perversely, this alternative achieves the information objectives claimed for consolidated financial statements, without the mystery and without the make-believe. It also removes some scope for the manipulations so evident in the corporate failures reviewed in this book. Users, consumers of the data, can treat the related companies as single entities if they choose. They can aggregate and disaggregate as they like. The data necessary to do that would be there. They can group and subgroup, as they see fit. They can do so without artificially lifting the veil of incorporation. They can peep under it or peer through it if they wish without offending the separate legal entity principle, for so long the foundation of 'British'-based company law.

SEVENTEEN

Fatal Attrition:
Accounting's Diminishing Serviceability

> 'Piece-meal patching will not make a worm-eaten craft
> seaworthy; neither will piece-meal tinkerings of
> individuals, boards and committees make cost-based
> valuations trustworthy.'
>
> *R.J. Chambers (1991)*

No matter from what angle corporate failure is observed, accountants and their accounting products deserve major attention – and for good reason. Without question, the financial implications of corporate failure have an impact upon the welfare of the community irrespective of the causes or the personal culpability of the major participants in the corporation's affairs.

In the aftermath of the greedy eighties, the levels of criticism and litigation against accountants, auditors in particular, evidence the perceived involvement of accountants and auditors in failures and in some instances their perceived responsibility for it (Table 17.1).[1] Undoubtedly the accounting profession is extremely sensitive to its members' exposure to litigation in the aftermath of the 1980s corporate failures. Ongoing attempts by the professional bodies to have legislation limit accountants' liability for negligence bear witness to that.[2]

So too does the increased public comment on behalf of those bodies of the need for closer definition and monitoring of the ethical conduct of accountants.[3] Since the late 1980s, office holders in the ICAA and (what now is) the ASCPA have been quick to voice their allegiance to a more detailed ethical code.

Life after litigation

Upon commencing his term of office, the incoming 1993 president of the ASCPA was quite open on that score with the reported comment that by becoming involved in the 'tax scams of the '70s and the entrepreneurial corporate collapses of the '80s' the profession's highly prized self-regulation was put at risk, and with it the very essence of professionalism: 'The threat of increased outside regulation of the profession is ever

232

present. . . . Many members don't understand that once we lose self-regulation, we are no longer a profession; we become artisans working to a cookbook provided by others.'[4] A question we shall return to is whether this means that the profession should produce its own cookbook of procedures, to be followed come what may. If so, one must ask whither professional judgement?

Senior members of the regulatory bodies have pursued a similar line. Henry Bosch led the criticism of the unethical behaviour of many of the 1980s entrepreneurs – 'corporate cowboys' in his terms. It would seem he saw business evil at every turn whilst others saw none.

He notes that when he first joined the NCSC 'a few flamboyant entrepreneurs were perceived as folk heroes' and that their apparent 'dramatic financial success' received acclaim. 'Cautionary words from regulators were received with surprise and distaste.'[5] True enough. But those warnings regarding Bond, Skase, Goward, and the like, were generally late coming, low key, *sotto voce*.

In the public rhetoric generally the emphasis has been upon deviant, unethical behaviour. It is questionable whether all, or even the majority, of the behaviour complained of is deserving of being labelled deviant. Not so, at least, in so far as it implies behaviour which always entailed an improper departure from the accounting norm. Evidence has been provided here that much of the publicly-disclosed accounting by failed companies was in accord with the then established and compulsory rules. Much accounting was *creative* – but compliant. Other misleading accounting practices were possibly *feral*.

The profession has acknowledged that some of the behaviour of its members in those collapses was less than professional. Disciplinary actions against members have occurred, but the process has been criticised for the hearings being slow to commence and not open to the public. There is a push to revise the nature of those disciplinary proceedings.[6]

Commingling creative and feral accounting practices within complex corporate structures ensures that the financial outcomes are nearly impossible to unravel – a nightmare for investors, directors and auditors. It is a recipe for the use of a dart to choose an appropriate profit figure. Unprofessional auditing, if it occurs, simply adds to the muddle.

Without doubt, many conventional accounting rules allowing optional treatments were, and remain, deviant with respect to common financial sense and experience. But they are compliant with the mandatory Accounting Standards. In many respects Bosch's corporate cowboys have been made the scapegoats as far as accounting is concerned. Rather, some of the blame (at least) could properly be levelled at the financial information system responsible for cementing those practices into commerce in the first place.

Table 17.1 Selected negligence claims, notifications lodged with insurers and reported settlements

Plaintiffs (clients and liquidators of clients of)	Defendants	Damages claims/(result) $m
Duke Group	Ernst & Young, KPMG Peat Marwick & Ors, settled out-of-court reportedly for $35 million	$175 ($35)
Farrow Finance Company	ASC civil action against ANZ Executors Trustee Co. and the auditors, Day Neilson Jenkins	$50
Rothwells	KMG Hungerford	$40
National Safety Council	Horwath and Horwath	$263
Estate Mortgage unitholders	Priestley and Morris and Ors	$650
Estate Mortgage Financial Services	Tyshing Price and Co.	$25
Deposit and Investment Group	KPMG Peat Marwick	$73
Battery Group	Deloitte Ross Tohmatsu, settled out-of-court reportedly for $12 million	$132 ($12)
AWA	The initial judgment against Deloitte Ross Tohmatsu of $23.9 million was appealed and settled out-of-court reportedly for $12 million	$50 ($12)
Titan Hills	Coopers and Lybrand & Ors, settled out-of-court reportedly for $17 million	($17)

Client	Auditors / notes	$ million
State Bank of Victoria	Day Neilsen Jenkins, Ian Johns & Ors	$900
Spedley Securities	Priestley and Morris & Ors, settled out-of-court reportedly for $22 million	$320 ($22)
Tricontinental	KPMG Peat Marwick, settled out-of-court reportedly paying the Victorian Government $136 million	$1,094 ($136)
Independent Resources	Deloitte Ross Tohmatsu	$44.5
Adelaide Steamship	Deloitte Ross Tohmatsu and former directors; appeal of auditors against validity of ASC action was successful in April 1996 but the ASC successfully overturned the decision on appeal	$340
Bond Corporation Holdings	Arthur Andersen	$276.1
Colombia Tea and Coffee	Nelson Parkhill	Nominal damages
Keydata	Coopers & Lybrand & Westgarth Baldick	$17 ($17)
Linter Group	Price Waterhouse, concerns deals worth $320 million	$300
State Bank of South Australia	KPMG Peat Marwick	$3,100
Westmex	Thomson Douglas	$60

Sources: 'Clients – and liquidators of clients – sue firms for damages totalling $2 billion plus', *Chartac*, September 1991; and miscellaneous newspaper articles, including: I. Ries, 'Auditors find themselves in the hottest seat of all', *Australian Financial Review*, 10 January 1992, p 44; M. Gill and B. Pheasant, 'Record claim against KPMG', *Australian Financial Review*, 2 June 1992 and J. Falvey, 'Spedley claim may be $750 million', *Daily Telegraph Mirror*, 10 June 1992, p 36; 'ASC seeks $20m. damages in Farrow case', *Australian Financial Review*, 24 March 1993, p. 3; B. Pheasant, 'Auditors in danger from $2.5 billion claims', *Australian Financial Review*, 30 June 1993, pp. 1 & 6 and B. Pheasant, 'Accountants want to stop the damage', *Australian Financial Review*, 30 August 1993, p. 14. See also W. Hogan, 'Accounting Introspection', *Australian Accounting Review*, November 1994, pp. 54–64, especially Table 1. Figures in this table are as at October 1996.

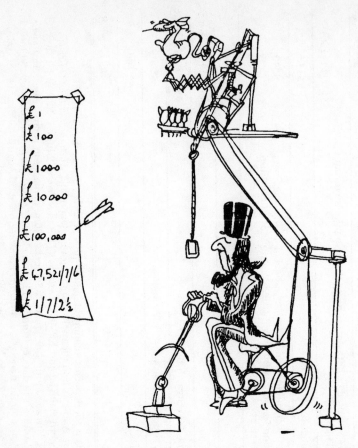

'What profit do you want?', *Company Accounting Standards*, a Report of the
Accounting Standards Review Committee, 19 May 1978, p. 54. Subject to
Crown copyright; reproduced with the permission of the Crown.

Nonetheless, over the past 30 years the accounting profession in
Australia has been keen to sheet home the blame for accounting failure
to virtually everybody outside of the accounting profession. Chapter 2
noted that its 1966 response to the spate of Australian failures during the
1960s exposed a virulent predisposition to 'tip the bucket' on whom-
soever happened to be in sight. Managers primarily were blamed for
those 1960s failures. Some aspects of the quality of company accounting
and disclosure came under attack in that report. But sloppy-to-bad
management attracted most of the profession's invective.[7]
    Auditing received some criticism, with an emphasis on strengthening
the hand of the auditor and requiring complete independence from any
unwarranted pressures that might be brought to bear by directors.[8]

There were other reforms proposed, including recognition of the need for the parent company auditor also to be the auditor of the subsidiary companies. Yet there was no suggestion of the type we propose here that the group structure be prohibited or in some ways constrained nor that consolidated accounting be dumped.

The general structure of historical cost accounting came in for only limited criticism.[9]

Overall, the impression to be gained was not all that different from commentaries on the 1980s breed of entrepreneurs – the escapades of Christopher Skase, Alan Bond, Russell Goward and John Spalvins, to name a few. The cult of the individual was strongly emphasised also in the 1960s press, when Herbie Palmer and the Catel brothers were in the dock, and when the name of Stanley Korman was prominent. They may well have deserved considerable attention. But focusing on the individuals diverted attention from how the underlying frameworks of accounting and auditing, institutional, legal and regulatory mechanisms facilitated deception, masked pending failure, and frequently exacerbated the disastrous financial outcomes.

But then, press exposure of the frailties, the mistakes, the ineptitude, the peccadilloes of the individuals made – and still make – for better reading and more entertaining viewing. They do nothing, however, towards rectifying the underlying problems in the system. In fact, they push solutions further from sight. The failures and their consequences sit in the wings ready to be repeated at a later date – as they were in Australia in the 1970s and again in the 1980s, with the predictable but unjustified dismay, surprise and indignation of politicians, investors, corporate regulators, accountants and auditors. It was a convenient but costly case of 'out of sight, out of mind'.

No doubt the 1966 report spurred on those in the profession who perceived the need to specify a more definitive set of rules for the processing of accounting data in the 'professional cookbook' fashion implied earlier. Indeed, the push for a complex set of Statements of Accounting Standards and the push for compulsory compliance with them in Australia might well be based on it. And along with it the beginning of the Australian slide in respect of corporate regulation.

In consumer protection terms the slide was southwards – from an emphasis on the rights of the consumers of financial information to receive serviceable data and towards promulgation of an accounting checklist, conducive to effecting regulation but devoid of any prospect of disclosing the wealth and financial progress of corporations. That slide in Australian accounting has been noted even from within the profession: '[accounting firm] staff . . . faced with a transaction, rigorously leaf through the rule books to try and find where it fits, and do not sit back and say what really happened. So we have this focus on the rule book rather than the commercial reality.'[10] Meanwhile, outsiders, including the deputy governor of the Bank of Scotland, tell a similar story with respect to the recent corporate failures: '[M]any accountants have failed to properly exercise judgement, are too anxious to conform and are too caught up in the technicalities of accounting standards rather than their overall objectives.'[11]

That is happening when others within the profession are claiming that there is adherence to substance over form in accounting for transactions, and that substantial reforms improving the system's checks and balances either have been, or will be shortly, implemented.

Our view is that contemporary responses from corporate regulators and from the accounting profession to the failures during the 1980s and early 1990s have been repeat performances. The 1966 report was a preview. Whereas the rhetoric has been couched in newer terms, the fundamental message has been the same. Bad management and the unethical behaviour and dishonesty of some entrepreneurs have been singled out as the primary causes of failure. The causes implied have a familiar ring, as does the remedy: promulgation of more Accounting Standards, now with statutory back-up to ensure compliance, has become the formula for regulating the disclosure of financial information. Specification of more compulsory Standards has become the current fad, the flavour of the decade – despite the lack of evidence that it is likely to succeed now, particularly so in Australia, when it has been so ineffective here and elsewhere in the past.

Henry Bosch, both during his time at the NCSC and since, has vigorously pursued more Accounting Standards as a mechanism for the regulation of financial disclosure. Australia has conformed to the pattern elsewhere in the English-speaking world in this respect. In the United States the promulgation of standard accounting practices proceeded initially through the operation of the American Institute of Certified Public Accountants' Accounting Principles Board to the current out-pourings of the Financial Accounting Standards Board – with nearly 130 Standards published to date. Regulation through threat of sanction for non-compliance with the prescribed rules appears to have been spawned by the push for a formula approach to financial disclosure – the 'cookbook approach'. Central to that theme has been the philosophy that the greater the number of rules, the more predictable the regulators' behaviour, the less accountants exercise professional judgement – the more effective the regulation. Perversely, the greater the regulation the less reliable accounting has become, and a fatal attrition of accountants' professional judgement has become more of a reality than a mere possibility.

More and tighter rules governing the behaviour of corporate mana-gers and directors have been high on the agenda, too. *Corporate*

governance is a new-age buzz-phrase within commerce generally. Definition of the principles of good practice in corporate governance also has
entertained analysts of corporate failure. It is claimed that the nebulous
bad management would be overcome by applying the principles of
corporate *best practices*. That analysis sits nicely with the 1991 monograph
on 'Company Failure'[12] commissioned by the ICAEW, which declares
that failure cannot be sheeted home either to inadequate audit or to
accountancy in general; management, changing economic conditions,
product failure and the like, all stand more accused. Our concern is with
the relative weightings given to those factors, and specifically the down-
playing in analyses of the role of accounting in corporate collapse.

A thrust in many institutional prescriptions has been that companies'
financial data should be used to anticipate failure. If only they were a
reliable enough indicator of failure or success. However, the truth is that
the present contents of companies' published income statements and
balance sheets are not serviceable for determining their current
financial positions or for discovering how they arose. Nor are those data
indicative of the critical financial characteristics of companies. If they do
mesh into reasonable predictions it is simply a case of serendipity.
Without knowledge of a company's present financial position and how it
arose, one is in a difficult position to predict likely future financial
positions and periodic outcomes, including failure.

One product of the 'better corporate governance' movement is the
1992 wisdom of the Cadbury Committee in the United Kingdom, in
particular its 'Code of Best Practice'. Ultimately, however, the code
amounts to little more than a series of motherhood statements regarding
the virtues directors must display and be seen to display, plus the
recommendation for audit committees to be mandatory for all public
companies. Essentially the Cadbury 'Best Practice' code presumes that
company managers now possess less integrity, have more questionable
ethics, and are more inept and more easily compromised than the community at large. Overall, the inevitable impression to be gained is that
bad, dishonest or unethical conduct by managers, directors and the like,
are the major causes of corporate failure – and that the code will set that
right. At best, that is a pious hope.

No sustainable evidence has been forthcoming that managers' ethical
behaviour is less acceptable than that of any other cross-section of the
Australian (or UK) community, or that it is at a lower ebb now than it
was in the past. Reference was made earlier to many instances of un-
scrupulous and unethical business practices in the past. It is likely the
current gang of corporate cowboys is no worse than its predecessors.[13]

It is wrong to consider the current problems as new phenomena.
Commonly suggested remedies take little heed of lessons of the past. The
UK's Cadbury code is typical. Significantly, nowhere does the code

explain how the appointment of audit committees will ensure that the financial information disclosed by companies will be indicative of their wealth and progress. Curiously, though, the code specifies that directors must present 'a balanced and understandable assessment of the company's position' (para. 4.1) and the Final Cadbury Report on *The Financial Aspects of Corporate Governance* declares its support for the cardinal principle of financial reporting, '. . . that the view presented should be true and fair . . . [aimed at] the highest level of disclosure'. commitment to the 'true and fair' criterion by the Committee stands in stark contrast with its official professional abandonment in Australia.

Despite all that, it is likely that eventually a similar code will be introduced into Australia following, amongst other works, Professor Hilmer's discourse on corporate governance in his *Strictly Boardroom*, the series of 'Bosch Codes' (*Corporate Procedures and Conduct*) and the general paranoia in the financial press. If past history is a guide, we must expect it would have little effect. We might expect no greater fidelity on the part of managers by virtue of the watchdog activities of the Cadbury-type audit committees and greater compliance with the approved Accounting Standards. Perversely, as a consequence we must expect also a greater incidence of creative accounting by virtue of the consequential stricter compliance with the plethora of Accounting Standards.

Corporate managers are placed in a no-man's-land, between a rock and a hard place. The cure is likely to be worse than the complaint. In this setting the ASX's reluctance to adopt the Cadbury recipe in favour of compulsory disclosure and explanation by directors of their corporate governance measures is to be applauded.

Consumerism

Accusing the directors and auditors for the post-1980s crop of failures is unreasonable. Disciplinary actions by the profession against some of its members imply some unprofessional activity.

Our case analyses do not explore that aspect. They demonstrate that compliance with the Accounting Standards was as likely to produce data which were not serviceable for the making of the ordinary financial assessments regarding solvency, liquidity, rate of return, asset backing, debt to equity and general financial viability, as when there was deviation from them.

Clearly corporate regulators and the spokesperson for the accountancy bodies do not see it that way. Henry Bosch, and his predecessors and successors at the NCSC and ASC, appear to be obsessed with the idea that we need more accounting rules of the kind currently in vogue. Changes to the national companies legislation requiring compliance with the

Accounting Standards, ASC surveillance, UIG wisdom statements, and consequent actions against firms and auditors for not complying with them, are indicative of that 'magnificent' obsession.

Against that background the inevitable conclusion is a widespread presumption that accounting practice provides management with serviceable financial data. Certainly the US Treadway Commission, the UK Cadbury Committee and proposals by Professor Hilmer in his *Strictly Boardroom* seem to hold that view. If so, then virtually all those inquiries into how directors ought to direct, how managers ought to manage, how audit committees ought to audit, are not much to the point. Cadbury's 'Code of Best Practice' strongly recommends that all companies have audit committees.

Supposedly an audit committee would ensure that the current, incorrectly directed Accounting Standards are complied with. If so, then companies and the public at large would be better off without audit committees. It is odds-on that compliant accounting will be creative, whereas there is a chance of something serviceable coming from non-compliance, subject to the rigours of the market and professional audit oversight to ensure that truthful accounts are presented.

There is very little evidence to demonstrate how more of the same variety of accounting data can improve the state-of-play. Analysts, for example, declared that until (and unless) Adsteam published consolidated statements a reliable understanding of its financial position was impossible. Precisely the opposite was more likely the case. The previous chapter explained that fiction-laden consolidated statements are the artifact *par excellence* of accounting, a proven longstanding vehicle for deceit and distortion.

None of the contemporary observers of the present corporate state (in their public utterances, at least) indicates awareness that the long history of *unexpected* corporate collapse contradicts the view that all we need is more of the same variety of public financial information. None has explained why the financial information relevant to administrators' assessments and evaluations when a company is known to be in financial distress, is treated as if it were irrelevant when the company is regarded as a going concern. Nor is it explained how such perceptions of financial distress or health are formed by administrators in the first place without current selling price data. Yet there are examples which expose awareness of what is required, though often the logic is astray.

Ernst & Young's 1990 *A Guide for the Company Director* enshrined the peculiar and pervading logic. It explained that directors of a *failing* company 'must have reliable and up-to-date information on the company's financial position . . . liabilities scheduled by due date [and] of realisable values of assets'.[14] True enough. But, they need that information continuously, in good and bad times. How else can anybody, inside or outside a company, assess whether it is failing, or when it is necessary to take steps to reverse the decline? Under the Corporations Law, directors are required to possess knowledge of an entity's current and expected solvency positions – an onerous task. However, it is one in which accounting has a major role to play. Recourse continuously to the market resale prices of assets (marking-to-market) would appear an imperative – albeit insufficient of itself – in meeting that legal obligation. Conventional accounting certainly does not produce information serviceable for those purposes, even on an annual basis.

Accounting and the consumer

Accounting practice enjoys a peculiar insulation from the conventional idea in Western law that consumers may presume goods and services to possess the characteristics making them fit for the uses commonly made of them. Why accounting retains this exception is impossible to understand. Moreover, the denial of ordinary rights enjoyed in most other settings is being institutionalised. Consider the following disclaimer in the 1995 revised Australian Auditing Standard AUS 202: 'Although the auditor's opinion enhances the credibility of the financial report, the user cannot assume that the opinion is an assurance as to the future viability of the entity nor the efficiency or effectiveness with which management has conducted the affairs of the entity.'[15]

What purpose that statement serves is difficult to deduce. The import of the second part of the sentence appears to contradict what is professed in the first. An auditor's opinion regarding a company's state-of-affairs lacks credibility if it cannot be relied upon by those making predictions about the company's future financial viability. If it cannot be relied upon, then the financial information to which the auditor's opinion refers does not deserve the credibility claimed of it.

In that context an auditor's opinion contrasts dramatically with quality assurances usually given to consumers of ordinary goods and services. Whereas the products of the accounting process are not goods of the kind contemplated in the usual consumer laws, those who use financial data set out in published financial statements do so with expectations reasonably identical to those who purchase the usual run of goods and services. It is reasonable that those who draw financial inferences from raw financial statement data do so with the expectation that they are fit for that use, that they are serviceable. With respect to the absolute amounts set out in the financial statements, it would appear reasonable that the data may be used to inform readers regarding the nature, composition and contemporary monetary worths of both the liquid and physical assets and the contractual amounts of the various liabilities, of the business entity to which they relate. A presumption of serviceability applies to financial relationships, too.

It is reasonable to expect that accounting data are fit to be used to calculate a variety of financial ratios whose products will be indicative of the company's financial characteristics – solvency, liquidity, the relative contributions of debt to equity in financing the operations, the asset backing for the equity interests, rate of return, the interest cover given by the level of profits, the financial implications of the relationships between the separate and aggregative amounts of the different classes of assets, and between the different classes of liabilities. Each of those matters relates to a specified date. In this respect accounting is like every system of instrumentation. The readings must correspond to changes in the external matter being depicted.

Drawing financial inferences from published financial data and from the products of calculations made with them is indisputably an everyday practice in commerce. Invariably, financial press around the world publish lists of financial ratios and offer comment on those relationships whenever the results of companies are announced. Invariably published financial statements expected to have been prepared within the framework of procedures specified by the national Accounting Standards are the source of the data used. Unquestionably that is the case with respect to those absolute amounts and ratios produced around the world. Brokers' broad-sheets on companies' financial positions, progress and prospects draw primarily from that source; as do the financial analysts and ratings agencies which specialise in tracking the financial results of companies' operations and selling their conclusions as services on a regular basis: for example, Moody's, Dun and Bradstreet, Standard and Poor's. So do those who incorporate it on an *ad hoc* basis as part of a wider variety of financial journalism, the financial press in general.

Virtually every textbook on financial accounting published in the English language over the past 70 years contains sections on analytical techniques requiring such calculations to be made from data drawn from companies' published accounts. It is reasonable to presume that the endurance of those expositions in teaching materials is indicative of a demand for the skills involved and indicative also of at least a pervading belief that the data can be used properly in that manner.

Likewise the publication of similar calculations, schedules of conventional ratios and aggregates, is commonplace in the annual reports of companies in many countries. Frequently, as in Australia's Statex, ten-year (or more) summaries are published inviting the inference that comparisons are expected to be made and that the data are serviceable for that purpose. A considerable portion of distress prediction research requires the making of similar calculations from data similarly derived. In fact, doing so is the emphasised thrust of that research. The presumed use of published financial data in those ways seems to have the unqualified endorsement of the financial markets, the regulatory agencies, commercial agencies, the financial press, teachers, scholars and the community in general.

None of the Accounting Standards is set within an explicit framework of data serviceability. Accounting quality control proceeds in a manner completely different from other systems of product control. That is curious when the professional bodies enthusiastically endorse a study of such matters as total quality control and total quality management as part of accreditation programmes. Even more so when every accredited teaching programme in Australia, and the professional courses and examinations in the United Kingdom and the United States, require the successful study of consumer law. Accounting students in these programmes have to understand how manufacturers are to produce goods of merchantable quality, but they are not exhorted to produce accounting data possessing the same basic quality.

The idea of serviceability enjoys unqualified public and government support, by far exceeding that of the notion of *caveat emptor*. The latter notion, so evident in the extract above from Auditing Standard AUS 202, can only serve to warn those who have the competence to assess for themselves technical and qualitative characteristics. *Caveat emptor*, however, is of no help to the inexpert. For the lay person, it merely is a warning to be wary. In every other setting it always is secondary to the general principle of serviceability. Lay persons reasonably expect professionals to protect them from having to make uninformed judgements and assessments. Evoking a *caveat emptor*-like shield would appear to contradict the ethos of every profession.

Recourse to the consumer law's notion of merchantable quality (fitness for use, serviceability) in the context of accounting is apt. Users of published financial data are consumers, albeit of a particular kind. Financial data are, in a sense, economic goods.[16] In the same way that peanut butter must be fit for its ordinary use – safe for human consumption – data from published financial statements might reasonably be expected to be fit for the uses we know are ordinarily made of them.

Consumers and consumer protection agencies concentrate on products, not the processes from which they emerge. Possibly the specification of serviceability evokes a natural selection mechanism by which a common production process emerges. If it does – then so be it. If not – does it matter? If there were a number of different ways of achieving the same thing, it would not matter if one producer used one method and a second chose another. Accounting regulation might well benefit from adopting a similar approach.

Financial data serviceability

Features which make financial data serviceable are readily identified. Primary assessment of a company's solvency (for both going concerns and distressed companies) necessitates the comparison of its immediate debt and the current money's worth of its available assets. Debt to equity ratios relate debt (actual money owing) to the money's worth of the aggregate of the shareholders' stakes in the company. Security for borrowing is assessed, *inter alia*, through the comparison made of the proposed borrowing and the money's worth of the assets pledged or available for debt cover. Asset-backing, for example, is assessed by relating the number of shares issued to the difference between the amounts of the company's debt and the aggregate of its money balances and the money's worth of its physical assets.

Each of those assessments and evaluations reduces to a comparison (of one kind or another) of amounts of actual money owed, money possessed or legally obtainable, and approximations of the money's worth of physical assets. Comparable rates of return of the type specified are calculated meaningfully only as the rate of increase in the money's worth of the net assets. Again, that necessitates (*inter alia*) comparison of contemporary amounts of actual money and approximations of the money's worth of physical assets, with the similar aggregates contemporary at a prior time.

Nobody with experience of the real world is likely to dispute such things. Nor, in order to understand them, do they require the invention of a special 'conceptual framework'. Everybody who has bought and sold, handled money, faced prices and price structures, or experienced the differential impact of changing prices and price levels would find such things unexceptional. They are common commercial knowledge, not peculiar to accounting.

Each of the financial indicators refers to commonly considered aspects of contemporary relationships between the financial features of a firm at a specified date, its financial position or changes that have occurred in that position over time. With respect to those primary, elementary and expected uses, only data indicative of actual amounts of money, or claims to money by or from the firm, or indicative of approximate money's worth of its physical assets (and their derivatives), are serviceable. Only such data are pertinent for the identification of the financially sound company, the company at financial risk and the company already in financial trouble. As shown in the above examples from healthy, ongoing firms and in the post-mortems on the failed, many of the products from conventional accounting were not serviceable for doing that.

That leads to the inevitable proposition that accounting data ought to satisfy the same general serviceability criterion of quality that applies elsewhere in the consumer society – that they must be fit for the uses ordinarily, knowingly and predictably made of them.

EIGHTEEN

Ethos Abandoned, Vision Lost: Accounting at the Professional Crossroads?

'We should speak . . . of the immorality of accounting; for it has been the quirks of accounting that have provided many of the opportunities for misdemeanours of . . . corporate officers.'

R.J. Chambers (1991, pp. 16–17)

Talking ethics has become a 1990s growth industry. Not surprisingly, the accounting profession sought also to blame a decline in moral standards amongst corporate managers as a major factor contributing to corporate collapse. Regulators of corporate activity, the financial press and politicians, also have been quick to jump on the ethics bandwagon. Immediate post-1980s headlines in the financial press are representative of the ethics push: 'Ethics becoming the buzzword of the 90s',[1] 'Call for higher business ethics',[2] 'Ethics rise in the West',[3] 'Corporate ethics come under the microscope',[4] 'Accounting education in "chronic neglect"'[5] and 'Big business elders crusade for higher ethics';[6] as are subsequent accounts: 'Declining ethics . . . bad company',[7] 'Profession begins to get serious about its ethics',[8] 'Society needs dose of ethics to purge its "moral chaos"',[9] 'Phillips bows out with call for code of ethics',[10] 'Another counselling centre for ethically troubled accountants',[11] 'Ethics is a tricky business',[12] 'The selling of ethics'[13] and 'Where does the buck stop?'[14]

One could well ask, where indeed?

Against that background, the issue of corporate and professional ethics might have been perceived as a relatively simple matter with which to come to grasp. As Roslender noted, accountants' quest for professional recognition should have pointed them immediately towards the social orientation – a primary duty to the public – which is universally accepted to be a primary characteristic of the professional.[15] Or so one might imagine. Ever since the specification of accounting provisions in the 1844 UK _Companies Act_, the explicit legislative theme has been that published financial information in the form of a company balance sheet and subsequently the income statement were to be _full and fair_ representations of the company's financial state of affairs and changes therein. Truthful accounts were deemed a *quid pro quo* of incorporation. Unquestionably, the ethos of corporate accounting was that those interested in a company's financial affairs were to be accurately informed through the annual financial statements made public. Beyond question, that was the explicit charge emerging from the Gladstone Committee of Enquiry which preceded the 1844 Act and followed a series of major joint stock company collapses.

Over time the 'full and fair' phrase has undergone minor changes – for example, *full and correct* and *true and correct* in the 1936 NSW *Companies Act*, *true and fair* in the 1948 UK *Companies Act* and in the 1961 Uniform Companies Acts, and similar phrases used elsewhere. But there has never been compelling argument that the original ethos was no longer the pervading essence, despite lengthy debate in the literature as to precisely what the phrases mean, and whether the words should be read separately or as one.[16] Accordingly, notwithstanding countless changes in recommended accounting practices since the 1960s, then promulgation of prescribed Accounting Standards, changes in the Standards-setting mechanism,[17] and successive revisions of Australian company laws up to 1992, the overriding requirement has been that a company's published accounting data were to show a *true and fair* view of its state of affairs at a stipulated date and its financial performance in the period prior to that date.

Camouflage the facts!

Typically, few are letting the facts get in the way. Consideration of ethics by the profession has been a whirlwind, faddish movement which has diverted attention from accounting's core activities. Nobody on behalf of the accounting profession appears to have spelled out what form ethical behaviour is to take in the corporate arena. Ethical behaviour has become something which everybody is expected to understand, a code to which everybody (except the offenders) automatically and voluntarily adheres. Hence, the ethics push has proved to be a red-herring, a diversion. Sceptically one commentator has claimed it is a 'defensive strategy necessary to assuage public fears that a State-granted trade monopoly and self governance will not be abused in favour of a profession's members . . . a shield behind which various forms of behaviour can be "tolerated" '.[18]

In the Western world embracing the tenets of market-driven commercial activity, it is less than clear what is ethical commercial behaviour and what is not. With a set of secular laws in place and voluntary compliance with the principles of the underlying Judeo-Christian framework, staying within the law and being constrained financially by the market are the final determinants of the manner in which Western commerce proceeds. Consider Professor David Fischel's attack on 'greed bashing' and the 'greed is good' stance forming the basis of his support for the actions of the embattled Michael Milken, the 1980s 'junk-bond king'.[19]

Motherhood statements have characterised the ethics push. Talk of corporate responsibility to protect the environment, responsibility to warn customers of limits on the serviceability of products, obligations to provide community services, contributions to charities, and the like, are rather empty platitudes without legal force or the force (sometimes) of common sense. First, it is interesting to note how the personification of corporate activity sheets home the blame for what is considered a dubious corporate activity to the legal entity itself, not to its human agents – its directors, managers, employees, accountants and auditors.[20] Yet, surely only the human agents can conceive, implement and follow through the actions complained of, only they make the choices between alternative proposals, only they direct the manner in which the corporate vehicle interacts with other corporations and real individuals within the community. Second, there can be considerable doubt whether corporate managers are acting in the best interest of the corporation if its resources are diverted from the market-driven financial objectives.

Cause and effect have been a preoccupation in the regulators' analyses of corporate collapses. Although cause and effect is a hotly disputed relationship in the discipline of history, the superficial histories accorded many corporate collapses embrace a rather strong willingness by observers to jump to simplistic explanations. Corporate regulators in Australia, the NCSC and its successor the ASC, the accounting profession and, say, the Cadbury Committee in the UK, have been quick to sheet home many of the problems to declining ethical behaviour by managers and financiers.[21] Of course, accountants who have departed from the prescribed Accounting Standards have been targeted deviants, as engaging in creative accounting. We have argued in this book that some may have been precisely the opposite, that creative accounting as likely arose from complying with those Standards as from deviating from them.

In any event, whether the moral behaviour of businessmen has declined is contestable.[22] Matters already discussed suggest that there is good reason to support that it has not. In the past, as now, the practices of leading businessmen and accountants have been the subject of criminal, civil and professional disciplinary investigations.[23]

Distinguishing business ethics as a class of behaviour of its own is a curious fad of the commentators on corporate failure. Business activity is really only one of many facets of human endeavour. No good reason exists why business ought to be different, with respect to how it proceeds regarding the relations of one participant to another, from how other human relations proceed. A delineation of business ethics from other human behaviour has skewed the debate from the real issue deserving attention – the features of the general commercial and financial framework in which corporate fraud and unexpected failure have occurred. Concentrating on the financial shenanigans of a few individuals who have either set out, or by dint of unfortunate temporary financial circumstances were forced to deceive, has little to commend it. It has been a fertile ground producing many 1990s reports (codes) including, in Australia, several editions of Bosch's *Corporate Procedures and Conduct*; in the UK, *Cadbury's Code of Corporate Governance*; and in the US, the American Law Institute's *Principles of Corporate Governance: Analysis and Recommendations*. Missing has been an exhaustive discussion of the framework within which, and the processes by which, a commercial society may proceed about its business in a reasonably well informed manner, fairly and equitably. Of course, one is in trouble immediately by making such comments. The terms *reasonably well informed, fairly* and *equitably* are open to definition and virtually every definition will attract complaint and dispute. At the other end of the scale, nobody could claim that the publication of unserviceable financial data is informing fairly and equitably.

There can be no doubt that the behaviour of some entrepreneurs of failed 1980s enterprises was less than a fulfilment of their fiduciary responsibilities. Descriptions of the collapses and the observations of the judiciary (for example, regarding Bond Corporation, Estate Mortgage, Spedley and Hooker) and the laying of charges by the ASC (at Qintex, Rothwells, Interwest, Linter, Duke, Equiticorp, Westmex, Budget and Independent Resources) pointed to action and inaction of managers, directors, accountants and auditors, which was questionable at least morally, and in other cases legally, in so far as it affected the fortunes of investors.

But then, what of those investors? What of the shareholders, noteholders, creditors and particularly the financial institutions who stumped up so much of the financial wherewithal to allow projects, schemes and the speculation (especially in property) to proceed? What might be said of their motives for investing in the prospective high-return ventures? Managers and directors whose behaviour is now under the microscope, those corporate cowboys of the 1980s, might well be said to have been buoyed along on the encouragement of the investors who supported their ventures, who were happy to hunt with the pack in the pursuit of expected high returns. It is but a short step from that scenario to a proposition that the investors generally were quite content with the *modus operandi*, so long as they did not have to share the blame if it came unstuck. It is instructive to note that initially few were publicly vocal in their questioning of the entrepreneurial push. Just the opposite, it was almost universally applauded.[24] As were those who were driving it. They were fêted nationally and internationally, seemingly never short of friends and admirers, many in high places.

We have suggested that the behaviour of many 1980s Australian entre-preneurs was no worse than that of their counterparts in the previous two decades. The history of corporate failure is replete with allegations of scallywags and con-men, cheats, swindlers and crooks, who set out from day one to deceive investors, deliberately so regarding the financial state of their companies, and deliberately manipulated accounting records and reports. Many were referred to earlier, whilst the 1990s exposes its own high-rollers – for example, Leeson (Barings' derivatives trader), Iguchi (Daiwa's bond trader), Benson (Metallgesellschaft's oil futures trader) and Hamanaka (Sumitomo's copper trader).[25]

In contrast, it might be argued, in mitigation of the questionable deeds of Australia's 1980s entrepreneurs, that they were spurred on by an investing public and even governments, right behind them, supportive of, applauding their ventures. And, we might presume, even applauding their tactics. A contentious view is that it would not have mattered too much what the entrepreneurs' intentions were, for if they had complied with the official Accounting Standards their financial reports were bound to be creative and potentially misleading. Deceit and evil intent mattered little in so far as investors were fed misleading financial signals about the financial wealth and progress of public entities. It was going to happen anyway. That is important, for it begs the question as to who ultimately should have ended up in the dock on trial.

Perhaps the personal ethics of the main public players in Australia's corporate collapses ought not to be on trial, or at least on trial as much as they are, and in particular not in so far as accounting is an issue. In the Australian financial press, Hugh McKay succinctly noted a theme we have pursued here: 'The exploitation of morality is one of the most corrosive of contradictions.'[26] Media attention on the individuals – we referred to it earlier as the 'cult of the individual' – has turned public attention away from the whales and toward the minnows to capture the human-interest angle.[27] Such attention is short-lived. Those individuals will leave the scene anyway, to be replaced by others – inevitably, unless the circum-stances in which they operated are changed to prevent it.

What ought to be under close scrutiny are the principles and practices in the loose framework in which commerce and industry proceeds and is supposed to be accountable, for that will be enduring unless deliberate action is taken to alter it. Attention ought to be on the relationship of commerce and industry and society as a whole, not on the personal strengths and weaknesses of individual members of it.

True and fair: fare-thee-well

Neither accountants nor corporate managers should have had any
doubts as to their overriding ethos. The *true and fair* override is
consistent with a commonly held view embodied in this dictum: 'To be
effective as a stimulus to ethical thought and behaviour, a code of ethics
should set out principles, ideals, virtues and values. What it should not
do is prescribe behaviour through a set of rules and regulations.'[28] Under
the *true and fair* ethos, ethical behaviour by accountants necessitated that
they produce financial information indicative of the financial characteristics it is held out to show. Few professional groups have as explicit an
ethical charge presented to them as that, and few have had it embodied
consistently (over 150 years) in legislation as widely used as the companies laws. One might have expected accountants and corporate
managers to have jealously guarded that edict.

Just the opposite has occurred. It has been abandoned. Described by
one regulator as an 'accounting anachronism', it has been replaced by
industry and professionally developed codes and rules (Standards) of
practice. Already an accounting textbook has referred to it as being
carried forward in legislation 'as something of a museum piece'.[29]

Without vehement objection by the accounting profession to its most
explicit ethical peg being thus demoted, the current Corporations Law has
relegated the *true and fair* override clause in respect of the financial
statements to a second-order imperative to enforce stricter compliance
with the profession's Accounting Standards. If directors or auditors are of
the view that the published data are not true and fair, they are to report to
that effect, not in the accounts proper, but in the notes to the accounts.
Not surprisingly, some maverick practitioners and corporate managers
have reacted quickly and strongly. Two good examples to date are the
tactics of the directors of Westfield Holdings, and the QBE and NRMA
Insurance groups. QBE, for example, having been refused court
exemption from compliance with the Standard covering Accounting for
General Insurance Business (AASB 1023), reported its 1992 results under
two heads – as per the Accounting Standards, and according to the
directors' preferred method of accounting.[30] The directors at Westfield
exercised their judgement to satisfy their true and fair Corporations Law
obligations when they 'derecognised' management agreements as an asset
– a sensible move, we would assert. However, their action did not accord
with Australian Accounting Standards. But to complicate matters even
further, it *was* in accord with international accounting standards. Life for
directors was certainly not meant to be easy.

It is surprising that the accounting profession generally has traded
such a unique ethical benchmark for the misguided safe-harbour

afforded by compliance with its Standards. However, the trade fits neatly into the concurrent attempts by accountants legislatively to limit liability arising from their professional work. As an aside, it was reported that recent action by the Director of Public Prosecutions has resulted in charges being laid (mostly under provisions of the old Companies Code) 'against several company officers for breaches of the "true and fair view" provisions'.[31]

Limiting liability – if the cap fits, wear it!

There should be little doubt that the level of professional indemnity insurance corporate directors and auditors take out is the primary factor limiting the extent to which damages for negligence might be extracted through litigation. Those individuals' personal wealths are unlikely to amount relatively to much. Divesting of property ownership is expected to mitigate exposure to personal loss. In the wake of past litigation and with the prospect of more to come, it is to be expected that insurance cover will be increased and premiums will continue to rise.[32] Accountants in general and auditors in particular are finding the insurance slug unpalatable. Their responses, whilst predictable, are somewhat questionable. As professionals, they claim sizeable fees for their services, but appear unwilling to accept the relationship between the level of fees and the risk for which it compensates.[33] Whilst it might be claimed that fees have increased to meet the high insurance premiums, it is far from clear that the fees were correspondingly lower before the spate of litigation or the surge in indemnity premiums. The same is true of company directors and valuers; insurance premiums are high, but then so are directors' and valuers' fees.[34] Many seem to want to have their cake and eat it too.

To that end, following similar moves overseas, accountants in Australia have pursued having financial liability for the consequences of their professional services limited by statute. A statutory cap on their liability arising through actions under the Corporations Law has been sought.[35] Such a proposal has an approximately 70-odd-year history.[36] The matter remains under parliamentary review – perhaps even given new life by the change of federal government in early 1996. A separate document (*Professional Liability in Relation to Corporations Law Matters*), prepared in June 1993 (updated in March 1996) by the Working Party of the Ministerial Council for Corporations, canvassed the professional bodies' alternative mechanisms to statutory capping, *inter alia*: combining self-regulation and auditor rotation, placing a limit on the useful life of financial accounts, permitting accountants to incorporate with consequential limited liability, and permitting companies to pay directors' indemnity premiums so as to split the claims on auditors by having directors well insured too.[37] Whilst the 1990s NSW and WA legislation supposedly restricts liability, accounting firms are not satisfied as the federal *Trade Practices Act* is perceived still – due to several claims against auditors during the mid-1990s – to provide users of accounts with the opportunity to seek damages of an unlimited amount.

Most of that *brouhaha* appears to be clutching at phantoms. It is questionable whether financial statements prepared in compliance with the profession's Accounting Standards ever had a useful life to limit. In the final analysis that is the root cause of many grounds for the litigation. Incorporation by professionals runs counter to the exercise of individual judgement, the very hallmark of professional behaviour – that which distinguishes the professional from the artisan. Nonetheless, it looms as the most likely outcome. Incorporation, in part, damages accountants' claims to professional status. Proposals for proportionate liability ensuring that directors with sufficient insurance cover would share the damages with accountants are reasonable, provided the objective is to increase the recovery of financial losses by the aggrieved. But they are less than honourable if undertaken as an alternative to rectifying a primary cause for the actions in the first place. It is difficult to imagine how accountants, directors or valuers can gain public respect by limiting liability.

It is even more difficult to understand how such actions can remedy unethical behaviour. Public opinion is more likely to view them as adding to it. Directors and valuers cannot expect to collect sizeable fees and not fulfil their fiduciary obligations in return. Accountants and auditors cannot expect to collect large fees and then not deliver quality products, with impunity. It has been suggested, perhaps unkindly, that those who are finding it too hot in the kitchen ought to get out.[38] Notwithstanding directors' and accountants' desires, neither can enjoy their commercial status and receive their financial rewards, but not accept the risks.

Technical subservience: professionalism lost?

Attacks on the professionalism of auditors and accountants following corporate collapses are now commonplace. Whereas Australians are said not to be litigious by nature, they have found it in their water in recent times to launch numerous negligence suits against members of the accounting profession. Avowed litigants (presumably by nature) in the US no doubt have shown the way, been good teachers. But the locals have been willing students. Claims in the United States have generally dwarfed those in Australia and the UK, in the past. In the United States, for example, in 1991 the seventh-largest accounting firm, Laventhol & Howarth, was placed in bankruptcy owing to the settlement of litigation claims.[39] Claims against auditors catalogued in Table 17.1 are also of alarming proportions. Indeed, it is no wonder Australia recently ranked number two in the world after the United States in the litigation-against-auditors stakes.[40]

A common thread in the reporting of those claims is the theme that auditors have acted unprofessionally, that they have been negligent in carrying out their audits or that their ethics have declined. In certain cases this may have been so. However, explanations of what auditors generally were expected to do that they did not, how they were expected to behave differently, are curious omissions in most of that reportage. Actually, there are no good explanations within the framework of accounting and auditing rules with which accountants have to comply, and the framework in which they are to work. Exposure to litigation is inherent in the former and risk to their professional status in the latter. That is a tragic outcome for a professional group. They are on a hiding-to-nothing from the start – a 'mission impossible'.

Auditors are in a no-win situation The count is over before they even enter the ring. The inherent creativity of conventional accounting data assures that even where fraud is absent, auditors are to provide unqualified reports when published income statements and balance sheets have been prepared in conformity with the prescribed Accounting Standards and to qualify when they do not, even though to do the opposite in many cases might be the more prudent. Curiously, no action alleging that the accounts were misleading because they were the product of complying with the Accounting Standards has arisen in the litigation surrounding corporate collapse, though such an action may well eventuate within that setting when the impact of compliance on the published financial data of some failed companies becomes more apparent.

If this comes to pass, argument as to whether compliance with professional rules is a strong defence against negligence claims will be riveting stuff – reminiscent of the events surrounding the 1931 UK *Royal Mail* case, but with the benefit of over 65 years of case studies to draw upon. It could damage accountants' professional status considerably. It might also evoke a hasty about-face by the legislators regarding the compulsory compliance with the prescribed Standards. Facing those prospects, auditors may well be as diligent as possible within the framework in which they are forced to work, but incur uncontrollable exposure to litigation; damned for certain if they do not comply and likely to be damned some day if they do.

Some of the blame for that situation must be borne by the auditors themselves. Specification of Standards within which they are to work has been embraced by many as a kind of safe-harbour against litigation.[41] In this regard some auditors have been willing travellers with the regulators who have found sets of rules convenient benchmarks against which to test corporate reporting performance. Neither can have it both ways. If the auditors and accountants are to have any defence against claims that their compliance with the 'cookbook' Accounting Standards was itself negligent, they need to distance themselves from the Standards as quickly as possible. Likewise the regulatory watchdogs. It is not beyond the realms of possibility that their enforcement of compliance with the Accounting and Auditing Standards currently in force could, some time in the future, be viewed as negligence on their part. If watchdogs do not protect the community at large as they are expected to, then it is common sense for them to be replaced.

So, too, may the Accounting Standards-setters be replaced. For when it is realised how inadequate the Standards are for producing serviceable accounting data, the work of those who devised them may well attract more attention from the financial victims of corporate failures than that of the directors, managers, accountants or auditors. It is sobering to note in US product liability cases how the manufacturers are being sued for poor-quality products. For example, it is the manufacturers of breast implants who are being sued, rather than the surgeons!

Both the Crown and the professional accountancy bodies, legal draftsmen and the Standards-setters may be sitting on a time-bomb ready to explode.

Like most maturing professions, accountancy wants to get there fast. In this respect the professional accountancy bodies in Australia, as else-where before them, have spent considerable time and fortune over the past two decades trying to create a public image of their not-to-be-denied professional status. It probably has changed the image, though likely not for long. The trouble is, the professional bodies appear to believe their own propaganda – the product so needing an overhaul remains virtually unchanged. Centres-of-excellence are emerging under ASCPA patronage – in financial accounting, management accounting, public sector accounting and treasury, not in recognition of excellence, but to seek it. It is credentialism at its extreme. They would not appear to have spent anywhere near as much on either the education of entrants to the profession, by way of untied grants and the like, or on funding pure research.

One strategy of the AARF has been to commission monographs, either to give the existing practices the appearance of having the underpinning force of a body of theory or to pave the way for 'official' solutions to accounting problems. Both have further entrenched the accounting and reporting *status quo*, shown over three decades in the inspectors' and other official inquiries into corporate failures, and reportage in the financial press, to fall far short of the *true and fair* ethos. This deficiency prevails notwithstanding a long recognition of its existence.

Sociologist Bernard Barber identified the features of emerging or maturing professions: middle ranking in respect of generalised knowledge and community orientation, heterogeneous membership, the struggle to enforce their own rules of conduct and ethics.[42] Accountancy would seem to fit those characteristics well. Conformity to that pattern sends an important message to the commercial world regarding the efficacy of accounting products to be used for the assessment and evaluation of the financial health, the wealth and progress of companies – those products are technically very crude.

Few groups act with as much faith in the power of their own rhetoric. Attempts to talk away the supposed gap between what accountants and auditors do and what they are expected by the public at large to be doing is apposite. We are told that what accountants do and how they do it is not questionable, it is more the case that everybody other than members of the profession and regulators has unreasonable, misguided, expectations – there is an *expectation gap*.[43] A gap, that is, between what the consumers unreasonably expect from accounting and auditing, and what they get.

That is true enough. One would think a better way of fixing the image would be to improve the product, improve what the consumers get, or at least argue it is not a hazard – as the tobacco lobby is doing. What is inexplicable is the promotion of the idea that the way to repair the damaged image of accounting and auditing is to have consumers understand that accounting data are not serviceable, that published financial statements are limited in their function – do not disclose the wealth and progress of companies; and that whereas they are to be declared *true and fair*, they are no such thing. That is, to explain that there is not so much an expectation gap as what amounts to a *performance gap*. That is tantamount to the tobacco lobby agreeing that smoking is dangerous and that smokers merely have false expectations – set them right and the danger will be gone. Possibly there is a message from the anti-smoking movement: perhaps the way forward for accounting reform is to have income statements and balance sheets labelled *financial hazards*.

Accounting at the professional crossroads

Corporate accounting is 'in crisis'.[44] It is in a chaotic state as the evidence in this volume demonstrates.[45] Further testimony to this state are the settlements of claims against audit firms, including one of over $135 million (Tricontinental), litigation claims pending against auditors, including one of $3.1 billion (State Bank of South Australia), the $276.1 million damages claim by the liquidators against the auditors of Bond Corporation alleging breach of duties and failure to warn the company of its impending demise, and even the recent *smaller* $60 million claim by Bankers Trust and several Westmex shareholders against Westmex's 1987/88 auditor and partners, seeking damages for negligence and misleading and deceptive conduct. The Westmex action was brought under the Trade Practices legislation limb pertaining to negligence. However, that legislation potentially has a wider ambit.

It is reasonable to suggest that many of the data which appear in income statements and balance sheets prepared in compliance with the Accounting Standards do not meet the criteria contained in section 52(1) of the Australian *Trade Practices Act* – that, 'A corporation shall not, in trade or commerce, engage in conduct that is misleading or deceptive or is likely to mislead or deceive'. The recent NRMA prospectus case indicates that the Act can be invoked in respect to the companies' financial affairs. Publishing financial statements containing misleading data of the kind we have described would appear to be apposite. Intent to mislead is not necessary (*Hornsby Building Information Centre Pty Ltd v Sydney Building Information Centre Pty Ltd* (1978) 140 CLR 126 at 223 per Stephen J.); and that meshes with many of the outcomes of diligent compliance with the Accounting Standards without any intention to deceive. The focus of the Act is the class of consumers likely to be affected by the conduct (*Parkdale Custom Built Furniture Pty Ltd v Puxu Pty Ltd* (1982) 149 CLR 191 at 199). It is not unreasonable to place the consumers of accounting data in that setting. It has been held (*Taco Co of Australia v Taco Bell Pty Ltd* (1982) 42 ALR 177) that those who might be considered misled extends to 'the public, including the astute and the gullible, and the intelligent and the not so intelligent, the well educated and the poorly educated'; that clearly would capture the reasonable recourse to companies' published financial statements by those without any technical understanding of the machinations of accounting in general or the Accounting Standards in particular. It would appear that recourse to the *Trade Practices Act* by the consumers of companies' published financial data is a time-bomb waiting to be detonated.

From the published financial statements it remains impossible to assess the wealth and progress of a company, virtually impossible to calculate reliable indicators of solvency, rate of return, asset backing, gearing, and the like. Published financial statements contain data which are mere artifacts of the processing rules imposed upon accountants through the compulsory imposition of Accounting Standards, some of which lead to data being pure fiction. The latter are not merely unrepresentative of what they describe; they have nothing to describe, no referent in the real world. The discussion on creative accounting in Chapter 2 and the instances of *creative* and *feral* accounting described in Chapters 3 to 14 from the 1960s to the 1980s demonstrate the continuing unserviceable state of accounting information. Is it any wonder that there is a crisis?

That evidence leads to an almost inevitable proposition: notwithstanding the best of intentions and the highest integrity, compliance with many Accounting Standards will almost certainly lead to creative (untruthful) accounting; deliberate deviation from historical-cost based, fiction-laden Standards is necessary to produce serviceable (truthful) financial information. All of which begs further questions: Whither regulation, whither quality, whither professionalism?

No evidence has been produced by the professional bodies or the corporate regulators to support the idea that the quality of accounting data and reporting can be guaranteed through compelling compliance with prescribed practices. It is reasonable to presume that the regulation is intended to protect the users of the data in company accounts from, rather than expose them to, financial peril. It is inexplicable why, in the face of what we believe to be irrefutable evidence that the accounting data emerging from the existing regulated process fail to inform and hence to protect, the regulators push for more of the same.

In a reasonably well ordered society one would expect, indeed demand, regulation to be directed to achieving quality, reliability, fitness for use – serviceability of the product, rather than mere standardisation of the processing rules. That standardisation is a virtue *per se* is a contestable proposition at the best of times. Yet, the accounting profession appears to have led the field in the pursuit of standardisation divorced from the pursuit of serviceability. Latest moves by the international Accounting Standards-setting body to have the IASC Standards adopted world-wide indicates the malaise is universal. Accountants would do much better for themselves were they to adopt the current vogue and have mission statements and the like directed towards producing serviceable data. As it is, they have 'mission impossible' forced upon them.

Apparently, compliance with prescribed processes (the Accounting Standards) is assumed to be an effective regulatory mechanism. Missing is the link between the prescribed practices and the quality of the end product. So, whereas there is regulation of process, the quality of the end product is not assured. Not one of the Accounting Standards, nor the Statement of Accounting Concepts,[46] specifies *a* general quality serviceability characteristic (pp. 242–245), which the emerging data are to possess, singly or in combination. This is at a time when quality, quality of outcomes in particular, is the general desideratum virtually everywhere. The notion of quality is somewhat like the Holy Spirit; except that whereas the Holy Spirit is everywhere, quality is the characteristic pursued everywhere – except, it seems, in accounting!

With some justification we might also question whether compulsory compliance with prescribed processing standards is compatible with the notion of a profession. Professional activity is differentiated from that of the artisan. Artisans ply their craft according to hands-on experience, use regular and proven technology known to all in the craft without necessarily understanding why it is used, methods handed down from artisan to artisan. Their knowledge and skill, though considerable, is a common matter, rarely idiosyncratic. By contrast, the distinguishing feature of a professional is the exercise of the accumulated skill and wisdom, the out-of-the-ordinary, extraordinary expertise applied equally to both the ordinary and out-of-the-ordinary, the extraordinary circumstances. Professionals and their professions are distinguished from others by the exercise of the *differentia specifica* of their practices which set them apart from the rest of the community. That entails recognition of a social obligation, to apply one's skill and wisdom for the general benefit – requiring independent judgement as to how best to proceed.

Specifying compulsory rules (Standards) for processing accounting data, without also specifying necessary end qualities or characteristics to be achieved, poses a serious threat to accountants' claims to professional status. So does the pursuit of limited liability for the consequences for their actions. That leads to other propositions: compulsory compliance with Accounting Standards which concentrate on processes, not outcomes, is not necessarily conducive to producing serviceable financial data; and, in any event, compulsory compliance with the prescribed processing Standards is incompatible with professional activity.

Conventional accounting practices complying with the prescribed Standards have masked impending failure, exacerbated losses to creditors and shareholders, and provided regulators with a recurring dilemma.

Regulators of corporate activity have not heeded the lessons of history – the wailing, the gnashing of teeth and the rhetoric of indignation at the sequential episodes of corporate failure have been recurrent, but ineffective, responses. Possibly, the current litigation against corporate officers, accountants and auditors is only the first phase of inevitable outcomes for those whose actions further entrench the *status quo* in respect of corporate financial reporting.

It is not difficult to imagine that somewhere, somehow, some day, an alert judge will question the serviceability of conventional accounting data. A 1996 NSW Supreme Court judgment by McLelland C.J. suggests it is nigh – he described the untangling of one Standard prescription on goodwill as 'almost a metaphysical problem'.[47] Against financial common sense, the financial nonsense promoted in the Accounting Standards will be nigh impossible to defend.

Postscript: deregulation, serviceability, professionalism

Our case for reform outlined in Chapters 16, 17 and in this chapter pursues the less detailed regulation of processes, but the more effective regulation of outcomes. Accounting Standards of the kind generally in force are conducive neither to producing serviceable accounting information nor to ensuring true professional endeavour. Regulation through the compulsory compliance with Standard processes and formats has not improved the quality of accounting data. There is no evidence even that it has achieved the comparability which is claimed as its virtue. Indeed, there is disturbing evidence to the contrary.

Notwithstanding continuing pleas by spokespersons of the profession to continue to improve the quality of accounting, the road being followed is *more* of the same – increased compliance, now in respect not only of national, but also of international, Accounting Standards.

One would have thought it obvious that the present regulatory framework has failed to achieve the overall quality of accounting data, let alone improve it. The only regulatory defence for compulsory Accounting Standards is that they would improve the serviceability of accounting information. One would pursue that line with the expectation that the more Standards, the less the complaint and criticism of accounting from consumers, and the fewer the instances of creative accounting. We have more prescribed procedures now than at any time in our history, nationally and internationally. One would have thought that there would be evidence of a decline in the dissatisfaction with the data accountants are producing – evidence of less creative accounting. The opposite has occurred (nationally and internationally).

Against that background it is most curious that the ASC is reported to be determined to 'enforce the rules and apply them strictly as worded', even it seems if the 'ASC might say privately what you have to do does not make sense'. Whether it makes sense, according to the ASC, 'is not the issue'.[48] To the contrary, it *is* the issue! The ASC has the opportunity to be a public voice on consumer protection in respect to financial information. It looks as if financial nonsense will continue to be protected in the safe-harbour of the Accounting Standards.

The many *unexpected* corporate collapses reviewed in this book exposed gross anomalies and continuing generic defects of existing accounting practice.

Accounting information as a serviceable product and accountancy as a professional endeavour are undeniably at the crossroads. Without change, users will continue to lament that 'corporate accounting does not do violence to the truth occasionally, and trivially, but comprehensively, systematically, and universally, annually and perennially'.[49]

Notes

1 Swindlers' list?

1 D. Light *et al.*, 'The secret society which sank Australia', *Sydney Morning Herald*, 28 July 1990, p. 63. The term 'high-fliers' draws more on the personalities (Bond, Skase, Hawkins, *inter alia*) heading the companies than on particulars of the companies.

2 T. Sykes, *Bold Riders* (Sydney: Allen & Unwin, 1994), p. 571.

3 H.Y. Izan, 'Corporate distress in Australia', *Journal of Banking and Finance*, June (1984), pp. 303–320.

4 A.E. Hussey, *Shareholder and General Public Protection in Limited Liability Enterprises from 1856 to 1969* (Unpublished MEc Thesis, University of Sydney, 1971).

5 Dun and Bradstreet Corporation, *The Business Failure Record* (New York: Dun and Bradstreet Corporation, miscellaneous issues). Also E.I. Altman, *Corporate Financial Distress* (New York: Wiley, 1983), p. 32.

6 T. Sykes, *Two Centuries of Panic: A history of corporate collapses in Australia* (Sydney: Allen & Unwin, 1988), p. 548.

7 Anon, *Institutional Investor*, November 1989, p. 127; Anon, 'Alan and his mates: Lessons from the drawn-out collapse of the Bond businesses', *The Economist*, 13 January 1990, pp. 14–15; *The Financial Times*, 5 January 1990, p. 19. These, and similar 1990s laments by H. Bosch, *The Workings of a Watchdog* (Melbourne: William Heinemann, 1990), prompted responses by spokespersons of the profession, viz. W. McGregor and J. Paul, 'Corporate collapses: Who's to blame?', *Charter*, September (1990), pp. 8–10 and 13; W. McGregor, 'True and fair view – an accounting anachronism', *Company and Securities Law Journal*, December (1991), pp. 414–418; and P. Howard, 'Auditors in clash over standards', *Financial Forum*, August 1994, pp. 1–2.

8 S. Cronje *et al.*, *Lonrho: A portrait of a multinational* (London: Penguin, 1976), pp. 136 and 141, respectively.

9 C. Brooks, *The Royal Mail Case* (Toronto: Canada Law Book Co., 1933; reprinted New York: Arno Press, 1980), p. xiii summarises the RMSP Co. saga; and our Chapter 15.

10 Anon, 'Finding the facts', *Sydney Morning Herald*, 25 November 1965.

11 Sykes, *Two Centuries of Panic*, p. 424; and our Chapter 8.

12 C. Ryan, 'Going for broke', *Sydney Morning Herald*, 20 May 1989, pp. 75 and
    78 at 75.
13 J. Gilmour quoted in S. Fitzgerald and C. Jones, 'Accountants come under
    fire', *Sun-Herald*, 23 September 1990, pp. 12–13 at 12.
14 T. McCrann, 'Westpac takes its medicine', *Daily Telegraph Mirror*, 21 May 1992,
    pp. 27–28 at 27.
15 M. Walsh, 'Lending binge was institutional hubris', *Sydney Morning Herald*,
    21 May 1992, p. 29.
16 B. Pheasant, 'Auditors in danger from $2.5bn claims', *Australian Financial
    Review*, 30 June 1993, pp. 1 and 6 at 6. The phrase 'in crisis' was used in a
    document submitted in May 1993 by the joint task force of the two major
    accounting bodies, the ICAA and the ASCPA, to a federal government
    working party on professional liability.
17 ASCPA and ICAA, *A Research Study on Financial Reporting and Auditing –
    Bridging the Expectations Gap* (Sydney and Melbourne: ASCPA and ICAA,
    1993); followed in 1966 by *Beyond the Gap*.
18 D. Greatorex *et al.*, *Corporate Collapses: Lessons for the future*, (Sydney: ICAA,
    March 1994).
19 D. Miller, *The Icarus Paradox: How exceptional companies bring about their own
    downfall* (New York: Harper Business, 1990), p. 2.
20 As suggested by Mark Burrows on Andrew Olle's 2BL (ABC Radio) morning
    programme, 8 April 1992.
21 Bosch, *The Workings of a Watchdog*, pp. 123–124.
22 Anon, 'Bean-counters fight back', *The Economist*, 14 December 1991,
    pp. 79–80. Also P. Sikka *et al.*, 'Guardians of knowledge and the public
    interest: Evidence and issues in the UK accountancy profession', *Accounting,
    Auditing and Accountability Journal*, Vol. 2 No. 2 (1989), pp. 47–71; R.A.
    Chandler, '"Guardians of knowledge and public interest": A reply',
    Accounting, Auditing and Accountability Journal, Vol. 4 No. 4 (1991), pp. 5–13;
    F. Mitchell *et al.*, 'Accounting for change: Proposals for reform of audit and
    accounting', *Fabian Discussion Paper*, No. 7, 1991; and P. Sikka *et al.*,
    '"Guardians of knowledge and public interest": A reply to our critics',
    Accounting, Auditing and Accountability Journal, Vol. 4 No. 4 (1991), pp. 14–22.
23 T. McCarroll, 'Who's counting?', *Time*, 13 April 1992, pp. 48–50 at 49. See
    also W. Sternberg, 'Cooked books', *The Atlantic Monthly*, January (1992), pp.
    20–22, 24, 26, 35 and 38.
24 Public Oversight Board, *Issues Confronting the Accounting Profession: A Special
    Report by the Public Oversight Board of the SEC Practice Section* (Stamford, CT:
    AICPA, 5 March 1993), emphasis added.
25 Respectively: C. Ryan, 'Auditors are being called to account', *Sydney Morning
    Herald*, 29 April 1989, pp. 41 and 48; Anon, 'The accounts are a joke', *Sydney
    Morning Herald*, 29 May 1989; T. Sykes, 'Audit served no useful purpose',
    Australian Business, 12 September 1990, p. 6; R. Walker, 'What makes an audit
    "true and fair"?', *Business Review Weekly*, 11 January 1991, p. 61; T. Kaye,
    'Uproar on accounting proposals', *Australian Financial Review*, 29 March
    1993, pp. 1 and 35; B. Pheasant, 'Auditors in danger from $2.5 bn claims',
    Australian Financial Review, 30 June 1993, pp. 1 and 6; and B. Pheasant,
    'Accountants want to stop the damage', *Australian Financial Review*, 12 August
    1993, p. 14.
26 W. P. Birkett and R. G. Walker, 'Response of the Australian accounting pro-
    fession to company failure in the 1960s', *Abacus*, Vol. 7 No. 2 (1971), pp.
    97–136. And, for example, in the 1970s: 'Cambridge fall calls joint accounting

into question', *Australian Financial Review*, 19 January 1976; 'The need for a new spirit of realism in accounting', *Australian Financial Review*, 5 April 1979; and 'What in hell's name happened?', *Australian Financial Review*, 14 February 1979. Reference to *déjà vu* was discussed in F.L. Clarke and G.W. Dean, 'Chaos in the counting house: Accounting under scrutiny', *Australian Journal of Corporate Law*, Vol. 2 No. 2 (1992), pp. 177–201 and again in R.G. Walker, 'A feeling of déjà vu: Controversies in accounting and auditing regulation in Australia', *Critical Perspectives in Accounting*, Vol. 4 (1993), pp. 97–109.

27 See, *inter alia*, B. Pheasant, 'Ripples on the corporate front', *Australian Financial Review*, 11 March 1992. 'Fuzzy law' is discussed in J.M. Green, 'Rogues – how to keep them out of the boardroom', *Company and Securities Law Journal*, December (1990), pp. 414–419; '"Fuzzy law" – a better way to stop "snouts in the trough"', *Company and Securities Law Journal*, June (1991), pp. 144–157; 'A fair go for fuzzy law', Parliamentary Joint Committee on Corporations and Securities Conference, March 1992; and D. Forman, 'A fuzzy route to greater clarity?', *Business Review Weekly*, 9 July 1993, pp. 34–35.

28 W. McGregor, 'True and fair view – an accounting anachronism', *The Australian Accountant*, February (1992), pp. 68–71; W. McGregor, 'The conceptual framework for general purpose financial reporting', *The Australian Accountant*, December (1990), pp. 68–74; D. Waller, 'Time to get rid of true and fair?', *The Accountants' Magazine*, December (1990), p. 53; and, say, A. Kohler, 'Tony Hartnell throws a spanner into the works', *Australian Financial Review*, 28 March 1991, p. 56.

29 *Interim Report . . . into the Affairs of Reid Murray Holdings Limited and Certain of its Subsidiaries* (Melbourne: Victorian Government Printer, 1963), p. 10.

30 Finance Editor, 'Learning the hard way: The Reid Murray Lesson', *The Sun*, 4 December 1963.

31 Committee of General Council of the Australian Society of Accountants, *Accounting Principles and Practices Discussed in Reports on Company Failures* (Melbourne: ASA, 1966).

32 Cases are described in E. Woolf, *Auditing Today* (London: ICAEW, 1982).

2 Creative accounting

1 B. Sidhu describes professional developments in Australia and overseas in 'The new "deferred tax": A comment on AARF Discussion Paper 22 "Accounting for Income Tax"', *Australian Accounting Review*, March (1996), pp. 37–49, and F.L. Clarke, 'Deferred tax is still hocus pocus', *The Accountant* (1977), pp. 523–526, discusses the unserviceability of tax effect accounting.

2 T. Boreham, 'Regulator takes a new look at abnormal items', *Business Review Weekly*, 25 September 1995, pp. 96–97.

3 *Ibid.*

4 R.J. Chambers, 'Information and the securities market', *Abacus*, Vol. 1 No. 1 (1965), pp. 3–30 at 16. A similar view in the 1960s was held by a leading American practitioner, Leonard Spacek.

5 R.J. Craig and F.L. Clarke, 'Phases in Australian Accounting Standards Setting: Control, capture, co-existence and coercion', *Australian Journal of Corporate Law*, Vol. 3, No. 1 (1993), pp. 50–66 at 60.

6 Chanticleer 1977a, 'Accountants dream of the BHP statement of profitability', *Australian Financial Review*, 25 July 1977 (as cited in J.J. Staunton, 'Widows, orphans and lessons for accounting', *Management Forum*, June (1978), pp. 134–139 at 134.

7   Chanticleer 1977b, *Australian Financial Review*, 25 July 1977 (as cited in Staunton, 'Widows, orphans . . .').

8   Bosch, *The Workings of a Watchdog*, p. 121.

9   Staunton, 'Widows, orphans and lessons for accounting', provides some instances of this international characteristic, as does Bosch, *The Workings of a Watchdog*, p. 121.

10 A. Briloff, 'Unaccountable accounting revisited', *Critical Perspectives in Accounting*, Vol. 4 No. 4 (1993), pp. 301–335.

11 Synonyms used include *cooking* the books and *window-dressing*. Similar observations appeared in Australia and overseas in the late 1980s, even prior to the October 1987 share market crash: H. Killen, 'A correction for creative accountants', *Australian Financial Review*, 15 May 1987, p. 10, and Anon, 'Amateur accountants: Britain's Accounting Standards Committee is under-financed, under-staffed and under-powered', *The Economist*, 11 April 1987, pp. 14 and 16. A commentary on creative accounting in Britain in the 1980s appeared in D. Tweedie and G. Whittington, 'Financial reporting: Current problems and their implications for systematic reform', *Accounting and Business Research*, Winter (1990), pp. 87–100.

12 G. Breton and R.J. Taffler, 'Creative accounting and investment analyst response', *Accounting and Business Research*, Spring (1995), pp. 81–92.

13 J. Argenti, *Corporate Collapse* (Maidenhead: McGraw Hill, 1976), pp. 141–142.

14 References to authors cited and others in date order: W.Z. Ripley, *Main Street and Wall Street* (New York: Little Brown and Company, 1927; reproduced Kansas: Scholars Book Co., 1974); A.A. Berle Jr and G.C. Means, *The Modern Corporation and Private Property* (New York: Macmillan, 1932); A. Andersen, 'Present day problems affecting the presentation and interpretation of financial statements', *Journal of Accountancy*, November (1935), pp. 330–344; C. Blough, 'Some accounting problems of the Securities and Exchange Commission', *The New York Certified Public Accountant*, April (1937); Twentieth Century Fund, *Abuse on Wall Street: Conflicts of interest in the securities markets* (Westport, CT: Quorum Books, 1937; 1980); A. Barr, 'Accounting and the SEC', in A. Barr, *Written Contributions of Selected Accounting Practitioners, Volume 3 Alabama* (1959); A. Briloff, *Unaccountable Accounting* (New York: Wiley, 1972), *More Debits Than Credits* (New York: Harper & Row, 1976) and *Truth About Corporate Accounting* (New York: Wiley 1981); E. Stamp and C. Marley, *Accounting Principles and the City Code: The case for reform* (Altrincham: Butterworths, 1970); Chambers, 'Financial information and the securities market'; and R.J. Chambers, *Securities and Obscurities* (New York: Gower Press, 1973) reproduced as *Accounting in Disarray* (New York: Garland Publishing Inc., 1986).

15 M. Stevens, *The Accounting Wars* (New York: Collier Books, 1986); I. Griffiths, *Creative Accounting: How to make your profits what you want them to be* (London: Allen & Unwin, 1986); M. Jameson, *A Practical Guide to Creative Accounting* (London: Kogan Page, 1988); Tweedie and Whittington, 'Financial reporting: Current problems and their implications for systematic reform'; I. Kellogg and L.B. Kellogg, *Fraud, Window Dressing and Negligence in Financial Statements* (New York: McGraw-Hill, 1991); T. Smith, *Accounting for Growth: Stripping the camouflage from company accounts* (London: Century Business, 1992); and H.M. Schilit, *Financial Shenanigans: How to detect accounting gimmicks and fraud in financial reports* (New York: McGraw-Hill, 1993).

16 Jameson, *A Practical Guide . . .*, p. 20.

17 *Ibid.*

18 Griffiths, *Creative Accounting*, p. 5, emphasis added.

19 *Ibid.* 'Foozle' was used by H. Russell, *Foozles and Fraud* (Altamone Springs, FL: Institute of Internal Auditors, 1978) to designate the action of a manager portraying a company in the best light, bordering on that fine line between what is regarded as legal and illegal.

20 R.G. Walker, 'Ten (legal) ways to cook your books', *Business Review Weekly*, 2 June 1989, pp. 50–53 and 55.

21 Bosch, *The Workings of a Watchdog*, p. 29.

22 *Ibid.*

23 *Ibid.*

24 *Ibid.*, p. 123.

25 The significance of this standard was discussed by J. Trowell, 'Asset valuation: Recoverable amount and measurement error', *Australian Accounting Review*, November (1992), pp. 27–33. The actual variety of methods used is discussed in R. Begum and B. West, 'Non-current asset valuation: An Australian survey', *Charter*, February (1996), pp. 49–51.

26 M. Stevens, 'Winners in the race for recovery', *Business Review Weekly*, 23 April 1993, pp. 64–71 at 67.

27 *Ibid.*

28 See T. Blue, 'Now it's open season on directors', *Australian Business*, 3 July 1991, pp. 54–55.

29 S. Ellis, 'Westpac hits $2.2 bn brick wall', *Sydney Morning Herald*, 21 May 1992, p. 29, emphasis added. Several finance studies have examined whether the share market can forecast the declining fortunes of companies, notwithstanding the picture painted in the reported accounts. A summary appears in R.H.A. El Hennawy and R.C. Morris, 'Market anticipation of corporate failure in the UK', *Journal of Business Finance and Accounting*, Vol. 10(3) (1983), pp. 359–372. Also, articles have examined whether audit qualifications act as a signal or red flag to failure (W. Hopwood *et al.*, 'A test of the incremental explanatory power of opinions qualified for consistency and uncertainty', *The Accounting Review*, January (1989), pp. 28–48).

30 B. Jamieson, *Accounting Jungle* (Sydney: Business Review Weekly Publications, 1995).

31 Neil Chenoweth, 'The great profit recovery', *Australian Financial Review*, 11 September 1995, pp. 1 and 24.

32 Boreham, 'Regulator takes a new look at abnormal items'.

33 T. Kaye, *Sydney Morning Herald*, 29 June 1996, p. 79.

34 Trowell, 'Asset valuation'.

35 F.L. Clarke and G.W. Dean, 'Company officers at risk', *Corporate Management*, February (1995), pp. 13–16.

36 It is unclear in some cases exactly what revaluation basis was relied upon by directors. With the 1992 Westpac revaluation it is clear. In releasing the results, it was stated that the property and loan-related asset write-downs were to bring them in line with the *amount realisable from a willing buyer to a willing seller* allowing up to two years for settlement.

37 R.G. Walker, 'ASC must tackle misleading valuations', *New Accountant*, 23 January 1992, p. 9. The revaluation in May 1992 by Westpac of its property portfolio provides further support for this claim.

3 The corporate 1960s

1 Birkett and Walker, 'Response of the Australian accountancy profession to company failure in the 1960s', p. 104.

2 *Ibid.*, p. 108.

3 *Ibid.*

4 See Argenti, *Corporate Collapse*; S. Holmes and D. Nicholls, *Small Business and Accounting* (Sydney: Allen & Unwin, 1990); Miller, *The Icarus Paradox*; and S. Makridakis, 'What can we learn from corporate failure?', *Long Range Planning*, August (1991), pp. 115–126. In Australia, recently, the same claim was made in the Greatorex *et al.* study.

5 Similarly, McGregor and Paul, 'Corporate collapse'; McGregor, 'True and fair view'; C. Cohn, 'Brian Waldron – new ASCPA National President', *The Australian Accountant*, May (1991), pp. 20–22; and C. Pratten, *Company Failure* (London: ICAEW, 1991). All suggest that accounting was not a major contributing factor in 1980s company collapses in Australia and the UK, respectively. In the 1970s *Cambridge Credit Corporation* case the defendants also adopted this line of reasoning, suggesting that 'bad management' and 'economic circumstances' were the primary cause of failure. An *Australian Financial Review* editorial speculated that in the pending (1990s) court cases involving auditors of 1980s corporate collapses, defence counsel will be adopting similar pleading. It is sceptical of the likely success of this approach ('Auditors v. 1980s' excesses', 27 May 1992, p. 18). Several letters to the editor were generated, viz. G.H. Bennett, 'Auditors check prepared books', *Australian Financial Review*, 3 June 1992, p. 16; D. Smithers, 'Urgent need for national laws to protect auditors', *Australian Financial Review*, 5 June 1992, p. 16, M. Macleod, 'Takes two to do the audit tango', *Australian Financial Review*, 12 June 1992, p. 18; and A. Roff, 'Ensuring auditors stay independent', *Australian Financial Review*, 17 June 1992, p. 15.

6 Australian Bankers Association, *Corporate Failures* (1990) and R.J. Chambers, 'Accounting and corporate morality – the ethical cringe', *Australian Journal of Corporate Law*, Vol. 1 No. 1 (1991), pp. 9–21.

7 General Council of the Australian Society of Accountants, *Accounting Principles and Practices Discussed in Reports on Company Failures*, pp. 6–8. The UK accounting profession commissioned a similar inquiry 25 years later (Pratten, *Company Failure*) following the flurry of the high-profile corporate collapses and what the profession perceived to be the ill-informed comment they had drawn.

8 *Ibid.*, p. 7.

9 Chambers, 'Accounting and corporate morality – the ethical cringe', p. 18.

4 Reid Murray

* The *Reid Murray* case draws on the official reports of the inspectors appointed by the Victorian government: B.J. Shaw, *Final Report of an Investigation . . . into the Affairs of Reid Murray Holdings Limited* (Melbourne: Victorian Government Printer, 1966). B.L. Murray and B.J. Shaw, *Interim Report of an Investigation . . . into the Affairs of Reid Murray Holdings Limited* (Melbourne: Victorian Government Printer, December 1963), B.L. Murray and B.J. Shaw, *Interim Report of an Investigation . . . into the Affairs of Reid Murray Holdings Limited* (Melbourne: Victorian Government Printer, March 1965); *Interim Report of an Investigation . . . into the Affairs of Reid Murray Holdings Limited* (Perth: WA Government Printer, 1963); and University of Sydney class notes prepared by Professor Emeritus Ray Chambers, expert witness in litigation following the collapse of the Reid Murray group.

1 P.H. Karmel and M. Brunt, *The Structure of the Australian Economy* (Melbourne: Cheshire, 1963).
2 Shaw, *Final Report . . . into Reid Murray*, pp. 70–71.
3 *Ibid.*, p. 63.
4 M. Kidman, 'Acacia to pursue Solpac takeover', *Sydney Morning Herald*, 13 April 1996, p. 84.
5 Murray and Shaw, *First Interim Report . . . into Reid Murray*, pp. 40–43.
6 Murray and Shaw, *First Interim Report . . . into Reid Murray*, p. 95.
7 The price illustrated is the last sale for every other month as disclosed in the *Sydney Stock Exchange Gazette.*
8 Murray and Shaw, *First Interim Report . . . into Reid Murray*, p. 107, emphasis added.
9 Chapter 9 demonstrates that a similar series of events and current asset reporting occurred at Cambridge Credit Corporation only a decade later.
10 Murray and Shaw, *First Interim Report . . . into Reid Murray*, p. 109.
11 *Ibid..*
12 Sykes, *Two Centuries of Panic*, p. 323.
13 *Ibid.*, p. 298.
14 *Ibid.*, p. 303.
15 Shaw, *Final Report . . . into Reid Murray*, p. 93.
16 Murray and Shaw, *Interim Report . . . into Reid Murray*, p. 92, emphasis added.

5 Stanhill

1 Sykes, *Two Centuries of Panic*, p. 327.
2 It changed its name to Banyule Australia Pty Ltd during 1963. It was the antecedent of an incestuous web of companies named Stanhill, some of which would be public and some private. Many investors in the public companies would see much of their money disappear into the private ones owned by the Korman family.
3 Sykes, *Two Centuries of Panic*, p. 328.
4 P. Murphy, *Third and Final Report of an Investigation . . . into the Affairs of Stanhill Development Finance Limited . . .* (Victorian Government Printer, November 1967), p. 18.
5 *Ibid.*, p. 19
6 *Ibid.*, p. 20.
7 Donaldson; acting chairman of Tufton Corporation – as reported in Murphy, *Stanhill Final Report*, p. 36.
8 *Ibid.*, p. 72.
9 *Ibid.*, p. 77.
10 *Ibid.*, p. 82.
11 *Ibid.*, p. 149.
12 *Ibid.*, p. 169.

6 H.G. Palmer

* This chapter is based on F.L. Clarke, University of Sydney BEc Honours major essay, 1969, and H.G. Palmer 1965 Statement of Affairs.
1 T. Fitzgerald, 'H.G. Palmer: The outlook now', *Sydney Morning Herald*, 14 December 1965, p. 18.

2 Other businessmen referred to in this collection having a similar indenture period were O'Grady (Reid Murray) and Stanley Korman (Stanhill group).

3 Anon, 'Prospectuses . . . should be true and accurate', *Australian Financial Review*, 5 June 1969, pp. 4 and 6 at 4.

4 Sykes, *Two Centuries of Panic*, p. 371: 'Both groups were started by individuals during the Depression; both blossomed in the 1950s; both remained under executive control of their founders. More importantly both were really financiers rather than retailers. But, whereas Reid Murray diversified widely, Palmer stayed . . . a financier of retail sales.'

5 Anon, '"Bolt from the blue" bid by M.L.C. for Palmer', *Australian Financial Review*, 9 April 1963, p. 3.

6 *Ibid.*

7 Anon, 'H.G. Palmer sets records', *Australian Financial Review*, 23 April 1964, p. 20.

8 Anon, 'A matter of gearing', *Australian Financial Review*, 21 March 1963, p. 20.

9 Anon, '"Bolt from the blue"', p. 3.

10 Sykes, *Two Centuries of Panic*, p. 372.

11 R.R. Hirst and R.H. Wallace (eds), *Studies in the Australian Capital Market* (Melbourne: Cheshire, 1964), pp. 414–423 noted that only after the early 1950s were debentures and other forms of long-term debt issued commonly by publicly listed companies. By 1954/55, £27.6 million was raised, increasing to over £200 million by 1959/60 (p. 408).

12 *Ibid.*, p. 409. Other critics included R. Chambers, 'Information and the securities market'.

13 Anon, 'H.G. Palmer shareholders on clover', *Daily Telegraph*, 31 August 1958.

14 Anon, *Australian Financial Review*, 5 October 1961.

15 Anon, 'Palmer progress', *Daily Telegraph*, 8 April 1962, emphasis added.

16 These scandals are summarised in Bloomberg, 'Mr Copper: From high-roller to has been', *Sydney Morning Herald*, 15 February 1996, p. 88.

17 Report of evidence before S.M. Scarlett, 7 July 1966, cited in *Sydney Morning Herald*, 8 July 1966, pp. 7 and 8. Anon, 'H.G. Palmer case – witness tells of 1964 forecast: Bad debt situation "must show up"', *Sydney Morning Herald*, 8 July 1966.

18 Sykes, *Two Centuries of Panic*, p. 375.

19 Anon, 'Palmers a good buy', *Australian Financial Review*, 7 August 1964, p. 18.

20 Brooks, *Royal Mail Case*, p. xiv; and our Chapter 15.

21 Anon, 'H.G. Palmer, gets 4 years . . . auditor 3 years – Prospectuses should be true and accurate', *Australian Financial Review*, 5 June 1969, pp. 4 and 6 at 4.

22 Walker, 'A feeling of déjà vu', p. 107.

7 Going for broke in the 1970s

1 Accounting Standards Review Committee Report, Chairman R.J. Chambers, *Accounting Standards* (Sydney: NSW Government Printer, 1978), covering letter with the Report.

2 L. Wood, 'Corporate tax-rate cut to play havoc with results', *Australian Financial Review*, 10 June 1993, p. 23.

3 D. Janetzki, *The Gollins Years* (Brisbane: Privately published, 1989).

8 Minsec

* Analysis is based on University of Sydney Department of Accounting course notes prepared by I. Eddie with assistance from G. Dean, and from Inspectors' Report, *Investigating the Affairs of Mineral Securities Ltd. . . . ,* Vols 1–3 (NSW Parliament, 3 March 1977); *Report of the Senate Select Committee on Securities and Exchange, Australian Securities Markets and Their Regulation,* Vol. 1 (Commonwealth Parliament, 1974; *Rae Report*); T. Sykes, *The Money Miners: Australia's Mining Boom 1969–1970* (Sydney: Wildcat Press, 1978); J. Byrne, 'The Minsec Affair: Parts 1–6', *The Australian,* 23–28 April 1973; G. Souter, 'The rise and fall of the House of Minsec: Parts 1, 2 & 3', *Sydney Morning Herald,* 20, 22 and 23 February 1971; W. Horrigan and C.R. Weston, 'Australian money markets: The aftermath of Minsec', *The Banker,* January 1977, pp. 43–47; and Sykes, *Two Centuries of Panic.*

1 G. Souter, *ibid.,* Part 2, p. 7.
2 Miller, *The Icarus Paradox.*
3 *Rae Report,* p. 14.1. Arguably, the subsequent rise and fall of Compass Airlines (twice!) within 18 months in the early 1990s may have eclipsed Minsec.
4 *Inspectors' Report,* Vol. 1, p. 10.
5 *Ibid.*
6 *Rae Report,* p. 14.15.
7 S. Salsbury and K. Sweeney, *The Bull, the Bear & the Kangaroo: The history of the Sydney Stock Exchange* (Sydney: Allen & Unwin, 1988), pp. 350–354.
8 AARF ED 59, 'Accounting for Financial Instruments' (1993) is a break from the tradition of not requiring stocks to be marked-to-market; however, its purview is limited to financial instruments of banks and financial institutions.
9 *Rae Report,* p. 14.42.
10 *Inspectors' Report,* Vol. 1, p. 18. There are similarities with the disclosure/non-disclosure of items revealed at the *Royal Mail* trial some 40 years earlier in the UK (see Chapter 15).
11 Clarke and Dean, 'Chaos in the counting-house'.
12 *Inspectors' Report,* Vol. 1, p. 167.
13 Back-to-back loans were a common practice in the affairs of 1980s corporate failures. They were referred to in analyses of one of those collapses, Bond Corporation, as 'BBs' or 'Brigitte Bardots'.
14 *Rae Report,* p. 14.75.
15 *Ibid.* Back-to-back loans figured prominently in C. Raw's account in *Moneychangers* of Robert Calvi's 1970s fraud involving Banco Ambrosiano, the Vatican's IOR and entities connected with both.
16 *Inspectors' Report,* Vol. 1, p. 50.
17 *Rae Report,* p. 14.123.
18 *Inspectors' Report,* Vol. 1, p. 72.
19 Complicating this saga is whether the *market* was being *made* by the dealings of the Minsec group of companies.
20 *Rae Report,* p. 14.63.
21 *Ibid.,* p. 14.67.
22 *Ibid.,* p. 14.74.
23 *Inspectors' Report,* pp. 199–200.
24 Announcement to Sydney Stock Exchange, 3 February 1971.
25 Sykes, *Two Centuries of Panic,* pp. 424–425.
26 This rescue operation is described in Reid, *The Secondary Banking Crisis.*
27 *R v. M* [1980] 2 NSWLR 195 (January 1981)
28 *Ibid.*

9 Cambridge Credit

* Analysis is based on G. Dean, 'Accounting for real estate development: Cambridge Credit Corporation case study', pp. 140–172 in R.T.M. Whipple (ed.) *Accounting for Property Development* (Sydney: The Law Book Co. Ltd, 1985); Report of Inspectors, *First Interim Report by the Corporate Affairs Commission into the Affairs of Cambridge Credit Corporation Limited and Related Corporations* Vol. 1 (Sydney: NSW Government Printer, No. 222, 25 August 1977; *Inspectors' 1st Report*); and Report of Inspectors, *Second Interim Report by the Corporate Affairs Commission into the Affairs of Cambridge Credit Corporation Limited and Related Corporations* Vol. 2 (Sydney: NSW Government Printer, No. 23, 13 September 1979; *Inspectors' 2nd Report*).

1 See *Sydney Stock Exchange Investment Service*, C29 (1963), p. 6.
2 Graphical illustrations of the complexity of the group structure are provided by the Inspectors. See *Inspectors' 1st Report*, pp. 286–287 and *2nd Report*, p. 290.
3 *Inspectors' 1st Report*, p. 22.
4 *Ibid.*, p. 23.
5 *Ibid.*, p. 24. Unearthing this penchant for 'a one-man show' operation is a recurring feature of investigations following collapses of large public companies.
6 *Inspectors' 2nd Report*, pp. 21–22.
7 Further details are provided below and in the *Inspectors' 2nd Report*, pp. 59–63.
8 *Inspectors' 1st Report*, para. 2.148 (specific examples of this channelling of losses appear at paras 2.96 ff.).
9 *Inspectors' 2nd Report*, p. 29.
10 *Ibid.*, p. 281.
11 *Ibid.*, p. 29.
12 *Ibid.*, 'Conclusions', pp. 277–283; specifically, paras 6.35–6.37 and Appendix III.
13 *Ibid.*, pp. 51–52, emphasis added.
14 *Ibid.*, p. 52.
15 *Inspectors' 1st Report*, p. 65.
16 Securities and Exchange Commission (1965): *Accounting Series Release No. 95*, USA.
17 Securities and Exchange Commission (1975): *Accounting Series Release No. 173*, USA.
18 *Inspectors' 1st Report*, pp. 65 ff.
19 *Ibid.*, p. 52; para. 4.8 at p. 168; para. 8.199 at p. 278 and *Inspectors' 2nd Report*, pp. 272–273. Reliance on substance over form has been promoted by accountants in Australia, the United States and the United Kingdom – see APB, *Opinion No. 4* (1970); in the UK ICAEW *Technical release, TR 603*, 'Window dressing and substance v. form' (1985); and in S.J. Martens and J. McEnroe, 'Substance over form in auditing and the auditor's position of public trust', *Critical Perspectives in Accounting*, December (1992), pp. 389–401.
20 *Inspectors' 2nd Report*, pp. 38–39, 148–150 and 269–270.
21 See *Cambridge Credit Corporation. Ltd v. Hutcheson and Ors* (1983) 8 ACLR 123 at 133–158 and *Inspectors' 2nd Report*, pp. 151–247.
22 8 ACLR 123 at 162.
23 *Inspectors' 2nd Report*, p. 43.
24 Anon, 'Auditors not liable for damages', *Sydney Morning Herald*, 17 September 1983, p. 7.
25 *Inspectors' 2nd Report*, p. 20, para. 2.3, emphasis added.

26 *Ibid.*, pp. 251–252 and 278.

27 *Ibid.*, p. 251.

28 In 1973, for the first time in ten years, the total borrowings due exceeded by
    $30 million the total receivables due. Interestingly, even then management
    was able to *report* the *two-year cover* at around 1.03.

29 *Inspectors' 2nd Report*, p. 16.

30 *Ibid.*, p. 17.

31 *Ibid.*, p. 277, para. 6.4 and Table 9.4 in this book.

32 Sykes, *Two Centuries of Panic*, p. 466, is critical of the delay in criminal
    proceedings against Cambridge's directors, Hutcheson, Whitbread, Davis-
    Raiss and its auditor, Purcell: as is Bosch, *The Workings of a Watchdog*.

33 Details are provided in the 1994–1995 ASC *Annual Report*, pp. 32–41.

34 *Cambridge Credit Corporation Ltd v. Hutcheson and Ors* (1985); unreported
    Supreme Court of NSW, No. 3462 of 1977, 25 March 1985, pp. 68–69,
    emphasis added.

10 Uncoordinated financial strategies at Associated Securities Ltd

*   This chapter draws on F.L. Clarke and G.W. Dean, 'Uncoordinated financial
    strategies: The experience of ASL', in R.J. Jüttner and T. Valentine (eds), *The
    Economics and Management of Financial Institutions* (Melbourne: Longman
    Cheshire, 1987), pp. 437–453; and from a more detailed post-mortem of the
    collapse of ASL by G.W. Dean and F.L. Clarke, *Working Paper*, 'Anatomy of a
    Failure: A Methodological Experience – The Case of ASL', Centre for Studies
    in Money, Banking and Finance, Macquarie University, July 1983 (hereafter
    Working Paper).

1   R. Meadley, 'What in hell's name happened?', *Australian Financial Review*,
    14 February 1979, p. 4.

2   This was a common reaction of investors and creditors immediately after the
    announced collapses at H.G. Palmer, Reid Murray, Minsec and Cambridge
    Credit Corporation, to name a few.

3   R. Gottliebsen *et al.*, 'The inside drama of a $300 million crash: The ASL
    story', *The National Times*, 10 March 1979, pp. 22–25 and 27 at 22.

4   Trends in finance company borrowings (1945–1963) are outlined in R.R.
    Hirst and R.H. Wallace, *Studies in the Australian Capital Market* (Melbourne:
    F.W. Cheshire, 1964), pp. 154–159. Trends for the 1960s and 1970s are
    provided in the Australian Finance Conference (AFC) members' submission
    to the *Australian Financial System of Inquiry* (1979); and M.T. Skully, *Working
    Paper*, 'Finance Companies in Australia: An Examination of Their Develop-
    ment, Operation and Future', Centre for Studies in Money, Banking and
    Finance, Macquarie University, February 1983.

5   Gottliebsen *et al.*, 'The ASL Story', p. 22.

6   *Ibid.*, p. 23.

7   M.T. Daly, *Sydney Boom or Bust: The city and its property market 1850–1981*
    (Sydney: Allen & Unwin, 1982), pp. 91–92. For further details of ASL's land
    operations, see Dean and Clarke, 'Uncoordinated financial strategies: The
    experience of ASL', p. 13.

8   Gottliebsen *et al.*, 'The ASL Story', p. 23.

9   A phrase coined by the *Australian Financial Review* when Sir Reginald Ansett,
    Sir Henry Bolte and Sir Cecil Looker along with the other directors of Ansett
    made the decision to stop further injections of Ansett money to prop up ASL.

10 Comprising finance to developers for the acquisition and development of raw land into residential blocks and, to builders, investors and owner occupiers for housing construction.

11 Australian Finance Conference – Member companies of the AFC (including ASL) account for more than 85 per cent of the total assets of *all* finance companies and general financiers. For further details, see P.J. Barker and P.J. Mair, 'Finance companies', *Reserve Bank of Australia Bulletin*, August 1982, p. 76 where there is further evidence of finance companies' increasing investment in leasing.

12 For illustrations of the share market's response to ASL operations from January 1971 to February 1979, see Dean and Clarke, *Working Paper*, especially Appendices II and III. Sykes, *Two Centuries of Panic*, p. 493 notes that in October 1973 'the first whisper went around that all was not well at ASL and the share price was marked down from $1.80 to $1.30'. It was on a downhill slide thereafter until the collapse in 1978.

13 Daly, *Sydney, Boom or Bust*, p. 103. Contrary to the suggestion by Sykes, *Two Centuries of Panic*, p. 494, the Royal Bank of Scotland, with its less than 30 per cent capital in ASL, was 'never perceived as [ASL's big brother] and it was not'. These support actions and continuing investment in ASL by the bank provided some form of assurance to the market.

14 Daly, *ibid.*, p. 74.

15 Evidence supporting this proposition is found in Daly, *ibid.*, pp. 71–82, and Baker and Mair, 'Finance Companies', pp. 75–83.

16 For details refer to Daly, *Sydney, Boom or Bust*, Table 3.6 at pp. 80–81; Reid, *The Secondary Banking Crisis, 1973–75*; and R.A. Schotland, 'Real Estate Investment Trusts', in Twentieth Century Fund, *Abuse on Wall Street: Conflicts of interest in the securities markets* (Westport, CT: Quorum Books, 1980), pp. 158–223.

17 Daly, *Sydney, Boom or Bust*, p. 73.

18 Gottliebsen *et al.*, 'The ASL Story', p. 22.

19 Daly, *Sydney, Boom or Bust*, p. 73.

20 *Ibid.*

21 W. Guttmann and P. Meehan, *The Great Inflation* (London: Saxon House, 1975), pp. 14–17; and G. Dean, F. Clarke and F. Graves, *Replacement Costs and Accounting Reform in Post-World War I Germany* (New York: Garland, 1990).

22 C. Bresciani-Turroni, *The Economics of Inflation* (London: Allen & Unwin, 1937), p. 28.

23 *Ibid.*

24 Guttmann and Meehan, *The Great Inflation*.

25 Reported in *The National Times*, July 1978.

26 Sykes, *Two Centuries of Panic*, p. 498.

27 The belief of the ASL's directors in the advantages of having the Royal Bank of Scotland as an investor are impregnated on the minds of the reader of any ASL annual report for the years 1960–1976.

28 F.L. Clarke *et al.*, 'Testing failure trajectories – European/Non-European contrast', 17th European Accounting Association Annual Congress, Venice, 1994.

11 The 1980s: Decade of the deal?

1 J. McManamy, *The Dreamtime Casino* (Melbourne: Schwartz and Wilkinson, 1990).

2 P. Barry, *The Rise and Fall of Alan Bond*, p. 286.

3 J. Green, 'Fuzzy Law – a better way to "stop snouts in the trough"?', *Company and Securities Law Journal,* June (1991), pp. 145 and 149, emphasis added.
4 Other criteria include relevance, materiality, consistency and prudence. All require directors', accountants' and auditors' judgements.
5 R.W. Gotterson, *Report of a Special Investigation into the Affairs of Ariadne Australia Limited & Ors* (Sydney: NSW Government Printer, 1989).
6 T. Sykes, Editorial, *Australian Business,* 12 September 1990, p. 6.
7 Public Oversight Board Report, 'Issues Confronting the Accounting Profession'.
8 Reported view of former KPMG Peat Marwick partner, Stuart Grant, upon his appointment to the ASC as Executive Director Accounting Policy in 1993, cited in B. Pheasant, '"True and fair" change seen as backward step', *Australian Financial Review,* 16 November 1992, p. 18.

12 Adsteam on the rocks

1 Respectively A. Kohler, 'Adsteam a humiliation for the accounting profession', *Australian Financial Review,* 2 April 1991, pp. 1 and 52, and G. Burge, 'Adsteam's $4.49 billion loss is biggest ever', *Sydney Morning Herald,* 1 October 1991, p. 25.
2 M. Stenberg, 'DJs will not go cheap, says Adsteam', *Sydney Morning Herald,* 20 November 1993, p. 41.
3 M. Meagher and F. Chong, 'One-man bands?: How their companies would fare without them', *Business Review Weekly,* 20 February 1987, pp. 44–45, 47–48, 51, 53, 55–56, 59 and 63 at 59.
4 P. Rennie, 'Charting a course for Adsteam', *Business Review Weekly,* 26 August 1988, p. 125.
5 *In the Matter of The Adelaide Steamship Company Limited v. James Gunars Spalvins and Ors,* No. SG3036 of 1994 in the Federal Court of Australia, SA District Registry, General Division, December 1994. See also J. Parker, 'ASC appeals in ASC case', *Sydney Morning Herald,* 6 May 1996, p. 35.
6 T. Sykes, 'Adsteam unmasked', *Australian Business,* 19 April 1989, pp. 16–19.
7 R. Gottliebsen, 'Spalvins, the quiet acquirer', *Business Review Weekly,* 28 April 1989, pp. 20–25.
8 M. Peers, 'Intricacies cloud Adsteam's losses', *Australian Financial Review,* 13 February 1990, p. 16.
9 P. Rennie, 'What's the problem? Spalvins wonders', *Business Review Weekly,* 16 February 1990, pp. 29–30.
10 R. Gottliebsen, 'Spalvins' fatal flaw', *Business Review Weekly,* 3 May 1991, pp. 40–51.
11 M. Peers, 'Adsteam loses another 36c as panic spreads', *Australian Financial Review,* 20 September 1990, pp. 1 and 8 at 8.
12 A. Kohler, 'Now it's full steam ahead into retailing for Spalvins', *Australian Financial Review,* 31 October 1990, p. 68.
13 Rennie, 'What's the problem?', p. 30.
14 T. Sykes, 'Adsteam accounting made clear', *The Bulletin,* 14 April 1992, p. 93.
15 Anon, 'Accountancy Hotline: Spalvins judgement', *Business Review Weekly,* 1 June 1990, p. 110.
16 I. McIlwraith, 'John Spalvins out of steam', *Australian Financial Review,* 5 July 1991, pp. 27 and 29 at 29.
17 Sykes, *Bold Riders,* p. 435, emphasis added.
18 J. Parker, 'Taking Adsteam apart', *Australian Business,* 25 July 1990, pp. 16–19.

274 NOTES (PAGES 164–174)

13 Bond Corporation Holdings Ltd (Group)

1 Assistance by M. Tan in preparing the acquisition and divestment details of the Bond group of companies is gratefully acknowledged. Sources are cited throughout the text, including the publicly disclosed extracts from the ASC's Sulman Report presented in early 1992 but not publicly released; P. Barry, *The Rise and Fall of Alan Bond*; T. Maher, *Bond* (Melbourne: William Heinemann, 1990); the SSE Investment Review Service; and articles by M. Maiden, 'Bond's triumphs and troubles', *Australian Financial Review*, 4 December 1989, pp. 19, 20, 69, 70, and R. Gottliebsen, T. Treadgold and J. Kavanagh, 'Trapped in the web of WA Inc', *Business Review Weekly*, 8 September 1989, pp. 20–24. Alan Bond was convicted of fraud involving the purchase of *La Promenade*. Another investigation by the ASC into transactions around the time of the Bell Resources '$1.2 billion deposit' resulted in Alan Bond (together with two other BCH directors, Messrs Coates and Mitchell) being charged with fraud in January 1995. As this book went to print, Bond pleaded guilty and is awaiting sentencing; the others face trial in April 1997.

2 J. McGlue, 'Final nail driven into Bond Corp', *Sydney Morning Herald*, 24 December 1993, p. 13.

3 Barry, *The Rise and Fall of Alan Bond*.

4 J. McGlue, 'Bond Corp auditor sued', *Sydney Morning Herald*, 11 April 1996, p. 25.

5 Miller, *The Icarus Paradox*.

6 As suggested by Mark Burrows on ABC broadcaster, Andrew Olle's 2BL morning programme on 8 April 1992.

7 Interestingly, troubled assets seem attracted to troubled companies. Land held by the Korman and Reid Murray groups was found in the asset portfolios of troubled companies in the 1970s and 1980s, including Cambridge Credit and Tricontinental and Bond's purchase of Robe's shares.

8 Barry, *The Rise and Fall of Alan Bond*, pp. 70–80.

9 Maiden, 'Bond's triumphs', p. 19.

10 Consortium members (respective interests) were Bond Corporation (50 per cent), Dallhold (10 per cent), Endeavour Resources (30 per cent), Amalgamated (5 per cent) and Leighton Mining N.L. (5 per cent).

11 A. Cromie, 'Bond keeps it in the family', *Business Review Weekly*, 2 July 1993, pp. 40–47 at 41. Other transactions discussed formed the basis of an ABC *Four Corners* programme (26 July 1993) detailing aspects of Alan Bond's bankruptcy.

12 Barry, *The Rise and Fall of Alan Bond*, pp. 193–208.

13 Sotheby's, who sold the *Irises* painting, provided the majority of finance for the purchase of *Irises*. With this painting Alan Bond was described as one of the 75 biggest art collectors of the eighties. The collection was acquired through a web of dealings between BCH group companies and Dallhold Investments. Clearly, 'there is nothing new under the sun', as further evidenced by the liquidation of the Bond Corporation empire's burgeoning Impressionist art collection. This had parallels with the 1941 'sale of the century' of William Randolph Hearst's collection, including Van Dyck's *Queen Henrietta Maria*.

14 Gottliebsen *et al.*, 'Trapped in the web of WA Inc', p. 21.

15 *Ibid.*, pp. 21–22.

16 *Ibid.*, p. 22.

17 A. Nolan, 'The position of unsecured creditors of corporate groups: Towards a group responsibility solution which gives fairness and equity a role', *Company and Securities Law Journal*, December (1993), pp. 461 ff. at 468.
18 This was achieved by way of a 93-page document, 'The Bond Group of Companies: A Financial Analysis by Lonrho Plc', November 1988.
19 M. Stevens, T. Treadgold, N. Way and D. Uren, 'Bond Corp all at sea', *Business Review Weekly*, 12 January 1990, pp. 16–19. Financial journalist A. Cromie notes, 'Beckwith, Oates and Mitchell were Bond's key men. The value placed on them was shown in 1987': A. Cromie, 'Bond's men rise from the ashes', *Business Review Weekly*, 17 September 1993, pp. 62–68 at 63.
20 As reported in G. Haigh, 'UK judge chides Bond over lack of Bell records', *Sydney Morning Herald*, 22 July 1989, p. 41, and Anon, 'Bond tells jury of problems with memory', *Sydney Morning Herald*, 6 August 1996, p. 4.
21 Reported in Shaplen, *Kreuger: Genius and Swindler.*
22 For example, in the Lonrho document all debt in BCH was aggregated into one figure, including debt of a non-recourse nature.
23 Nolan, 'Towards group responsibility', p. 489.
24 See Barry, *The Rise and Fall of Alan Bond*, and H. Armstrong and D. Goss, *The Rise and Fall of a Merchant Bank*. (Melbourne: Melbourne University Press, 1995).
25 An insight is provided in R. Gottliebsen and M. Stevens, 'Why the banks lent Bond \$7 billion', *Business Review Weekly*, 8 December 1989, pp. 24–26 and 29.
26 M. Stevens, D. Uren and J. Kavanagh, 'Bond's biggest creditors', *Business Review Weekly*, 7 July 1990, pp. 20–22 and 26, and T. Sykes and T. Blue, 'The bankers behind Bond', *Australian Business*, 13 September 1989, p. 19.
27 M. Meagher and F. Chong, 'One-man bands? How their companies would fare without them', *Business Review Weekly*, 20 February 1987, pp. 44–45, 47–48, 51, 53, 55–56 and 59 at 45.
28 P. Rennie, 'Bond sails through the crash', *Business Review Weekly*, 11 December 1987, p. 141.
29 R.G. Walker, 'Brought to account: Normal items? Extraordinary!', *Australian Business*, 10 February 1988, pp. 95–96 at 96.
30 R.G. Walker, 'Window-dressing at Bond Corp', *Australian Business*, 24 February 1988, pp. 77–78 at 77.
31 BCH, *Annual Report* (1986/87), p. 86, note 10.
32 *Ibid.*, p. 114, note 29(i).
33 Walker, 'Window-dressing', p. 78.
34 BCH, *Annual Report* (1986/87), p. 87 note 10.
35 *Ibid.*
36 B. Dunstan, 'Eagle eye on company accounts', *Australian Financial Review*, 7 March 1988, pp. 75–76.
37 Walker, 'Window-dressing', p. 77.
38 *Ibid.*, pp. 77–78.
39 M. Stevens, 'London waits for Bond's response', *Business Review Weekly*, 9 December 1988, pp. 39–40 at 39.
40 T. Sykes, 'Inside the Bond accounts', *Australian Business*, 19 October 1988, pp. 36 and 38 at 38.
41 T. Sykes and T. Blue, 'Bond's big sell-off', *Australian Business*, 13 September 1989, pp. 18–20 at 20. Those transactions are also discussed in R.G. Walker, 'A feeling of déjà vu: Considerations of accounting and auditing regulation in Australia', *Critical Perspectives on Accounting* 4 (1993), pp. 97–109 at 102–103; Maher, *Bond*, pp. 281–284; and Barry, *Rise and Fall of Alan Bond*, pp. 243–248.

42   Barry, *The Rise and Fall of Alan Bond*, p. 261.
43   T. Sykes, 'The End of Bond Corp?', *Australian Business*, 10 May 1989, pp. 16–18 and 20 at 16.
44   J. Wainwright, *Sunday Telegraph*, 22 October 1989, p. 23.

14 Westmex Ltd

1   Y. van Dongen, *Brierley: The man behind the corporate legend* (Auckland: Viking/Penguin Books, 1990), p. 177.
2   *Ibid.*, pp. 233 ff.
3   A 'closed group' usually comprises a parent company and one or more of its wholly-owned subsidiaries agreeing to be bound by a deed of cross guarantee formally approved by a regulatory body (first the NCSC and now the ASC). Refer J. Hill, 'Cross guarantees and corporate groups', *Company and Securities Law Journal*, 10 (1992), pp. 312–317; J. Hill, 'Corporate groups, creditor protection and cross guarantees: Australian perspectives', *Canadian Business Law Journal* (April 1995); and G. Dean, F. Clarke and E. Houghton, 'Cross Guarantees and the Negative Pledges: A Preliminary Analysis', *Australian Accounting Review* (May 1995), pp. 48–63.
4   Figure 14.1 depicts only 21 companies – the other 15 companies within the 'closed group' were shelf companies with zero assets and liabilities.
5   Westmex, *Annual Report*, Chairman's Report, 1988/89, pp. 4–16 at 4.
6   For a listing of those fads since the end of World War II, refer M. McGill, *American Business and the Quick Fix* (New York: Henry Holt and Company, 1988), and F. Hilmer and L. Donaldson, *Management Redeemed* (Sydney: Simon & Schuster, 1996).
7   *Ibid.*
8   Westmex, *Annual Report*, 1988, p. 6, emphasis added.
9   P. Rennie, 'Goward continues to impress', *Business Review Weekly*, 3 February 1989, pp. 91 and 92 at 91.
10   C. Chapel, 'Since Black Tuesday, cash is kingmaker', *Business Review Weekly*, 13 May 1988, p. 89
11   P. Rennie, 'Goward continues to impress', p. 91.
12   R. Baker, 'Westmex: Acorn award – outstanding new entrant', *Australian Business*, 5 April 1989, pp. 62–63 at 62.
13   Henry Bosch, as cited in B. Hills, 'Sex, Lies & Ticker Tape', *Sydney Morning Herald*, 28 September 1991, p. 39. See also T. Blue, 'When to blow the whistle', *Australian Business*, 21 August 1991, pp. 61–62.
14   Reported in Hills, *ibid.*
15   C. Wood, 'Plan for open disciplinary hearings on auditors', *Business Review Weekly*, 1 July 1996, pp. 78–79.
16   M. West, 'BT sues auditors for $60 million', *Sydney Morning Herald*, 31 January 1996.
17   Hills, 'Sex, Lies & Ticker Tape', p. 39.
18   Details of companies taking advantage of the accounting and audit relief provisions are given in Clarke, Dean and Houghton, 'Cross guarantees'.
19   (1991) 9 ACLC 1483. This case was not contested. J.N. Taylor Holdings Ltd was a BCH satellite acquired late in 1988 and placed in liquidation in 1990.
20   Uncertainty was not wholly alleviated by the 1992 judgment of McLelland J in the NSW Supreme Court case, *Westmex Operations Pty Ltd (In liq.) v. Westmex Ltd (In liq.) & Ors* (1992) 10 ACLC 1179 and its confirmation by the 1993 NSW Supreme Court of Appeal in *Westmex Operations Pty Ltd (In liq.) v. Westmex Ltd*

In liq.) & Ors. This issue is explored elsewhere and in the next chapter. See G.W. Dean, P.F. Luckett and E. Houghton, 'Notional calculations in liquidations revisited: The case of the ASC class order cross guarantees', *Company and Securities Law Journal*, August 1993, pp. 204–226; 'Case Note: *Westmex Operations Pty Ltd (In liq.) v. Westmex Ltd (In liq.) & Ors'*, *Company and Securities Law Journal*, December (1993), pp. 448–451; and in P. Luckett, G. Dean and E. Houghton, 'Cross debts and group liquidations: A cross claim *liquidation model'*, *Pacific Accounting Review*, December (1995), pp. 73–102.

15 Groupthink: Byzantine corporate structures

* This chapter and the next draw on Clarke and Dean, 'Law and accounting: The separate legal entity principle and consolidation accounting', 21 *Australian Business Law Review*, August (1993), pp. 246–269; Clarke and Dean, 'Chaos in the counting-house: Accounting under scrutiny'; and Dean, Luckett and Houghton, 'Notional calculations in liquidations revisited'.

1 Respectively, (1977) 3 ACLR 529 at 532 and (1991) 3 ACSR 531 at 540.

2 M.A. Eisenberg, 'Corporate groups', paper, Conference on Corporate Groups, the Centre for Commercial and Resources Law, Perth, 12–13 June 1991, p. 4. See also Nolan, 'The Position of unsecured creditors of corporate groups: Towards a group responsibility solution which gives fairness and equity a role' and J.M. Landers, 'A unified approach to parent, subsidiary and affiliate questions in bankruptcy', *University of Chicago Law Review*, 42(4) (1975), pp. 589–652.

3 *Ibid.*

4 A. McGee, 'The true and fair view debate: A study in the legal regulation of accounting', *Modern Law Review*, Vol. 54 (1991), 769 at p. 874.

5 Figure 5.1 illustrates the nature of the 1960s Korman round robin. A brief description of it appears also in Clarke and Dean, 'Law and accounting'.

6 Editorial, 'Coles: Trouble at the top', *Sydney Morning Herald*, 14 September 1995, p. 16.

7 C. Ryan, 'Coles Myer: A loveless marriage gone mad', *Sydney Morning Herald*, 9 March 1996, pp. 53 and 58. A lengthy ASC investigation of the Yannon transaction examined, *inter alia*, the conclusion of Alan Goldberg QC that Solomon Lew 'knew nothing of Yannon' (as reported in M. Gawenda, 'What makes Solly run', *Sydney Morning Herald Good Weekend*, 10 August 1996, pp. 31–37).

8 R. Baxt, 'Tensions between commercial reality and legal principle – Should the concept of the corporate entity be re-examined?', *Australian Law Journal* (1991a), pp. 352–353; and R. Baxt, 'The need to review the rule in Salomon's case as it applies to groups of companies', *Company and Securities Law Journal*, 9 (1991b), pp. 185–187. See also J. Hill, 'Corporate groups, creditor protection and cross guarantees: Australian perspectives', *Canadian Business Law Journal* (February 1995), pp. 321–356.

9 J. Green succinctly describes the four major types of 1980s corporate abuses: '(i) "skimming" or "value shifting"...; (ii) "toys for the boys"...; (iii) "window dressing"... (iv) "market rigging/insider trading"....' ('"Fuzzy law" – a better way to stop "snouts in the trough"', *Company and Securities Law Journal* 9 (3) (1991), 144 at p. 149.

10 Brooks, *The Royal Mail Case*, p. xv. Consider also A.A. Berle, 'The theory of enterprise entity', *Columbia Law Review*, 47 (1947), p. 343; A.A. Berle,

'Subsidiary corporations and credit manipulation', *Harvard Law Review*, 41 (1941), p. 874; and the summary article by Landers, 'Unified Approach'.

11 K. Brice, 'Linter battle delayed as judge grants time for settlement talks', *Australian Financial Review*, 28 March 1996, p. 4

12 P. Blumberg, *The Law of Corporate Groups* (New York: Little Brown and Co., 1983); H. Collins, 'Ascription of legal responsibility to groups in complex patterns of economic integration', *Modern Law Review*, 53 (1990), p. 731; and G. Tuebner, 'Unitas multiplex: Corporate governance in group enterprises', in D. Sugarman and G. Tuebner (eds), *Regulating Corporate Groups in Europe* (1990); M. Pittard and R. McCallum, 'Superannuation funds, interlocking corporations and industrial disputes', *Australian Business Law Review*, 21 (1993), pp. 71 ff. at 74; and B. Fisse and J. Braithwaite, *Corporations, Crime and Accountability* (Cambridge; Melbourne: Cambridge University Press, 1993).

13 L.C.B. Gower, *Gower's Principles of Modern Company Law*, 3rd ed. (London: Stevens and Co., 1969), p. 216; see also 4th ed. (1979), p. 137.

14 Lord Denning, M.R., *Littlewoods Mail Order Stores Ltd v. IRC* [1969] 1 WLR 1254.

15 Baxt, 'Tensions', p. 352.

16 Hill, 'Corporate Groups'.

17 Baxt, 'Tensions', p. 352. However, 'in *Industrial Equity Ltd v. Blackburn* (1977) 137 CLR 567 the High Court of Australia confirmed the need to preserve, as a matter of law, a rigid demarcation between wholly-owned subsidiaries in the same group of companies as well as their holding company', *obiter* in NSW Supreme Court in *Qintex Australia Finance Ltd v. Schroders Australia Ltd* (1991) 3 ACSR 267 at 268–269, and 9 ACLC 109 at 110.

18 NSW Supreme Court in *Qintex Australia Finance Ltd v. Schroders Australia Ltd* (1991) 3 ACSR 267 at 268–269, and 9 ACLC 109 at 110.

19 *Briggs v. James Hardie & Co. Pty Ltd* (1989) 16 NSWLR 549 at 577.

20 *Re Southward and Co. Ltd* [1979] 1 WLR 1198 at 1208. Other instances are noted in Gower, *Modern Company Law*, under the subsection 'Associated companies', pp. 128–133. *The Report of the UK Review Committee on Insolvency Law and Practice* (Cork Report) in 1982 at Chapter 51, pp. 434–444.

21 Hadden, 'Regulation of Corporate Groups'.

22 These issues are discussed in J. Farrar and A.B. Darroch, 'Insolvency and Corporate Groups: The problem of consolidation', in J.P.G. Lessing and J.F. Corkery (eds), *Corporate Insolvency Law* (Gold Coast: Taxation and Corporate Research Centre, 1995); Hadden, 'Regulation of corporate groups'; and Nolan, 'Towards group responsibility'.

23 *ASC Digest, Update 41*, 'Report on the Public Hearing on Accounts and Audit Relief for Wholly-owned Subsidiaries' (1991), para. 31.

24 Figures from NCSC *Annual Reports* for the years, 1987–1991.

25 Bosch, *The Workings of a Watchdog*, pp. 54 and 68. Some of the claims raised by Bosch are addressed in Clarke and Dean 'Chaos in the Counting-house' (1992) and 'Law and Accounting: Separate legal entity and consolidation accounting' (1993); and Dean, Luckett and Houghton, 'Notional calculations in liquidations revisited'.

26 *ASC Digest, Update 41*, 'Report on the Public Hearing on Accounts and Audit Relief for Wholly-owned Subsidiaries' (1991), para. 31.

27 B. Pheasant, 'ASC request on accounts queried', *Australian Financial Review*, 20 August 1993, p. 26. The ASX and the ASC were unsatisfied with Washington H. Soul Pattinson's (WHSP) initial refusal to consolidate into the parent company's accounts its 49.8 per cent share of Brickworks Ltd. The

ASX eventually accepted Pattinson's compromise to provide as a separate note in its accounts for the year ended 30 June 1993 a set of consolidated accounts including Brickworks Ltd. (See E. Mychasuk, 'Regulators battle over Soul accounts', *Sydney Morning Herald*, 11 June 1993, p. 23.) As from 31 July 1993, directors of WHSP agreed to a further request from the ASC to consolidate Brickworks into the accounts of WHSP even though in their opinion this would not 'provide a true and fair view'.

28 G. Garnsey, *Holding Companies and their Published Accounts* (London, Gee and Co., 1923); reproduced as *Holding Companies and their Published Accounts: Limitations of a Balance Sheet* (New York: Garland Publishing Inc., 1982). Garnsey put forward several alternatives to account for groups: separate publication of subsidiaries' balance sheets; publication of consolidated balance sheets embracing both holding companies and their subsidiaries.

29 D.W. Locascio, 'The dilemma of the double derivative suit', *Northwestern University Law Review*, 83 (3) (1989), pp. 729 ff. at 757.

16 Groupthink – group therapy

1 Hadden, 'Regulating corporate groups', p. 72.

2 J. Hill, 'Cross guarantees and corporate groups', *Company and Securities Law Journal*, October (1992), pp. 312 ff. at 317 lists some critics.

3 Gower, *Modern Company Law*, pp. 118–119, emphasis added.

4 *Littlewoods Mail Order Stores Ltd v. IRC* [1969] 1 WLR 1254.

5 *D.H.N. Ltd v. Tower Hamlets* [1976] 1 WLR 852, emphasis added.

6 *Industrial Equity Ltd v. Blackburn* (1977) 137 CLR 567.

7 ASC Media Release 91/64, Issues Paper 29, *Public Hearing: Accounting Relief for Wholly-Owned Subsidiaries*, para. 3, note 4.

8 S. Jemison, 'Why not sack Clark, SBSA director asked', *Australian Financial Review*, 22 May 1992, p. 55. Details of the complexity of these off-balance sheet operations were revealed in T. Maher, 'Why the State Bank went south', *Australian Business*, 20 February 1991, pp. 12–16, and in S. Jemison, 'Counsel turn up the heat as ex-director gives evidence', *Australian Financial Review*, 25 May 1992, p. 48.

9 Mason J. in *Industrial Equity Ltd v. Blackburn* (1977) 137 CLR 567.

10 This is reinforced by the financial imbroglios in 'closed-group' liquidations where attempts to administer regulatory-approved class order cross guarantees have proven nigh impossible. It would seem that, in respect of 'liquidated' and 'going concerns', a 'state of affairs' presupposes a 'legal' form.

11 R.G. Walker, *Consolidated Statements: A history and analysis* (New York: Arno Press, 1978) documents the numerous functions of consolidated statements. A condensed version appears in R.G. Walker, 'An evaluation of the information conveyed by consolidated statements', *Abacus*, December (1976), pp. 77–115.

12 Hadden, 'Regulating corporate groups', p. 72.

13 Walker, *Consolidated Statements*, p. 277, emphasis added.

14 First put succinctly in Chambers, *Securities and Obscurities*, pp. 225–228, reproduced as *Accounting in Disarray*, and summarised in the 1978 report to the NSW Attorney General, *Accounting Standards*, pp. 123–136.

15 A somewhat similar, radical move – prohibiting the operation of holding companies across state borders – occurred in the United States following the abuses perpetrated by virtue of complex group structures such as Ivar

Kreuger's international match labyrinth and utility company group structures operating sub-subholding companies across state boundaries. Many
congressmen at the US Congressional Hearings before the Senate Committee on Banking and Practice into the 1920s holding company abuses
expressed concerns about complex group structures – some of which are
reproduced in Clarke and Dean, 'Chaos in the Counting-house'.

16 For details of pre-1980 company failures in Australia see Sykes, *Two Centuries
of Panic*, whilst more recent controversial consolidation accounting practices
are revealed in R.G. Walker, 'Off-balance sheet financing', *UNSW Law
Journal*, Vol. 15(1) (1992), pp. 196–213; Hadden, 'Regulating corporate
groups'; and Sykes, *The Bold Riders*.

17 Chambers, *Securities and Obscurities*, p. 225.

18 *Spedley Securities Limited (in Liquidation) v. Greater Pacific Investments Pty Limited
(in Liquidation) & Ors, 50177 of 1991: The October Transactions*, p. 10.

19 B. Pheasant, 'Goldberg trust held Brick and Pipe stake', *Australian Financial
Review*, 12 February 1992, p. 23.

20 B. Pheasant, 'Backdating gave Goldberg $160 million', *Australian Financial
Review*, 14 February 1992, p. 19; the judgment in the Victorian Supreme
Court by Southwell J., *Linter Group Limited v. A. Goldberg and Zev Furst & Ors*,
No. 2195 of 1990, 4 May 1992; and B. Pheasant, 'Former Goldberg
accountant tells of "warehousing"', *Australian Financial Review*, 30 August
1993, p. 4. The latter recounts another deal with the potential to benefit
private companies controlled by Goldberg at the expense of the shareholders
of public companies. For details of the Rothwells transactions, see McCusker
Report, *Report of the Inspector on a Special Investigation into Rothwells Limited
Pursuant to Companies Code (W.A.), Part VII – Part 1*, (Perth: WA Government
Printer, 1989); for details of the Spedley Holdings round robin, see
J. Manson and T. Sykes, 'Lucky Brian', *Australian Business*, 16 May 1990, pp.
16–19; for the particulars involving Unity Corporation and the private
company, Carter Holdings Pty Limited, see C. Fox, 'Carter "siphoned off"
$17 million, hearing told', *Australian Financial Review*, 4 February 1992, p. 17.

21 Walker, 'Off-balance sheet financing', and 'A feeling of déjà vu'.

22 Hadden, 'Regulating corporate groups', p. 72. Importantly, each public
company within a corporate group is required to prepare a separate annual
report to be lodged with the ASC.

17 Fatal attrition

1 For example, comments attributed to national audit partner of Coopers and
Lybrand, Bob Lynn, in P. Howard, 'Auditors in clash over Standards',
Financial Forum, August (1994), 1.

2 D. Hrisak and M. Dobbie, 'US Big Six limits partner liability', *Financial Forum*,
December (1994), p. 7.

3 M. Dobbie, 'Doomed to repeat mistakes?', *Financial Forum*, December
(1994), p. 7.

4 Report of an interview by A. Ivanov, 'Introducing Graham Paton', *Australian
Accountant*, April (1993), pp. 22–24 at 23.

5 Bosch, *The Workings of a Watchdog*, p. 24. A similar line courses through the
analysis of P. Brokensha, *Corporate Ethics: A guide for Australian managers*
(Adelaide: Social Science Press, 1993).

6 Wood, 'Plan for open disciplinary hearing on auditors'.

7 General Council, Australian Society of Accountants, *Accounting Principles and Practices Discussed in Reports on Company Failures*, p. 7.
8 *Ibid.*, p. 37.
9 *Ibid.*, p. 38.
10 B. Pheasant, '"True and fair" change seen as backward step', *Australian Financial Review*, 16 November 1992, p. 18.
11 Cited in B. Madden, 'Change or shut up', *New Accountant*, November (1994), p. 1.
12 Pratten, *Corporate Failure*.
13 Green, 'Keeping snouts out of the trough', p. 145.
14 Ernst & Young, *A Guide for the Company Director: Role, Duties and Liabilities* (1990).
15 AUS 202, 'Objective and General Principles Governing an Audit of a Financial Report', ICAA 1966, para .03.
16 The information economics literature is replete with references to accounting being an economic good.

18 Ethos abandoned: Accounting at the professional crossroads?

1 C. Fox, 'Ethics becoming the buzzword of the 90s', *Australian Financial Review*, 12 June 1990, p. 44.
2 A. Boyd, 'Call for higher business ethics', *Australian Financial Review*, 24 May 1990, p. 4.
3 Anon, 'Ethics rise in the West', *The Bulletin*, 5 June 1990, p. 22.
4 J. Hurst, 'Corporate ethics come under the microscope', *Australian Financial Review*, 29 January 1990, p. 3.
5 S. Lewis, 'Accounting education in "chronic neglect"', *Australian Financial Review*, 5 July 1990, p. 10.
6 T. Stephens, 'Big business elders crusade for higher ethics', *Sydney Morning Herald*, 26 May 1990, p. 6.
7 J. Collins, 'Declining ethics . . . bad company', *The Australian*, 10 July 1990, p. 13.
8 M. Lyons, 'Profession begins to get serious about its ethics', *Business Review Weekly*, 21 February 1992, pp. 73 and 75.
9 T. Forester, 'Society needs dose of ethics to purge its "moral chaos"', *The Australian*, 14 May 1991, p. 46.
10 T. Kaye, 'Phillips bows out with call for code of ethics', *Australian Financial Review*, 3 April 1992, p. 61.
11 M. Lawson, 'Another counselling centre for ethically troubled accountants', *Australian Financial Review*, 27 March 1992, p. 3.
12 H. Mackay, 'Ethics is a tricky business', *Australian Financial Review*, 23 March 1993, p. 15.
13 M. Niemarck, 'The selling of ethics' – special issue on ethics, politics and academic accounting, *Accounting, Auditing and Accountability*, Vol. 8 No. 3 (1995), pp. 81–96. See also J.A. Gaa, *The Ethical Foundations of Public Accounting* (Vancouver, BC: Canadian Certified General Accountants Research Foundation, 1993).
14 K. Edwards, 'Where does the buck stop?', *Time*, 19 April 1993, pp. 24–29.
15 R. Roslender, *Sociological Perspectives on Modern Accountancy* (London: Routledge, 1992).
16 Two articles by R. Chambers and P. Wolnizer, 'A true and fair view of financial position', *Company and Securities Law Journal*, December (1990),

pp. 353–368 and 'A true and fair view of financial proposals and results: The historical background', *Accounting, Business and Financial History*, March (1991), pp. 197–213, provide detailed references to many others which are reproduced in a recent anthology by R.H. Parker, P. Wolnizer and C. Nobes, *Readings in True and Fair* (New York: Garland, 1996).

17   Clarke and Craig, 'Phases in accounting standards'.
18   A. Lovell, 'Moral reasoning and moral atmosphere in the domain of accounting' – special issue on ethics, politics and academic accounting, *Accounting, Auditing and Accountability*, Vol. 8 No. 3 (1995), pp. 60–80.
19   D. Fischel, *Payback: The conspiracy to destroy Michael Milken* (New York: Harper Business, 1995).
20   Graphically illustrating this was the 1950s mercury poisoning at Minamata by the Japanese chemical company, Chisso. For decades, victims seeking compensation were fighting an amorphous corporate giant. It was *as if* humans had played no role in the poisoning of the sea around Minamata (see W.E. Smith and A.M. Smith, *Minamata* (New York: Holt, Rinehart & Winston, 1975)). In Australia this issue was considered by senior federal and state law officers resulting in a proposed new legal code, avoiding the need to prove criminal intent, but to 'jail dirty corporates' (Rowly Spiers, 'New law to jail dirty corporates', *Australian Financial Review*, 16 September 1992, p. 3). Legal commentators Fisse and Braithwaite summarise the individualism versus corporate criminality perspectives discussed in legal and cognate disciplines (*Corporations, Crime and Accountability*, especially Chapters 2 and 3).
21   For example, Bosch, *The Workings of a Watchdog*, pp. 24–39.
22   A similar view was recently put by R. Tomasic and S. Bottomley, *Directing the Top 500: Corporate governance and accountability in Australian companies* (Sydney: Allen & Unwin, 1993). Consider also the headline covering the recent arrest of a leading 1970s US corporate cowboy, 'Robert Vesco . . . a man who makes Christopher Skase look like Mother Theresa', in Marcus Casey, 'Wall Street swindler's pals finally desert him', *Sunday Telegraph*, 18 June 1995, p. 131.
23   The current evidence is captured in the following: 'Poseidon chief faces charges', *Sydney Morning Herald*, 24 December 1993, p. 11, just after that business chief had been voted 1993 ABM Businessman of the Year; and in the same issue, '$66 million theft: Elliot charged' and, referring to former WA Premier 'Burke on $124,585 charge', as well as the headlines regarding the Budget Corporation case.
24   Notable exceptions included financial consultants such as M. Burrows and A. Donnelly, regulators like Bosch, and certain journalists noted in the accounts of failure in this book.
25   Bloomberg, 'From high-roller to has-been'.
26   Mackay, 'Ethics is a tricky business'.
27   K. Edwards, 'Where does the buck stop?', *Time*, 19 April 1993, pp. 24–29.
28   Mackay, 'Ethics is a tricky business'.
29   P. Jubb and S. Haswell, *Company Accounting* (Melbourne: Nelson, 1993), p. 163.
30   QBE Insurance Group, *Annual Report* (1992).
31   Walker, 'A feeling of déjà vu', p. 107.
32   It has been reported that, in 1993 and 1994, premiums rose by 15 per cent each year, following a 20 per cent rise in 1992 – S. Clafton, 'Professional bodies review call for liability limits', *Business Review Weekly*, 1 April 1996, pp. 68–69.
33   This view is implicit in an interview by S. Harrison of ASC Chairman, Alan Cameron, in the April 1993 issue of *Charter*, 'Civil or criminal remedies and the ASC', pp. 10–12.

34 J. Este, 'Interchase claim worsens valuers' indemnity problem', *The Australian*, 2 July 1995, p. 3.

35 The cap in the NSW Bill may be set at an amount or at a multiple of fees. Professional bodies must seek permission for the cap by applying to the Professional Standards Council. In the UK the DTI has proposed a limit on auditors' liability through changes to the companies laws. It has suggested that regulations will be made under s. 310(4) of the *Companies Act* 1985 (Anon, 'DTI acts on auditors' liability', *Accountancy*, April (1993), p. 13).

36 C. Napier, 'The antecedents of unlimited liability in the United Kingdom: A study of corporate governance', paper, 19th EAA Congress, Bergen, May 1996.

37 These and other proposals are listed in Working Party of the Ministerial Council for Corporations, *Professional Liability in Relation to Corporations Law Matters*, June 1993, especially pp. 10–35.

38 M.C. Wells, reported comment in proceedings of *Crime and the Professions – The Accountancy Profession*, Institute of Criminology Seminar, 18 September 1985.

39 For an account of this bankruptcy see C.W. Wootton and S.D. Tonge, 'Where do clients go when an accounting firm goes bankrupt?: The case of Laventhol & Howarth', *Abacus*, September (1993), pp. 149–159.

40 M. Lawson, 'Accountants "top for claims"', *Australian Financial Review*, 2 August 1993, p. 3.

41 See M. Moonitz, *Obtaining Agreement on Standards in the Accounting Profession*, Studies in Accounting Research, American Accounting Association, 1974.

42 B. Barber, 'Some problems in the sociology of the professions', *Daedalus*, Fall (1963), pp. 669–688. (An issue devoted to discussing the professions.)

43 See the professional booklet, International Federation of Accountants, *Understanding Financial Statement Audits* (Melbourne: AARF, 1990).

44 B. Pheasant, 'Auditors in danger from $2.5bn claims', *Australian Financial Review*, 30 June 1993, pp. 1 and 6 at 6.

45 This crisis has been long recognised (see Chambers, *Securities and Obscurities* and Briloff (1970, 1976 and 1981)). This label was used in the December 1993 AICPA/ASCPA monograph, *A Research Study on Financial Reporting and Auditing – Bridging the Expectations Gap, op. cit.*, and in a 1994 Ernst and Young Foundation monograph, *Measurement Research in Financial Accounting*, reporting the workshop proceedings, 30 September to 1 October 1993. The workshop had discussed the 'crisis in accounting research' claimed in an unpublished pamphlet by six leading US academic researchers – for further details, see R. Mattessich, *Critique of Accounting* (Westport, CT: Quorum Books, 1995).

46 M. Dobbie, 'ASB wants SACs to be mandatory', *Financial Forum*, August (1993), p. 1. SAC 4, which was put on hold in 1994 after vehement opposition from practitioners and their clients, was intended to prescribe the concepts to underpin accounting practices. It was rereleased in 1995 but this time its application was voluntary.

47 As reported by K. Bice, 'Judgement reserved on Acacia Part A', *Australian Financial Review*, 27 March 1996, p. 28.

48 T. Boreham, 'Mockers of rules better beware of the watchdog', *Business Review Weekly*, 19 March 1993, pp. 92–93.

49 Chambers, 'Accounting and corporate morality – the ethical cringe', p. 17.

Bibliography

Accounting Standards Review Committee, *Company Accounting Standards*, under chairmanship of R.J. Chambers (Sydney: NSW Government Printer, 1978).

Altman, E.I., *Corporate Bankruptcy in America* (Lexington, Mass.: Heath Lexington Books, 1971).

Altman, E.I., *Corporate Financial Distress: A complete guide to predicting, avoiding and dealing with bankruptcy* (New York: John Wiley & Sons Inc., 1983; 2nd ed., 1993).

American Law Institute (ALI), *Principles of Corporate Governance, Analysis and Recommendations* (New York: ALI, 1992).

Argenti, J., *Corporate Collapse: The causes and symptoms* (London: McGraw-Hill, 1976).

Argenti, J., *Predicting Company Failure*, Accountants' Digest No. 93 (London: ICAEW, 1985).

Armstrong, H. and Gross, D., *Tricontinental: The rise and fall of a merchant bank: The first full account of one of the biggest disasters in Australian banking* (Melbourne: Melbourne University Press, 1995).

Australian Bankers Association, *Corporate Failures* (Sydney: ABA, 1990).

Australian Society of Accountants, *Accounting Principles and Practices Discussed in Reports of Company Failures* (Sydney–Melbourne: ASA General Council, 1966).

Australian Society of Certified Practising Accountants (ASCPA) and The Institute of Chartered Accountants in Australia (ICAA), *A Research Study on Financial Reporting and Auditing – Bridging the Expectations Gap* (Melbourne: ASCPA and ICAA, 1993).

Barchard, D., *Asil Nadir and the Rise and Fall of Polly Peck* (London: Victor Gollancz Ltd, 1992).

Barry, P., *The Rise and Fall of Alan Bond* (Sydney: Bantam Books, 1990).

Berle, A.A. and Means, G.C., *The Modern Corporation and Private Property* (New York: Macmillan, 1932).

Blumberg, P., *The Law of Corporate Groups* (Boston: Little, Brown and Co., 1983).

Bosch, H., *The Workings of a Watchdog* (Melbourne: William Heinemann Australia, 1990).

Bosch, H., *Corporate Procedures and Conduct* (Sydney: Institute of Directors, 1991, 1993).

Bower, T., *Maxwell: The outsider* (London: Mandarin Paperbacks, 1991).

Bresciani-Turroni, C., *The Economics of Inflation* (London: Allen & Unwin, 1937).

Briloff, A.J., *Unaccountable Accounting* (New York: Harper & Row, 1972).

Briloff, A.J., *More Debits Than Credits: The burnt investor's guide to financial statements* (New York: Harper & Row, 1976).

Briloff, A.J., *Truth about Accounting* (New York: Harper & Row, 1982).

Brokensha, P., *Corporate Ethics: A guide for Australian managers* (Adelaide: Social Science Press, 1993).

Brooks, C., *The Royal Mail Case* (Toronto: Law Book Co., 1933).

Cadbury Committee, *Code of Corporate Governance* – Interim and Final (London: HMSO, 1991, 1992).

Chambers, R.J., *Securities and Obscurities: A case for reform of the law of company accounts* (Melbourne: Gower Press, 1973a); reproduced as *Accounting in Disarray* (New York: Garland Publishing Inc., 1986).

Chambers, R.J., 'Observation as a method of inquiry – the background of *Securities and Obscurities*', *Abacus*, December 1973b.

Clarke, F.L and Dean, G.W., *Contributions of Limperg and Schmidt to the Replacement Cost Debate in the 1920's* (New York: Garland Publishing Inc., 1990).

Companies and Securities Advisory Committee, *Discussion Paper No. 3: Civil Liability of Company Auditors* (Sydney: NSW Government Printer, 1985).

Craswell, A.T., *Auditing* (New York: Garland Publishing Inc., 1986).

Cronje, S. *et al.*, *Lonrho: A portrait of a multinational* (London: Penguin, 1976).

Daly, M.T., *Sydney Boom, Sydney Bust: The city and its property market 1850–1981* (Sydney: Allen & Unwin, 1982).

Dean, G.W. and Clarke F.L., 'Anatomy of a Failure: A methodological experiment – the case of ASL', in M. Juttner, and T. Valentine (eds), *The Economics and Management of Financial Institutions* (Sydney: Longman Cheshire, 1987).

Dean, G.W., Clarke, F.L and Graves, O.F., *Replacement Costs and Accounting Reform in Post-World War I Germany* (New York: Garland Publishing Inc., 1990).

Dirks, R.L. and Goss, L., *The Great Wall Street Scandal* (New York: McGraw-Hill, 1974).

Dun and Bradstreet Corporation, *The Business Failure Record, 1981* (New York: Dun and Bradstreet, 1982).

Fischel, D., *Payback: The conspiracy to destroy Michael Milken* (New York: Harper Business, 1995).

Fisse, B. and Braithwaite, J., *Corporations, Crime and Accountability* (Cambridge; Melbourne: Cambridge University Press, 1993).

Ford, H.A.J., *Principles of Company Law*, 5th ed. (Sydney: Butterworths, 1990).

Gaa, J.A., *The Ethical Foundations of Public Accounting* (Vancouver, B.C: Canadian Certified General Accountants Research Foundation, 1993).

Garnsey, G., *Holding Companies and Their Published Accounts* (London: Gee & Co., 1923), reproduced as *Holding Companies and Their Published Accounts: Limitations of a Balance Sheet* (New York: Garland Publishing Inc., 1982).

Gower, L.C.B., *Gower's Principles of Modern Company Law*, 3rd ed. (London: Law Book Co., 1969).

Gower, L.C.B., *Gower's Principles of Modern Company Law*, 4th ed. (London: Stevens and Co., 1979).

Greatorex, D. *et al.*, *Corporate Collapses: Lessons for the future* (Sydney: The Institute of Chartered Accountants in Australia, 1994).

Greising, D. and Morse, L., *Brokers, Bagmen and Moles: Fraud and corruption in the Chicago Futures Markets* (New York: John Wiley & Sons, Inc., 1991).

Griffiths, I., *Creative Accounting: How to make your profits what you want them to be* (London: Allen & Unwin, 1986).

Guttmann, W. and Meehan, P., *The Great Inflation* (London: Saxon House, 1975).

Haigh, G., *The Battle for BHP* (Melbourne: Allen & Unwin Australia Pty Ltd, 1987).

Haldane, A., *With Intent to Deceive* (Edinburgh: William Blackwood, 1970).

Hilmer, F., *Strictly Boardroom* (London: Gollancz, 1993).

Hirsch, E.D., *Cultural Literacy* (Melbourne: Schwartz Publishing, 1989).

Hirst, R.R. and Wallace, R.W., *Studies in the Australian Capital Market* (Melbourne: Cheshire, 1964).

Holmes, S. and Nicholls, D., *Small Business and Accounting: Building a profitable relationship between owner/managers and accountants* (Sydney: Allen & Unwin, 1990).

Hussey, A.E., *Shareholder and General Public Protection in Limited Liability Enterprises from 1856–1969*, Unpublished MEc Thesis (University of Sydney, 1971).

International Federation of Accountants, *Understanding Financial Statements* (Melbourne: Australian Accounting Research Foundation, 1990).

Jameson, M., *The Practical Art of Creative Accounting* (London: Kogan Page, 1988).

Jamieson, B., *The Accounting Jungle* (Sydney: Business Review Weekly Publications, 1995).

Janetzki, D., *The Gollin Years* (Brisbane: Don Janetzki, 1989).

Jubb, P. and Howell, S., *Company Accounting* (Melbourne: Nelson, 1993).

Juttner, M. and Valentine, T. (eds), *The Economics and Management of Financial Institutions* (Melbourne: Longman Cheshire, 1987).

Karmel, P.H. and Brunt, M., *The Structure of the Australian Economy* (Melbourne: Cheshire, 1963).

Keats, C.B., *Magnificent Masquerade* (New York: Funk & Wagnalls, 1964).

Kellogg, I. and Kellogg, L.B., *Fraud, Window Dressing and Negligence in Financial Statements* (New York: McGraw-Hill, 1991).

Kharbanda, O.P. and Stallworthy, E.A., *Corporate Failure: Prediction, panacea and prevention* (Whitstable, Kent: McGraw-Hill, 1985).

Levi, E.H., *Point of View: Talks on education* (Chicago: University of Chicago Press, 1969).

McDonald, F., *Insull* (Chicago: Chicago University Press, 1962).

McGill, M., *American Business and the Quick Fix* (New York: Henry Holt and Company, 1988).

McManamy, J., *The Dreamtime Casino* (Melbourne: Schwarz and Wilkinson, 1990).

Maher, T., *Bond* (Melbourne: William Heinemann Australia, 1990).

Mantle, J., *For Whom the Bell Tolls: The scandalous inside story of Lloyd's crisis* (London: Mandarin Paperbacks, 1993).

Mattessich, R., *Critique of Accounting* (Westport, CT: Quorum Books, 1995).

Miller, D., *The Icarus Paradox: How exceptional companies bring about their own downfall* (New York: Harper Business, 1990).

Moonitz, M., *Obtaining Agreement on Standards in the Accounting Profession*, Studies in Accounting Research, American Accounting Association, 1974.

Naser, K.H.M., *Creative Financial Accounting* (London: Hemel Hempstead, Prentice Hall International, 1993).

Oliver, K.G., *Australian Corporate Failures 1946–88: A random sample of thirty listed industrial companies assessed in the light of Argenti's trajectories*, Honours Thesis, Department of Economic History (University of Sydney, 1990).

Parker, R.H., Wolnizer, P.W. and Nobes, C., *Readings in True and Fair* (New York: Garland Publishing Inc., 1996).

Pecora, F., *Wall Street under Oath: The story of our modern money changers* (New York: Simon & Schuster Inc., 1939).

Pelikan, J., *The Idea of a University: A reexamination* (New Haven: Yale University Press, 1992).

Peters, T.J. and Waterman Jnr, R.H., *In Search of Excellence: Lessons from America's best run companies* (Sydney: Harper and Row, 1982).

Pratten, C., *Company Failure* (London: ICAEW, 1991).

Public Oversight Board, 'Issues in Confronting the Accounting Profession', *Report by Public Oversight Board of the SEC Practice section* (Stanford, CT: AICPA, 1993).

Raw, C., *Slater Walker* (London: Andre Deutsch Ltd, 1977).

Raw, C., *The Moneychangers: How the Vatican Bank enabled Roberto Calvi to steal $250 million for the heads of the P2 Masonic Lodge* (London: Harvill, 1992).

Reid, M., *The Secondary Banking Crisis, 1973–74: Its causes and course* (London: Macmillan, 1982).

Ripley, W., *Main Street and Wall Street* (Lawrence, Kan.: Scholars Book Co., 1927, 1974).

Roslender, R., *Sociological Perspectives on Modern Accountancy* (London: Routledge, 1992).

Ross, B., *The Ariadne Story: The rise and fall of a business empire* (Elwood, Victoria: Greenhouse Publications, 1988).

Ross, J.E. and Kami, M.J., *Corporate Management in Crisis: Why the mighty fall* (Englewood Cliffs, NJ: Prentice-Hall Inc., 1973).

Rothchild, J., *Going for Broke: How Robert Campeau bankrupted the retail industry, jolted the junk bond market and brought the booming eighties to a crashing halt* (New York: Simon & Schuster, 1991).

Russell, B., *The Problems with Philosophy* (London: Oxford University Press, 1912, 1959).

Russell, H.F., *Foozles and Fraud* (Altamone Springs, Fla: Institute of Internal Auditors, 1978).

Salsbury, S., *No Way to Run a Railroad: The untold story of the Penn Central crisis* (New York: McGraw-Hill, 1982).

Salsbury, S. and Sweeney, K., *The Bull, the Bear and the Kangaroo: The history of the Sydney Stock Exchange* (Sydney: Allen & Unwin, 1988).

Schilit, H., *Financial Shenanigans: How to detect accounting gimmicks and fraud in financial reports* (New York: McGraw-Hill, 1993).

Shaplen, R., *Kreuger: Genius and Swindler* (1961; reproduced by Garland Publishing, New York, 1990).

Smith, T., *Accounting for Growth: Stripping the camouflage from company accounts* (London: Century Business, 1992).

Smith, W.E. and Smith, A.M., *Minamata* (New York: Alskog Sensorium – Holt, Rinehart and Winston, 1975).

Stamp, E. and Marley, C., *Accounting Principles and the City Code* (London: Butterworths, 1970).

Stevens, M., *The Accounting Wars* (New York: Colliers Books, 1986).

Stewart, J.B., *Den of Thieves* (New York: Simon & Schuster, 1991).

Sugarman, D. and Tuebner, G. (eds), *Regulating Corporate Groups in Europe* (Firenze: European University Institute, 1990).

Sykes, T., *The Money Miners: Australia's mining boom 1969–70* (Sydney: Wildcat Press, 1978).

Sykes, T., *Two Centuries of Panic: A history of corporate collapses in Australia* (Sydney: Allen & Unwin, 1988).

Sykes, T., *The Bold Riders* (Sydney: Allen & Unwin, 1994; 2nd ed. 1996).

Toffler, A., *Adaptive Corporation* (London: Pan Books, 1984).

Tomasic, R. and Bottomley, S., *Directing the Top 500 – Corporate governance and accountability in Australian companies* (Sydney: Allen & Unwin, 1993).

Truell, P. and Gurwin, L., *BCCI – The Inside Story of the World's Most Corrupt Financial Empire* (London: Bloomsbury Publishing Ltd, 1992).

Twentieth Century Fund, *Abuse on Wall Street: Conflicts of interest in the securities markets* (Westport, CT: Quorum Books, 1937, 1980).

Van Dongen, Y., *Brierley: The man behind the corporate legend* (Auckland: Viking Press, 1990).

Walker, R.G., *Consolidated Statements: A history and analysis* (New York: Arno Press Inc., 1978).

Whipple, R.T.M. (ed.), *Accounting for Property Development* (Sydney: Law Book Co., 1986).

Woolf, E., *Auditing Today* (Englewood Cliffs; London: Prentice-Hall, 1982).

Working Party of Ministerial Council for Corporations, *Professional Liability in Relation to Corporations Law Matters* (Canberra: Commonwealth Government Printer, 1993).

Index